Teach Yourself
► dBASE III PLUS® ◄

Teach Yourself
►dBASE III PLUS®◄

Charles Ackerman

Osborne McGraw-Hill
Berkeley New York St. Louis San Francisco
Auckland Bogotá Hamburg London Madrid
Mexico City Milan Montreal New Delhi Panama City
Paris São Paulo Singapore Sydney
Tokyo Toronto

Osborne **McGraw-Hill**
2600 Tenth Street
Berkeley, California 94710
U.S.A.

Osborne **McGraw-Hill** offers software for sale. For information on translations or book distributors outside of the U.S.A., please write to Osborne **McGraw-Hill** at the above address.

dBASE and dBASE III PLUS are registered trademarks of Ashton-Tate Corporation.

Teach Yourself dBASE III PLUS®

Copyright © 1990 by McGraw-Hill, Inc. All rights reserved. Printed in the United States of America. Except as permitted under the Copyright Act of 1976, no part of this publication may be reproduced or distributed in any form or by any means, or stored in a database or retrieval system, without the prior written permission of the publisher, with the exception that the program listings may be entered, stored, and executed in a computer system, but they may not be reproduced for publication.

234567890 DOC 99876543210

ISBN 0-07-881680-7

Information has been obtained by Osborne **McGraw-Hill** from sources believed to be reliable. However, because of the possibility of human or mechanical error by our sources, Osborne **McGraw-Hill**, or others, Osborne **McGraw-Hill** does not guarantee the accuracy, adequacy, or completeness of any information and is not responsible for any errors or omissions or the results obtained from use of such information.

To Caroline

▶ Contents ◀
At a Glance

	Why This Book Is for You	1
1	Getting Started	3
2	The Assist Interface	13
3	Creating a Database	37
4	Entering Data	59
5	Editing Data	85
6	Locating and Calculating Records	109
7	Deleting Records	139
8	Modifying a Database	157
9	Organizing a Database	183

10	Simple Printing	209
11	Creating and Using Formats	229
12	Creating and Using Reports	263
13	Creating and Using Labels	293
14	Creating and Using Queries	315
15	Managing Files	337
A	Installing dBASE III PLUS	351
B	Answer Section	363
C	ASCII Character Chart	417
	Index	427

▶ Contents ◀

Introduction		xv
Why This Book Is for You		1

1 Getting Started — 3

1.1	BECOME FAMILIAR WITH DATABASES	4
1.2	BECOME FAMILIAR WITH dBASE III PLUS	5
1.3	LOAD AND UNLOAD dBASE III PLUS	7

2 The Assist Interface — 13

2.1	BECOME FAMILIAR WITH THE ASSIST SCREEN	14
2.2	WORK WITH MENUS	19
2.3	MEET THE DOT PROMPT	26
2.4	ACCESS HELP	28

3 Creating a Database — 37

3.1	DESIGN A STRUCTURE	39
3.2	INSERT CHARACTER FIELDS	42
3.3	INSERT NUMERIC FIELDS	48
3.4	INSERT DATE, LOGICAL, AND MEMO FIELDS	51
3.5	SAVE AND VIEW THE STRUCTURE	54

4 Entering Data — 59

| 4.1 | OPEN A DATABASE | 60 |

4.2	BECOME FAMILIAR WITH THE APPEND SCREEN	66
4.3	INSERT INFORMATION	70
4.4	WORK WITH MEMO FIELDS	76

5 Editing Data — 85

5.1	USE THE EDIT SCREEN	86
5.2	BECOME FAMILIAR WITH THE BROWSE SCREEN	91
5.3	USE THE BROWSE SCREEN MENU	97
5.4	GO DIRECTLY TO RECORDS	102
5.5	DISPLAY RECORDS	104

6 Locating and Calculating Records — 109

6.1	USE THE POSITION AND SEARCH/SCOPE MENUS	110
6.2	SKIP RECORDS	115
6.3	LOCATE RECORDS	117
6.4	SPECIFY A SCOPE	124
6.5	REPLACE RECORD INFORMATION	126
6.6	CALCULATE NUMERIC FIELDS	129

7 Deleting Records — 139

7.1	MARK AND RECALL A SINGLE RECORD	140
7.2	MARK AND RECALL A GROUP OF RECORDS	147
7.3	PACK A DATABASE	152

8 Modifying a Database — 157

8.1	INSERT FIELDS	159
8.2	CHANGE EXISTING FIELDS	167

	8.3	DELETE FIELDS	177

9 Organizing a Database — 183

9.1	INDEX A DATABASE	185
9.2	USE THE SEEK COMMAND	194
9.3	SORT A DATABASE	196
9.4	COPY DATABASE FILES	200

10 Simple Printing — 209

10.1	PRINT A SINGLE SCREEN	212
10.2	USE THE LIST COMMAND	215
10.3	USE THE DISPLAY COMMAND	222

11 Creating and Using Formats — 229

11.1	BECOME FAMILIAR WITH THE CREATE FORMAT SCREEN	231
11.2	SELECT A DATABASE	236
11.3	DESIGN AND USE FORMAT FILES	239
11.4	MODIFY AND ENHANCE FORMAT FILES	246
11.5	CREATE MORE COMPLEX FEATURES	252

12 Creating and Using Reports — 263

12.1	BECOME FAMILIAR WITH THE CREATE REPORT SCREEN	265
12.2	DESIGN REPORTS	275
12.3	PRINT REPORTS	283
12.4	MODIFY REPORTS	288

13 Creating and Using Labels — 293

- 13.1 BECOME FAMILIAR WITH THE CREATE LABEL SCREEN — 295
- 13.2 CREATE LABELS — 301
- 13.3 PRINT LABELS — 305
- 13.4 MODIFY LABELS — 309

14 Creating and Using Queries — 315

- 14.1 BECOME FAMILIAR WITH THE CREATE QUERY SCREEN — 316
- 14.2 CREATING AND USING QUERY FILES — 320
- 14.3 MODIFYING QUERIES — 329

15 Managing Files — 337

- 15.1 CHANGE DRIVES AND LIST DIRECTORIES — 338
- 15.2 COPYING, RENAMING, AND ERASING FILES — 341
- 15.3 IMPORTING AND EXPORTING INFORMATION — 345

A Installing dBASE III PLUS — 351

- STEPPING THROUGH THE INSTALLATION — 352
- CHECKING THE PACKAGE CONTENTS — 352
- MAKING BACKUP COPIES — 354
- Making Backup Copies on a Dual Floppy Disk System — 354
- Making Backup Copies on a Hard Disk System — 355
- READING THE README.TXT FILE — 356
- MINIMUM SYSTEM REQUIREMENTS — 357
- RUNNING THE ID PROGRAM — 358
- INSTALLING ON A HARD DISK — 359
- INSTALLING ON A FLOPPY DISK — 360

| | PLACING dBASE IN YOUR DOS PATH STATEMENT | 361 |
| | RUNNING THE TUTORIAL PROGRAM | 362 |

B Answer Section — 363

C ASCII Character Chart — 417

Index — 427

► Acknowledgments ◄

I can't understand how authors develop swollen heads about their books; they usually put in less than half the labor required.

For the production of this book I would first of all like to thank Liz Fisher for thinking of me when Osborne decided to do a book on dBASE III PLUS® for the Teach Yourself series. Next, I'd like to thank Gwen Goss for all her patient guidance. Dusty Bernard gets credit for straightening out my grammatical and syntactical mistakes; and Michael Katz gets credit for straightening out my technical mistakes, which, in a book with so many examples and exercises, proved to be a major undertaking. Finally, hats off to Janis Paris, who pulled all the parts together and drove the book home to printing.

▶ Introduction ◀

dBASE III PLUS® is the single most popular computer database management program in use today. It's held the number one position for over half a decade, and it continues to be the leader in the face of competition from the product that was supposed to replace it—dBASE IV.

Interestingly enough, most of the competition for dBASE III PLUS comes from within the fold—from programs that call themselves "dBASE III PLUS compatible." There's FoxBase and FoxPro, dBXL, and Clipper, to name just the most popular. There's also Microsoft Works and PC Tools Deluxe, which contain dBASE III PLUS engines. These let you create, read, and write dBASE III PLUS data files and perform other routine database handling techniques, letting you work easily with the most popular database format.

If you're going to work with a computerized database, you must know something about dBASE III PLUS. This is certainly true if your company has the program and you must use it at work. It's also true if you want to learn to work with data the way most other people do.

It's also important to know something about dBASE III PLUS even if you plan to work with another database management program. dBASE III PLUS has its fans as well as its detractors—but all of them know dBASE III PLUS.

There will be times when you have to work with dBASE® database files regardless of what program you use. These can be data files your company uses, or which you purchase, or which are given to you by someone else. There will also be times when you need to export data from your program to the dBASE standard for someone else to use. The more you know about dBASE, the more you'll be able to bridge the gap between the database program used by millions of users and the database program you use.

ABOUT THIS BOOK

Teach Yourself dBASE III PLUS is designed to get you up-and-running with dBASE quickly and to understand the important features of the program. The ideal reader is a new user to dBASE III PLUS who's just starting out, or someone who has worked with the program sporadically and now realizes there's real value in learning more about it.

Learning about database management can be one of the more difficult tasks to learn on a computer. Most people have written letters before, so working with a word processor comes naturally. And many people have worked with numbers before, so building a spreadsheet makes sense. But fewer people have managed data in any sort of organized fashion. It's this initial step that deters many people from ever tackling database management, and it hinders new users from developing their skills beyond the most rudimentary level.

Fortunately, dBASE III PLUS is a menu-driven program. This book guides you through these menu commands using practical examples that you can put to work right away. Along the way you'll learn certain basic concepts regarding database structure and organization that can illuminate your work. This will help you understand what you're doing as opposed to just learning from memory.

You don't need to know anything about databases—or even computers—when you first start out reading this book. When you finish, you'll be skilled enough to perform all routine database management work as well as to flirt with the idea of writing dBASE programs.

HOW THIS BOOK IS ORGANIZED

Teach Yourself dBASE III PLUS is organized into 15 chapters and 3 appendixes. The book has been organized around the central task of building your skills. Each chapter describes a specific task that moves you one step closer to mastery of the program. Each chapter provides examples and exercises for your own work, exercises that build on information you learned in previous chapters.

The first two chapters help you get started with the dBASE III PLUS program. Chapter 1 describes the concept of databases in general and dBASE III PLUS in particular, introduces you to features in dBASE III PLUS, and describes how you load and unload the program. Chapter 2 gives you more details about the menu-driven interface called the Assist, which you'll work with for most of the rest of the book.

Chapters 3, 4, and 5 describe how you design and create a database structure, then how you enter data into the structure and edit the data when you want to change it. These are the most fundamental tasks you can perform in database management.

Chapters 6 through 10 describe how you actually manage data on a routine basis—locating specific information, deleting out-of-date records, modifying the database structure, organizing the display of data, and printing out the information.

Chapters 11 through 14 describe how you work with more sophisticated features in dBASE III PLUS, such as formatting the display of information on your screen, designing reports and labels, and creating queries that automatically select the information you want to work with.

Chapter 15 describes how you manage the various files you have learned to create. Most of these involve the normal DOS file housekeeping commands.

There are also three appendixes. Appendix A describes what you get in the dBASE III PLUS program package as well as how to install the program on your computer using either a hard disk or a two-floppy disk drive system.

Appendix B provides answers to Skills Checks and exercises you'll find throughout each chapter. These answers consist of the sequence of keystrokes (including menu commands) you must follow to complete the Skills Check or exercise correctly. You should try to perform the Skills Checks and exercises before checking the answers, and then only after tackling the exercise should you check your results against the correct answers supplied in the book.

Appendix C is a chart of ASCII characters, which you will use in data management.

Each chapter of the book includes these items:

- An introduction and list of objectives or section titles that list what you'll learn while reading the chapter

- A Skills Check at the beginning of every chapter (beginning with Chapter 3), which is a list of skills you should review before starting the chapter (you can find the answers in Appendix B)

- A set of examples at the end of each chapter section putting to work the information you just learned in the section

- A set of exercises after each set of examples so you can test your skills and see how much you've retained (again, you can find the answers in Appendix B)

CONVENTIONS USED IN THIS BOOK

Teach Yourself dBASE III PLUS is just one in a series of books published by Osborne/McGraw-Hill that's designed to let you teach yourself a major popular software program. The design of these books has been formulated around a specific plan. You learned something about the structure of this book in the previous section.

In addition, there are several design elements that you should become familiar with. Most of them are readily apparent and understandable. We'll describe these elements here.

- Keycaps (for example, [Shift] and [F1]) are used to designate the key or combination of keys you should press to perform a command, example, or exercise. You'll find these keycaps throughout the book. In the answers provided in Appendix B, these keys will appear as small caps (for instance, SHIFT and F1).

- Menu or screen commands appear with initial caps, such as the Select command; or within quotation marks, as in "Quit dBASE III PLUS."

- Messages you'll see on your display screen appear in typewriter format (also called Courier or monospaced type), like this:

    ```
    *** END RUN    dBASE III PLUS
    ```

- The basic steps to perform a command are displayed in an alphabetical list, like this:

    a. Press [S] to open the Set Up menu.
    b. Highlight "Quit dBASE III PLUS."
    c. Press [Enter].

OTHER OSBORNE/McGRAW-HILL BOOKS OF INTEREST TO YOU

As you advance in your knowledge of dBASE III PLUS, you might find one or more of the following books by Osborne/McGraw-Hill helpful.

dBASE III PLUS Made Easy by Miriam Liskin refreshes you on the basics of dBASE III PLUS and introduces you to more sophisticated techniques.

Every dBASE III PLUS command function and feature is listed in alphabetical order in *dBASE III PLUS: The Complete Reference*, by Joseph-David Carrabis, making this book invaluable to those who use their program often. And *dBASE III PLUS: The Pocket Reference*, by Miriam Liskin, is a handy portable encyclopedic reference to dBASE features.

For network users or those who simply wish to increase the performance of their program, *dBASE III PLUS: Power User's Guide*, by Edward Jones, is a must. Also by Edward Jones, *The dBASE Language Reference* discusses the similarities and differences between the various dBASE and dBASE-compatible products on the market.

Osborne/McGraw-Hill also publishes a variety of titles on dBASE IV, as well as other popular database management programs and computer subjects.

Why
This Book Is for You

THIS BOOK'S OBJECTIVES

If you're a new dBASE III PLUS user, you'll find this book ideal for getting started the first time. If you've worked with dBASE III PLUS before but need practice, you'll find this book a handy way to become more familiar—and friendly—with the program.

Using this book, the reader is guided through a carefully constructed sequence of self-teaching tasks that impart sufficient knowledge to handle routine database management using dBASE III PLUS. The best way to learn anything is by example, and this book is full of examples. Each step is described clearly and succinctly, supported with an example, and then tested with an exercise. The reader can find answers for every exercise at the end of the book, so it is possible to use this book as a class coursebook.

Readers can also use this book as a reference, to refresh their skills, clear up certain points, or to double-check a procedure.

Getting Started

▶1◀

CHAPTER OBJECTIVES

In this chapter you will

▶ Become familiar with databases   1.1

▶ Become familiar with dBASE III PLUS   1.2

▶ Load and unload dBASE III PLUS   1.3

You'll start out in this chapter learning some basic facts about databases in general and dBASE in particular. Then you'll learn how to load the program into your computer and then unload it. This will prepare you for the next chapter, where you will learn how to work in dBASE III PLUS.

Before you start working with dBASE III PLUS, you should understand what a database is and how dBASE developed into the most popular personal computer database management system.

1.1 BECOME FAMILIAR WITH DATABASES

The term *database* is just a fancy name for a group of facts. It's a base of data that you want to maintain, such as a list of people's names and their addresses, items or services that you buy or sell for your business, or anything else you want to keep track of. You've used databases before, even if you've never worked with a computer. Your personal address book is a database of names you like to keep track of, such as members of your family, personal friends, and business associates. The telephone book is a much larger example of the same thing. These database examples are books of some sort.

Databases can take other forms as well. For example, if you save your tax deductible receipts in a manila envelope, the envelope is a type of database because it stores and maintains receipts for tax purposes. If you cook regularly, then you probably have a collection of recipes you've organized in some manner. This is a database of recipes.

The definition of a database arose with the advent of computers when data—or information—went electronic. Before computers, information was maintained in tangible items such as books and bags, something you could get your hands on when you needed to. When computers first came into routine use in the 1960s, they were applicable only to the largest sorts of databases, such as national census information and federal tax records. As computer technology became accessible to more people, particularly as microcomputers became popular, they opened the powerful world of database management to small companies and individuals who wanted to store important information electronically.

Databases are considered one of three primary applications for microcomputers. The other two are spreadsheets and word processors. In fact, all three types of applications are designed to save and display data. Spreadsheets display data as financial figures, and word processors display data as readable text. Databases are the purest form of data display, since you can work with both financial figures and text, as well as with many other types of information.

Exercises

1. List examples of databases you use regularly.

2. List examples of databases that you don't use directly, but that involve activities affecting your life, such as your checking account.

BECOME FAMILIAR WITH dBASE III PLUS — 1.2

dBASE III PLUS was first introduced in 1985. It remains the premier database program for personal computer users, even though the program has hardly changed since the day it was first released. There's something remarkable about dBASE III PLUS. When it was released, it instantly took over the PC database market from its predecessor, dBASE III, but it hasn't yielded much to its successor, dBASE IV.

There are two fundamental facts you should know about the program:

- It provides a choice of *interfaces,* or ways you can work with the program: the *Assist* screen, which provides pull-down menus to activate commands, and the *dot prompt,* which requires that you type in every command you want to use.

- It's a *relational database program,* which means that you can relate information among varied database files.

Even though dBASE III PLUS is a relational database program, you won't work with more than one file at a time in this book. You can do most of your routine work in dBASE III PLUS without relating data between two or more databases.

The dot prompt is present in all versions of the dBASE family of programs, from dBASE II through dBASE IV. It was the first and only way you could work with the program until the Assist interface was introduced in dBASE III PLUS. dBASE IV has an entirely different user interface called the Control Center, which built extensively onto features in Assist.

You'll learn how to work in Assist in Chapter 2, where you'll also take a quick look the dot prompt.

Examples

1. Relating two or more databases lets you select various parts of each database and combine the information for more detailed views of special items. If you keep a complex set of records for a business that sells merchandise, you might want to put customer information in one database, supplier information in a second database, and merchandise information in a third database. You would then relate the three databases so you could find out what merchandise goes to which customers and whom you get the merchandise from.

2. Popular database programs that are not relational are Q&A from Symantec, Inc., Reflex from Borland International, and RapidFile from Ashton-Tate. These are usually called *file managers,* as opposed to relational database management programs, because you can work with only one database file at a time.

Exercises

1. Name the two ways you can work with dBASE III PLUS.

2. Name the various versions of the dBASE family of programs.

3. Which is the most recent version?

4. Which is the most widely used?

LOAD AND UNLOAD dBASE III PLUS | 1.3

Before you can take a look at either Assist or the dot prompt, you must load dBASE III PLUS into your computer's memory. You need a minimum of 284K RAM in your computer if you're using a 2.x version of DOS. You need a minimum of 384K RAM to load dBASE III PLUS into your computer if you're using a 3.x version of DOS.

If you work with a minimum amount of RAM, dBASE will take more time to perform certain activities, such as working with large files. You'll need more memory if you want to create particularly large database files, or if you also want to use terminate-and-stay-resident (TSR) programs such as SideKick and PC Tools Deluxe.

You can load dBASE III PLUS two different ways, depending upon whether you want to use the program on a hard disk or on a floppy disk. Since more people use hard disks, you'll learn that method first.

To load dBASE III PLUS from a hard disk:

a. Begin at the C prompt, which probably looks something like this on your display screen: C\>.

b. Type **DBASE**. You can use uppercase or lowercase characters. This book shows all commands typed at DOS in uppercase.

c. Press [Enter]. This moves you into the copyright screen.

d. Press [Enter]. This removes the copyright screen and moves you into the dBASE program.

When dBASE is fully loaded into your computer, your screen should look like the one in Figure 1-1. It is a display of what is called the Assist screen. You will see the Set Up menu each time you enter the Assist screen. This is one of eight pull-down menus you can use to access commands in the dBASE III PLUS program. You can see the

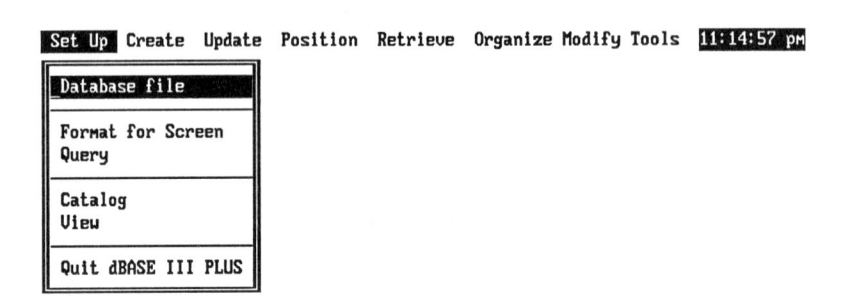

```
 Set Up  Create  Update  Position  Retrieve  Organize  Modify  Tools   11:14:57 pm
        ┌─────────────────────┐
        │ Database file       │
        ├─────────────────────┤
        │ Format for Screen   │
        │ Query               │
        │                     │
        │ Catalog             │
        │ View                │
        │                     │
        │ Quit dBASE III PLUS │
        └─────────────────────┘




 ASSIST              <C:>              Opt: 1/6
 Move selection bar - ↑↓. Select - ↵.  Leave menu - ←→. Help - F1. Exit - Esc.
                          Select a database file.
```

FIGURE 1-1. | The Assist screen

names of all eight menus along the top line of your screen. You don't need to pay attention to details on this screen right now. Chapter 2 will tell you more about the Assist screen and how to select commands using the pull-down menus.

If, after loading the program, your screen does not look like the one in Figure 1-1 but instead displays only a dot before the cursor (in the lower left corner of the screen), you've moved directly to the dot prompt screen. This means that your version of the program has been customized to display the dot prompt screen rather than the Assist screen directly upon loading. If this happens, press F2 to move to the Assist.

Many people, particularly programmers, prefer working at the dot prompt. You'll learn a little about the dot prompt in Chapter 2. All your work in this book, however, will be done by using commands in the Assist screen.

For now, if you are at the dot prompt screen, move back to the Assist screen by pressing [F2]. This inserts the command ASSIST at the dot prompt and automatically executes it. You've moved to Assist when your screen looks like the one in Figure 1-1.

To quit dBASE after loading it from a hard disk:

a. Make sure the Set Up menu is displayed. If another menu is showing, press [S] to open the Set Up menu.

b. Highlight the command Quit dBASE III PLUS. You can do this by pressing [↑] once. This moves the highlight bar over the top and down to the bottom command of the Set Up menu.

c. Press [Enter].

When the program is unloaded from your computer's memory, it will give you this message on screen:

```
*** END RUN    dBASE III PLUS
```

Quitting dBASE while working in the dot prompt interface is even easier. First, load dBASE from your DOS prompt, as described earlier in this chapter. If you see the screen shown in Figure 1-1, press [Esc]. This closes the Assist screen and opens the dot prompt screen. With your cursor blinking to the right of the dot prompt:

a. Type **QUIT**.

b. Press [Enter].

You'll get the same message as when you quit from Assist.

You can also run the dBASE III PLUS program from a floppy disk. If you're going to use dBASE on a floppy disk, the disk must have a minimum capacity of 720K. This includes all 3 1/2-inch disks and quadruple density 5 1/4-inch disks formatted for 1.2 MB, or more.

There are advantages and disadvantages to using dBASE on a floppy disk. The program takes longer to load from a floppy disk, and it also takes dBASE longer to perform its work. However, you gain an extra measure of security since you can take your program and data disks out of the computer to keep people from using—and perhaps damaging—them.

When you do work in dBASE that needs to access data on disk frequently (such as indexing a database), it will take you much longer if you're using a floppy disk. After you become more familiar with dBASE, you'll be able to identify these disk-intensive activities. You can tell when your computer is accessing your disk because the disk drive light will be on.

To load dBASE III PLUS from a floppy disk, you need to insert two disks: a program disk and a data disk. The *program disk* contains your dBASE III PLUS program files. The *data disk* contains the data you want to use or will hold the data you create. The program won't load unless there are certain files on the program disk. You can find the names and descriptions of the files necessary to run the program from a floppy disk in Appendix A.

NOTE: You can run dBASE III PLUS from a single 720K or 1.2 MB floppy disk, but it is recommended that you keep your program and data files on separate disks.

To load dBASE from a floppy disk:

a. Place your program disk in drive A.

b. Place your data disk in drive B.

c. Type **A:** (that's A and then a colon) and press (Enter) to log onto the A drive. Make sure the DOS prompt A> is showing on your screen.

d. Type **DBASE** and press (Enter) to load the program into your computer's memory. The Assist screen, as shown in Figure 1-1, will appear. This is always the first screen to appear when you load dBASE III PLUS, regardless of whether you load the program from a floppy or a hard disk.

It will take a bit longer for dBASE to load when it's working from a floppy disk. Nevertheless, most personal computer programs can no longer work from floppy disks, so dBASE is particularly handy for people who still haven't upgraded to a hard disk.

To quit dBASE after loading it from a floppy disk:

a. Make sure the Set Up menu is open. If some other menu is open, press [S] to open the Set Up menu.

b. Press [↑] to highlight the bottom command, Quit dBASE III PLUS.

c. Press [Enter].

When the program is unloaded from memory, it will give you this message on screen:

*** END RUN   dBASE III PLUS

You quit from the dot prompt in this way:

a. Type **QUIT**.

b. Press [Enter].

Exercises

1. Are the steps for loading dBASE III PLUS from a hard disk and a floppy disk exactly the same?

2. What are the advantages of loading dBASE from a hard disk?

3. What are the advantages of loading dBASE from a floppy disk?

The Assist Interface
▶2◀

CHAPTER OBJECTIVES

In this chapter you will

▶ Become familiar with the Assist screen — 2.1

▶ Work with menus — 2.2

▶ Meet the dot prompt — 2.3

▶ Access help — 2.4

dBASE is a powerful database management program that is still flexible enough to let you begin at your own level of skill and confidence. You're given two choices of interface to use: a menu-driven interface called Assist and the dot prompt, which behaves like your DOS command line.

The Assist screen appears by default when you first load the program and includes all the commands you need to perform routine database management work. You'll spend most of your time in this chapter and the rest of the book working in Assist.

The dot prompt is an alternative interface that is used mostly by advanced users and programmers. You'll learn a little more about the dot prompt in this chapter.

Once you've loaded dBASE into your computer, you can begin working with it right away. All you need to know is how to access and use the correct commands.

Exercises

1. Begin at the DOS command line and load dBASE. Make sure the Assist screen is showing.

2. Quit dBASE using the Set Up menu; then reload the program so the Assist screen reappears.

2.1 BECOME FAMILIAR WITH THE ASSIST SCREEN

Assist serves as a central switchboard for controlling the dBASE III PLUS program.

NOTE: The Assist screen is referred to by two different names at various locations in the documentation published by the manufacturer: Assist and Assistant. This book refers to it as Assist, which is the way its name appears on the Assist screen.

The Assist screen is what is called a *nested menu-driven interface*. You can understand this more clearly if you take each term in reverse order and discover its definition. The term "interface" is just a fancy word for

Chapter 2   The Assist Interface

the way you communicate with a program. This includes all the keys you press to send commands to the program, as well as the way the program responds by displaying messages on the screen or carrying out your command. You communicate in the Assist screen by opening the pull-down menu you want to use and selecting a specific command on the menu. Pull-down menus are the eight menus whose names appear on the top line of your screen. dBASE III PLUS is therefore called a "menu-driven" program. In some cases, the command you select will lead to another menu that presents you with more commands or options. This is where the term "nested" applies, when one menu is nested within another. These subsidiary menus are called *pop-up menus* and are distinguished from pull-down menus because they pop up in various locations on your screen.

When you load dBASE III PLUS, the Assist screen will appear automatically and look like the one in Figure 2-1. The Set Up menu is always open when the Assist screen first appears, and the command

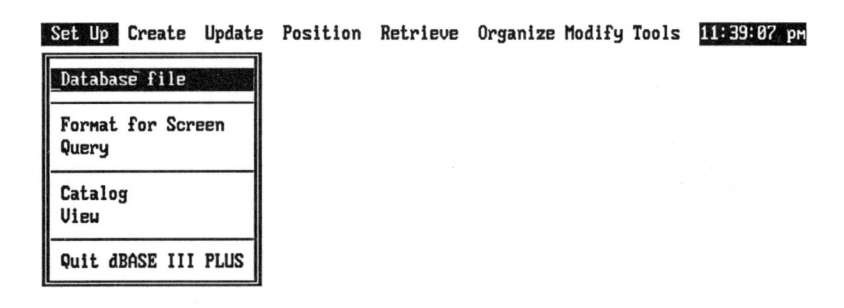

FIGURE 2-1.   The Assist screen

"Database file" at the top of the menu is highlighted by default. The top line of your screen is called the *menu bar.* There you will find the names of all eight available pull-down menus.

Now take a look at the bottom three lines on your screen. These three lines will appear in almost every dBASE screen. The very bottom line says "Select a database file." This is called the *message line*; it defines the command that is highlighted. In this case, it defines the command "Database file" on the Set Up menu. This command lets you select a database file to use.

The definition on the message line will change as you highlight different commands. Press [↓] to highlight the command Format for Screen, and your screen should now change to look like the one in Figure 2-2.

Notice that the definition on the message line now reads, "Select a screen design for updating with APPEND and EDIT." Don't worry about what this means—some dBASE terminology can seem pretty

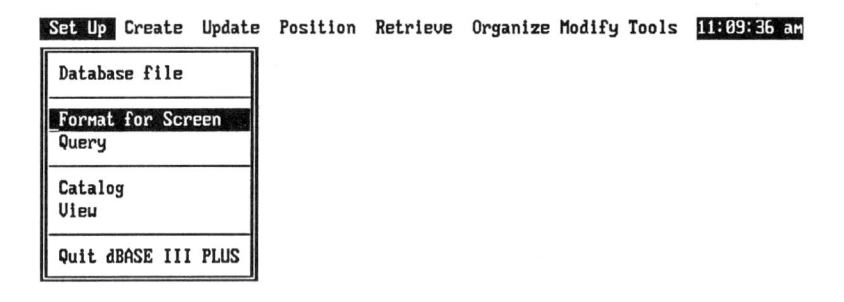

| FIGURE 2-2. | The command Format for Screen highlighted |

obscure the first time you run across it. Just notice how the definition changed for the new command. You'll find out more about what each command means at the appropriate time.

The second line from the bottom of your screen is called the *navigation line*. This line tells you how to navigate in your current situation. It is the line where dBASE displays its security prompts and error messages, in case dBASE wants to confirm your course of activity or let you know you've done something wrong. Notice that the information on the navigation line in Figures 2-1 and 2-2 is identical and can be interpreted using the following definitions:

Move selection bar	Press ↑ or ↓ to move the selection bar. This highlights an adjacent command in the open menu, either above or below the initially highlighted command, depending upon which arrow key you press.
Select	Press Enter to select and execute the highlighted command.
Leave menu	Press ← or → to leave the current menu. When you do this while viewing a pull-down menu, you'll move to the adjacent menu to the right or left, depending upon which arrow key you press. When you do this in a pop-up menu, you close the menu and return to the previous menu. You'll see how this works when you begin to work with pop-up menus later in this chapter.
Help	Press F1 to view help information or a more detailed description of the highlighted command. You'll learn more about this, as well as how to access other forms of help, later in this chapter.
Exit	Press Esc to exit from the Assist screen. This switches you to the alternative interface, the dot prompt.

You'll use all of these commands in this chapter.

The third line from the bottom is called the *status bar* because it shows the current status of your activities in dBASE III PLUS. The term ASSIST on the left side of the line shows you're working in the Assist screen. <C:> shows that the C drive is the current drive. Opt: 2/6 shows that the second of six options is highlighted in the current menu. The information on the status line will change as you start to do different things in the program. Press [↑] to highlight the top command on the Set Up menu, "Database file." You'll see the option information change to Opt: 1/6. When you load a database to start working with it, the name of the database will appear on the status line. Information about record numbers will replace the menu option information.

An additional line of information called the *action line* will appear just above the status bar when you select a command. As an example, select the command "Database file" on the Set Up menu (highlight the command name and press [Enter]). If the command "Database file" on the Set Up menu isn't already highlighted, press [↑] to highlight it now, and then press [Enter] to select the command. Notice the new line, Command: USE, which is displayed in Figure 2-3. This refers to the command you would use if you were trying to select a database from the dot prompt. You needn't pay any attention to the action line for your work in this book. Later, if you decide you want to become more proficient using the dot prompt, you can use information displayed on the action line as a means of learning specific dBASE programming language terms.

Before you continue, press [Esc] to remove the action line from your screen.

Exercises

1. What does the term "interface" mean?

2. What does the status bar do?

3. Which line is the status bar on?

4. What does the navigation line do?

5. What does the message line do?

Chapter 2   The Assist Interface   **19**

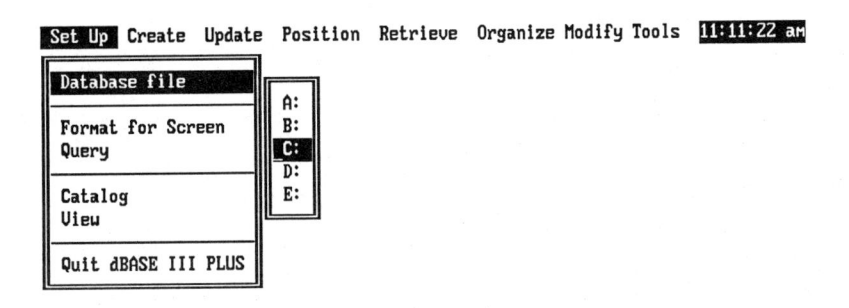

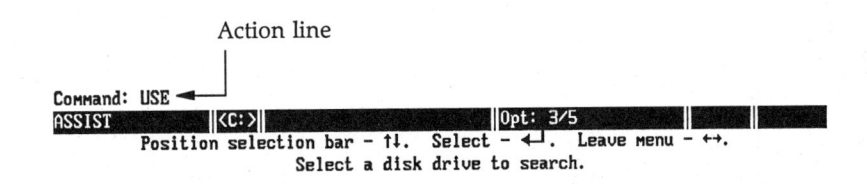

```
        Set Up  Create  Update  Position  Retrieve  Organize  Modify  Tools   11:11:22 am
       ┌─────────────────┐
       │ Database file   │  ┌────┐
       │                 │  │ A: │
       │ Format for Screen│ │ B: │
       │ Query           │  │ C: │
       │                 │  │ D: │
       │ Catalog         │  │ E: │
       │ View            │  └────┘
       │                 │
       │ Quit dBASE III PLUS │
       └─────────────────┘


                         Action line
                            │
           Command: USE ◄───┘
           ASSIST            <C:>              Opt: 3/5
                    Position selection bar - ↑↓.  Select - ↵.  Leave menu - ↔.
                           Select a disk drive to search.
```

| FIGURE 2-3. | The action line |

WORK WITH MENUS | 2.2 |

There are two types of menus you can use in dBASE III PLUS: pull-down and pop-up. There are eight pull-down menus, and they are all unique. Figure 2-4 shows the contents of all eight menus. You'll never be able to see all eight open on your screen like this, since you can open and work with only one menu at a time. Press ⟶ once now to open the Create menu. Press ⟶ again and you'll open the Update menu. Pressing ⟵ works the same but in a leftward direction.

You can also open a specific pull-down menu directly by pressing the key that matches the first letter of the menu name. For example, to open the Retrieve menu, press R. You can use Ctrl-key combinations

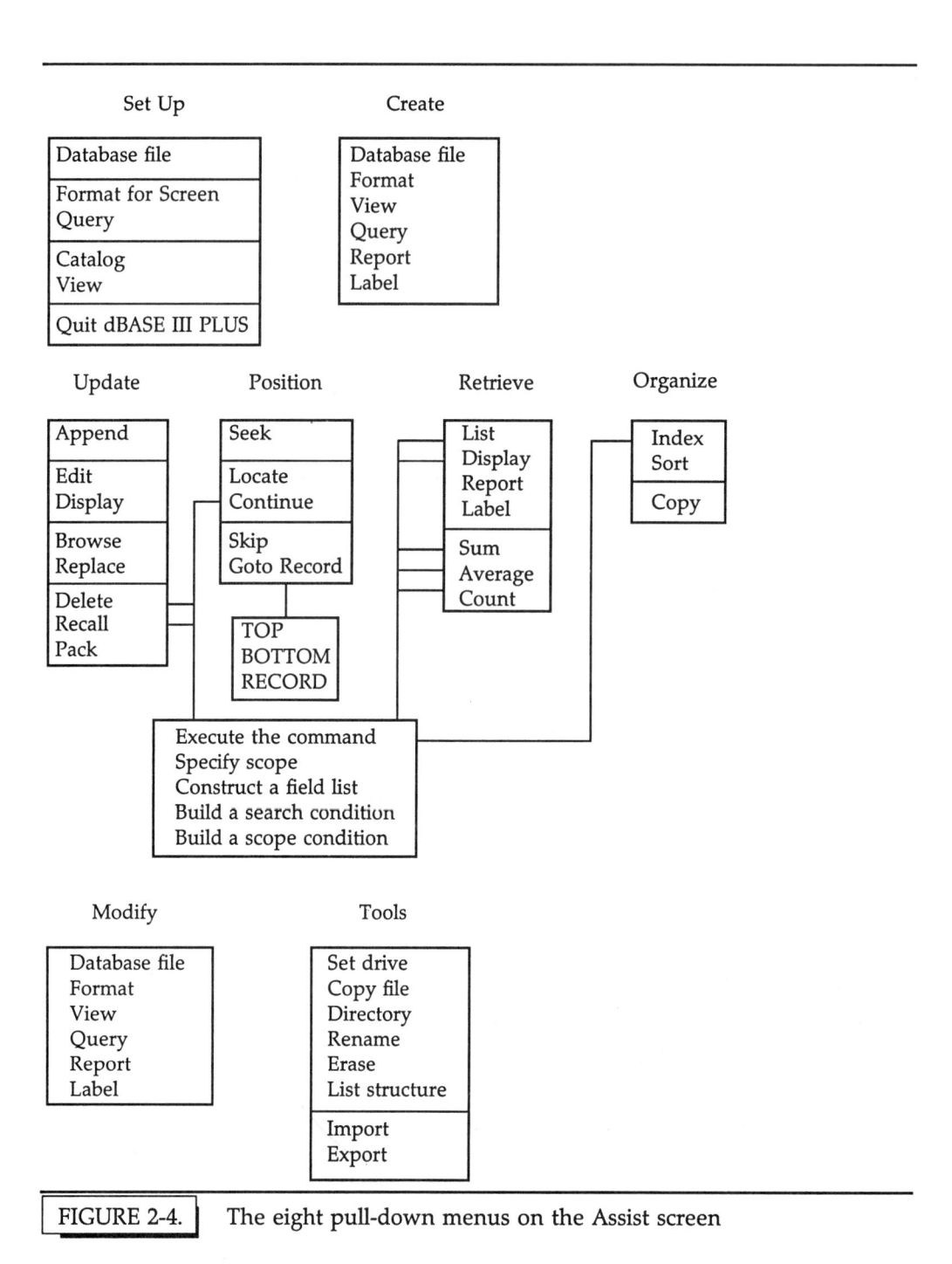

Set Up
- Database file
- Format for Screen
- Query
- Catalog
- View
- Quit dBASE III PLUS

Create
- Database file
- Format
- View
- Query
- Report
- Label

Update
- Append
- Edit
- Display
- Browse
- Replace
- Delete
- Recall
- Pack

Position
- Seek
- Locate
- Continue
- Skip
- Goto Record
- TOP
- BOTTOM
- RECORD

Retrieve
- List
- Display
- Report
- Label
- Sum
- Average
- Count

Organize
- Index
- Sort
- Copy

Execute the command
Specify scope
Construct a field list
Build a search condition
Build a scope condition

Modify
- Database file
- Format
- View
- Query
- Report
- Label

Tools
- Set drive
- Copy file
- Directory
- Rename
- Erase
- List structure
- Import
- Export

FIGURE 2-4. The eight pull-down menus on the Assist screen

to open pull-down menus, too. For example, pressing [Ctrl]-[F] opens the Tools menu. Table 2-1 shows all the commands you can use to open pull-down menus and select commands on the menus. You'll learn how to select individual commands in just a moment.

You might notice that the [Ctrl]-key combinations are grouped together on the left side of your keyboard. This allows rapid typists to open pull-down menus without moving their fingers from the typewriter keys.

The second type of menu, pop-up menus, are menus attached to specific commands; they provide for more control of complex commands. Pop-up menus are not unique. The same menu can pop up for different commands. As an example, select the command "Database file" on the Set Up menu. (Press [S] to open the Set Up menu if it isn't open already.) The top command on each pull-down menu will always appear highlighted by default when the menu first appears, so the command "Database file" should be highlighted. Press [Enter] to select the command. This opens a subsidiary menu displaying a list of the disk drive letters you can use, as shown in Figure 2-5. You can open this same menu for a variety of pull-down menu commands.

NOTE: The disk drive that is currently in use will always appear highlighted when this menu appears. Figure 2-5 shows the C: drive highlighted because it is the current drive.

TABLE 2-1.	Controls for Pull-down Menus		
Movement		**Cursor Keys**	[Ctrl]-**Keys**
Right one menu		[→]	[Ctrl]-[D]
Last menu		[End]	[Ctrl]-[F]
Left one menu		[←]	[Ctrl]-[S]
First menu		[Home]	[Ctrl]-[A]
Down one command		[↓]	[Ctrl]-[X]
Bottom command		[PgDn]	[Ctrl]-[C]
Up one command		[↑]	[Ctrl]-[E]
Top command		[PgUp]	[Ctrl]-[R]

22 Teach Yourself dBASE III PLUS

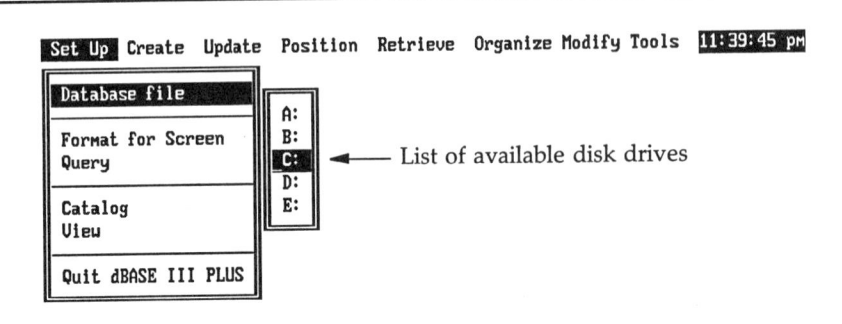

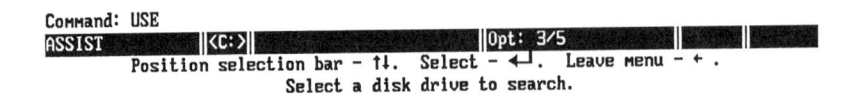

```
 Set Up  Create  Update  Position  Retrieve  Organize  Modify  Tools   11:39:45 pm
┌─────────────────────┐
│ Database file       │ ┌───┐
├─────────────────────┤ │A: │
│ Format for Screen   │ │B: │
│ Query               │ │C: │ ◄────── List of available disk drives
│                     │ │D: │
│ Catalog             │ │E: │
│ View                │ └───┘
├─────────────────────┤
│ Quit dBASE III PLUS │
└─────────────────────┘




Command: USE
ASSIST            <C:>                       Opt: 3/5
            Position selection bar - ↑↓.  Select - ↵.  Leave menu - ←.
                          Select a disk drive to search.
```

FIGURE 2-5. | List of available disk drives

The eight different pull-down menus in Assist have been divided into broad but specific activity groups and are fairly easy to remember. For example, to create a database, open the Create menu and select the command "Database file." The number of commands in each menu and the activities they control are defined here:

Set Up   Six commands that let you set up your current dBASE environment, including exiting the program completely.

Create   Six commands that let you create six different types of dBASE III PLUS files. Each command moves you into a separate component of the program that takes over the screen and provides you with a unique set of menus and commands.

Update   Eight commands that let you update the database you're currently working with. You'll learn how to use all of these commands as soon as you create your first database in Chapter 3.

Position   Five commands that let you find and move to specific records in the database you're working with. Some of these are elementary, such as going to a specific record or entry in the database. Others are more sophisticated, such as locating the next record or entry in a group with similar characteristics.

Retrieve   Seven commands that let you retrieve and display a variety of items. These items include specific database information, report and label files, and calculations based upon numbers in specific fields.

Organize   Three commands that let you organize information in the database you're working with or copy the information to another database in a different order.

Modify   Six commands that let you modify the different types of dBASE III PLUS files. Each command moves you into a separate component of the program that takes over the screen and provides you with a unique set of menus and commands.

Tools   Eight commands that let you perform certain routine DOS housekeeping activities, such as changing current drives, copying, renaming, and erasing files, listing the structure of the current database, and exporting and importing information.

These 49 commands provide you with a wide range of database management activities. You already used one of them in the last chapter: the command Quit dBASE III PLUS on the Set Up menu.

As you move through various menus, both pull-down and pop-up, you'll notice that some of the commands appear brighter than others. The brightness of the command reflects whether a specific command is enabled or disabled. You can't use some commands until you've created a certain type of dBASE environment.

As an example, you can't use any of the commands that work with databases until you open a specific database. You can see this most dramatically by switching between the Create and Update menus. Press [C] to open the Create menu. All the commands are enabled in this menu. This means dBASE is ready to create any type of file you want. Now press [U] to open the Update menu. No commands are enabled on this menu, because the Update menu lets you update information in a database, and no database is currently open or loaded into dBASE III PLUS. Notice how the highlight bar doesn't appear in a menu with all commands disabled (such as the Update menu). You can only highlight enabled commands.

Press [S] to open the Set Up menu. When you work in a menu with enabled commands, you can highlight different commands by using controls similar to those when you work with menus. In fact, the highlight bar behaves quite a bit like the cursor in a word processing program. Pressing [↓] moves the highlight bar down one command. Pressing [↑] moves the highlight bar up one command. You can also use [Ctrl]-key combinations. Refer to Table 2-1 for the keys you can use to select commands on menus.

Examples

1. You can use [→] or [←] to scroll through the pull-down menus. Hold down [→] and the menus appear in sequence rather quickly. When you move in a rightward direction, the Set Up menu opens after the Tools menu. When you move in a leftward direction, the Tools menu will open after the Set Up menu.

    Pressing [Ctrl]-[D] also opens the next pull-down menu to the right. Pressing [Ctrl]-[S] opens the next pull-down menu to the left. Holding these keys down scrolls you through the series of menus quickly.

2. Press [O] to open the Organize menu. Press [C] to open the Create menu. Press [T] to open the Tools menu. Press [S] to open the Set Up menu. You can also open the Set Up menu directly by pressing [Ctrl]-[A]. And you can open the Tools pull-down menu directly by pressing [Ctrl]-[F].

3. Once a menu is open, you can move the highlight bar over lower commands by pressing [↓]. When you get to the bottom command and press [↓] once again, the highlight bar moves back to the top command. If you hold the key down, you'll move down through commands quickly.

   This happens in the reverse order as well. If you press [↑] until the top command is highlighted, pressing [↑] once again highlights the bottom command.

4. Press [Ctrl]-[X] to move the highlight bar down one command. Press [Ctrl]-[E] to move it up one command. Pressing [Ctrl]-[C] highlights the bottom command automatically. Pressing [Ctrl]-[R] highlights the top command automatically.

Exercises

1. How many pull-down menus are there?

2. Begin in the Set Up menu and scroll through all eight pull-down menus going from left to right using one key; then return to the Set Up menu.

3. Open the Modify menu using a letter key.

4. Open the Tools menu using a [Ctrl]-key combination.

5. Open the Set Up menu using a [Ctrl]-key combination.

6. Highlight the second command on the Set Up menu.

7. Highlight the very bottom command on the Set Up menu.

8. Highlight the very top command on the Set Up menu by pressing one arrow key.

2.3 MEET THE DOT PROMPT

The dot prompt, present in all versions of dBASE, is the only interface that was available in dBASE II and dBASE III. The Assist was introduced with the release of dBASE III PLUS and was designed to assist new users in learning how to work with dBASE more quickly and easily. You're going to use the dot prompt in this section only. The rest of the book is devoted to commands you can use in the Assist interface.

Advanced dBASE users prefer the dot prompt because they can use commands that are unavailable in the Assist interface. Don't worry about being limited to the Assist. You can do all your routine database management by using commands in the Assist.

To switch to the dot prompt when the Assist screen is showing, just press (Esc). You might have to press (Esc) several times if you've selected a command in the Assist screen, to back out of the command first.

When the dot prompt appears, note that your screen is almost blank. There's not much to this interface—just the lonely dot in the lower left corner of your screen followed by the blinking cursor.

You work at the dBASE dot prompt the same way you work at the DOS prompt: You type an acceptable command and press (Enter) to execute the command, or you press a function key assigned to the command you want to use.

If you want to experiment with a dot prompt command, use one now to move back to the Assist screen:

a. Type **ASSIST**.

b. Press (Enter).

This moves you directly back to the Assist screen. Press (Esc) to return to the dot prompt.

Commands can be typed at the dot prompt in either upper- or lowercase letters. This means that "ASSIST" is identical to "asSIST" and "assist."

When using the dot prompt, you can also enter the ten most frequently used dBASE commands by using the function keys (F1) through (F10). When you press a function key, you do not need to press

[Enter]. dBASE executes [Enter] automatically. The ten commands assigned to function keys while working in the dot prompt are just the most popular. There are many more dBASE commands than these ten.

Examples

1. You can move from the dot prompt to the Assist screen by typing **ASSIST** and pressing [Enter]. You can also move from the dot prompt to the Assist screen by pressing [F2]. Try that now. Notice how dBASE automatically inserts the command ASSIST after the dot prompt and then executes the command.

2. There is no menu command in the Assist pull-down menus that lets you move to the dot prompt. The only way you can do so is by pressing [Esc]. If you've selected one or more commands in the Assist, you'll have to press [Esc] first to back out of the commands and then press [Esc] one more time to move to the dot prompt. You can move back and forth quickly and conveniently between the dot prompt and Assist by pressing [Esc] in Assist and [F2] at the dot prompt.

3. The most interesting function key command is [F6], "display status." At the dot prompt, press [F6]. This begins a two-screen display, the first of which looks like the one in Figure 2-6. This screen displays the status of your dBASE environment. The only part of this environment you might recognize at this point is the default disk drive, C:. You'll learn about the other elements of the dBASE environment later in this book.

    Press any key to see the second screen of the "display status" command. Your screen should change to look like the one in Figure 2-7. This screen displays the status of various settings you can change, as well as a list of nine of the ten commands assigned to the function keys at the dot prompt. You might want to remember the "display status" command, [F6], in case you don't have this book

```
. display status

File search path:
Default disk drive: C:
Print destination: PRN:
Margin =      0
Current work area =    1

Press any key to continue...
Command Line    |<C:>|

            Enter a dBASE III PLUS command.
```

| FIGURE 2-6. | The first screen of the "display status" command |

handy and want to know the other function key commands. The [F1] key accesses help. You'll learn about this key in the next section.

Exercises

1. With the dot prompt showing, move to the Assist screen by typing a command.

2. Move back to the dot prompt.

3. Move to the Assist screen by using a function key.

| 2.4 | ## ACCESS HELP |

We all need help at one time or another. Before you go any further, you should know how to access the help information provided as part of the program.

```
ALTERNATE - OFF   DELETED    - OFF   FIXED     - OFF   SAFETY     - ON
BELL      - ON    DELIMITERS - OFF   HEADING   - ON    SCOREBOARD - ON
CARRY     - OFF   DEVICE     - SCRN  HELP      - ON    STATUS     - ON
CATALOG   - OFF   DOHISTORY  - OFF   HISTORY   - ON    STEP       - OFF
CENTURY   - OFF   ECHO       - OFF   INTENSITY - ON    TALK       - ON
CONFIRM   - OFF   ESCAPE     - ON    MENU      - ON    TITLE      - ON
CONSOLE   - ON    EXACT      - OFF   PRINT     - OFF   UNIQUE     - OFF
DEBUG     - OFF   FIELDS     - OFF

Programmable function keys:
F2  - assist;
F3  - list;
F4  - dir;
F5  - display structure;
F6  - display status;
F7  - display memory;
F8  - display;
F9  - append;
F10 - edit;
```

Command Line   <C:>

Enter a dBASE III PLUS command.

FIGURE 2-7. The second screen of the "display status" command

You can obtain help five ways while working in dBASE III PLUS:

- While working in the Assist screen, you can view help information that's automatically displayed on the message and navigation lines of the Assist screen. These are the bottom two lines on your screen.
- While working in the Assist screen, you can press [F1] to view more detailed information about a specific command. This pops open a help window that provides on-line context-sensitive help describing the command. *On-line* means the help is ready at the touch of a key. *Context-sensitive* means that dBASE keeps track of what you're doing in the program and displays help appropriate to your current work.
- While working in the dot prompt, you can access the Help Main Menu by pressing [F1]. This is the most extensive form of help in the program and can serve as an introductory tutorial.

- While working in the dot prompt, if you mistype a command, dBASE will ask if you need help. You can press [N] or [Enter] to cancel help and type the command a second time. Or you can press [Y], and dBASE will present a description of the command it thinks you're trying to use.

- While working in a full-screen component of the program, you can automatically view a table of help information.

Some of this help is provided automatically, while the rest is optional. You'll take a closer look at these five types of help now. First, you'll work with the two types of help in the Assist screen. Then you'll explore help at the dot prompt. Finally, you'll see help that's available in a full-screen component of the program.

Switch to the Assist screen now if you're not already looking at it. (Press [F2] if you're working with the dot prompt.) Your screen should look like the one in Figure 2-1.

The best way to get help about individual commands is to highlight the command name and press [F1]. dBASE will give you a window of information about the command. For example, if you highlight the command "Database file" on the Set Up menu and press [F1], you'll see the window of information displayed in Figure 2-8.

This information might not make much sense to a new user of dBASE. What does the USE command have in common with the "Database file" command? The Set Up menu lets you *set up* your dBASE working environment, but when you select the "Database file" command, you're asking dBASE to load a specific database file you want to *use*.

Notice how the navigation line, the second line from the bottom on your screen, keeps current with new circumstances on your screen. The definition of the current menu command remains the same on the bottom line, but the description of what you can do in your present position as shown in the navigation line does change. It states "Press any key to continue work in ASSIST." This means that after you're finished reading the information displayed in the help window, you should close the window and return to work in Assist by pressing any key. Try that now. Press any key.

```
Set Up  Create  Update  Position  Retrieve  Organize  Modify  Tools   11:35:28 pm

                                  USE

        USE selects the active database file and its index files from existing
        files.  Subsequent commands operate on this database file until another
        one is selected.  If a new file is needed, use the Database File option
        in the Create menu.

            Command Format:   USE [<database file name>/?]
                              [INDEX <index file name>] [ALIAS <alias name>]




ASSIST          |<C:>|                    |Opt: 1/6 |
                    Press any key to continue work in ASSIST._
                            Select a database file.
```

FIGURE 2-8.	On-line context-sensitive help in Assist

Now switch to the dot prompt to explore the two types of help you can use there. Press [Esc] as many times as necessary to view the dot prompt on screen. Begin with the help tutorial available at the dot prompt: Press [F1]. This inserts the command HELP and automatically executes it. dBASE will display the Help Main Menu, as shown in Figure 2-9. The first choice, Getting Started, is highlighted. To explore the contents of this option, press [Enter]. You can view more information on this option by pressing [PgDn]. To exit this help, press [Esc], and you'll return to the dot prompt. You might want to explore the various options in the Help Main Menu at your leisure. You can do this by pressing the number of the option you want to explore, reading the information, and then selecting another option by pressing its number. You can press [Esc] at any point when using the Help Main Menu if you want to return to the dot prompt. Much of the information can serve as an introductory tutorial to dBASE III PLUS.

You can access a second type of help at the dot prompt when you type an incorrect command. For example:

a. Type **AS** and press [Enter]. This is not enough letters to indicate the ASSIST command, so dBASE reports that it doesn't recognize the command you've used and asks on the navigation line, "Do you want some help?"
b. Press [Y]. dBASE displays information about the ASSIST command. The program was smart enough to figure out that was the command you wanted to use.

If dBASE can't guess what command you want to use, it opens the Help Main Menu shown in Figure 2-9.

If you type a command incorrectly but you don't want help, just press [N] or [Enter] when dBASE asks if you want help. This returns the dot prompt to your screen. You should follow this procedure when you mistype a command and then realize your mistake.

The fifth type of help in dBASE requires that you enter a full-screen feature in the dBASE program. Examples of full-screen features you'll

```
                                                        MAIN MENU

         Help Main Menu


              1 - Getting Started
              2 - What Is a ...
              3 - How Do I ...
              4 - Creating a Database File
              5 - Using an Existing Database File
              6 - Commands and Functions




HELP         ||<C:>||
      Position selection bar - ↑↓. Select - ↵. Exit with Esc or enter a command.
              ENTER >
```

| FIGURE 2-9. | The Help Main Menu |

Chapter 2 The Assist Interface **33**

use are the Append and Edit screens and the Create screen, although there are many others in the program. Since you can open the Append and Edit screens only if you have access to a database in the current directory, you should open instead the Create screen as an example:

a. Make sure you're viewing the Assist screen.
b. Press C to open the Create menu.
c. Press [Enter] to select the "Database file" command, which is the top command on the menu, highlighted by default.
d. Press [Enter] again to accept the default drive letter.
e. Type **TEST** and press [Enter]. This tells dBASE to begin creating a database file called TEST.

dBASE will open the Create screen, which looks like the one in Figure 2-10. Don't worry about the details in this screen in this

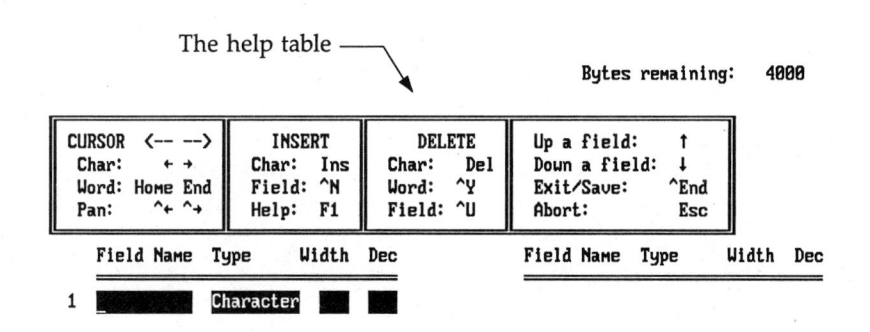

```
                    The help table
                                                    Bytes remaining:    4000

    ┌─────────────────┬─────────────────┬─────────────────┬─────────────────┐
    │ CURSOR  <-- -->│ INSERT          │ DELETE          │ Up a field:   ↑ │
    │ Char:     ← →  │ Char:    Ins    │ Char:    Del    │ Down a field: ↓ │
    │ Word: Home End │ Field:   ^N     │ Word:    ^Y     │ Exit/Save:  ^End│
    │ Pan:   ^← ^→   │ Help:    F1     │ Field:   ^U     │ Abort:      Esc │
    └─────────────────┴─────────────────┴─────────────────┴─────────────────┘

        Field Name   Type      Width  Dec        Field Name   Type     Width  Dec
        ─────────────────────────────────        ─────────────────────────────────
     1  ▮▮▮▮▮▮▮▮▮▮  Character  ▮▮    ▮▮




    ┌──────────┬─────────┬──────────────┬──────────┐
    │ CREATE   │<C:>│TEST │ Field: 1/1   │          │
    └──────────┴─────────┴──────────────┴──────────┘
                       Enter the field name.
    Field names begin with a letter and may contain letters, digits and underscores
```

FIGURE 2-10. The Create screen showing the help table

chapter. You'll start working with it in Chapter 3. The feature to notice is the table at the top of the screen. This provides information about how you work in the screen. You can leave this table displayed (on) when you first start working in the Create screen. Once you become familiar with the table and want more space on your screen to work in, press [F1] to toggle off the table information. Notice how you're given more room to work in the screen. Press [F1] a second time to toggle the help information back on.

Return to the Assist screen now.

a. Press [Esc] to exit the Create screen. dBASE asks you on the navigation line if you really want to abandon your current work.

b. Press [Y]. This confirms your exit and returns you to the Assist screen.

Examples

1. Explore the differences between the navigation line and the message line. Move to Assist. With the Set Up menu showing, highlight each command in turn and watch your navigation and status lines. This means you need to press [↓] five times while keeping your eyes on the bottom two lines of your screen. Notice that information on the navigation line remains the same for each command but changes on the message line.

2. Switch to the dot prompt. Press [F1] to open and explore the Help Main Menu. Highlight option 4—Creating a Database File. Read each screen and then press [PgDn] to view each succeeding screen. This should prepare you for Chapter 3.

Exercises

1. Find out what on-line context-sensitive help has to say about the six commands on the Create menu.

2. Find out what on-line context-sensitive help has to say about the Query and View commands on the Set Up menu. Be sure to close the last help window.

3. Move to the dot prompt. Open the Help Main Menu. Find out what information is given for the second option: "2 — What Is a . . . ."

4. Find out more information about option "7 — Records" in the "What Is a . . ." screen.

5. Return to the dot prompt.

6. Enter the command HEP and see what dBASE does.

7. Return to Assist.

Creating a Database
► 3 ◄

CHAPTER OBJECTIVES

In this chapter, you will learn how to

► Design a structure	3.1
► Insert character fields	3.2
► Insert numeric fields	3.3
► Insert date, logical, and memo fields	3.4
► Save and view the structure	3.5

Before you can begin entering data into a database, you must create the structure of the database. The backbone of a database, the structure determines the form and shape of the database. Without the correct structure, you won't be able to insert the information you want to keep track of.

Before you can create the structure, you must have a clear idea in your head of exactly what type of information you want to save in the database. This includes the type of characters you want to use (text, numbers, or symbols) and their format in the database (dates, currency), as well as certain conditions (true/false, male/female).

In this chapter you'll begin working with the dBASE program by designing a structure for a simple name-and-address database. You'll use this example to learn more about the dBASE concepts of fields, records, and files.

Follow these three steps each time you want to create a database:

a. First, design the structure. This is where you conceptualize the type of information you want to save.

b. Next, give the database a valid name.

c. Finally, create the structure. When you create a structure, you insert and define various fields you want to use.

Exercises

SKILLS CHECK

1. Load dBASE into your computer's memory.

2. Open the Create menu.

3. Find out what on-line context-sensitive help says about the command "Database file" at the top of the Create menu.

DESIGN A STRUCTURE

| 3.1 |

The two main elements of a database structure are fields and records. A *field* contains a discrete piece of information you want to save. For a database of people you know, one field would contain the name, another the street address, and a third the phone number. You could include additional fields for the city and state names if you wanted to save information with that level of detail.

A *record* contains a set of fields for an individual entry. You would create a record for each person you want to place into your database. Each record would contain the individual's name, street address, city, state, and phone number. You'll get a better idea of the relationship between fields and records when you create your first database and begin entering information into it.

To design a database correctly, you need to know what type of information you want to save, and in some cases how much of it you want to save. Once you have a clear idea of the type and amount of information you want to save, you define and insert the fields that are appropriate.

Different types of information must be inserted into different types of fields. You can use the following five types of fields in dBASE III PLUS: character, date, numerical, logical, and memo.

- A *character field* is the most commonly used type and can contain any alphanumeric information, which means all letters and numbers you can type from your keyboard.

- A *date field* can contain calendar dates only.

- A *numerical field* can contain numbers only. This is a more specialized form of the character field type; you can perform calculations on numerical fields but you can't on character fields.

- A *logical field* can contain only a true (T) or false (F) entry or a yes (Y) or no (N) entry.

- A *memo field* is designed to contain more text than can fit into a character field.

You can insert a minimum of one field or a maximum of 128 fields into a single database. When you use character or numeric fields, you must also specify the field length—the maximum number of characters you plan to put into these fields. dBASE III PLUS uses a *fixed file format,* which means you can't enter more characters into a character or numeric field than you've specified as the width of the field. You can always enter less information than the maximum. You can even decline to enter any information into a field. But if you declare a character field to be 30 spaces wide, you can't enter 31 characters into the field.

Two of the field types, date and logical, have fixed formats. You must enter six numbers into a date field, which uses the format mm/dd/yy (month/day/year). The two slashes are added automatically by dBASE.

You can enter only one character into a logical field, either T, F, Y, or N. You use a logical field to specify one of two conditions, such as whether the account is paid or unpaid, whether the person is male or female, and whether the record has been updated or not.

The rules for naming fields are fairly restrictive. First of all, the name of each field in a database must be unique. This means you can't use the same name twice in the same database.

You can use only alphanumeric characters and the underline symbol (_). This means all alphabetic characters, numbers, and one symbol, the underline (_). This totals 37 characters: the 26 alphabetic characters, the ten digits 0 . . . 9, and the underline symbol. You must use at least one character in a name, but you can't use more than ten characters. The field name must begin with an alphabetic character, such as A, B, or C. You can use numbers beginning in the second position, such as N12, NAME1, and so on.

The only nonalphanumeric character you can use, the underline symbol, lets you separate two short words and make them more intelligible, such as FIRST_NAME and LAST_NAME. You can't use any spaces in field names.

Don't feel that you're bound irrevocably to the structure you first create. You can always modify the structure of a database if you have to. But there's no substitute for thinking clearly beforehand and saving yourself the trouble of modifying a database more often than you need to.

Examples

1. Different types of databases contain different types of fields. A personal name-and-address database needs only five fields: name, street address, city, state, and ZIP code. These can all be character-type fields.

    A vendor database file, however, might contain other types of information. You might want to keep track of prices, which require numeric fields. You might want to use a date field to show when you last bought an item. You might want to use a logical field to show whether or not you ordered recently from the vendor (yes/no) or if the vendor is a reliable supplier (true/false).

2. Use field names that serve as mnemonic reminders of the field contents. NAME is fine for a name field in a personal phone book file, but if the database contains both a company name and the name of a person you contact at the company, you should probably use COMPANY for company name and CONTACT for the contact person. Each field name in a database must be unique.

3. You might want to use identical types of fields to contain similar, but not identical, information. For example, you might want to use several date fields, one to record a birth date, another to record an anniversary date, and a third to show when you last updated the record. This is the time to use field names that distinguish the contents of the field precisely. The first field could be called BIRTH or BORN_DATE. The second field could be called ANNIVERSAR or ANN_DATE, and the third could be called UPDATE.

Exercises

1. What are the most appropriate six fields for a personal phone book database? Think about the information you save for your friends.

2. What are the most appropriate types of fields for the following information:

INV	COMPANY	TITLE	TYPE	QUANT	PRICE	IMPORT	ORDERED
4127	ACME	12 Golden Songs	record	5	$5.00	T	08/12/88
4135	BLUE TUNES	Jazz Favorites	record	5	$5.50	F	07/22/89

```
4119 BLUE TUNES      25 from Waller    cd       10   $8.75  F   01/16/90
4002 BLUE TUNES      More from Fats    record    5   $4.50  F   02/02/89
4012 QUEBECOIS       Daniel Lanois     record   12   $5.00  T   11/23/88
4015 STRANGE CHARM   Sweet Dreams      tape      8   $4.50  F   12/13/88
```

3. If you were to add the telephone number to the above database, what type of field would you use?

3.2 INSERT CHARACTER FIELDS

The first database you'll create is a name-and-address database. You'll use this to keep track of various people you know. Your first step is to insert six fields that will contain the name of each person, the street address, the city, the state, the ZIP code, and the phone number. Later you'll insert more fields that let you store other types of information about these people.

Your first step is to load dBASE into your computer's memory. The second step is to open the Create screen.

To open the Create screen, use the Create pull-down menu:

a. If you're viewing the Set Up menu on screen, press [→] once to open the Create menu. This is the second menu from the left in the Assist screen. (You explored the definitions of each command on this menu in Chapter 2, when you opened on-line context-sensitive help for each of the six commands on this menu.)

b. Press [Enter] to select the command "Database file." This command is highlighted by default when the Create pull-down menu first appears. Selecting the command "Database file" opens the disk drive selection menu with the current drive highlighted by default.

c. Press [Enter] to select the default drive. dBASE opens a prompt box that asks you to declare the name for the database you want to create.

d. Type **NAD** (for name and address) and press [Enter].

Chapter 3 Creating a Database **43**

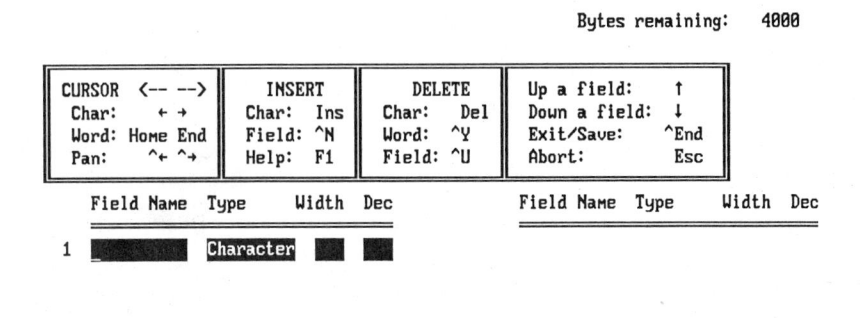

```
                                               Bytes remaining:    4000

        ┌─────────────────────┬─────────────────┬─────────────────┬──────────────────────┐
        │ CURSOR    <-- -->   │   INSERT        │   DELETE        │ Up a field:     ↑    │
        │ Char:      ← →      │ Char:    Ins    │ Char:     Del   │ Down a field:   ↓    │
        │ Word: Home End      │ Field:   ^N     │ Word:     ^Y    │ Exit/Save:     ^End  │
        │ Pan:     ^← ^→      │ Help:    F1     │ Field:    ^U    │ Abort:          Esc  │
        └─────────────────────┴─────────────────┴─────────────────┴──────────────────────┘
            Field Name   Type    Width   Dec        Field Name   Type    Width   Dec
        1   ▓▓▓▓▓▓▓▓   Character  ▓▓      ▓


        ▓CREATE▓▓▓▓▓▓▓▓▓▓<C:>▓NAD▓▓▓▓▓▓▓▓▓▓▓▓▓▓Field: 1/1▓▓▓▓▓▓▓▓▓▓▓▓▓▓
                              Enter the field name.
        Field names begin with a letter and may contain letters, digits and underscores
```

FIGURE 3-1.	The Create screen

dBASE will now display the Create screen, shown in Figure 3-1.

Familiarize yourself with features on this screen so you can work in it with confidence. Some of the elements also appear in other dBASE III PLUS screens.

Starting at the bottom, notice the three lines you first learned about in the Assist screen. These are the status bar as the top line, the navigation line below that, and the message line at the bottom. These three lines keep you advised as to your current environment and activity in all dBASE screens.

The left side of the status bar shows you're in the Create screen. The rest of the status bar shows that the current drive is C, the database NAD is active, and you're creating the first field (Field 1/1).

The navigation line tells you that your next step is to enter a field name. The message line tells you what characters you can use to enter a field name. The middle of the screen is where you insert fields and view them on screen.

| TABLE 3-1. | Help Instructions in the Create Screen |

Keys	Action
←	Cursor left one space
↑	Cursor up one line
→	Cursor right one space
↓	Cursor down one line
Home	Left one word
End	Right one word
Ctrl - ←	Left end of line
Ctrl - →	Right end of line
Ins	Insert mode
Ctrl - N	Insert new field
F1	Toggle help on/off
Del	Delete character
Ctrl - Y	Delete whole word
Ctrl - U	Delete field
Ctrl - End	Exit and save current structure
Esc, then Y	Abandon create

The top of the screen provides a table of help instructions telling you what you can do in the Create screen. You first saw this table in Chapter 2, when you learned how to get help in dBASE. Table 3-1 shows the help information presented in the Create screen. To turn the help table off, press F1. Figure 3-2 shows what the Create screen looks like when help is turned off.

By removing the table of help at the top, you expand the area you can work in. Whenever you want to view help, press F1 again. Pressing F1 toggles help on and off. You won't need much space to create your first database, so keep help on. Make sure your Create screen looks like the one in Figure 3-1.

The right side of the very top line in the Create screen shows that you have 4000 bytes remaining. This is the maximum number of characters you can use to define a database structure. Each character in a field name occupies one space. The structure information is stored at

Chapter 3   Creating a Database

```
                                            Bytes remaining:    4000

         Field Name   Type    Width  Dec        Field Name  Type    Width  Dec
         ═══════════════════════════════        ═══════════════════════════════
      1  ▓▓▓▓▓▓▓▓▓▓  Character ▓▓▓▓  ▓▓




  ┌─────────────┬─────────┬─────────────┬────────────────┬──────┬──────┐
  │ CREATE      │ <C:>    │ NAD         │ Field: 1/1     │      │      │
  └─────────────┴─────────┴─────────────┴────────────────┴──────┴──────┘
                            Enter the field name.
          Field names begin with a letter and may contain letters, digits and underscores
```

FIGURE 3-2.	The Create screen with help turned off

the front of the database file to let dBASE know what structure it's working with. You'll find that 4000 bytes of structure information is quite a lot. You'll hardly touch this amount for your first database.

You'll find the cursor blinking under the column marked Field Name for field 1 when the Create screen first appears. To insert a character field, you must declare the name of the field, the type of field, and the size of the field, using these three steps:

a. Type the name of the first field you want to use and press [Enter]. This moves you to the next column, called Type.

b. Declare the type of field you want to use. There are five types, but "Character" appears by default since this is the type you will use most often. To accept this field type, just press [Enter]. The cursor moves to the third column, called Width.

c. Type the number of spaces you want the field to contain. dBASE uses what's called a fixed field format, which means that once you declare the number of spaces for a field, that number remains the same unless you modify the field. Modifying fields is described in Chapter 8.

Field size for character fields is often more important than the name you give the field. When you start filling the field with information, you can use only as many characters as will fit in the size you've declared for the field. dBASE III PLUS allows a maximum of 254 characters in a character field, 19 in a numeric field. You can use fewer characters than the size, but you can't use any more. They simply won't fit. Therefore, always keep in mind the maximum size of the information you want to save in the field. For state names, this is a simple decision. You'll always use two characters for the accepted postal code abbreviations (CA for California, NY for New York, and so on).

For ZIP code fields, you can use either five or ten spaces, depending upon whether you want to use the five-digit or ten-digit code. Declaring a width of ten spaces lets you use either five or ten digits, but it also builds a bigger database. Five spaces might not seem like much, but if you insert 10,000 records, it could cause some problems. If you declare a ZIP code field width of ten spaces and use only five, there will be 5K of wasted space. If each field has superfluous space, the waste can build up rapidly.

When you're finished declaring the field width for character fields, press [Enter] to move the cursor down to the beginning of the next field.

Examples

1. Insert your first field in the NAD database: Type **NAME** and press [Enter]. (Field names always appear in uppercase letters, regardless of how you enter them.) The cursor moves into the second column, Type. Notice how the field type is predefined as "Character." You can explore the four other field types by pressing SPACEBAR. Notice how "Character" changes to "Numeric." Press SPACEBAR three more times. You'll pass through Date and Logical and end up with Memo. You might want to cycle through the list a second time, but keep your eyes on the message line as you do so. You'll notice the definition for each field type appear in sequence. Keep pressing SPACEBAR until you return to the character field type. This is the type you want to use.

Chapter 3   Creating a Database

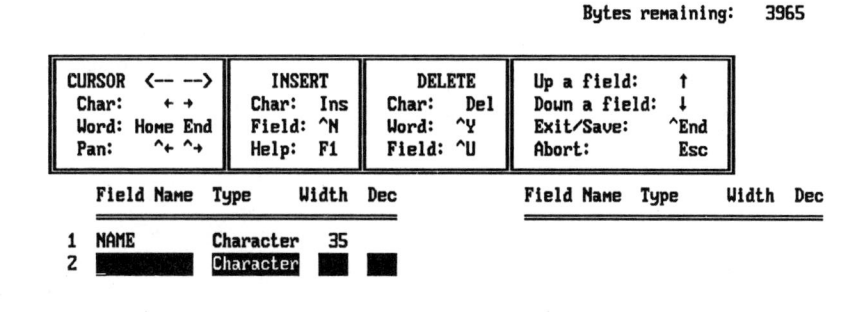

```
                                       Bytes remaining:  3965

   ┌─────────────────┬────────────────┬───────────────┬─────────────────┐
   │ CURSOR  <-- -->│ INSERT         │ DELETE        │ Up a field:   ↑ │
   │ Char:    ← →   │ Char:    Ins   │ Char:   Del   │ Down a field: ↓ │
   │ Word: Home End │ Field:    ^N   │ Word:    ^Y   │ Exit/Save:  ^End│
   │ Pan:    ^← ^→  │ Help:      F1  │ Field:   ^U   │ Abort:       Esc│
   └─────────────────┴────────────────┴───────────────┴─────────────────┘
        Field Name   Type    Width  Dec      Field Name  Type   Width  Dec

      1 NAME         Character   35
      2 ▌            Character

   CREATE    ||<C:>||NAD                  ||Field: 2/2 ||
                        Enter the field name.
   Field names begin with a letter and may contain letters, digits and underscores
```

FIGURE 3-3.   The first field in NAD

    Press (Enter). This accepts the character field type and moves the cursor to the Width column. The message line describes minimum and maximum settings for width. The navigation line tells you to enter a specific width. This means the maximum number of characters you'll want to use—the longest name. As an experiment, don't enter a value this time.

    Press (Enter). Did you hear the beep? dBASE has alerted you to a problem. The bottom two lines say you've entered an illegal data length so you should press any key to continue. Press (Enter) (or any other key) and type **35**. This is a good length for names, at least when you start out. Press (Enter). This last step completes all the information for the first field and moves your cursor down one line so you can begin creating the second field. Your screen should now look like the one in Figure 3-3.

2. Insert a second character field called ADDRESS: Type **ADDRESS** and press (Enter) twice. The first inserts the field name; the second

accepts the field type as character. Type **35** and press [Enter]. This declares the field to be 35 characters wide and moves you down to the third field.

3. Insert a third field called CITY. Type **CITY** and press [Enter] twice. Type **20** and press [Enter].

Exercises

1. What's the difference between the Create pull-down menu and the Create Database screen?

2. What are the three categories of characters you can use for field names?

3. What are the minimum and maximum sizes for character fields?

4. Insert a fourth character field, called STATE, with a field width of two characters.

5. Insert a fifth character field, called ZIP, with a field width of five characters.

6. Insert a sixth character field, called PHONE, with a field width of 15 characters.

3.3 INSERT NUMERIC FIELDS

Numeric fields are fields designed to hold numbers that will be calculated. They aren't designed simply to hold information containing numbers, such as addresses (123 West Street), ZIP codes, and phone numbers because these numbers will not be calculated. They are numbers used for reference only.

Information appropriate for numeric fields are numbers that represent some value. If you're a businessperson, these would be quantities, prices, and costs (or almost all currency figures). If you're a scientist, these would be degrees of angles or temperature. Numeric fields have been designed to contain figures that you add, subtract, and calculate in various other ways to obtain more information—the results of the calculation.

Numeric fields can be as small as 1 space and as wide as 19 spaces. If you use a decimal point, you're limited to 18 characters because one is used for the decimal point.

If you use a decimal point, there are two other requirements you should keep in mind. First, once you've defined the field as numeric, you must declare the size of the entire field; then you must declare how much of that space will be used by decimal numbers. Second, you need to reserve a minimum of two spaces to the left of the decimal point, leaving room for at least one integer and the decimal point itself since the decimal point must occupy one of those spaces.

Example

1. Expand the structure of NAD by inserting a numeric field (before you begin, your screen should look like the one in Figure 3-4): Type **MONEY** and press [Enter]. This is the name of the numeric field you'll use. Press SPACEBAR once to display Numeric. Notice that the bottom line of your screen describes the type of information you can place into a numeric field. Press [Enter] and type 6. This is the width of the total numeric field. Since this numeric field will contain money amounts, a width of six will let you enter up to $999.99. Press [Enter]. This moves the cursor into the Dec column.

    The Dec column stands for decimal points or places. You can enter a value into the Dec column when you create a numeric field. Type **2** and press [Enter]. This is the number of decimal numbers you want to use. Two decimal numbers lets you insert cents. Fields containing money amounts usually have two decimal numbers. The structure for NAD should now look like that shown in Figure 3-5.

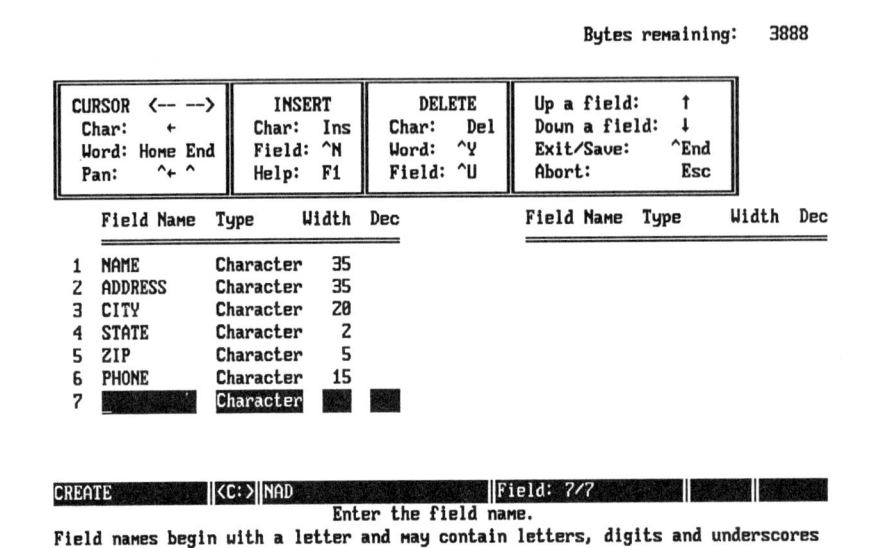

```
                                                    Bytes remaining:   3888

        CURSOR  <-- -->  ║  INSERT       ║  DELETE      ║  Up a field:    ↑
        Char:      ←     ║  Char:   Ins  ║  Char:  Del  ║  Down a field:  ↓
        Word: Home End   ║  Field:  ^N   ║  Word:  ^Y   ║  Exit/Save:    ^End
        Pan:    ^← ^→    ║  Help:   F1   ║  Field: ^U   ║  Abort:         Esc

            Field Name  Type       Width  Dec        Field Name  Type   Width  Dec
          1 NAME        Character   35
          2 ADDRESS     Character   35
          3 CITY        Character   20
          4 STATE       Character    2
          5 ZIP         Character    5
          6 PHONE       Character   15
          7             Character

        CREATE        ║<C:>║NAD              ║Field: 7/7  ║
                              Enter the field name.
        Field names begin with a letter and may contain letters, digits and underscores
```

FIGURE 3-4.   NAD with the first six fields

Exercises

1. Suggest some types of numbers that are inappropriate for numeric fields.

2. Suggest some examples of numbers that are suitable for numeric fields.

3. What are the minimum and maximum field sizes you can use for numeric fields without decimal numbers?

4. What is the minimum field size you can use for a numeric field with five decimal numbers?

5. How many decimal numbers can be used in a numeric field that is ten spaces wide?

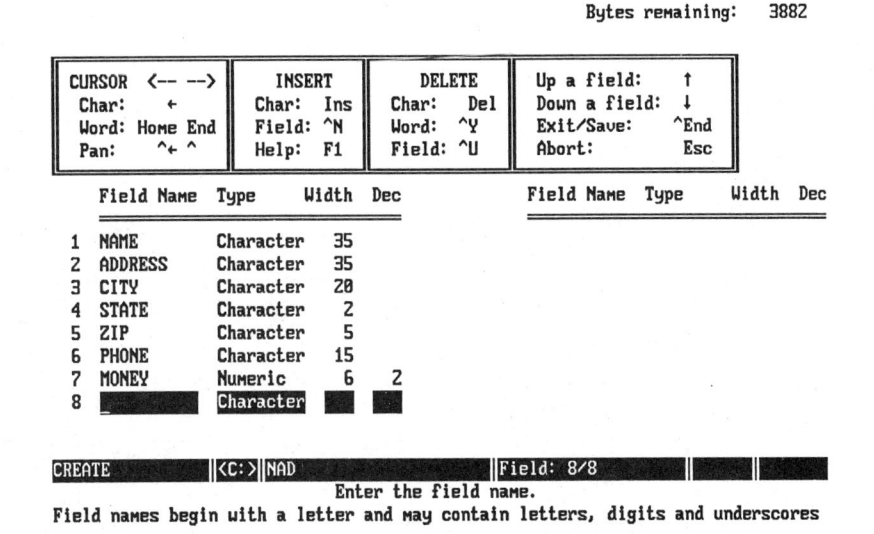

```
                                                     Bytes remaining:   3882

       ┌─────────────────┬─────────────────┬─────────────────┬──────────────────────┐
       │ CURSOR  <-- -->│     INSERT      │     DELETE      │ Up a field:     ↑    │
       │ Char:      ←   │ Char:     Ins   │ Char:     Del   │ Down a field:   ↓    │
       │ Word: Home End │ Field:    ^N    │ Word:     ^Y    │ Exit/Save:      ^End │
       │ Pan:    ^← ^→  │ Help:     F1    │ Field:    ^U    │ Abort:          Esc  │
       └─────────────────┴─────────────────┴─────────────────┴──────────────────────┘
           Field Name   Type     Width  Dec        Field Name   Type    Width  Dec
         ─────────────────────────────────────    ─────────────────────────────────
       1  NAME         Character   35
       2  ADDRESS      Character   35
       3  CITY         Character   20
       4  STATE        Character    2
       5  ZIP          Character    5
       6  PHONE        Character   15
       7  MONEY        Numeric      6    2
       8  ▇▇▇▇▇▇▇     Character  ▇▇    ▇

    ┌─────────┬────────┬────────────────┬──────────────┬──────────┐
    │ CREATE  │ <C:>NAD│                │ Field: 8/8   │          │
    └─────────┴────────┴────────────────┴──────────────┴──────────┘
                         Enter the field name.
         Field names begin with a letter and may contain letters, digits and underscores
```

FIGURE 3-5.   NAD with a numerical field

INSERT DATE, LOGICAL, AND MEMO FIELDS — 3.4

The three remaining field types are date, logical, and memo fields. While these three types of fields are very different from one another, you can insert a date, logical, or memo field into a database structure with ease. All you need to do is give the field a name and select the type. The format for each field is fixed by dBASE.

The date field type contains eight characters in the format mm/dd/yy (month/day/year). The slash marks are entered automatically. When you begin to insert information into a date field, all you do is enter the six digits of the date. For example, when you want to see the date 10/30/90, you type **103090**. dBASE will jump over the slash marks.

NOTE: dBASE will not recognize your entry in the date field unless you type in all 6 digits, including any zeroes that precede a single day or month entry. For example, April 2, 1990 should be entered as **040290**.

The logical field type contains one character only. This can be any one of four characters: T, F, Y, and N (for true, false, yes, and no).

The memo field type is unusual. It has been designed to contain text that won't fit into a character type field, usually because the text is too long or too undifferentiated. You can insert a maximum of 254 characters into a character field, but you can insert up to 5000 characters into a single memo field. You can even insert carriage returns and tab marks into memo field text to make the text easier to read.

When you insert a memo field, dBASE assigns to it a width of ten spaces. When you begin inserting information into the database, you won't enter anything into the spaces after a memo field, as you will with all other types of fields. Instead, dBASE automatically creates a second file, using the same name as the database file but adding the extension .DBT, for database text file. This is the only way dBASE can accommodate text longer than 254 characters. When you begin inserting information into a memo field, dBASE moves you to the second file, where the information will be saved. You'll see how this works in Chapter 4, when you begin inserting information.

Examples

1. Insert an eighth field into NAD, using the date field type, and call it DATE. Type **DATE** and press [Enter]. Press SPACEBAR two times to select Date, and then press [Enter]. You'll notice that dBASE automatically assigns this field eight spaces.

2. Insert a ninth field, using the logical field type, and call it AGAIN. Type **AGAIN** and press [Enter]. This field will keep track of whether or not you want to call this account again. Press SPACEBAR three times to select Logical, and then press [Enter]. dBASE automatically assigns this field one space.

3. Insert a tenth field, using the memo field type, and call it NOTES. Type **NOTES** and press [Enter]. Press SPACEBAR four times to select Memo, and then press [Enter]. This is where we'll write information

Chapter 3 Creating a Database 53

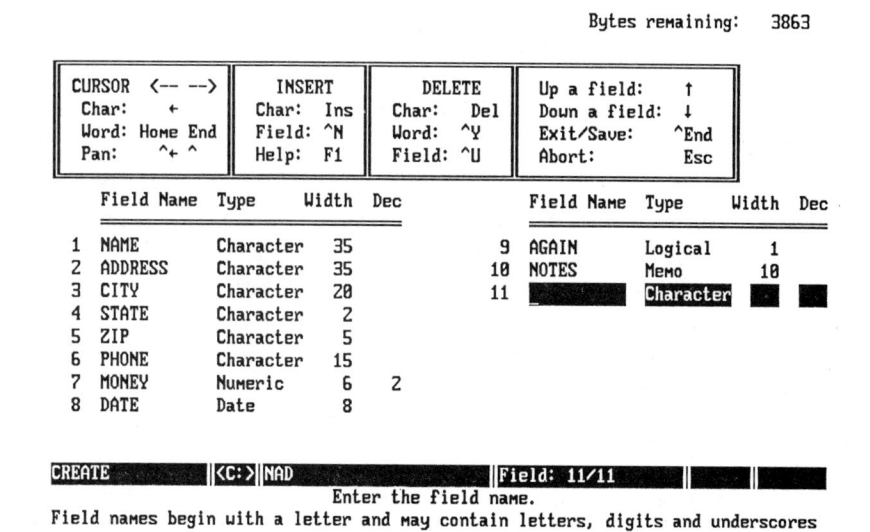

```
                                                     Bytes remaining:  3863

     ┌─────────────────┬─────────────────┬─────────────────┬──────────────────────┐
     │ CURSOR  <-- -->│    INSERT       │    DELETE       │ Up a field:     ↑    │
     │  Char:     ←   │  Char:    Ins   │  Char:    Del   │ Down a field:   ↓    │
     │  Word: Home End│  Field:   ^N    │  Word:    ^Y    │ Exit/Save:     ^End  │
     │  Pan:    ^← ^→ │  Help:    F1    │  Field:   ^U    │ Abort:          Esc  │
     └─────────────────┴─────────────────┴─────────────────┴──────────────────────┘
        Field Name   Type      Width  Dec         Field Name   Type      Width  Dec
        ══════════════════════════════════         ══════════════════════════════════
      1 NAME         Character   35              9 AGAIN        Logical     1
      2 ADDRESS      Character   35             10 NOTES        Memo       10
      3 CITY         Character   20             11 ▓▓▓▓▓▓▓      Character  ▓▓  ▓▓
      4 STATE        Character    2
      5 ZIP          Character    5
      6 PHONE        Character   15
      7 MONEY        Numeric      6    2
      8 DATE         Date         8

     ▐CREATE▌    ▐<C:>▌▐NAD▌              ▐Field: 11/11▌
                        Enter the field name.
        Field names begin with a letter and may contain letters, digits and underscores
```

| FIGURE 3-6. | The completed structure of NAD in the Create screen |

that doesn't fit into any of the other fields. dBASE assigns this field ten spaces. The structure for NAD should now look like the one in Figure 3-6.

Exercises

1. How many spaces does dBASE assign to a date field?

2. How many spaces to a logical field?

3. What characters can you insert in a logical field?

4. What is the purpose of a memo field?

3.5 SAVE AND VIEW THE STRUCTURE

When you've expanded NAD to include the four new field types, and the structure looks like that shown in Figure 3-6, you're ready to view it for errors and then save the structure. Once you've created a structure you want to use, you save it to disk. Up to this point, the structure has been created only in your computer's memory. If your computer were to fail now, you'd lose all your work up to this point.

Before you actually save the structure, you should check it for errors. You can always move the cursor back over any item you've declared and change it. This means that you can edit field names and change field types. You can also change the field widths of character and numeric fields. However, dBASE does not allow you to change the widths of date, logical, or memo fields.

To save a database structure in the Create screen:

a. Press [Ctrl]-[End]. dBASE asks if you want to append any records.

b. Press [N]. (You'll begin adding records in Chapter 4.) This should return you to the Assist interface.

Notice that dBASE gives you the option of inserting information into a newly designed structure as soon as you save it. This lets you create and fill databases "on the fly." You could do that for this example, but it's better to proceed methodically with your first example.

You can view the structure of a database in the Assist screen once you've saved it to disk:

a. Press [T] to open the Tools menu.

b. Press [↓] five times to highlight the command "List structure" and press [Enter]. Your screen should display the structure shown in Figure 3-7.

Once you've created and saved a database structure, you can modify it if you want to. This procedure is described in Chapter 9, "Organizing a Database." You should always try to put as much thought as possible into creating a database structure, but you can always change the structure if you want to.

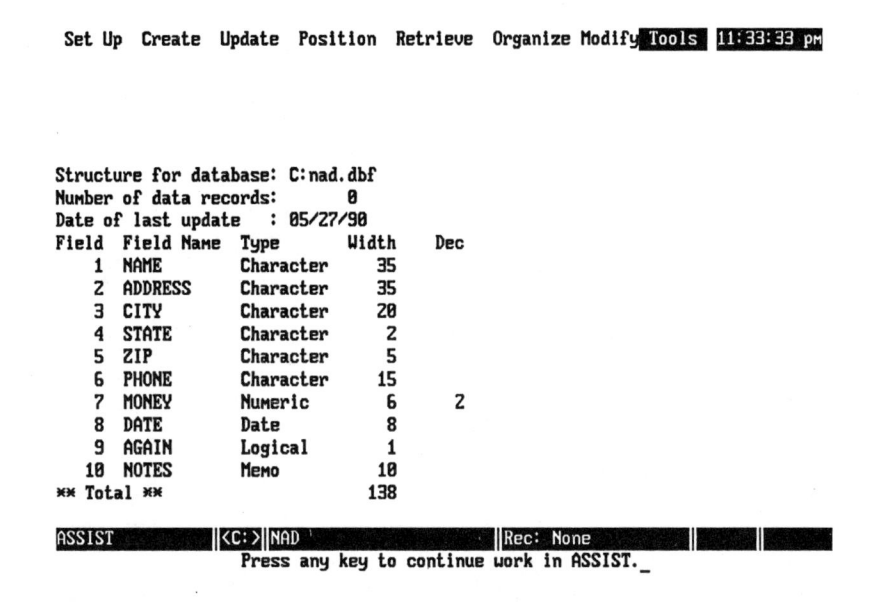

Chapter 3   Creating a Database

```
        Set Up  Create  Update  Position  Retrieve  Organize  Modify Tools  11:33:33 pm


        Structure for database: C:nad.dbf
        Number of data records:      0
        Date of last update    : 05/27/90
        Field  Field Name  Type       Width   Dec
            1  NAME        Character    35
            2  ADDRESS     Character    35
            3  CITY        Character    20
            4  STATE       Character     2
            5  ZIP         Character     5
            6  PHONE       Character    15
            7  MONEY       Numeric       6     2
            8  DATE        Date          8
            9  AGAIN       Logical       1
           10  NOTES       Memo         10
        ** Total **                    138
        ASSIST        |<C:>|NAD                    |Rec: None
                    Press any key to continue work in ASSIST._
```

FIGURE 3-7.   The structure of NAD listed on screen

Exercises

1. Is a database structure automatically saved to disk?

2. Can you start inserting information into records directly after you've created a structure?

3. Can you view a structure in the Assist screen before you have saved it?

4. Are you irrevocably bound to the structure of a database once you've saved it?

```
                                                    Bytes remaining:   3946

 ┌─CURSOR  <-- -->─┬──INSERT──────┬──DELETE──────┬─Up a field:      ↑──┐
 │ Char:    ← →    │  Char:  Ins  │  Char:  Del  │ Down a field:    ↓  │
 │ Word: Home End  │  Field: ^N   │  Word:  ^Y   │ Exit/Save:     ^End │
 │ Pan:    ^← ^→   │  Help:  F1   │  Field: ^U   │ Abort:          Esc │
 └─────────────────┴──────────────┴──────────────┴─────────────────────┘
         Field Name   Type     Width  Dec        Field Name   Type     Width  Dec

    1    ITEM         Character   30
    2    DATE         Date         8
    3    PAID         Logical      1
    4    QUANTITY     Numeric      5    0
    5    COMMENTS     Memo        10
    6                 Character

 CREATE      |<C:>|TEST                    |Field: 6/6 |
                        Enter the field name.
         Field names begin with a letter and may contain letters, digits and underscores
```

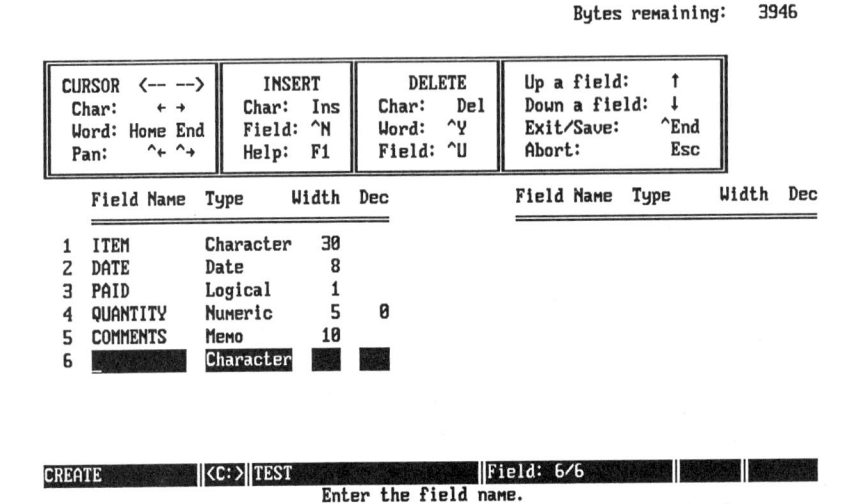

FIGURE 3-8. | The structure of TEST

EXERCISES

MASTERY SKILLS CHECK

1. Begin with the Set Up menu showing. Create a database structure called TEST.

2. Insert the first field as a character field called ITEM of 30 spaces.

3. Insert a second field, a date field called DATE.

4. Insert a third field, a logical field called PAID.

5. Insert a fourth field, a numeric field called QUANTITY. Use a width of five integers and no decimals.

6. Insert a fifth field, a memo field called COMMENTS. The structure for TEST should now look like the one in Figure 3-8.

7. Save TEST to disk and exit the Create screen.

8. List the structure of TEST in the Assist interface, and then return to Assist.

1. Quit dBASE, and then reload it. Find help information about the "Database file" command on the Create menu and then close the help window.

   INTEGRATING SKILLS CHECK

2. Suppose you were a salesperson who wanted to create a database containing the following information: Customer name, customer number, street address, mailing address, city, state, country, ZIP code, phone number, fax number, monthly purchase total, annual purchase total, buyer contact, billing contact, date last paid, and whether the account was paid this month, paid within 60 days, paid within 90 days. What types of fields would you assign to these?

3. Why would you use decimal spaces in a numeric field that shows money?

4. Find help information about the "List structure" command on the Tools menu, and then close the help window.

Entering Data

▶4◀

CHAPTER OBJECTIVES

In this chapter you will learn how to

▶ **Open a database** 4.1

▶ **Become familiar with the Append screen** 4.2

▶ **Insert information** 4.3

▶ **Work with memo fields** 4.4

Entering the correct information into a database is the single most important task in database management. It's a tedious chore, but the value of database information is only as good as its accuracy. If you put garbage in, you get garbage out.

In this chapter you'll load the database you just created into dBASE III PLUS, view the contents of the database in the Append screen, and begin entering information into individual records. Once you create a few records, you'll have a clearer idea of the relationship between fields and records.

Exercises

SKILLS CHECK

1. If you are continuing to read this chapter directly after creating NAD, exit dBASE now and return to the DOS prompt.

2. Load dBASE III PLUS and find help information for setting up a database file.

3. How many fields are there in NAD? List them from memory by name.

4. Identify each field in the list by its specific type of field.

4.1 OPEN A DATABASE

Once you've created a database structure and saved it to disk, you can start entering information into records. You can enter information only into existing fields. That's why it's important to prepare beforehand by determining the types of fields you want to use. The best way to find out whether or not you've created the right structure is to begin filling it with information.

You can enter information in two ways in dBASE: immediately after you create the structure and then save it to disk, or by exiting the Create screen, returning to Assist, and opening the database to add records later on.

dBASE asks you which method you want to use. As soon as you press [Ctrl]-[End] to save the new structure to disk, you'll see a prompt on the navigation line asking "Input data records now? (Y/N)." Press [Y] to begin entering information into records immediately. Press [N] to exit the "Create Database file" screen and return to the Assist screen. When you reached this step at the end of the previous chapter, you answered no by pressing [N].

This chapter uses the second method for two reasons:

- Adding records is a discrete step, one you should learn separately from that of creating a database structure. As you become more adept with dBASE, you can create a structure, save it, and begin adding records right away. For your first lesson, however, it's best to separate the two steps.

- You need to learn how to load a database file into dBASE, since this is the way you'll work with your database files most of the time.

In order to begin working with a specific database file, you must first open the database you want to work with. Use the command "Database file" on the Set Up menu to open a database:

a. Press [Ctrl]-[A] to open the Set Up menu, if it's not already showing.

b. Highlight the command "Database file" and press [Enter]. This opens the list of available disk drives, as shown in Figure 2-5.

c. Press [Enter] to accept the current drive selection, which is highlighted by default (presumably, drive C). This opens a window displaying the names of files ending with the extension .DBF in the current drive and directory, as shown in Figure 4-1.

   NOTE: The extension .DBF stands for "database file." dBASE automatically assigns different mnemonic letter combinations as the default extensions to all dBASE files so you can readily distinguish the type of file from its name. For example, report files end with .RPT and view files end with .VUE. You can create these files and specify other extensions if you want to, but only while working at the dot prompt. When you work in Assist, you must accept the default file extensions.

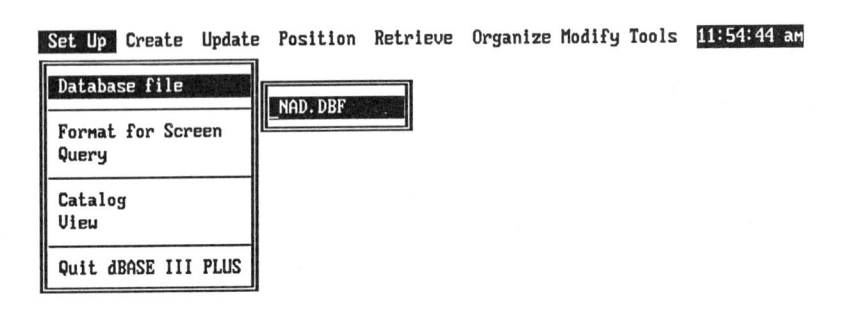

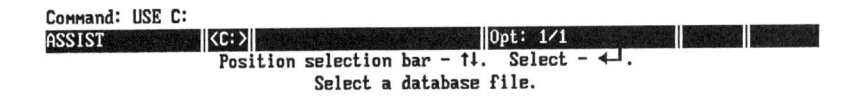

```
 Set Up  Create  Update  Position  Retrieve  Organize Modify Tools  11:54:44 am
┌──────────────────┐
│ Database file    │  ┌─────────┐
├──────────────────┤  │ NAD.DBF │
│ Format for Screen│  └─────────┘
│ Query            │
├──────────────────┤
│ Catalog          │
│ View             │
├──────────────────┤
│ Quit dBASE III PLUS│
└──────────────────┘




Command: USE C:
ASSIST          |<C:>|              |Opt: 1/1|
           Position selection bar - ↑↓.  Select - ↵.
                    Select a database file.
```

| FIGURE 4-1. | Window showing available database file names |

> Once this window is open, you can press [↓] or [↑] to highlight the file name you want to use and then press [Enter] to open the file.

d. Press [Esc] now to close all boxes and leave the Set Up menu showing on your screen.

Opening a database is the most basic procedure in dBASE. dBASE has been designed to let you open a database file quickly each time you load the dBASE program. Just type **DBASE** as your DOS prompt and press [Enter] four times. This loads the program name into DOS, moves you through the copyright screen, executes the command "Database file" on the Set Up menu, accepts the current drive letter, and opens the list of available dBASE database file names.

When you open a database, you're given access to many more commands in the Assist pull-down menus. When no database is open, you can access 21 of the 49 commands in the eight pull-down menus.

Once you've opened a database, however, you can access 47 of the 49 commands.

You must open a database if you want to use the database in any way. When you open one database to work with it and then open a second database to work with it, the first database is closed automatically. Actually, it is possible to open up to 15 databases at the same time, but you must take extra steps to do this. For more information on working with multiple databases—an advanced technique—see Miriam Liskin's *dBase III PLUS Made Easy* (Osborne/McGraw-Hill, 1990).

Remember that you don't need to open a database in order to create a new database. When you create a new database and then save it to disk, it is automatically opened by dBASE.

When you exit dBASE, the open database is automatically closed. This is the only way you can close a database in the Assist without opening another.

Examples

1. To find out which commands you can use when no database is open, first make sure this is the case: If NAD, TEST, or some other name shows in the middle of your status line, exit dBASE and then reload the program. To exit, press [Ctrl]-[A] to open the Set Up menu, press [Ctrl]-[C] to highlight the command Quit dBASE III PLUS, and press [Enter]. To load dBASE, type **DBASE** and press [Enter] twice.

   When the Assist screen appears with the Set Up menu displayed, repeatedly press [→] slowly to scroll through all eight pull-down menus. Notice that four pull-down menus—Update, Position, Retrieve, and Organize—don't present any enabled commands at all.

2. To open NAD.DBF, the database you created in the last chapter, begin with the Assist screen showing.

   Highlight NAD.DBF and press [Enter]. dBASE asks you the question "Is the file indexed? (Y/N)." Press [N]. (You'll learn about indexed files in Chapter 9.)

   When you press [N], you simply return to the Assist screen. Although it looks as if nothing has changed, you've actually loaded NAD.DBF into the dBASE program. Information about the database appears on the status bar, as shown in Figure 4-2. You can see the file name NAD in the middle of the line. To the right, the label

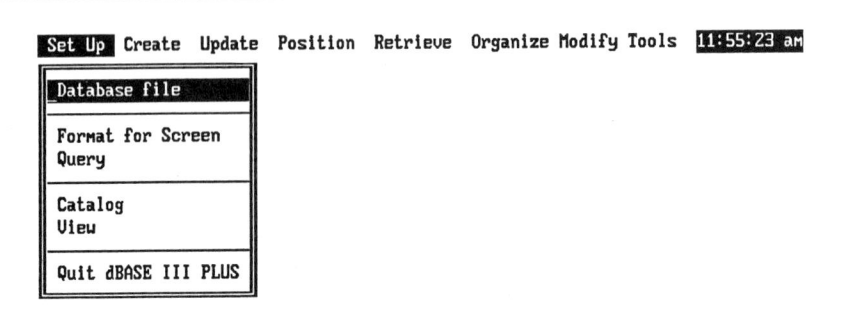

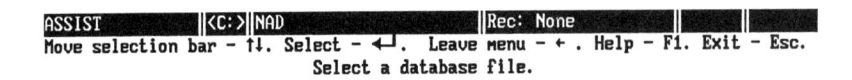

```
   Set Up  Create  Update  Position  Retrieve  Organize Modify Tools  11:55:23 am
   ┌─────────────────┐
   │ Database file   │
   ├─────────────────┤
   │ Format for Screen│
   │ Query           │
   │                 │
   │ Catalog         │
   │ View            │
   │                 │
   │ Quit dBASE III PLUS│
   └─────────────────┘




   ASSIST            <C:> NAD              Rec: None
   Move selection bar - ↑↓.  Select - ↵.   Leave menu - ←.  Help - F1. Exit - Esc.
                              Select a database file.
```

FIGURE 4-2. | Status bar showing current database file name

"Rec: None" shows there are no records in the database. When no database is open, no name will show in the middle of your status line, and the options for the current menu will appear on the right side.

3. With NAD.DBF open, you can now explore the range of commands that are enabled when a database is open. Begin with the Set Up menu showing. (Press Ctrl-A if it isn't open.) Now, repeatedly press → slowly to move through the eight pull-down menus from left to right. Notice that commands on the Update, Retrieve, and Organize menus are fully enabled. Two of the five commands on the Position menu, Seek and Continue, require an additional condition before you can access them.

4. With NAD.DBF as the current database file in use (the file name NAD appears in the middle of your status bar), you can now create a second database file and see how it becomes the current database.

Begin by opening the Create menu. Then highlight the command "Database file" and press [Enter] twice. This opens the prompt that asks you to name the database file. Type **TEST** and press [Enter]. This moves you into the Create screen.

A database structure must contain at least one field before you can save it to disk. Insert four character fields by using the example shown in Figure 4-3. Press [Ctrl]-[End] to save the structure to disk. Press [Enter] to confirm the save and then [N] to decline to append records. You will return to the Assist screen. Notice that the name TEST now appears in the middle of your status line. The file NAD.DBF has been closed automatically and has been replaced by TEST.DBF.

5. To close TEST.DBF and reopen NAD.DBF, press [Ctrl]-[A] to open the Set Up menu. Press [Enter] two times to open the list of available database file names. Highlight NAD and press [Enter] and then [N] (the file is not yet indexed). The file name NAD should now show in the middle of your status bar.

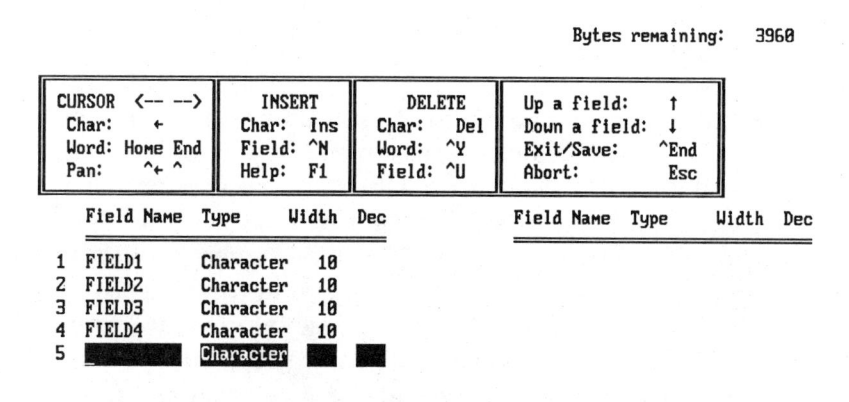

```
                                              Bytes remaining:   3960

    ┌─────────────────┬─────────────────┬─────────────────┬──────────────────┐
    │ CURSOR  <-- -->│ INSERT          │ DELETE          │ Up a field:    ↑ │
    │ Char:     ←    │ Char:    Ins    │ Char:    Del    │ Down a field:  ↓ │
    │ Word: Home End │ Field:   ^N     │ Word:    ^Y     │ Exit/Save:   ^End│
    │ Pan:    ^← ^   │ Help:    F1     │ Field:   ^U     │ Abort:       Esc │
    └─────────────────┴─────────────────┴─────────────────┴──────────────────┘

         Field Name   Type      Width  Dec         Field Name   Type      Width  Dec

      1  FIELD1       Character   10
      2  FIELD2       Character   10
      3  FIELD3       Character   10
      4  FIELD4       Character   10
      5               Character


    ║CREATE       ║<C:>║TEST                ║Field: 5/5         ║        ║
                          Enter the field name.
     Field names begin with a letter and may contain letters, digits and underscores
```

FIGURE 4-3.	Sample database called TEST

Exercises

1. Open TEST.DBF and then open NAD.DBF. Keep your eyes on the status bar for the currently open database file name.

2. Explore the definitions of three commands that are enabled when a database file is open. Open NAD. DBF or TEST.DBF, and then open the Update menu. Highlight Append and see how dBASE help defines this command. Then highlight the Edit and Browse commands in turn and see how dBASE help describes these commands.

4.2 BECOME FAMILIAR WITH THE APPEND SCREEN

A database has no value except for the information it contains. To make a database valuable, you must enter information into it that you want to save and manage.

When you insert new records into a database, you do what dBASE calls *appending* records. If you're creating a database of people you associate with, you need to add a record for each person you want to keep track of.

Appending records is a database management task that falls into the category of updating database information. One of the several ways you update a database is to add new records into it. This means you'll use the Update menu. Open that menu now so you can see the commands it provides. They are defined in Table 4-1. You'll learn about the Append command in this chapter. You'll learn about the other commands on the Update menu in Chapters 5, 6, and 7, which describe how you keep your database information current.

To append records to a database, you work in what is called the Append screen. This is one of the full-screen features in dBASE III PLUS. To work in the Append screen:

a. Open the Update menu by pressing [U].

b. Press [Enter]. This executes the top command on the Update menu, the command Append, which is highlighted by default when the Update menu first appears.

TABLE 4-1.	Commands on the Update Menu Defined
Append	Opens the Append screen, which lets you insert new records into the currently open database
Edit	Opens the Edit screen, which lets you view and edit existing records in a database one record at a time
Display	Displays all information about the current record in the Assist screen
Browse	Opens the Browse screen, which lets you view and edit a group of existing records in a database
Replace	Lets you replace information in records without viewing the records
Delete	Lets you mark records for deletion. The marked records remain in the database until you recall the records or pack the database. You'll learn about the terms "recall" and "pack" in Chapter 7
Recall	Lets you unmark records marked for deletion
Pack	Permanently removes marked records from a database and packs the remaining records into a small disk file

Remember, if you haven't yet opened a database, the Append command will not be enabled on the Update menu, and you won't be able to open the Append screen.

Examples

1. You should become familiar with the Append screen. Open it now. First make sure NAD.DBF is the current database. (Check your status bar to make sure NAD shows in the middle.) Then press [U] to open the Update menu and [Enter] to execute the top command, Append. Your screen will change to look like the one in Figure 4-4.

    The Append screen is similar to the Create screen but not identical to it. The similarities include the status bar at the bottom

68 Teach Yourself dBASE III PLUS

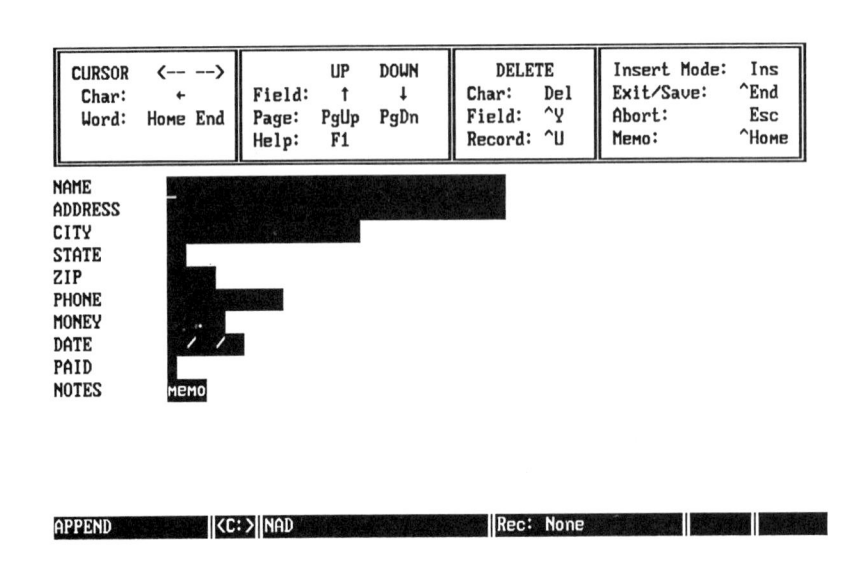

```
┌─────────────────┬──────────────┬──────────────┬─────────────────────┐
│ CURSOR  <-- --> │      UP DOWN │ DELETE       │ Insert Mode:    Ins │
│ Char:        ←  │ Field:  ↑  ↓ │ Char:   Del  │ Exit/Save:     ^End │
│ Word: Home End  │ Page: PgUp PgDn │ Field:  ^Y │ Abort:         Esc  │
│                 │ Help:   F1   │ Record: ^U   │ Memo:         ^Home │
└─────────────────┴──────────────┴──────────────┴─────────────────────┘
NAME      ▐▀▀▀▀▀▀▀▀▀▀▀▀▀▀▀▀▀▀▀▀▀▀▀▀▀▀▀▀▀
ADDRESS   ▐▀▀▀▀▀▀▀▀▀▀▀▀▀▀▀▀▀▀▀▀▀▀▀▀▀▀▀▀▀
CITY      ▐▀▀▀▀▀▀▀▀▀▀▀▀▀▀▀▀▀▀▀
STATE     ▐▀▀
ZIP       ▐▀▀▀▀▀▀▀▀▀
PHONE     ▐▀▀▀▀▀▀▀▀▀▀▀▀
MONEY     ▐▀▀▀▀▀▀
DATE      ▐ / /
PAID      ▐
NOTES     ▐MEMO

▐APPEND         ▐<C:>▐NAD              ▐Rec: None   ▐       ▐
```

| FIGURE 4-4. | The Append screen for NAD.DBF |

and the help table at the top. The status bar shows that you're working in the APPEND screen, that the current drive is C, that NAD is the current database, and that so far there are no records (Rec: None) in the database. You can toggle help off and on by pressing F1. Table 4-2 defines the commands displayed in the help table for the Append screen.

2. The most obvious difference between the Append screen and the Create screen is the way individual fields are displayed. In the Append screen, you can view the structure of the database in a more graphic display. The field names are listed vertically along the left margin of your screen. Extending to the right after each field name is a length of marked space equal to the width you defined for each field.

For example, you can see in Figure 4-4 that the NAME and ADDRESS fields are the same length. You might not be able to determine that they are both 30 spaces wide, but you can tell they

TABLE 4-2. Help Information in the Append Screen

Keys	Action
←	Left one space
→	Right one space
End	Right one word
Home	Left one word
↑	Up one field
↓	Down one field
PgUp	Up one screen
PgDn	Down one screen
F1	Toggle help on/off
Del	Delete character
Ctrl-Y	Delete current field
Ctrl-U	Mark current record for deletion
Ins	Toggle insert/typeover mode
Ctrl-End then Enter	Save text and exit
Esc	Abort or cancel
Move cursor to memo field	Open memo field editor
Ctrl-Home	

are the longest fields in the database, certainly longer than the CITY and STATE fields. You might be able to tell that the STATE field is only two characters wide.

3. When you work in the Append screen with the help table showing, you can view 11 fields in a single screen. You can increase the number of fields you can view to 17 if you turn help off by pressing F1. If the database you are viewing contains more than 17 fields, you'll need to press PgDn to see the second and subsequent screenfuls of fields and PgUp to scroll back through previous screenfuls of fields.

4. It's easy to distinguish the type of each field once you give it some thought. You can tell that the DATE field is a date type because it

contains the date format of six spaces divided into three groups by two slash marks (/ /). You can tell that the MONEY field is a numerical field because it contains a decimal point. And you can tell that the NOTES field is a memo field because the field type name "memo" appears next to the field name.

This leaves only character and logical fields to distinguish. Character fields are generally longer than most other fields, although they don't have to be. You could create a character field of one space to hold a letter code such as student grades running from A to F. Logical fields are only one space wide, but there's no way you can distinguish these from a character field of one space. The name of each field will help you remember which fields are what types. Keep this in mind when you choose names for specific fields.

Exercises

1. Do you have to open a database before you can begin appending records to the database?

2. Open the Append screen while TEST.DBF is the current database. (You created this database earlier in this chapter.) All four field lengths should be the same length; the Append screen shows this.

3. Open the Append screen while NAD.DBF is the current database. Your screen should look like the one in Figure 4-4.

4. View the structure of NAD.DBF in the Append screen. How many fields are showing?

5. How many fields are there for each type of field?

4.3 INSERT INFORMATION

Inserting information into most fields requires nothing more than your typing the information into fields. It is as easy as using a word processor. Just type the character keys you want to use. It's a bit more complicated when you work with memo fields, which are described in the following section of this chapter.

Whenever you insert information, you can use either the insert or typeover mode, although you'll probably find the typeover mode more convenient. Typeover is the default mode. It lets you type over existing characters, in case you want to correct information you just entered. Press [Ins] to switch from typeover to insert mode and back again. The label INS will show on the right side of your status line when you're in insert mode.

Regardless of which mode you use, you won't be able to move your cursor outside the field widths in which you enter information; but if you enter characters and then want to delete one or more of them, press [Backspace] to delete a character before the cursor and press [Ctrl]-[G] to delete a character the cursor is on.

You can only append information to records in a database by using fields that already exist. You cannot create new fields, nor can you change characteristics of existing fields in any way while working in the Append screen.

To begin inserting information into individual fields, simply type the information and press [Enter]. This inserts the information into the field and moves your cursor down to the next field. You'll see how this works in your first example.

When you've inserted all the information you want to save, make sure you press [Enter] and then [Esc] to close the Append screen. dBASE automatically saves all the new information to disk and returns you to the Assist screen.

Examples

1. Start adding information into the first field of NAD.DBF. Make sure NAD.DBF is the current database. Then open the Append screen by pressing [U] and [Enter]. You will see the cursor blinking in the first space of the first empty field.

    Type **Jeannie Iams** and press [Enter]. This inserts the characters into the field and moves the cursor down one line, to the beginning of the next field. Type **1234 Fox Lane** and press (Enter). This completes the ADDRESS field and moves you down to the CITY field. Type **Berkeley** and press (Enter). This completes the CITY field. Type **CA**. Notice that the cursor automatically pops down to the next field. This happens whenever you fill a field with information. Keep this in mind when you start defining specific widths for certain fields. If you know all your state fields will contain two characters, you can save having to press (Enter) by keeping all state fields two characters wide.

Continue inserting information. The next field is ZIP. Type **94704**. Again, the cursor automatically pops down. This completes the STATE and ZIP fields. Pause at this point and double-check your work. Your screen should look like the one in Figure 4-5.

2. Continue your work by filling in the phone number. The cursor should be at the beginning of the empty field for PHONE. Type **415-555-1212**.

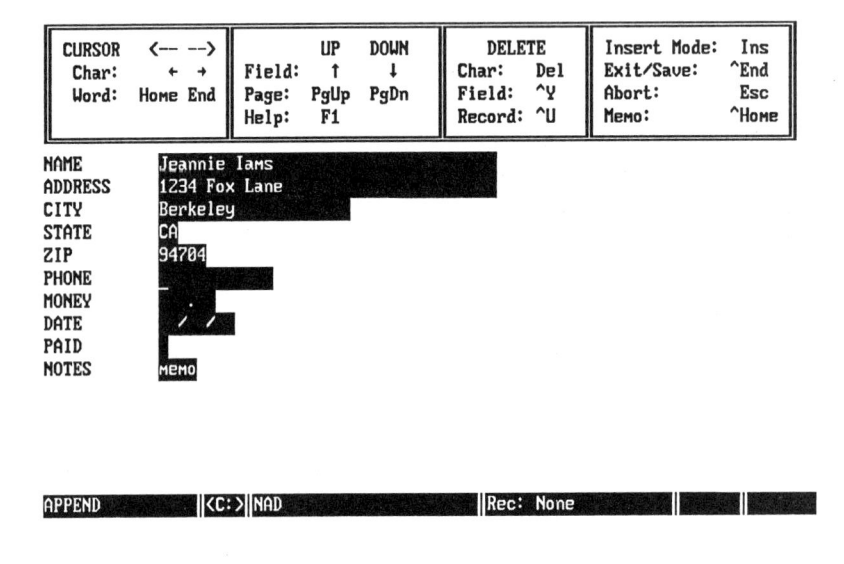

```
┌─────────────────────┬──────────────────────┬────────────────┬──────────────────────┐
│ CURSOR    <-- -->   │          UP    DOWN  │ DELETE         │ Insert Mode:  Ins    │
│ Char:      ←   →    │ Field:   ↑     ↓     │ Char:    Del   │ Exit/Save:    ^End   │
│ Word:    Home End   │ Page:   PgUp  PgDn   │ Field:   ^Y    │ Abort:        Esc    │
│                     │ Help:    F1          │ Record:  ^U    │ Memo:         ^Home  │
└─────────────────────┴──────────────────────┴────────────────┴──────────────────────┘
NAME      Jeannie Iams
ADDRESS   1234 Fox Lane
CITY      Berkeley
STATE     CA
ZIP       94704
PHONE
MONEY            .
DATE         /  /
PAID
NOTES     memo

APPEND        <C:> NAD              Rec: None
```

FIGURE 4-5.   The first part of record 1 in NAD.DBF

3. Inserting information into a numeric field is not much different from entering information in a character field, if you don't use decimal spaces. Just type the integers you want to save; if they don't fill the field completely, press [Enter] to move down to the next field.

   If the numeric field contains decimal spaces, as does the field MONEY in NAD.DBF, entering numbers takes more than one step. With the cursor on the first space of the MONEY field, type **100**. This fills in the three spaces for integers to the left of the decimal point and places the cursor on the first of the two spaces to the right of the decimal point. Press [Enter]. This inserts two zeroes for decimal numbers and moves the cursor down to the next field.

4. Date fields have a unique format that requires special handling. You'll use the date field in NAD.DBF to keep track of when people borrowed money from you.

   With your cursor on the first space of the DATE field, type **122589**. dBASE has already inserted the slash marks. All you have to do is enter the numbers corresponding to the month, day, and year you want to record. You'll skip over the slash marks automatically as you insert the numbers. Remember to include zeroes.

5. This brings you to the logical field PAID. You can enter only one of four characters into a logical field: T for true, Y for yes, F for false, or N for no. Type **F**. The cursor automatically pops down to the next field.

   Double-check your work again. It should look like the screen in Figure 4-6. You will be in the memo field, which is described in the next section.

6. You don't have to enter information into every field of a record, but you do have to enter at least one character into one field. Since you won't enter any information into the memo field NOTES until the next section of this chapter, press [Enter] to move to the next record. This moves you to the next record only when the cursor is in the last field of the current record. If you want to move to the next record before you get to the bottom of the current record, just press [PgDn].

   Notice that the right side of the status bar shows that you're now working in "Rec: EOF/1." This means that you're working at

74 Teach Yourself dBASE III PLUS

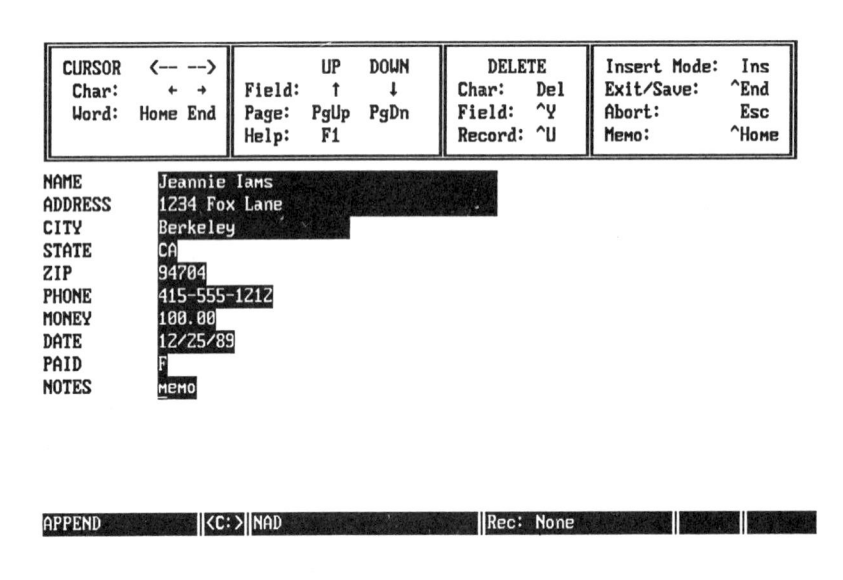

```
CURSOR    <-- -->           UP   DOWN      DELETE           Insert Mode:  Ins
  Char:    ←   →    Field:   ↑    ↓         Char:   Del      Exit/Save:   ^End
  Word:  Home End   Page:  PgUp PgDn        Field:  ^Y       Abort:        Esc
                    Help:   F1              Record: ^U       Memo:       ^Home

NAME      Jeannie Iams
ADDRESS   1234 Fox Lane
CITY      Berkeley
STATE     CA
ZIP       94704
PHONE     415-555-1212
MONEY     100.00
DATE      12/25/89
PAID      F
NOTES     memo


APPEND          |<C:>|NAD              |Rec: None
```

FIGURE 4-6.	More of record 1 in NAD.DBF

the end of the file and that one record already exists in the database. You aren't working in the second record until you have inserted some information into the blank Append screen and then either gone on to the next record (what will become the third record) or saved the information you added to the second record and quit the Append screen.

Exercises

1. If you decide while appending records that you need another field in the database, can you create the field in the Append screen?

2. Can you expand the length of a field while working in the Append screen?

Chapter 4　　　　　　　　　　　　　　　　　　　　　　　Entering Data　**75**

3. Enter the following information into the second record of NAD
   .DBF:

NAME	Walter Gomer
ADDRESS	560 San Jose
CITY	Kensington
STATE	CA
ZIP	94708
PHONE	415-456-7890
MONEY	150
DATE	01/07/90 (remember not to add the slash marks)
PAID	F

   Your screen should now look like the one in Figure 4-7. To move to the next record, place the cursor in the memo field NOTES and press [Enter].

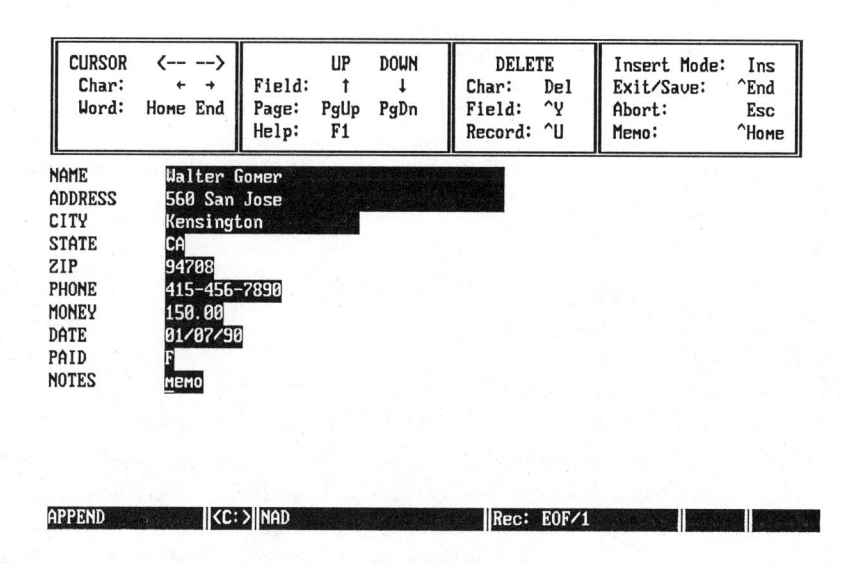

FIGURE 4-7.　　The second record in NAD.DBF

4. Insert the following information in the third record of NAD.DBF:

NAME	John McCord
ADDRESS	920 Evelyn
CITY	Albany
STATE	CA
ZIP	94706
PHONE	415-525-5614
MONEY	200
DATE	10/15/89
PAID	F

5. Move to record 4 and insert the following information:

NAME	Izzy Zagare
ADDRESS	350 Benvenue
CITY	El Cerrito
STATE	CA
ZIP	94530
PHONE	415-527-8745
MONEY	450
DATE	11/20/89
PAID	F

6. Save all the information by exiting the Append screen and returning to the Assist screen.

4.4 WORK WITH MEMO FIELDS

Entering information into memo fields requires a bit of extra work. This is due to the nature of memo fields and how dBASE handles them. You're limited to a maximum of 254 characters in a character field. This is more than enough characters for people's names, the names of companies, and other common sections of text that you want to save, but it is not long enough to hold sections of text such as several sentences or paragraphs that you want to save as part of your database information.

Memo fields have been devised to contain textual information that doesn't fit into the limited space of character fields. You can store a maximum of 5000 characters in a memo field. To enter information into a memo field, you use a feature of the dBASE program called the *memo field editor*. This is a scaled-down version of a word processor.

Because of the extraordinary capacity of memo fields, dBASE must handle them differently from other fields. When you insert information into a memo field, dBASE cannot place the information in the database you designed. dBASE must create a separate file and save the memo field text in that file. This separate file is given the same name as the original database, but it is given the extension .DBT, for DataBase Text file. For example, when you created NAD.DBF in the last chapter and inserted the memo field NOTES, dBASE created a second file on disk called NAD.DBT. This file will contain all the memo field information you insert into NOTES. If you insert more than one memo field in a database, all the memo field information is saved to the same single .DBT file.

A .DBT file actually isn't a text file at all, in the sense of a word processing file. It is a file that contains complex combinations of control codes and text characters that only dBASE can decipher.

To open the memo field editor for a memo field:

a. Place the cursor in the field width for the memo field you want to use.

b. Press [Ctrl]-[Home] to open the memo field editor. This key combination works only when your cursor is in a memo field width. As soon as the memo field editor appears, you can begin to type the text you want to save.

c. When you're finished typing, press [Ctrl]-[W] to save the text and return to the Append screen.

Although the memo field editor is an abbreviated word processor, it provides you with a surprising range of controls. You can enter and edit text easily by using the basic text keys. You can search for specific sections of text, called *text strings*, and you can reformat text lines that become misaligned when you change the text.

Examples

1. To open the memo field editor for the first record in NAD.DBF, first make sure NAD.DBF is open. Then press [U] to open the Update menu and [Enter] to execute the Append command. If the contents of the first record in NAD.DBF aren't displayed, press [PgUp] until they appear.

    You can press [↓] to move the cursor through various fields in the Append screen. Move the cursor so it appears in the width after the NOTES field.

    To open the memo field editor, press [Ctrl]-[Home]. Your screen should now look like the one in Figure 4-8. The label in the upper left corner (Edit: NOTES) shows that you are editing the NOTES field. Below that a help table displays the keys you can use while working in the memo field editor. You will see the cursor blinking in the first position beneath the help table. Table 4-3 describes the memo field editor keys and their functions.

Edit: NOTES

CURSOR: <-- -->		UP DOWN	DELETE		Insert Mode: Ins
Char: ←	Line: ↑ ↓	Char: Del	Insert line: ^N
Word: Home End	Page: PgUp PgDn	Word: ^T	Save: ^W Abort: Esc
Line: ^← ^→	Find: ^KF	Line: ^Y	Read file: ^KR
Reformat: ^KB	Refind: ^KL		Write file: ^KW

FIGURE 4-8. The memo field screen editor

TABLE 4.3 — Memo Editor Keys and Functions

Keys	Action
←	Left one space
→	Right one space
Home	Left one word
End	Right one word
Ctrl-←	Beginning of line
Ctrl-→	End of line
Ctrl-K-B	Reformat text
↑	Up one line
↓	Down one line
PgUp	Up one screenful
PgDn	Down one screenful
Ctrl-K-F	Find text
Ctrl-K-L	Look again
Del	Delete character
Ctrl-T	Delete next word
Ctrl-Y	Delete current line
Ins	Insert mode on/off
Ctrl-N	Insert new line
Ctrl-W	Save current text
Esc	Abort or abandon
Ctrl-K-R	Insert a file into the memo
Ctrl-K-W	Write text to a separate file

2. Entering information with the memo field editor is just like using a word processor. Start typing the text you want to save. You can use either insert or typeover mode. When you get to the right margin, word wrap will return the cursor to the beginning of the next line. When you get to the end of a paragraph, press Enter. This inserts a hard carriage return and moves your cursor to the beginning of the next line.

Type **She needed the money quickly, and said she would pay me as soon as she could.** Notice how word wrap controls the text when you get to the right margin.

Press [Enter] to move the cursor down one line and flush against the left margin of your screen. Notice that dBASE inserts a left-pointing bracket on the right edge of the screen on the line where you pressed [Enter]. This is a hard carriage return symbol that is helpful when you want to reformat lines of text. Your screen should now look like the one in Figure 4-9.

3. To save text inserted with the memo field editor, press [Ctrl]-[W]. dBASE saves the text and returns you to where you were in the Append screen when you opened the memo field editor.

You can delete this text in two ways. You can escape the change you've just made by pressing [Esc]. dBASE asks "Abort editing? (Y/N)." Press [Y] to return to the Append screen. If you want to delete the text in the memo field editor and remain working in the editor, place your cursor on the line you want to delete and press [Ctrl]-[Y]. Keep on deleting lines this way until you've removed all of the text.

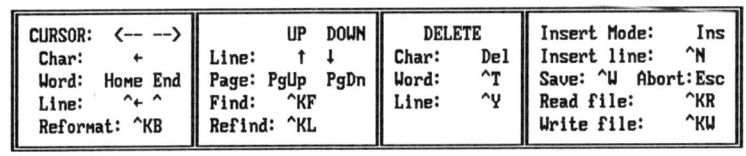

```
Edit: NOTES

CURSOR:   <-- -->        UP   DOWN      DELETE            Insert Mode:       Ins
Char:       +       Line:  ↑    ↓       Char:     Del     Insert line:       ^N
Word:    Home End   Page: PgUp PgDn     Word:     ^T      Save: ^W Abort:Esc
Line:      ^+ ^     Find:      ^KF      Line:     ^Y      Read file:         ^KR
Reformat: ^KB       Refind:    ^KL                        Write file:        ^KW
```

She needed the money quickly, and said she would pay me as soon
as she could.   <

-

FIGURE 4-9.   Memo field text for record 1

4. Now you can insert text into the NOTES field for the second record in NAD.DBF. Make sure NAD.DBF is current. Press [U] to open the Update menu and [Enter] to open the Append screen. Press [PgDn] or [PgUp] to go to the second record. Press [↓] to move the cursor into the width for the NOTES field. Press [Ctrl]-[Home] to open the memo field editor. Now type the text **He says he needed the money for the race track and will pay me back double on Thursday.**

To save the text and close the memo field editor, press [Ctrl]-[W].

Exercises

1. Can you insert characters into a memo field while viewing the Append screen?

2. Do you have to use the memo field editor to insert characters into a memo field?

3. What is the maximum number of characters you can insert into a memo field?

4. Does word wrap work in the memo field editor?

5. Can you insert text from another file into the memo field editor?

6. Insert the following text into the memo field of the third record in NAD.DBF: **Said he'd pay me back in two weeks.** Save the text and return to the Append screen and then the Assist screen.

EXERCISES

1. Which database is automatically made current when you first load dBASE?

   MASTERY
   SKILLS
   CHECK

2. What does the extension .DBF stand for?

3. Find out what dBASE help has to say about the Append command and then close the help window.

4. Make TEST.DBF current and open the Append screen. Turn help off and on. Exit the Append screen and return to the Assist screen.

5. Make NAD.DBF current and open the Append screen. Open the memo field editor for record 1. Turn help off and on. Close the memo field editor, exit the Append screen, and return to the Assist.

6. What does the extension .DBT stand for?

7. How is a .DBT file created?

8. Which database is current?

9. How can you tell?

INTEGRATING SKILLS CHECK

1. From the Assist screen, quit dBASE and then reload the program.

2. Which database is current?

3. If you want to save keystrokes, what's the ideal field width for ZIP codes that contain only five digits?

4. From the Assist screen, begin creating a database called TEMP.DBF with each of the five field types. FIELD1 is a character field with 20 spaces. FIELD2 is a numeric field of 5 integers, no decimals. FIELD3 is a date field. FIELD4 is a logical field. FIELD5 is a memo field. Save this structure to disk.

5. Move directly from the Create screen into the Append screen. Add the following information into the first record, save the information and return to the Assist Screen.

FIELD1	Toby Friar
FIELD2	100
FIELD3	122589
FIELD4	T
FIELD5	Said he needed the money for a book.

6. Create a database called MEMO.DBF with two memo fields, NOTES1 and NOTES2, and then save this structure and return to the Assist screen without entering any information into the database.

7. Insert the following information in NOTES1: **This is the first memo field**. Save this information and return to the Append screen.

8. Insert the contents of your CONFIG.SYS file in NOTES2. Save this information and return to the Append screen.

Editing Data
▶5◀

CHAPTER OBJECTIVES

In this chapter you will

- ▶ Use the Edit screen — 5.1
- ▶ Become familiar with the Browse screen — 5.2
- ▶ Use the Browse screen menu — 5.3
- ▶ Go directly to records — 5.4
- ▶ Display records — 5.5

Fully half of your time working with a database will be spent entering and editing information. Editing data means changing and updating existing information in a database. Information changes all the time; if you don't keep your databases current, they'll soon lose their value. For a database that contains the names and addresses of people you know, you'll edit records upon occasion to reflect changes of addresses and telephone numbers.

If you use a database for business, you'll find that you need to change the information much more often. If you keep track of payment accounts, you'll have to update fields that contain such information as the amount owed, payment due dates, amount paid, amount overdue, late payments, and penalties.

Editing data also includes deleting records, but these are complicated procedures, described in Chapter 7.

You've already learned how to add new records by using the Append screen. In this chapter you'll learn how to work in the Edit and Browse screens to view and edit record information. You'll access both these screens from the Update menu by using the commands Edit and Browse.

Exercises

SKILLS CHECK

1. Load dBASE and open NAD.DBF.

2. Find out what on-line context-sensitive help has to say about the Edit, Display, and Browse commands on the Update menu.

3. Find out what on-line context-sensitive help has to say about the Goto Record command on the Position menu.

5.1 USE THE EDIT SCREEN

The best way to edit individual records is to work in the Edit screen. To do so, you must first open the database you want to use. For your work in this chapter, make NAD.DBF the current database. Be sure the file

Chapter 5 — Editing Data

name NAD appears in the middle of the status bar. Whenever you make a database current, the first record will be the current record.

NOTE: You can make a database without records current, but you cannot view it in the Edit screen.

Now you're ready to open the Edit screen and display information in this screen from NAD.DBF.

a. Press [U] to open the Update menu.

b. Highlight the command Edit and press [Enter].
    Your screen should now look like the one in Figure 5-1. The current record is always displayed when you first enter the Edit screen.

The Edit screen looks and behaves a lot like the Append screen. The only apparent difference is that EDIT, instead of APPEND,

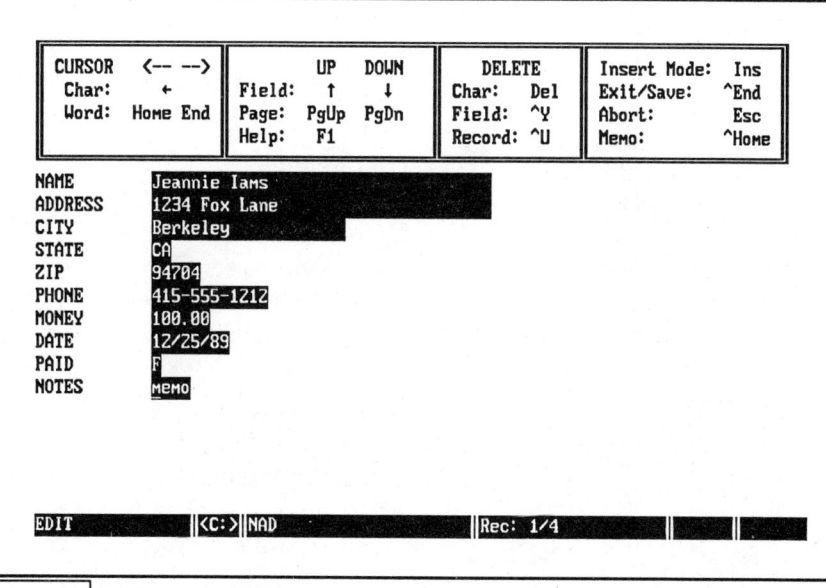

```
┌─────────────────────┬──────────────────┬──────────────────┬────────────────────┐
│ CURSOR   <-- -->    │        UP  DOWN  │ DELETE           │ Insert Mode:  Ins  │
│ Char:       ←       │ Field:  ↑   ↓    │ Char:   Del      │ Exit/Save:   ^End  │
│ Word:   Home End    │ Page:  PgUp PgDn │ Field:  ^Y       │ Abort:        Esc  │
│                     │ Help:   F1       │ Record: ^U       │ Memo:       ^Home  │
└─────────────────────┴──────────────────┴──────────────────┴────────────────────┘
        NAME     Jeannie Iams
        ADDRESS  1234 Fox Lane
        CITY     Berkeley
        STATE    CA
        ZIP      94704
        PHONE    415-555-1212
        MONEY    100.00
        DATE     12/25/89
        PAID     F
        NOTES    memo
```

`EDIT    |<C:>|NAD    |Rec: 1/4`

FIGURE 5-1. The Edit screen

appears on the left side of the status bar. Your controls for working in the Edit screen are also a bit different from those in the Append screen. You can find the controls described in the help table shown in Table 5-1.

Each time you enter the Edit screen, you'll start out working in typeover mode, which means that you'll type over any existing characters. This is the easiest way to edit data because you can type over existing characters without having to erase them first.

Using insert mode to edit information in the Edit screen is slightly different from using insert mode in other programs. In the Edit screen, insert mode is a blend of both insert and typeover modes. You press [Ins] to toggle insert mode on and off. The INS label will appear on the right side of your status bar when insert mode is on. When you press [Ins] to toggle insert mode on and then type new characters, characters

TABLE 5-1. Editing Controls in the Edit Screen

Keys	Action
[←]	Left one space
[→]	Right one space
[Home]	Left one word
[End]	Right one word
[↑]	Up one line
[↓]	Down one line
[PgUp]	Up one screenful
[PgDn]	Down one screenful
[F1]	Toggle help on/off
[Del]	Delete character
[Ctrl]-[Y]	Delete field
[Ctrl]-[U]	Delete record
[Ins]	Toggle insert on/off
[Ctrl]-[End]	Exit and save work
[Esc]	Abort or escape changes
[Ctrl]-[Home]	Open memo screen

to the right of your cursor will be pushed farther to the right. If you keep on typing, existing characters will be pushed right out of the field and disappear.

Moving around fields and records in the Edit screen is easy. You use the cursor keys, which you're probably familiar with from other activities on your computer. Unfortunately, you have no controls other than the cursor keys. This means that you can't move to a specific record directly. Instead, you must move through the records one by one until you reach the record you want.

When the help table is displayed in the Edit screen, you can view eight fields in one screenful. Pressing [F1] displays another 6 fields, for a total of 14. When your records grow to more than 14 fields, you'll have to move between screens to view all the fields, which can be inconvenient. When this happens, you'll probably want to begin creating and designing formats, which let you select and adjust the fields that are displayed on screen. You will learn how to create screen formats in Chapter 11.

Editing field information in dBASE is easy and flexible, but there are always some risks. You can type over existing information easily, which means that you may type over information you want to keep. You can move around fields and records easily, but if you start typing characters too quickly, or if you inadvertently touch keys on your keyboard, you may enter information you don't want to keep.

Always be aware that information you've typed that appears on your screen hasn't necessarily been saved to disk. Press [Ctrl]-[Enter] periodically just to make sure you're saving your new information to disk.

You can delete existing characters to the right of the cursor by pressing [Ctrl]-[G]. You delete characters to the left of the cursor by pressing [Backspace].

Examples

1. To type over the existing characters in the NAME field of the first record, start with your screen showing the first record in NAD.DBF, as shown in Figure 5-1. Type **Swarna Mitts**. Press [Enter]. This inserts

the new characters you just typed over the previous characters and moves the cursor down one field. Pressing [Enter] is crucial. Until you do so, the information you type on screen is only temporary. It doesn't actually replace the information existing on disk. This protects you from erasing information inadvertently.

2. You can escape any changes you make when editing a field up to the point that you press [Enter]. If you type characters and then decide you don't want the new information, press [Esc]. The new information will disappear, and the previous information will reappear.

   Try the technique now. Press [↑] to move your cursor up one field. Type **David Burt** and press [Esc]. You'll exit the Edit screen and return to the Assist screen. The Update menu will still be showing, with the command Edit highlighted. Press [Enter] to return to the Edit screen. When the Edit screen returns, it displays the first record. The first field, however, contains the information you typed over and not the information you just typed in.

   You can see information being saved to disk by keeping your eye on your current data disk drive. For hard disks, this is most likely drive C. For dual floppy disk systems, it is probably drive B. The disk drive light flashes on as the data in your computer's memory is saved to disk.

3. Experiment with some of the other Edit screen controls. Press [→]. This moves the cursor right one space. You can back up the cursor by pressing [←]. Press [↓]. This moves the cursor down one field. You can move back up by pressing [↑].

   Move to record 4 by pressing [PgDn] three times. The status line shows "Rec 4/5," which means you're viewing the fourth of five records.

   Move back to the first record in the database by pressing [PgUp] four times. If you keep pressing [PgUp] after you get to the first record, you'll exit the Edit screen and return to the Assist screen. Since the Update menu remains displayed and the Edit command highlighted, just press [Enter] to return to the Edit screen.

4. If you want to replace all the characters in a single field, move the highlight bar over the field whose contents you want to delete and

press Ctrl-Y. This deletes all the information in the field at once. When you work in insert mode, this is the best way to begin inserting entirely new information.

5. To edit the contents of a memo field, place your cursor on the word "memo" in the memo field and press Ctrl-Home. This opens the memo field screen editor, which behaves the same way as when you used it to append records in the Chapter 4.

   You'll probably need to realign your text lines when you edit text in memo fields. Inserting text jumbles up the original alignment. To realign text lines, press Ctrl-L. This aligns the text lines from your cursor position to the first hard carriage return.

Exercises

1. Can you view the contents of a database containing no records?

2. Do you move to the Edit screen as soon as you open a database?

3. From the Assist screen, how do you view the contents of the current database in the Edit screen ?

4. Move through a sequence of two records in the Edit screen and watch the record numbers change on the status line. Make sure you stop when you're viewing record 3.

5. Move back to record 1 and change the name to "Bill Bailey."

BECOME FAMILIAR WITH THE BROWSE SCREEN | 5.2

The Browse screen provides you with an alternative way to view and edit database information. It is called the Browse screen because you can use it to browse through database contents and view information in screenfuls. The Browse screen allows you to

- View the relationship between fields and records in a more graphic layout
- Position yourself within a group of records and view, compare, or edit information in related records
- Scroll through the same field in separate records and view, compare, or edit information in that field
- Lock specific fields on your screen so they always appear regardless of what other fields you're viewing
- Freeze a field so it's the only field you can change

To work in the Browse screen, load the database you want to use into dBASE and select the command Browse on the Update menu.

a. Load NAD.DBF into dBASE.

b. Press [U] to open the Update menu.

c. Highlight the command Browse and press [Enter].

Your screen should now which look like the one in Figure 5-2. The Browse screen displays the contents of each record on a single line running across your screen. Fields run up and down the screen in columns. Fields that don't fit into your screen scroll off the right side of your screen.

Most databases contain many more fields than can fit into a computer display terminal, so you have to pan or scroll through the fields to see what you're looking for. Panning to the right and left lets you view different fields on your screen. You scroll or pan to the right by pressing [Ctrl]-[→]. You scroll or pan to the left by pressing [Ctrl]-[←]. The list for all controls in the Browse screen are shown in Table 5-2.

The current record is highlighted. You can find the cursor blinking under the first character in the first field.

When the Browse screen first appears, it displays the help table. This leaves enough room for 11 records. To make room for 5 more records, press [F1] to toggle the help table off. You can view another screenful of records by pressing [PgDn]. Notice that you view the same fields as you move up and down in screenfuls. You can move back up in screenfuls by pressing [PgUp].

Chapter 5   Editing Data   **93**

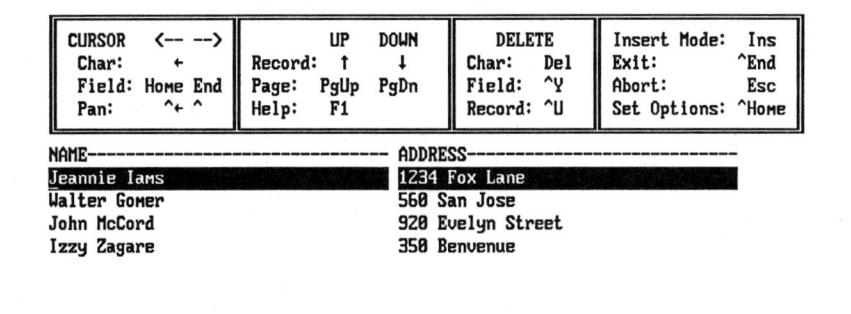

```
┌─────────────────────────┬─────────────────────┬─────────────────┬───────────────────────┐
│ CURSOR   <-- -->        │         UP    DOWN  │ DELETE          │ Insert Mode:   Ins    │
│ Char:     ←             │ Record:  ↑     ↓    │ Char:    Del    │ Exit:         ^End    │
│ Field: Home End         │ Page:   PgUp  PgDn  │ Field:    ^Y    │ Abort:         Esc    │
│ Pan:      ^← ^→         │ Help:   F1          │ Record:   ^U    │ Set Options: ^Home    │
└─────────────────────────┴─────────────────────┴─────────────────┴───────────────────────┘
 NAME------------------------------ ADDRESS------------------------------
 Jeannie Iams                       1234 Fox Lane
 Walter Gomer                       560 San Jose
 John McCord                        920 Evelyn Street
 Izzy Zagare                        350 Benvenue




 BROWSE         <C:>  NAD              Rec: 1/4
                        View and edit fields.
```

FIGURE 5-2.	The Browse screen

Most of these controls behave the same as they do in the Edit screen, with the following variations:

- [↑] and [↓] in the Edit screen move you between fields, but they move you between records in the Browse screen.

- [PgUp] and [PgDn] move you between records in the Edit screen, but they move you between screenfuls of records in the Browse screen.

- Pressing [Ctrl]-[Home] in the Edit screen opens the memo field editor (if your cursor is in a memo field), but it opens the top menu bar in the Browse screen. This menu provides you with controls for moving around records and manipulating fields displayed on screen.

New controls in the Browse screen are [Ctrl]-[→] for scrolling or panning right and [Ctrl]-[←] for scrolling or panning left.

TABLE 5-2. Editing Controls in the Browse Screen

Keys	Action
←	Left one space
→	Right one space
Home	Left one field/line
End	Right one field/line
Ctrl-←	Pan left one field
Ctrl-→	Pan right one field
↑	Up one record
↓	Down one record
PgUp	Up one screenful
PgDn	Down one screenful
F1	Toggle help on/off
Del	Delete character after the cursor
Backspace or Ctrl-G	Delete character before the cursor
Ctrl-Y	Delete field
Ctrl-U	Delete record
Ins	Toggle insert mode on/off
Ctrl-End	Exit Browse and save changes
Esc	Abort or escape changes
Ctrl-Home	Open the Set options menu in current database
(Options:)	
Bottom	Move to bottom or last record in current database
Top	Move to top or first record in current database
Lock	Lock field on screen
Record No.	Go to specific record number
Freeze	Freeze field to edit

Ctrl-End behaves the same in both the Browse and Append screens. It saves new data to disk and returns you to the Assist screen. If you're working in the the Browse screen, the Browse command remains highlighted. Just press [Enter] to return to your previous position in the Browse screen.

Since database information is valuable, you should practice using the three commands for deleting characters and fields

You can delete characters in a field in three ways. You can delete characters to the right of the cursor by pressing [Del]. This moves subsequent characters one space to the left. Continuing to press [Del] continues to delete characters to the right of the cursor. You can delete characters to the left of the cursor, up to the beginning of the current field, by pressing [Backspace] or [Ctrl]-[G]. You can delete all characters in a field by pressing [Ctrl]-[Y].

If you delete all the contents in a field by pressing [Ctrl]-[Y] and then decide you want the information back, press [Esc]. This returns you to the Assist screen with the Browse command highlighted. Press [Enter] to return to your previous position in the Browse screen, and the information you deleted will reappear. As when working in Edit screen, aborting your edits works as long as you don't move to another record or press [Ctrl]-[End] first.

The fourth delete command on the help table, [Ctrl]-[U], applies to deleting a record. Deleting a record is a powerful procedure, discussed in Chapter 7.

You can move the cursor easily among various fields. Press [End] to move the cursor forward one field in the current screen. Once you've reached the righmost field in the Browse screen, subsequent pressings of [End] move your cursor down one record at a time but keep it in the same field, always placing the cursor in the rightmost field of the current Browse screen.

Press [Home] to move the cursor back one field. When you arrive at the leftmost field in the current screen, subsequent pressings of [Home] move your cursor up one record each time, keeping the cursor in the leftmost field.

Press [PgDn] to move down by screenfuls. The highlight bar will remain in the same position on your screen. Press [PgUp] to move up by screenfuls.

Examples

1. Working in the Browse screen is a handy way to view and edit database information; you're given a wide range of ways to move

around records. You can get a better idea of the best controls by creating a database called SAMPLE.DBF that contains at least 10 fields and 21 records. Make each field a character-type field and name the sequence of fields FIELD1 through FIELD10. (Make one or more of these fields memo type to prepare you for Example 3.)

Place information in FIELD1 for each record, identifying the records as RECORD1, RECORD2, RECORD3, and so on. This information will help you identify your location within the database at a glance.

Once you've created and saved SAMPLE.DBF to disk, view the database contents in the Browse screen. It should look something like the screen in Figure 5-3 when it first appears. You'll use this database to practice moving around records. Press [PgDn] to move down a screenful and then press [PgUp] to move up a screenful.

2. Press [Ctrl]-[→] several times to pan to the right. Each time you press these keys, you'll display a new field to the right and remove the

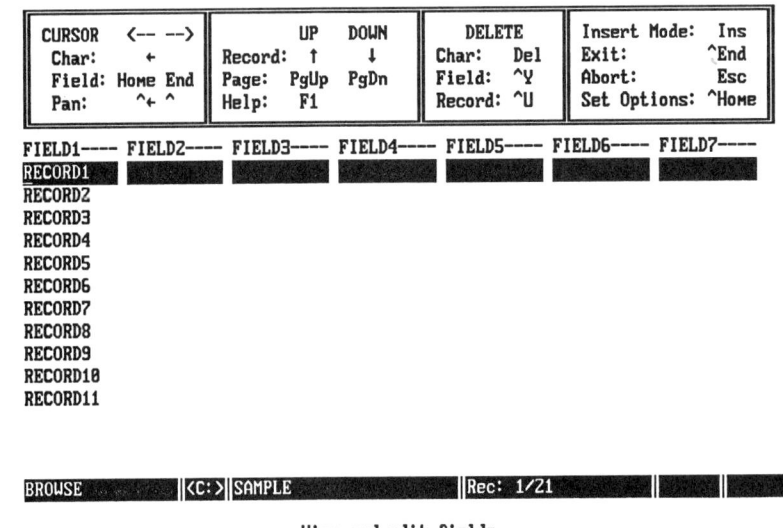

```
┌─────────────────────┬──────────────────┬──────────────────┬───────────────────────┐
│ CURSOR    <-- -->   │      UP   DOWN   │ DELETE           │ Insert Mode:    Ins   │
│ Char:       ←       │ Record:  ↑   ↓   │ Char:    Del     │ Exit:          ^End   │
│ Field: Home End     │ Page:  PgUp PgDn │ Field:   ^Y      │ Abort:          Esc   │
│ Pan:    ^←  ^→      │ Help:   F1       │ Record:  ^U      │ Set Options:  ^Home   │
└─────────────────────┴──────────────────┴──────────────────┴───────────────────────┘
 FIELD1---- FIELD2---- FIELD3---- FIELD4---- FIELD5---- FIELD6---- FIELD7----
 RECORD1
 RECORD2
 RECORD3
 RECORD4
 RECORD5
 RECORD6
 RECORD7
 RECORD8
 RECORD9
 RECORD10
 RECORD11

 BROWSE          <C:> SAMPLE              Rec: 1/21
                        View and edit fields.
```

FIGURE 5-3.   Contents of the top of SAMPLE.DBF in the Browse screen

last field on the left. This differs from the effect of pressing [End], which keeps your cursor within the currently displayed fields.

Now press [Ctrl]-[←] to pan to the left a field at a time.

3. You can't view the contents of a memo field while working in the Browse screen, which means you can't edit them either. If you place your cursor on a memo field and press [Ctrl]-[Home], you'll open the Browse menu bar instead. This is a major drawback to working in the Browse screen, but it also reflects the purpose of the Browse screen. You're supposed to use it to browse for information and edit only incidentally.

Exercises

1. Can you view a database that contains no records in the Browse screen?

2. What are the some of the advantages of working in the Browse screen?

3. Can you view or edit memo fields in the Browse screen?

4. What does panning or scrolling mean?

5. What's the difference between pressing [End] and pressing [Ctrl]-[→]?

USE THE BROWSE SCREEN MENU
5.3

The Browse screen contains a menu you can use to move around records in the current database, as well as to create special screen displays of record information. You use the Set Options command as defined in the help table to open this menu. Just press [Ctrl]-[Home] to open the Browse screen menu bar, which provides five commands:

Bottom	Moves you to the bottom or last record in the current database
Top	Moves you to the top or first record in the current database
Lock	Lets you lock one or more fields in the Browse screen. This allows you to scroll through other fields not currently displayed and continue to view the fields you locked. You do this to view and compare information in fields that can't normally be seen together in a single Browse screen
Record No.	Lets you go to the record number you specify
Freeze	Lets you freeze one or more fields. Frozen fields are the only fields you can edit, although you can continue to view other fields. Freezing a field or fields limits your activities to the frozen fields and prevents your accidentally changing data in other fields

NOTE: A sixth command, Find, will appear on the Browse menu bar when you're working with a database that has an attached index file. You'll learn about index files and how to work with them later in Chapter 9.

Once the Browse menu bar appears, you can select which command to use by pressing the letter key that matches the first letter of the command name. For example, to move to the top record, press [T] for Top. You can also select commands by pressing [→] or [←] to highlight the command and then pressing [Enter] to select it.

The commands Top and Bottom let you move to specific positions in the current database. The commands Lock, Record No., and Freeze require an additional step. After selecting one of these commands, you must specify which field or fields you want to work with.

Locking a field means that you lock it in place on your screen. You can lock only fields that are displayed on screen. You select the number of the field to lock by its position from the left margin. The first field is FIELD 1, the second FIELD 2, and so on, to the last field displayed at the right margin. In most cases, you can display only a few fields in the Browse screen. It is a good idea to position the field you want to lock on the left margin and then select FIELD 1 as the field you want to lock.

Once you've locked a field, you can scroll or pan far away from the original position of the locked field, but that field will always remain on your screen. This lets you lock a primary field, such as the name of the person, and browse through remote fields while keeping your eyes on the primary field. You can unlock fields as easily as you locked them, as shown in the examples.

The Record No. command allows you to go directly to a specific record. Press [R], type the record number you want to go to, then press [Enter] to go directly to that record.

Freezing fields lets you protect certain fields from being edited or changed inadvertently. You can edit only the contents of frozen fields. If you wanted to go through the records in NAD and change certain ZIP codes, but you wanted to make sure you didn't change any other data inadvertently, you would freeze the ZIP field. This lets you change data in the ZIP fields only. You can always view the contents of fields that aren't frozen—you just can't change their contents until you release all frozen fields, as shown in the examples.

Examples

1. To move to the bottom of the database, press [Ctrl]-[Home] to open the Browse menu bar. Press [Enter] to execute the Bottom command, which appears highlighted by default. (You can also press [B] to execute this command.) This moves you to the last record in the current database.

2. To move to a specific record in the Browse screen, use the command Record No. To go to record 12, press [Ctrl]-[Home], press [R], type 12, and press [Enter]. This moves your highlight bar to record 12.

3. To lock the first field in NAD.DBF, NAME, and then display the fields towards the end of the database, press Ctrl-Home to open the Browse menu bar. Press L to execute the lock command. This opens a box that asks you to "Change number of columns to lock to:" followed by a box that lets you specify the column number or numbers you want to lock.

   Since the NAME field is the first field on the left side of the Browse screen, type **1** and press Enter. This locks the first column, the NAME field, in its current position on your screen.

   Press Ctrl-→ twice to pan to the right. Notice that the NAME field remains locked on the left side of your screen. Unlocked fields scroll by from the right and then disappear. When you've panned to the right enough to display the last field, NOTES, your screen should look like the one in Figure 5-4.

4. You can lock more than one field at a time, but you can only lock the leftmost fields that are displayed on your screen. For example,

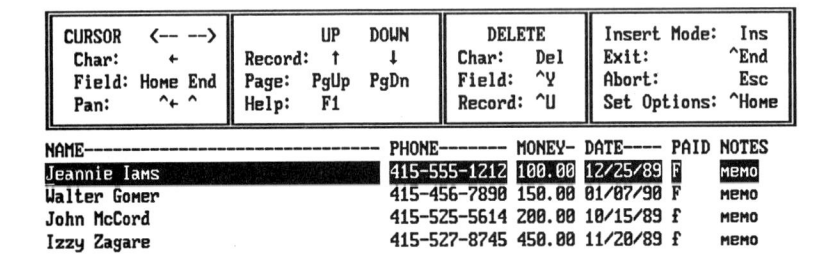

| FIGURE 5-4. | The NAME field locked in the Browse screen |

you can lock both the NAME and ADDRESS fields. Press [Ctrl]-[Home] to open the Browse menu bar, then press [L] to open the Lock prompt. Type **2** and press [Enter]. Now pan to the right by pressing [Ctrl]-[→]. Since the NAME and ADDRESS fields occupy most of your screen, you'll see only one field appear on the right side of your screen as you pan to the right, and only the smaller fields.

When you lock a field or fields, you can't scroll or pan to the left. You can only pan to the right. Consider this when you construct a database structure. If the ZIP field comes before the NAME field and you lock NAME on your screen, you won't be able to pan to the left to view the ZIP field and see what the ZIP code entry is for each NAME.

5. You'll want to unlock fields as often as you lock them. You can release locked fields in two ways: while working in the Browse screen and by exiting the Browse screen.

    To unlock a field while remaining in the Browse screen, go through the following procedure for locking 0 fields. Press [Ctrl]-[Home] to open the Browse menu bar. Press [L] to open the Lock prompt. (The prompt box is always empty when it first appears.) Press [Enter] without specifying any field numbers. This unlocks whatever fields are currently locked and returns the Browse screen to its normal display.

    Whenever you exit the Browse screen with one or more locked records, dBASE unlocks the records automatically. When you exit the Browse screen, you return to the Assist screen. Since the Browse command remains highlighted, just press [Enter] to return to your previous position in the current database.

6. To freeze the ZIP field, press [Ctrl]-[Home] to open the Browse menu bar, and then press [F] to execute the Freeze command. This opens a prompt asking you to "Enter field name to freeze" followed by a box where you enter the field name you want to freeze.

    Type **ZIP** and press [Enter]. Notice that the highlight bar disappears from your screen. The highlight bar appears only over the frozen field column. Since the ZIP field column doesn't appear on screen, there is no highlight bar. Press [Ctrl]-[→] once. This moves your cursor to the highlighted field, ZIP. As long as the frozen field appears on screen, the cursor will appear somewhere within the frozen field column. You can move up and down within the frozen field column by using the cursor control keys.

If you scroll far enough from the frozen field that it no longer shows on screen, the cursor will disappear. You can freeze only one field at a time.

7. To unfreeze a field, open the Browse menu bar, select the Freeze command, and press [Enter]. Practice freezing and unfreezing fields in SAMPLE.DBF. To freeze FIELD1, begin in the Browse screen and press [Ctrl]-[Home] to open the Browse menu bar. Press [F] to open the Freeze prompt box, type **1**, and press [Enter]. Make sure the field is frozen by scrolling to the right several fields and trying to enter information into other fields.

To unfreeze FIELD1, press [Ctrl]-[Home] to open the Browse menu bar, press [F] to open the Freeze prompt box, and press [Enter] twice.

Exercises

1. What are the five commands in the Browse menu?

2. How do you open this menu?

3. What is the difference between locking a field and freezing a field?

4. Lock FIELD10 on your screen.

5. Unlock FIELD10.

6. Freeze FIELD10 on your screen.

7. Unfreeze FIELD10.

5.4 GO DIRECTLY TO RECORDS

Going directly to specific records while working in the Assist screen facilitates your ability to display the contents of individual records in the Assist screen, which you'll learn about in the next section of this chapter. As the size of the current database grows, often you'll want to go directly to a specific record. To do this correctly, you should know something about the way dBASE keeps track of records.

When you go to a specific record, what you actually do is make the record current. dBASE uses a feature called the *pointer*, which always points at the current record. When you first load a database, the pointer always points at the first record. As you move from one record to another, you're actually moving the pointer. This is true whether you're working in the Edit, Browse, or Assist screen.

Use the command Goto Record on the Position menu to go to specific records quickly in the Assist screen. Using the command Goto Record on the Position menu is just as easy. To use this command:

a. Press [P] to open the Position menu.

b. Press [↑] to highlight the bottom command, Goto Record. This opens a pop-up menu giving you three commands: TOP, BOTTOM, and RECORD.

c. Select the appropriate command to go to the first or last record or to a specific record number.

Once you get the feel of working with the command Goto Record, you'll find going to records very easy.

When you use the command Goto Record and specify a record number that's beyond the number of records in the current database, dBASE will tell you "Record is out of range." If this happens, press any key and then repeat the steps to go to a specific record, using a valid record number. The total number of records in the current database is always displayed on the status line after the number of the current record.

Examples

1. To go to the bottom or last record in NAD.DBF, press [P] to open the Position menu, press [↑] to highlight the command Goto Record, and then press [Enter] to open the Goto Record menu. Press

⬇ and then [Enter] to accept the BOTTOM selection. Notice that "Rec: 5/5" appears on the right side of the status bar.

The contents of record 5 won't show on your screen because dBASE doesn't know how you want to display the data. You've only moved the dBASE pointer to the last record in the current database.

2. To go to the top or first record in NAD.DBF, press [Enter], (with the Position menu open and the command Goto Record highlighted). Press ⬇ to highlight BOTTOM and press [Enter]. You will see "Rec: 1/5" appear on the status bar.

3. To go specifically to record 3, press [Enter] (with the Position menu open and the command Goto Record highlighted), press ⬆ to highlight the RECORD selection, press [Enter], type 3, and press [Enter]. You will see "Rec: 3/5" appear on the status bar.

Exercises

1. What feature does dBASE use to keep track of the current record?

2. Which menu and which command do you use to go to a specific record in the current database while viewing the Assist screen?

3. How do you go to the bottom record of the current database?

4. Continuing directly from the previous exercise, how do you go to record 3 in the current database?

5.5 DISPLAY RECORDS

You can display the contents of individual records in the Assist screen without entering either the Edit or Browse screen. Displaying the contents of a record lets you confirm the contents of the current record. It also lets you view all the information for a single record at one time.

You can't always do this in the Edit screen, and you can rarely do it in the Browse screen.

You can't make any changes to a record's contents when you display them in the Assist screen. You have to use the Edit or Browse screen to make changes to records that can be observed on the screen. You have to use the command Replace on the Update menu to make unobserved changes, as described in the next section.

With the skills you've learned so far in this book, you can make a specific record current by entering the Browse screen, opening the Browse menu bar, and going to the specific record. From there, you can exit the Browse screen and run the Display command.

Use the command Display on the Update menu to display the contents of individual records. First make sure the record you want to view is the current record: Check the right side of the status bar and make sure the displayed record number is correct.

a. Press [U] to open the Update menu.

b. Highlight the Display command and press [Enter].

c. Press [Enter] again to accept the command "Execute Command," which is the default.

Your screen should change to look like the one in Figure 5-5.

This can be a confusing display if you're not familiar with the structure of the current database. The field names appear first in uppercase characters followed by the field entries. Blank spaces are added to each field entry to display the full width of each field.

To return to work in the Assist screen, press any key. The Update menu will reappear with the Display command highlighted.

The more fields in a record and the longer the field widths, the more confusing the record's display can be. If you forget the structure of a database, you can always view the structure using the "List structure" command on the Tools menu.

Examples

1. To display the contents of record 2 in NAD.DBF, first make record 2 current. Press [P] to open the Position menu, press [↓] to

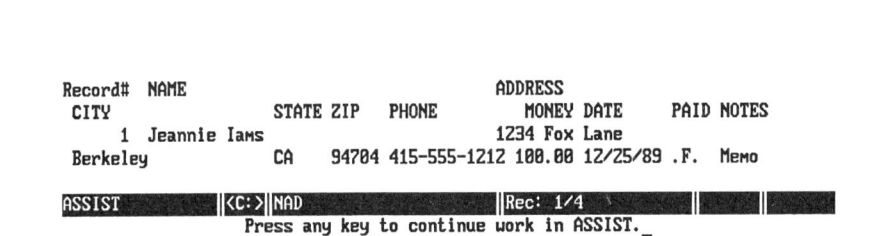

```
            Set Up  Create  Update  Position  Retrieve  Organize Modify Tools   01:08:12 pm




            Record#  NAME                              ADDRESS
            CITY                 STATE ZIP   PHONE         MONEY DATE    PAID NOTES
                 1  Jeannie Iams                      1234 Fox Lane
            Berkeley             CA    94704 415-555-1212 100.00 12/25/89 .F.  Memo
         ASSIST         ||<C:>||NAD                    ||Rec: 1/4  \
                        Press any key to continue work in ASSIST._
```

| FIGURE 5-5. | Displaying the contents of the current record |

highlight the command Goto Record, and press [Enter] to open the menu attached to this command. Press [↑] to highlight RECORD and press [Enter], type **2** and press [Enter]. Make sure record 2 shows on the right side of the status bar.

To display the contents of this record, press [U] to open the Update menu, press [↓] twice to highlight the command Display, and then press [Enter] twice to execute the command. Your screen should display the contents of record

2. When you're finished viewing the contents, press any key to return to the Assist.

Exercises

1. What is the advantage of displaying a record by using the command Display on the Update menu?

2. Can you edit a record displayed using the Display command?

3. Display the contents of record 1 in NAD.DBF, and then return to the Assist screen.

4. Display the contents of the bottom or last record in NAD.DBF, and then return to the Assist.

EXERCISES

1. Compare and contrast the ways you can replace information in a database by using the Edit and Browse commands.

    MASTERY SKILLS CHECK

2. Beginning in the Assist screen, open the Edit screen for NAD.DBF. Switch between Edit and Browse several times.

3. Open the Browse screen and go to record 7 in NAD.DBF. Close the Browse screen and open the Edit screen for record 7. Change the NAME field to show "Alan Vogle". Close the Edit screen and return to the Assist screen. Display the contents for record 7.

1. Begin in the Assist screen and check what dBASE on-screen help has to say about the commands Edit, Display, Browse, and Replace in turn.

    INTEGRATING SKILLS CHECK

2. Begin in the Assist screen. Append a new record to NAD.DBF. Use the following information:

    | NAME | Carol Hannah |
    | ADDRESS | 205 Martin |
    | CITY | Aptos |
    | STATE | CA |
    | ZIP | 95003 |

    Display the contents of this record in the Assist screen. Return to the Assist.

3. Begin in the Assist screen. Create a small database called AREA that saves major city names and their matching telephone area codes. The database should contain three character-type fields, one for CITY 20 spaces wide, one for STATE 2 spaces wide, and one for CODE 3 spaces wide. Append three records to this database directly after saving the structure, using this information:

CITY	STATE	CODE
San Francisco	CA	415
Seattle	WA	206
Honolulu	HI	808

Now scan the database using the Browse screen.

Locating and Calculating Records

►6◄

CHAPTER OBJECTIVES

In this chapter you will learn how to

- ▶ Use the Position and Search/Scope menus — 6.1
- ▶ Skip records — 6.2
- ▶ Locate records — 6.3
- ▶ Specify a scope — 6.4
- ▶ Replace record information — 6.5
- ▶ Calculate numeric fields — 6.6

Finding records that contain specific information, replacing information in records, and calculating information from numeric data are all important procedures in database management.

In this chapter, you'll learn how to use the Search/Scope menu to locate specific records and display their contents and then how to replace information in records quickly.

You'll learn how to obtain information based upon entries into numeric fields. dBASE can calculate numeric field information in three ways: by sum, by average, and by count.

Exercises

SKILLS CHECK

1. Load dBASE and make NAD.DBF the current database. Open the Edit screen and display record 4.

2. Open the memo field editor for record 4, insert the text "This is the memo field for record 4," and then save the text and close the memo field editor.

3. Exit the Edit screen and make sure record 4 is shown in the status bar. Go to record 1. Make sure the record number appears on the status bar.

4. Load the database SAMPLE.DBF. Open the Browse screen and move to the last or bottom record in the database. Move back to the top or first record. Move to record 3. Exit the Browse screen.

5. Replace the contents of the NAME field in record 4 with "Ziggy Zagare". Make sure the replacement was successful.

6.1 USE THE POSITION AND SEARCH/SCOPE MENUS

Before you begin learning how to locate records, you should become familiar with the Position menu and the Search/Scope menu that is attached to the command Locate. The Position menu is so named because you use it to move around to different positions, or records, in the current database.

To open the Position menu while working in the Assist screen, press P. You'll see these five commands:

Seek	Lets you search for the first record that matches your search criteria. You can use this command only when the current database also has an active index
Locate	Locates the next record that matches your search criteria
Continue	Lets you repeat the command Locate
Skip	Lets you skip a specified number of records
Goto Record	Lets you go to a specific record by location or number

You'll learn how to use the commands Locate, Skip, and Continue in this chapter. You'll learn how to use the command Seek in Chapter 9. You learned how to use the command Goto Record in the previous chapter.

If you haven't yet made a database current, you cannot use any commands on the Position menu. All five will be disabled. You have to open a database to enable some of the commands.

After you open a database and then press P to open the Position menu, three commands are enabled: Locate, Skip, and Goto Record. The Locate command will appear highlighted because it's the first enabled command. Seek remains disabled until you attach an index to the current database, as you'll learn in Chapter 9. Continue will become enabled as soon as you use the Locate command; it lets you continue to locate the next record matching your criteria.

The command Locate lets you go to a record based upon information contained within the record. To use this command while the Position menu is open, highlight the command Locate and press Enter. dBASE opens the Search/Scope menu, as shown in Figure 6-1. This menu lets you specify various characteristics for the record or records you're looking for.

```
Set Up  Create  Update  Position  Retrieve  Organize  Modify  Tools  04:12:53 pm
                          Seek
                                      Execute the command
                          Locate      Specify scope
                          Continue    Construct a field list
                                      Build a search condition
                          Skip        Build a scope condition
                          Goto Record




Command: LOCATE
ASSIST          |<C:>|NAD       ·        |Rec: 1/4
                     Position selection bar - ↑↓.  Select - ↵.
                     Perform the command displayed above the status bar.
```

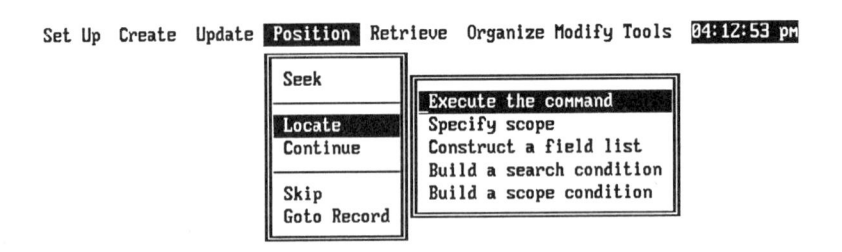

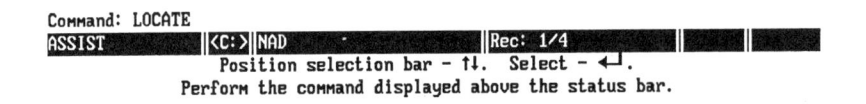

| FIGURE 6-1. | The Search/Scope menu for the Locate command |

The Search/Scope menu is one you'll run across frequently for various commands in dBASE III PLUS. You saw this menu for the first time in the last chapter when you used the command Display on the Update menu. You'll see it again at various points in this book, particularly when you work with commands on the Retrieve menu.

The Search/Scope menu contains the following five commands:

Execute the command   Executes the command that opened
                           the Search/Scope menu (Locate, De-
                           lete, List, and so on) according to the
                           search-and-scope conditions you set
                           by using other commands on this
                           menu

Specify scope   Opens a menu that lets you select a
                           scope or range of records

Construct a field list   Constructs a list of selected fields for handling. This command does not apply to locating records, but you will use it in Chapter 7, where you learn how to delete records

Build a search condition   Lets you specify certain fields, relational operators, and field information you want to base your search on

Build a scope condition   Lets you specify certain fields, relational operators, and field information you want to base your scope or range on

The Search/Scope menu is remarkably interactive. Commands become enabled and disabled from one step to the next, and the highlight bar moves automatically from one command to another, depending upon the progress of your work.

NOTE: Because you can't move around records until you've entered quite a few into a database, you should work with a large database for the examples in this chapter. Therefore, add more records to the file NAD.DBF. In order to follow the example, you should duplicate the records shown in Figure 6-2.

Examples

1. Open the Position menu without opening a database. If a database is open, quit dBASE and then reload the program. When the Assist screen appears, press [P] to open the Position menu. Notice that none of the commands on this menu are enabled.
   Now open NAD.DBF. Press [S] to open the Set Up menu, press [Enter] twice, highlight NAD, and press [Enter] twice more. Now press [P] to open the Position menu. Notice that three commands are enabled and that the highlight bar appears on the command Locate.

```
Jeannie Iams        1234 Fox Lane        Berkeley        CA 91010 415-456-7890 100.00 12/25/89 F
Walter Gomer        560 San Jose         Kensington      CA 94720 415-567-8900 150.00 01/07/90 F
John McCord         920 Evelyn Street    Albany          CA 94708 415-525-5614 200.00 10/15/89 F
Ziggy Zagare        560 Benvenue         El Cerrito      CA 94530 415-527-8745 450.00 11/20/89 F
Stan Freeberg       1 Chuckles Lane      Westport        CT 06530 203-567-5434  25.00 11/25/89 F
David Clark         288 Moody Lane       Oakland         CA 94612 415-899-0075  25.00 12/25/89 F
Launey Thomas       428 Birge            Berkeley        CA 94704 415-343-6978  50.00 07/11/89 F
Swarna Mitts        3489 Cricket Court   Richmond        CA 97540 415-785-6454 450.00 11/08/89 F
Richard Fallenbaum  343 Park Lane        Piedmont        CA 97455 415-333-1217 900.00 10/06/89 F
Christian Smith     2 Park Lane          San Francisco   CA 94017 415-678-4321 175.00 08/13/89 F
Judy Verlenden      4 Commodore Court    Carmel Valley   CA 93924 408-233-4554 235.00 07/10/89 F
Carol Hanna         19 Marin Lane        Aptos           CA 95003 408-567-3345 850.00 09/01/89 F
Dave Trollman       34 Sack Court        Redwood City    CA 94723 415-865-9090 600.00 09/19/89 F
Carol McGinnis      1234 Stagecoach Rd   Tucson          AZ 80650 602-873-4457 500.00 10/20/89 F
Margaret Smith      456 Primrose Place   Redwood City    CA 94565 415-645-9034 250.00 11/22/89 F
Roger Smith         567 Blake Street     Berkeley        CA 94710 415-896-6534 150.00 10/06/89 F
Cornelius Ragg      678 Sansome Street   San Francisco   CA 94710 415-743-6520 200.00 10/20/89 F
Charles Smith       6600 California      San Francisco   CA 94601 415-875-4567 340.00 12/20/89 F
Ahma Smith          34 Bentley           El Sobrante     CA 94567 415-734-5634 250.00 09/09/89 F
Pat Smith           45 Millwood          Mill Valley     CA 94784 415-785-6555 500.00 09/10/89 F
```

FIGURE 6-2.   NAD.DBF expanded to 20 records

2. To Open the Search/Scope menu for the command Locate, press [Enter] while the command Locate is highlighted. The top command, Execute, will be highlighted. Only the command "Construct a field list" will be disabled. This command does not apply to locating records.

3. Find out how interactive the Search/Scope menu is. While the Execute command is highlighted, press [Enter]. dBASE displays the message "Record = 1" above the status bar, which means that it has found record 1, or the current record, for you. Press any key to return to the Assist.

Notice that the command Continue has now become enabled. Don't execute the command just yet. Since you haven't built a search condition for the Locate command, it won't work.

Exercises

1. Where does the Position menu get its name?

2. What commands are on the Position menu?

3. What happens when you execute the command Locate?

4. What does the Position menu command Continue do?

SKIP RECORDS   6.2

The Skip command lets you skip over a specified number of records. For instance, you'll want to skip over certain records when you want to check the content of every *n*th record, such as every 10th record. This is a routine method for sampling a database or auditing the integrity of the database without checking every record. You can also skip a group of records if you have a fairly good idea of the contents of the records you are skipping.

You skip records by selecting the command Skip on the Position menu. dBASE then asks you how many records you want to skip. The value you enter is added to the current record number, and the sum will equal the record you go to. For example, if record 10 is current and you tell dBASE you want to skip five records, you'll move to record 15 (10 + 5 = 15).

You can skip both forward and backward through records. dBASE assumes you want to skip forward unless you place a minus sign before the number of records you want to skip.

If you try to skip more records than remain in the database, dBASE moves you to the end-of-file (EOF will show on the status bar), beeps, and tells you that you're at the end of the database file.

Examples

1. Use the command Skip to check the contents of every fifth record in NAD.DBF. First, make sure NAD.DBF is current, and make sure the first record is the current record number.

To check every fifth record, press [P] to open the Position menu, highlight the command Skip, and press [Enter]. dBASE asks you to specify a numeric value. This is the number of records you want to skip. For your first example, type 4 and press [Enter]. You'll see on the status bar that record 5 has become the current record. Remember, the numeric value you specify is the number of records you skip. To see every fifth record, you have to start out by skipping 4 the first time, then skipping every five.

2. Once you've moved to a new record, you can view its contents in the Edit screen, or you can display the contents on your screen by using the command Display. To display the record contents, press [U] to open the Update menu, highlight the command Display, and press [Enter] twice. Now press any key to continue working in the Assist screen.

  To skip to record 10, press [→] to open the Position menu, press [↓] to highlight the command Skip, press [Enter], type 5, and press [Enter]. To display the record, press [→], [↓], and then [Enter] again twice, view the display, and then press any key. You'll soon find yourself skipping and displaying records quickly and easily.

3. If record 10 is current and you want to skip to record 3, press [P], highlight Skip and press [Enter], type −7 and press [Enter]. Record 3 will show on the status bar. Remember to enter the minus sign to skip backward.

Exercises

1. What does the command Skip do?

2. How does dBASE calculate the record it skips to?

3. How do you skip backward?

LOCATE RECORDS

> 6.3

You can locate records in a database by specifying certain conditions in the record or records you want to locate. For example, if you don't know which record contains information for "Carol McGinnis", you can use the command Locate to move directly to the record that contains that name. You just specify that dBASE should search on the NAME field for "Carol McGinnis".

You locate records to view them individually on screen, to display them on your screen in a list, to print them to paper, or to delete them. You can also select a group of records to perform calculations upon them. This procedure will be described at the end of this chapter.

You can get a better idea of the power of the command Locate by using a broader example. If you want to locate all records for people living in California, you would build a search condition that locates all records with "CA" in the STATE field. dBASE would then take you to the first record in the group. If this wasn't the record you were looking for, or you want to go to other records for California, you would use the command Continue.

The first step towards using the command Locate correctly is to understand the difference between the terms "search" and "scope." You use *search conditions* to find records containing specific information. In the above examples, you specified "Carol McGinnis" in the NAME field and "CA" in the STATE field as your search criteria. Your search might find one record, several, or many. In some cases, it might not find any records. If your search finds any records, you can then view the contents of each record in turn and see if the record interests you.

You use *scope conditions* to specify the range of records you want to search through from a much larger group. In most cases, you won't use scope conditions unless you're working with a very large database.

The best way to start out locating records is to use the command "Build a search condition." Building a search condition is a three-step process:

a. Select the field you want to base your search on.
b. Select the conditional operator you want to use.
c. Define the condition.

The only new part to this process is selecting a conditional operator. You've worked with fields before, so selecting a field isn't difficult. In the examples that introduced this section, you selected the NAME field for "Carol McGinnis" and the STATE field for "CA". Defining the condition is perhaps the easiest of all. The condition is just the information you're looking for, for example "Carol McGinnis" or "CA".

You should understand how the six conditional operators behave so that you can control your searches more precisely. Table 6-1 describes each operator. These operators work with both numbers and alphabetic characters. Equal To has to be an exact match of the letter characters you specify. If you use the operator = Equal To, dBASE will only locate exact matches of the information you specify.

Less Than means letters below the letters you're searching for, with A being the lowest letter. Greater Than means letters above the letters you're searching for, with Z being the highest letter.

TABLE 6-1. Definition of Conditional Operators

Operator	Function
= Equal To	Searches for exact matches of all specified characters. This is the most precise form of searching
< = Less Than or Equal To	Searches for characters lower than or equal to the specified characters
< Less Than	Searches for characters that are less than the specified characters
> Greater Than	Searches for characters that are greater than the specified characters
> = Greater Than or Equal To	Searches for characters that are equal to or greater than the specified characters
< > Not Equal To	Searches for characters that are not equal to the specified characters. This is the least precise form of searching

When dBASE searches for records that match your criteria, it does so using the decimal value of the ASCII character. The ASCII character set contains the 256 characters you can display on your screen. It includes numbers, letters, and punctuation, as well as control codes and other characters you see from time to time on your screen, including the graphic characters that make up menu borders. Appendix C shows the complete ASCII character set.

The area most affected by the ASCII character set is the use of operators on uppercase and lowercase letters. In the ASCII table, all uppercase letters come before all lowercase letters (A = 41, Z = 90, a = 97, z = 122). When you use the conditional operator < Less Than and specify the letter "a" or a word that begins with "a", such as "able", dBASE will find all records that begin with uppercase characters, such as "Zycroft". This is an anomaly created by the arrangement of characters on the ASCII chart and not by dBASE.

When you search for information in a field with a fixed format, such as numeric and date fields, you have to enter the entire field contents. For example, to select a group of records based on the figure 5 cents in the decimal field, you have to enter .05.

When you try to locate records and dBASE doesn't find any records that match your search criteria, it displays the message "End of LOCATE Scope." When this happens, you should redefine your search criteria.

You can refine your search criteria by specifying more than one field. For example, you can locate records in NAD.DBF based upon the amount owed you by using the MONEY field and records based upon the date you loaned the money by using the DATE field. After you pick the first field you want to search, as well as the operator and the search criteria, dBASE opens a menu with three commands that allows you to either stop building search criteria or to refine the criteria further:

No more conditions	Returns you to the Search/Scope menu. Select this command when you don't want to specify any more search criteria
Combine with .AND.	Opens the field list box, which lets you select another field to search on
Combine with .OR.	Opens the field list box, which lets you select another field to include in the criteria

To refine your search, be sure you understand the difference between .AND. and .OR. Selecting the .AND. option narrows your search. It adds another condition that must be met before dBASE will locate the record. Selecting the .OR. option broadens your search. dBASE will locate all records that match any of the conditions you specify.

NOTE: The periods before and after the .AND. and .OR. commands reflect the way these commands are written by dBASE programmers.

When you execute the Locate command, it scans through the entire database from the first to the last record, looking for the first record that matches the conditions you've specified. Once a record is located, that record becomes the current record, and you can view its contents in the Edit or Browse menus or display the contents on your screen.

When you locate a record, you should display its contents by using the command Display on the Update menu, to make sure it's a record you're looking for.

If you want to continue locating subsequent records that match your current search criteria, use the command Continue. dBASE will then look for the next record in sequence until it finds the last matching record. The command Continue continues the search from the current record on.

Working with the various commands that let you go to specific records and find records containing specific information takes some getting used to. Once you work with these commands several times, you'll find them easier to use.

Examples

1. Locate the record in NAD.DBF that has "Carol McGinnis" in the NAME field. (This is a record you added to expand NAD.DBF.) First, make sure NAD.DBF is current. Press [P] to open the Position menu, and then highlight Locate and press [Enter]. Highlight the command "Build a search condition" and press [Enter]. This opens the "Build a search condition" screen, as shown in Figure 6-3.

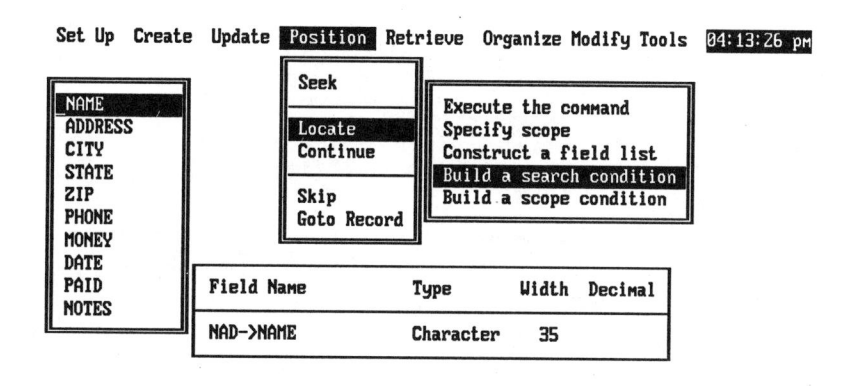

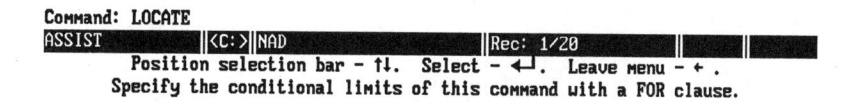

Chapter 6 Locating and Calculating Records **121**

```
              Set Up  Create  Update  Position  Retrieve  Organize  Modify  Tools   04:13:26 pm
           ┌─────────┐      ┌──────────────┐
           │ NAME    │      │ Seek         │    ┌──────────────────────────┐
           │ ADDRESS │      │              │    │ Execute the command      │
           │ CITY    │      │ Locate       │    │ Specify scope            │
           │ STATE   │      │ Continue     │    │ Construct a field list   │
           │ ZIP     │      │              │    │ Build a search condition │
           │ PHONE   │      │ Skip         │    │ Build a scope condition  │
           │ MONEY   │      │ Goto Record  │    └──────────────────────────┘
           │ DATE    │      └──────────────┘
           │ PAID    │    ┌──────────────────────────────────────────┐
           │ NOTES   │    │ Field Name        Type       Width  Decimal │
           └─────────┘    │                                          │
                          │ NAD->NAME         Character   35         │
                          └──────────────────────────────────────────┘


      Command: LOCATE
      ASSIST        |<C:>|NAD                  |Rec: 1/20  |           |
                  Position selection bar - ↑↓.  Select - ↵.  Leave menu - ←.
                Specify the conditional limits of this command with a FOR clause.
```

| FIGURE 6-3. | The "Build a search conditon" screen |

A list of the ten fields in NAD.DBF appears on the left side of your screen. This is where you select the field to search. The first field name, NAME, is highlighted. Details about the highlighted field appear in a second box in the lower middle of your screen. These details include the name of the highlighted field, the type of field, and the field width in spaces. (The field name is preceded by the name of the database file. This is significant only when you begin to relate information from multiple databases.) The decimal field in the lower box is empty because a character-type field has no decimal value. Press [Enter] to select the NAME field.

This opens the list of conditional operators, as shown in Figure 6-4. The second step of the process is to select one of six conditional operators. Press [Enter]. This accepts the operator = Equal To.

dBASE asks you to "Enter a character string (without quotes)." A *character string* is any group of characters you can type from your keyboard, including letters, numbers, and punctuation marks. You

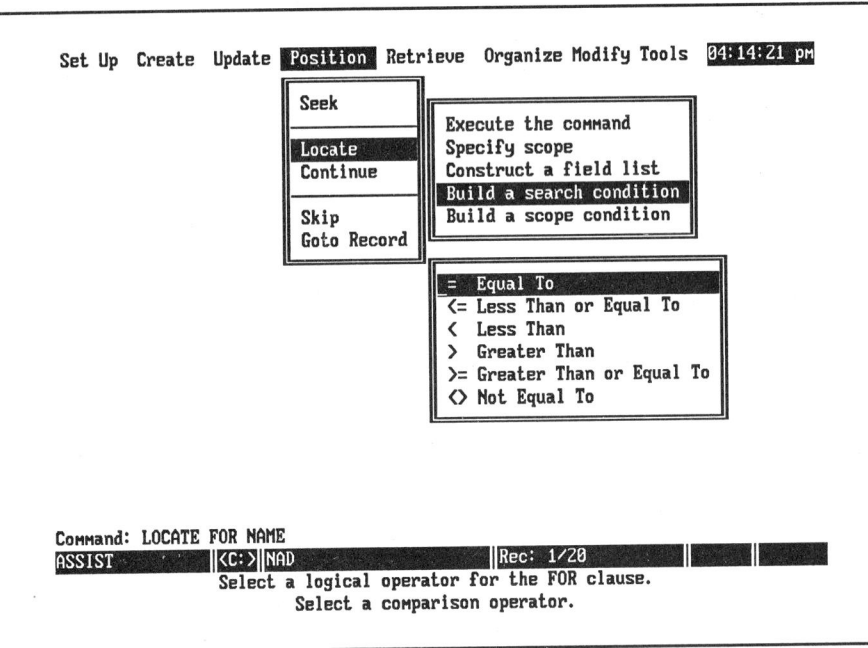

```
       Set Up  Create  Update  Position  Retrieve  Organize Modify Tools  04:14:21 pm
                              ┌─────────────┐
                              │  Seek       │ ┌──────────────────────────┐
                              ├─────────────┤ │ Execute the command      │
                              │  Locate     │ │ Specify scope            │
                              │  Continue   │ │ Construct a field list   │
                              ├─────────────┤ │ Build a search condition │
                              │  Skip       │ │ Build a scope condition  │
                              │  Goto Record│ └──────────────────────────┘
                              └─────────────┘
                                       ┌────────────────────────────────┐
                                       │ =  Equal To                    │
                                       │ <= Less Than or Equal To       │
                                       │ <  Less Than                   │
                                       │ >  Greater Than                │
                                       │ >= Greater Than or Equal To    │
                                       │ <> Not Equal To                │
                                       └────────────────────────────────┘

Command: LOCATE FOR NAME
ASSIST              |<C:>|NAD                |Rec: 1/20
                    Select a logical operator for the FOR clause.
                           Select a comparison operator.
```

FIGURE 6-4. Box of conditional operators

can enter up to 35 characters in this box because the NAME field in NAD.DBF has a maximum field width of 35 spaces.

Type **Carol McGinnis** and press [Enter]. This opens the menu that lets you tell dBASE whether you want to stop or continue adding additional search criteria. Press [Enter] to select "No more conditions." This returns you to the Search/Scope menu and automatically bumps the cursor down to the next command, "Build a scope condition." You'll learn about scope conditions in the next section. For now, press [↓] to highlight the top menu selection, "Execute the command," and press [Enter].

dBASE now tries to locate the first record with "Carol McGinnis" in the NAME field. If all goes well, dBASE will find record 14 with the information you've specified and display the record number just above the status bar. Press any key to return to the Assist. You can now view the contents of this located record in the Edit or Browse screen or display the record contents on your screen.

2. Highlight the command Continue, which should now be enabled, and press [Enter]. Presuming you have no more records in NAD.DBF containing the name "Carol McGinnis" in the NAME field, you should get the error message "End of LOCATE Scope."

3. Locate all records for people who have borrowed more than $200 and who have owed the money since the beginning of 1990. Press [P] to open the Position menu, highlight the command Locate, and press [Enter]. Highlight "Build a search condition" and press [Enter]. When the field list appears, highlight the MONEY field and press [Enter]. Select > Greater Than and press [Enter]. Type 200 and press [Enter]. This opens the menu that lets you refine your search criteria.

   Press [↓] to highlight "Combine with .AND.," and press [Enter]. Highlight the DATE field and press [Enter], and then highlight > Greater Than and press [Enter]. Type 89 and press [Enter]. Press [Enter] to select the command "No more conditions" and press [Enter] again. Press [↓] to highlight "Execute the command" and press [Enter]. dBASE will locate the first record that matches your refined search criteria (or tell you it couldn't find any records that fulfill your criteria).

Exercises

1. What is the difference between the terms "scope" and "search"?

2. What are the three steps towards building a search condition?

3. When you build a search condition, are letter characters ranked by their alphabetical order?

4. When can you use the command Continue?

5. Name the five conditional operators.

6. Locate the record in NAD.DBF with the name "John McCord" in the NAME field, display the contents, and return to the Assist screen.

6.4 SPECIFY A SCOPE

Using a scope condition lets you define a range of records dBASE will search through in the current database. This is useful only when you start working with large databases and don't want dBASE to waste time searching through all records. A search without a scope always goes through the entire database.

There are two commands you can use to specify a scope or range of records: "Specify scope" and "Build a scope condition." The first lets you declare a numerical range of records, and the second lets you refine a scope by using the same commands you use to build search conditions.

The command "Specify scope" opens a menu that lets you define the range of records by their numerical position in the database. It offers the following five options:

Default scope	Lets you continue to use the current scope condition
ALL	Selects all records to search through. This is disabled when you are using the Locate command because dBASE presumes a scope of all records when you want to locate a group of records
NEXT	Lets you specify a group of records by number, such as the next 4 records or the next 500 records
RECORD	Lets you enter a specific record number
REST	Specifies the rest of the records in the database after the current record

When you select either the NEXT or RECORD commands, you have to give dBASE a numerical value it will use to refine the scope. For example, selecting NEXT and typing **10** selects the next ten records as your scope. Selecting RECORD and typing **10** selects record 10 as the scope. The command REST simply selects the rest of the records in the database as the scope.

Once you declare a scope option and press [Enter], the Search/Scope menu reappears. The command "Build a search condition" is highlighted, and the "Specify scope" command is disabled. This moves you to the command that lets you specify any search criteria.

If you change your mind and decide you want to specify a different scope, press [Esc] to return to the Position menu, and then press [Enter] to reexecute the command Locate. When the Search/Scope menu reappears, the command "Specify scope" will be enabled.

Once you're satisfied with the scope, you can proceed to specify your search criteria. You don't have to specify a scope before your search criteria. You can specify the search criteria first, but it's more logical to specify scope first and then the search criteria.

You can continue to refine the scope of records in the same way you build a search condition. In this case, you build a scope condition. You specify the field, the operator, and the information for your scope.

Examples

1. To select a scope of the next ten records, press [P], highlight "Specify scope," and press [Enter]. Now highlight NEXT, press [Enter], type 10, and press [Enter]. You can now build the search condition you want to use. When you select "Execute the command," dBASE looks through the next ten records for information that matches your search criteria. If it locates a record that matches, it displays the record number on screen. Press any key to return to the Assist screen.

2. Using the "Specify scope" menu has no visible effects except when you use the command RECORD. Make sure record 1 in NAD.DBF is current. Press [P] to open the Position menu, and then press [Enter] (the command Locate should be highlighted by default). Highlight "Specify scope" and press [Enter], and then highlight RECORD, press [Enter], type 10, and press [Enter]. Now highlight "Execute the command" and press [Enter]. dBASE says it has found "Record = 10." Press any key to return to the Assist, and you'll see record 10 appear on the status bar.

3. You'll probably use the command "Specify scope" most often in conjunction with the REST command, which selects the rest of the records in the current database as the scope. To do this, press [P], [Enter], highlight "Specify scope" and press [Enter], and highlight REST and press [Enter].

Exercises

1. How many commands are there on the "Specify scope" menu?

2. Name the commands on the "Specify scope" menu.

3. Which command is disabled when you are locating records?

4. How do you specify a range of records as the scope?

6.5 REPLACE RECORD INFORMATION

Since editing database information is a routine and important procedure, you're given the ability to replace information in a record without entering either the Edit or Browse screen. You use the Replace command on the Update menu to do this.

You can replace information in records in two ways: one at a time or in a group. To replace field information in a single record, make the record current, and then replace the information.

To replace information in a group of related records or records with similar characteristics, you'll use the Search/Scope menu.

Whenever you change information in a group of records, you must make the same changes to each record in the group. dBASE will report back how many records were changed.

There are two differences between using the Replace command and using the Edit or Browse screen to replace information. One is an advantage, the other a disadvantage. The advantage of using the Replace command is that you can replace information in a lot of records and fields globally (all at the same time). The disadvantage is that you can't observe what changes are taking place when you use the Replace command. dBASE makes the changes automatically without displaying the results. You have to use the command Display on the Update menu to view the new contents.

You should use the Browse screen to change information in several adjacent records. You can view the same field for adjacent records in the Browse screen and change the information on screen. You can lock the primary field if you need to use that field to identify records, and then pan over to the field or fields you want to change.

Examples

1. Change the name in the NAME field for record 4. First make record 4 current by pressing [P] to open the Position menu, pressing [↑] to highlight RECORD, pressing [Enter], typing **4**, and pressing [Enter] again. Make sure record 4 shows on the status bar.

    Once you've made record 4 current, you can begin the replacement. Press [U] to open the Update menu, highlight the command Replace, and press [Enter]. This opens two boxes on your screen, which should look like the one in Figure 6-5. A list of all fields in the current database appears in the left window. Details about the highlighted field appear in the lower window. When these windows first appear, the field at the top of the list is highlighted.

    Press [Enter] to select the highlighted field for replacement, in this case the NAME field. dBASE asks you to "Enter a character string (without quotes):." You're limited to the width of the current field

```
 Set Up   Create  Update  Position  Retrieve  Organize  Modify  Tools   01:11:29 pm













       Record#  NAME                          ADDRESS
               CITY              STATE ZIP  PHONE      MONEY DATE    PAID NOTES
            4  Daniel Lanois                            350 Benvenue
               El Cerrito        CA    94530 415-527-8745 450.00 11/20/89 .F.  Memo
       ASSIST         |<C:>|NAD            |Rec: 4/4
                      Press any key to continue work in ASSIST._
```

FIGURE 6-5.   Results of replacing the NAME field

for the number of replacment characters. You can see the width of the field you want to replace in the lower window. The NAME field in NAD.DBF has a width of 35 spaces, which means you can replace up to 35 characters in that field.

Type **Daniel Lanois** and press [Enter]. The two boxes return, in case you want to select a second field to replace. Press [Esc] to tell dBASE that you don't want to replace any other fields. This opens the Search/Scope menu. You'll see this menu attached to many other commands in the Assist screen. When it first appears, the command at the top of the menu, Execute, appears highlighted. Press [Enter] to accept the top command. This executes the replacement you've defined for the current record only and returns you to the Assist screen.

2. You can't see the effect of your replacement until you look at the contents of the current record. As long as the record you just changed remains current, press [U] to open the Update menu, highlight the command Display, and press [Enter]. Your screen should look like the one in Figure 6-6.

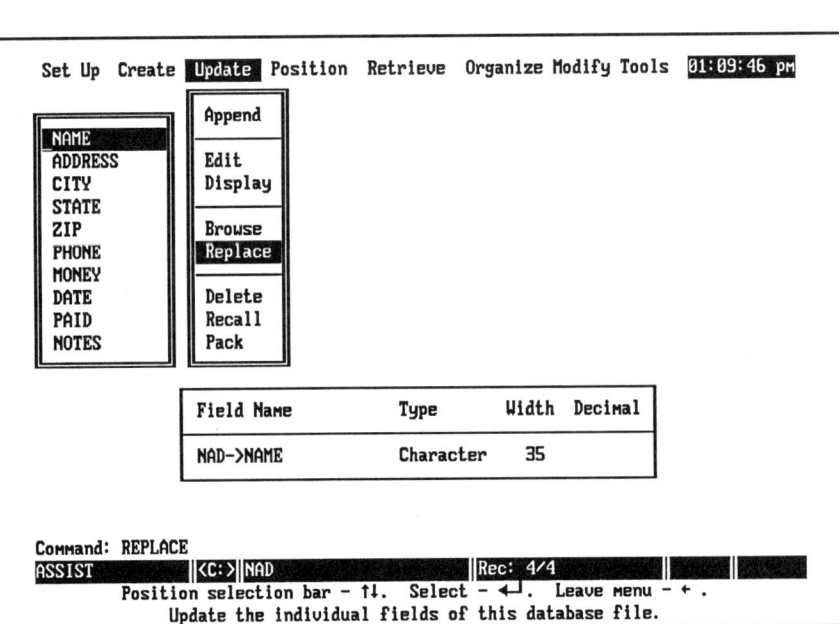

FIGURE 6-6. | The two Replace windows

3. Replace information in a group of records. We'll change the information for the STATE field for all records in California and put them in Texas.

Press [U], highlight Replace and press [Enter]. Highlight STATE, press [Enter], and type **TX**. Press [→]. Now highlight "Build a search condition" and press [Enter]. Highlight STATE and press [Enter] twice. This accepts the STATE field and the = Equal To conditional operator. Type **CA** and press [Enter]. This accepts "No more conditions." Highlight "Execute the command" and press [Enter]. dBASE will report back on the success of this replacement. It should show 18 records. Press any key to return to the Assist.

Before you go on, you should repeat the above example, only type **CA** in place of **TX**, and then **TX** instead of **CA**. This returns the correct information to the state names.

Exercises

1. Using NAD.DBF, replace the NAME field in record 1 with the information "Claudio Abau".

2. Check the results.

3. Replace the ADDRESS field in record 1 with the information "123 Adams Street".

4. Check the results.

5. Replace the CITY field in record 1 with the information "Berkeley".

6. Check the results.

CALCULATE NUMERIC FIELDS

6.6

dBASE lets you perform three types of calculations on numbers in numeric fields. You can't perform calculations on any other type of field.

You'll use three commands on the Retrieve menu to perform calculations. The Retrieve menu is designed to help you retrieve information from a database. When you press [R] to open the Retrieve menu, you'll see the following seven commands.

List	Lists to your screen or printer the contents of the records and fields you select using the Search/Scope menu
Display	Displays on your screen the contents of the records and fields you select using the Search/Scope menu
Report	Opens a report file and prints the report to your screen or the printer
Label	Opens a label file and prints labels to your screen or the printer
Sum	Adds up all numbers in the same numeric field for all records
Average	Calculates the mean average value for all entries in the same numeric field
Count	Counts the number of records in the current database. Since a count of all records calculated is given for all calculations, this lets you count the total of a group of records you've selected by building a search or scope condition

You'll use the bottom three commands in this section. You'll learn about the other commands in later chapters of this book.

To find and calculate all numeric fields in the current database:

a. Press [R] to open the Retrieve menu.

b. Highlight the calculation you want to perform.

c. Press [Enter]. This opens the Search/Scope menu attached to the Sum command, with the top selection, Execute, highlighted.

d. Press [Enter] to execute the calculation command. dBASE displays the results on your screen and also displays the number of records that were included in the calculation. Make note of the results.

e. Press any key to return to the Assist screen.

These steps work for all three calculation commands.

You can use the Search/Scope menu to build search and scope conditions that narrow down the records dBASE will use for calculation. You do this the same way you build search-and-scope conditions when you learned how to locate records earlier in this chapter.

By default, all numeric fields are calculated. You can narrow down the numeric fields that are calculated by using the command "Construct a field list." This lets you select which fields will be calculated. This command was disabled when you first worked with the Search/Scope menu to locate records. You can construct only a list of numeric fields. You cannot include other types of fields in this list. You should narrow down the list of fields to be calculated only when you work with a very large database. It takes dBASE some time to perform calculations on each field, but this delay only becomes noticeable with very large databases.

Once you've constructed a list of two or more numeric fields, the only way you can save a list of the field names you've created is to press ← or →. If you press Esc, you'll lose the entire list.

If you make a mistake while building a list, you cannot remove field names one by one. You have to exit the "Construct a field list" box by pressing Esc and then open it again and begin constructing the list anew.

The "Construct a field list" command is not available for the command Count because you don't need it. dBASE automatically displays the count of records calculated when it sums or averages the values in a specific field or list of fields.

You can also narrow down the range of records you calculate by building search-and-scope conditions using any type of field in the current database. For example, you can calulate all the money owed to you by people living in California only. You aren't limited to building a search or scope condition on numeric fields only.

Calculating the sum and average of numeric field information and counting selected records are the only types of calculations you can perform while working in Assist. You can perform other types of calculations on numeric field entries by using dBASE commands at the dot prompt.

Examples

1. First, calculate the sum of all values in the numeric field MONEY. Make sure NAD.DBF is current. Press [P] to open the Retrieve menu, highlight Sum, and press [Enter]. The results, including the count of all records calculated, are shown in Figure 6-7.

2. To calculate the average value of all entries in the MONEY field, highlight Average and press [Enter]. The results are shown in Figure 6-8.

3. Now calculate the count. Highlight Count and press [Enter]. The results are shown in Figure 6-9.

4. You can find out how much money you loaned in 1989 as recorded in NAD.DBF by building a search condition that selects only those records in which the DATE field is less than 1990 and then executing the Sum command.

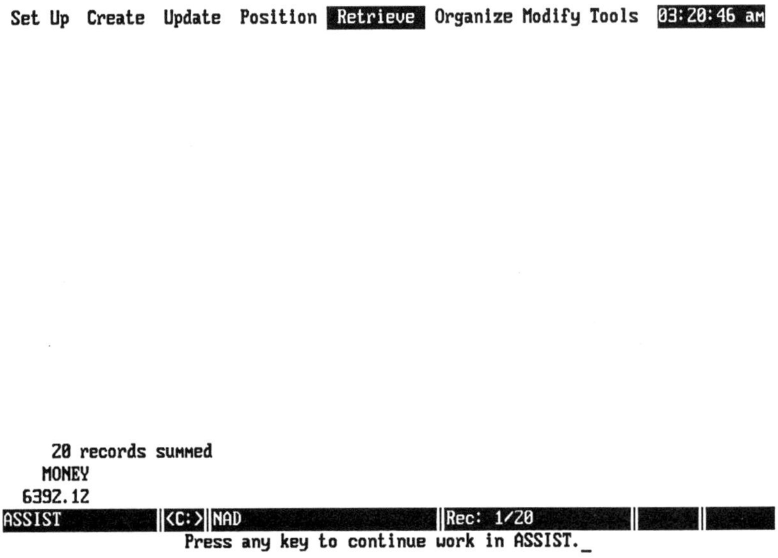

```
     Set Up  Create  Update  Position  Retrieve  Organize Modify Tools   03:20:46 am
```

```
        20 records summed
     MONEY
     6392.12
    ASSIST           |<C:>|NAD                    |Rec: 1/20
                Press any key to continue work in ASSIST._
```

FIGURE 6-7. | Results of running the command Sum

Chapter 6   Locating and Calculating Records   **133**

```
        Set Up  Create  Update  Position  Retrieve  Organize Modify Tools  03:21:29 am




           20 records averaged
        MONEY
        319.61
        ASSIST        |<C:>|NAD                    |Rec: EOF/20
                      Press any key to continue work in ASSIST._
```

| FIGURE 6-8. | Results of running the command Average |

Make sure NAD.DBF is current. Press [R] to open the Retrieve menu, highlight Sum, and press [Enter]. Highlight "Build a search condition" and press [Enter]. This opens the field list for NAD.DBF. Highlight MONEY and press [Enter], highlight < Less Than and press [Enter], and type **01/01/90** and press [Enter]. Highlight "Execute the command" and press [Enter]. dBASE displays the results on screen.

5. Running the three calculations on a database that contains a single numeric field is not as illustrative as calculating several different numeric fields in a single database. Create a database called VALUE.DBF with the following fields:

Field name	Field type	Width	Decimal
ITEM	Character	10	
UNITS	Numeric	5	
COST	Numeric	5	2
PRICE	Numeric	5	2

```
  Set Up  Create  Update  Position  Retrieve  Organize Modify Tools   03:21:48 am
```

```
            20 records
   ASSIST              |<C:>|NAD                  |Rec: EOF/20
                       Press any key to continue work in ASSIST._
```

FIGURE 6-9.	Results of running the command Count

Now enter information into all four fields for ten records, as shown in Figure 6-10. Once you've done this, calculate the sum of all numeric fields. Press [R] to open the Retrieve menu, highlight Sum, and press [Enter]. The results are shown Figure 6-11.

6. Calculate the sum of one numeric field in VALUE.DBF, the UNITS field. Press [R] to open the Retrieve menu. Highlight Sum and press [Enter]. Highlight "Construct a field list" and press [Enter]. This opens the "Construct a field list" screen. Notice that the three numerical field names UNITS, COST, and PRICE are highlighted in this screen, while the nonnumeric field names are dimmed. This shows that you can select only numerical fields when building a field list.

Press [↓] to highlight the UNITS field. Details about this field appear in the middle of your screen. Press [←] or [→] to exit the "Construct a field list" command. If you press any other key, all numerical fields will remain selected by default. Highlight "Execute the command" and press [Enter]. Your screen should look like the

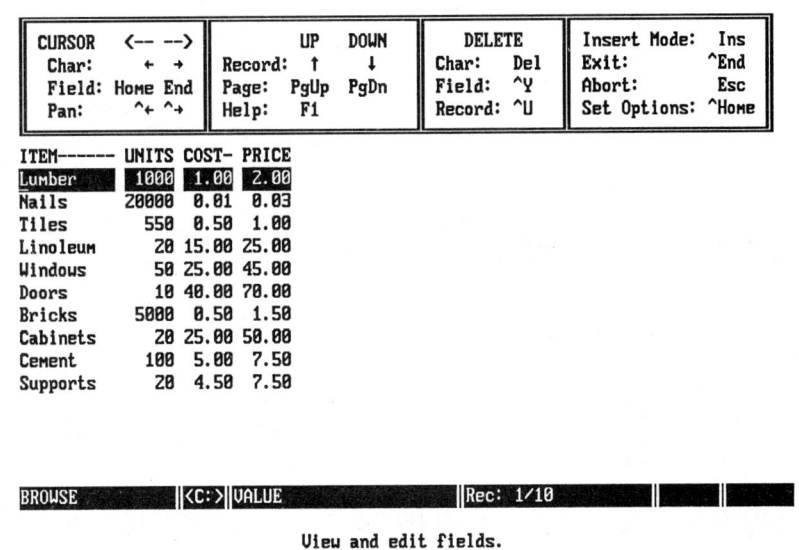

Chapter 6　　　　　　　　　　　　　　　　Locating and Calculating Records　　**135**

```
CURSOR   <-- -->          UP   DOWN    DELETE            Insert Mode:  Ins
  Char:   ←  →    Record:  ↑    ↓       Char:   Del      Exit:        ^End
  Field: Home End  Page:  PgUp PgDn     Field:  ^Y       Abort:        Esc
  Pan:    ^← ^→    Help:   F1           Record: ^U       Set Options: ^Home

ITEM------ UNITS COST- PRICE
Lumber      1000  1.00  2.00
Nails      20000  0.01  0.03
Tiles        550  0.50  1.00
Linoleum      20 15.00 25.00
Windows       50 25.00 45.00
Doors         10 40.00 70.00
Bricks      5000  0.50  1.50
Cabinets      20 25.00 50.00
Cement       100  5.00  7.50
Supports      20  4.50  7.50


BROWSE         |<C:>|VALUE              |Rec: 1/10
                      View and edit fields.
```

| FIGURE 6-10. | Ten sample records in VALUE.DBF |

one in Figure 6-12. Notice that only the UNITS field in VALUE.DBF was summed, and not any of the other numeric fields.

Exercises

1. What type of field information can you calculate using the commands Sum, Average, and Count on the Retrieve menu?

2. Can you calculate numbers placed into character fields?

3. What are the default conditions dBASE uses to calculate numerical fields in the current database?

4. Make VALUE.DBF current. Calculate the sum of all numerical field entries.

```
              Set Up  Create  Update  Position  Retrieve  Organize Modify Tools  03:22:26 am
```

```
         10 records summed
      UNITS    COST   PRICE
      26770   116.51  209.53
    ASSIST            |<C:>|VALUE              |Rec: 1/10
              Press any key to continue work in ASSIST._
```

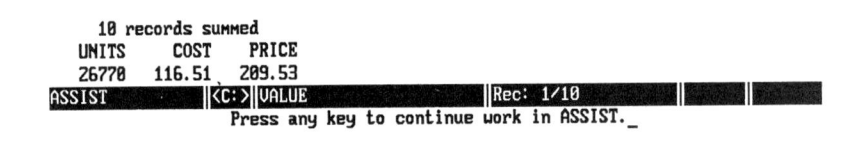

| FIGURE 6-11. | The sum of three numeric fields |

5. Calculate the sum of the UNITS field where UNITS is greater than 25.

EXERCISES

MASTERY SKILLS CHECK

1. Make NAD.DBF current. Locate all records in NAD.DBF that owe you money starting in 1990. Display the first record that dBASE finds.

2. Use the command Continue to display the second record. If dBASE finds a second record, view the contents, and then return to Assist.

3. Replace all records in NAD.DBF where AZ (Arizona) is in the state field with UT (Utah).

Chapter 6   Locating and Calculating Records   **137**

```
      Set Up  Create  Update  Position  Retrieve  Organize  Modify  Tools   03:23:00 am




       10 records summed
    UNITS
    26770
   ASSIST         |<C:>|VALUE                    |Rec: EOF/10
            Press any key to continue work in ASSIST._
```

| FIGURE 6-12. | Sum of UNITS field displayed |

4. Make VALUE.DBF current. Calculate the sum for all fields and view the results. Next calculate the average values for all fields and display the results.

5. Count all the records in VALUE.DBF, view the results, and then return to Assist.

6. Calculate the sum for UNITS in VALUE.DBF for all records where UNITS is equal to or greater than 25, view the results, then return to the Assist.

1. Make NAD.DBF current. Go to record 10 in NAD.DBF. Display the contents of this record. Go to the top record. Display this record. Go to the bottom record. Display this record. Return to Assist.

INTEGRATING SKILLS CHECK

2. Replace the amount in the MONEY field with 0 for all records where the MONEY field is less than $100.

3. Make VALUE.DBF current. Calculate the quantity of items that cost more than one dollar, view the results, and then return to Assist.

4. Make NAD.DBF current. Calculate the average of all the money owed to you. Calculate the sum of all money owed to you. Return to Assist.

Deleting Records
▶7◀

CHAPTER OBJECTIVES

In this chapter you will learn how to

▶ Mark and recall a single record 7.1

▶ Mark and recall a group of records 7.2

▶ Pack a database 7.3

An important part of keeping a database up to date is deleting records that you no longer need. If you don't delete out-of-date records, your database will grow to an unmanageable size. It takes extra time to load a large database and to calculate fields, search for fields, and perform other routine database management procedures.

This chapter describes how you delete records in a database. You'll learn how to use the commands Delete and Recall on the Update menu, and the command List on the Retrieve menu.

Deleting records is a routine procedure in database management. It lets you get rid of records that you no longer need or that don't apply to the database you're using. Deleting records from a database is just as important as adding new records to the database. A database must contain accurate information if it's going to be useful to you, which means it shouldn't contain useless or incorrect information.

Deleting records is a critical procedure. You don't want to delete records accidentally. To guard against this possibility, dBASE gives you two levels of protection. The first is to make deleting records a two-step procedure. The second is to create a backup file of your original database.

Exercises

1. Open NAD.DBF and go to record 10. Display the contents of the record on screen, view the results, and then return to Assist.

2. Locate the total number of records on the status bar. Double-check the figure by calculating the count of all records in the database, view the results, and then return to Assist.

3. View the contents of NAD.DBF in the Browse screen. Go to the bottom record and then the top record in the Browse screen. Return to the Assist.

7.1 MARK AND RECALL A SINGLE RECORD

To delete a record in dBASE, you first mark the record you want to delete. Then you *pack* the database, which removes all marked records.

You can recall—or unmark—a record marked for deletion before you pack the database if you decide you want to keep the record.

You can mark a record for deletion in three ways:

- You can use the Delete command on the Update menu.
- You can view the record in the Edit window and press [Ctrl]-[U].
- You can highlight the record in the Browse screen and press [Ctrl]-[U].

Regardless of which procedure you use, you can delete records only from the current database. To delete a record, first make current the database you want to use.

When you want to mark a single record by using the Update menu, begin with the Assist screen showing. Then

a. Press [U] to open the Update menu.

b. Highlight the command Delete. This opens the Search/Scope menu with "Execute the command" highlighted.

c. Press [Enter] to select "Execute the command." If dBASE marked the record successfully, it will display the message "1 record deleted" just above the status bar, as shown in Figure 7-1.

d. Press any key to return to working in the Assist.

The message dBASE gives you when you mark a record for deletion is really a misnomer. You have only *marked* a record for deletion. It hasn't yet been deleted. The record still exists in the database.

To mark a record for deletion in the Edit screen:

a. Press [U] to open the Update menu.

b. Highlight Edit and press [Enter].

c. Press [PgDn] or [PgUp] to move through records until you find the record you want to delete.

```
            Set Up  Create  Update  Position  Retrieve  Organize Modify Tools  10:21:41 pm




                    1 record deleted
            ASSIST         |<C:>|NAD           |Rec: 5/20
                         Press any key to continue work in ASSIST._
```

FIGURE 7-1.	dBASE reporting one record deleted

    d. Press Ctrl-U. Notice that the label "Del" appears on the right side of the status bar. The screen in Figure 7-2 shows that record 1 in NAD.DBF has been marked for deletion in this way. Ctrl-U serves as a toggle switch; if you press that key combination a second time, the label "Del" disappears. Press it again and the label reappears.

    e. Once the label "Del" appears for a record, press Enter once to fix the mark before you exit the Edit screen. Otherwise the record won't be marked.

    f. Press Esc to exit the Edit screen.

Marking a record for deletion in the Browse screen is similar to marking a record in the Edit screen.

    a. Press U to open the Update menu.

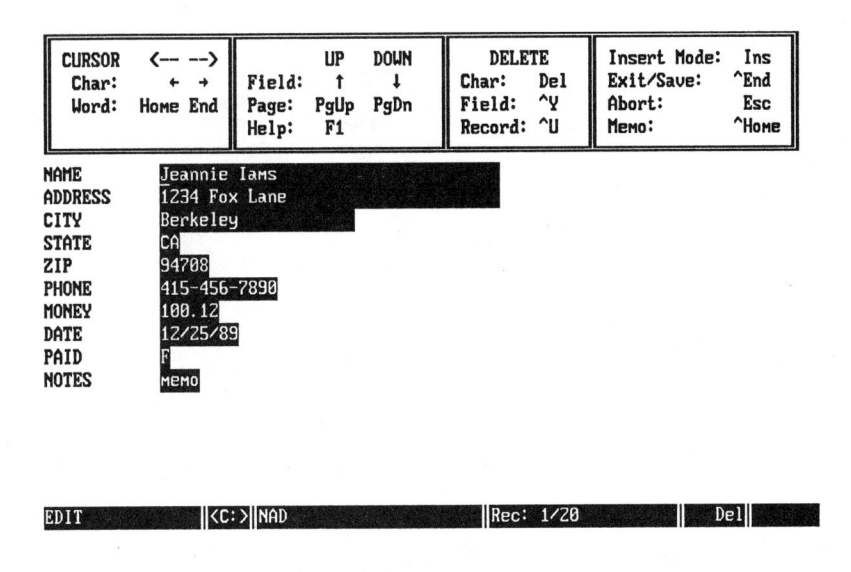

Chapter 7   Deleting Records **143**

CURSOR <-- -->	UP DOWN	DELETE	Insert Mode: Ins
Char: ← →	Field: ↑ ↓	Char: Del	Exit/Save: ^End
Word: Home End	Page: PgUp PgDn	Field: ^Y	Abort: Esc
	Help: F1	Record: ^U	Memo: ^Home

```
NAME     Jeannie Iams
ADDRESS  1234 Fox Lane
CITY     Berkeley
STATE    CA
ZIP      94708
PHONE    415-456-7890
MONEY    100.12
DATE     12/25/89
PAID     F
NOTES    memo
```

`EDIT           <C:> NAD              Rec: 1/20            Del`

FIGURE 7-2.   A record marked for deletion in the Edit screen

b. Highlight Browse and press [Enter].

c. Move the highlight bar over the record you want to mark for deletion and then press [Ctrl]-[U]. The label "Del" appears on the status bar for all marked records. The screen in Figure 7-3 shows record 1 marked for deletion in the Browse screen. As in the Edit screen, [Ctrl]-[U] acts as a toggle switch.

d. Press [Enter] once to fix the mark.

e. Press [Esc] to exit the Browse screen.

You can check a record to make sure it has been marked by using the command Display on the Update menu. As long as the marked record remains the current record:

a. Highlight Display.

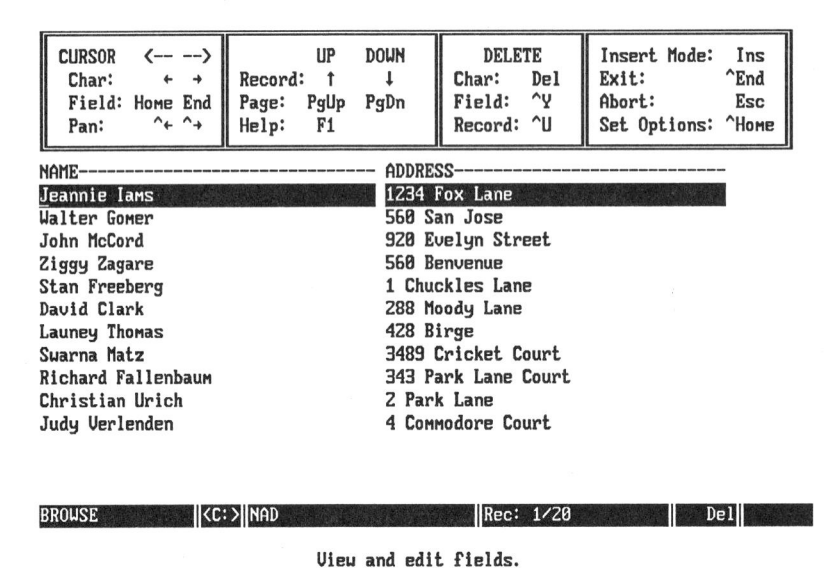

```
┌─────────────────────┬──────────────────┬────────────────────┬───────────────────────┐
│ CURSOR    <-- -->   │         UP  DOWN │   DELETE           │ Insert Mode:   Ins    │
│ Char:       ← →     │ Record: ↑    ↓   │ Char:      Del     │ Exit:          ^End   │
│ Field: Home End     │ Page:  PgUp PgDn │ Field:     ^Y      │ Abort:         Esc    │
│ Pan:       ^← ^→    │ Help:   F1       │ Record:    ^U      │ Set Options:   ^Home  │
└─────────────────────┴──────────────────┴────────────────────┴───────────────────────┘
NAME-------------------------------- ADDRESS--------------------------------
Jeannie Iams                         1234 Fox Lane
Walter Gomer                         560 San Jose
John McCord                          920 Evelyn Street
Ziggy Zagare                         560 Benvenue
Stan Freeberg                        1 Chuckles Lane
David Clark                          288 Moody Lane
Launey Thomas                        428 Birge
Swarna Matz                          3489 Cricket Court
Richard Fallenbaum                   343 Park Lane Court
Christian Urich                      2 Park Lane
Judy Verlenden                       4 Commodore Court


┌─────────┬────────┬───────┬─────────────────┬─────────┬────────┐
│ BROWSE  │ <C:>   │ NAD   │       Rec: 1/20 │   Del   │        │
└─────────┴────────┴───────┴─────────────────┴─────────┴────────┘
                          View and edit fields.
```

FIGURE 7-3. Record 1 marked for deletion in the Browse screen

> b. Press [Enter]. The screen in Figure 7-4 shows the results. Notice the asterisk that now appears between the record number and the NAME field information. The asterisk indicates that this record has been marked for deletion.
>
> c. Press any key to continue working in Assist.

You can also check a record to see if it is marked by opening the Edit or Browse screen, where you display the record. If "Del" shows on the status bar, the record is marked for deletion.

Remember that a record isn't deleted just because you've marked it. You will have to pack the database to remove all marked records.

As mentioned, you can recall a marked record in the same way that you mark the record when you use the Edit or Browse screen. Just make the marked record current and press [Ctrl]-[U] to toggle the label "Del" off.

Chapter 7 Deleting Records **145**

```
 Set Up  Create  Update  Position  Retrieve  Organize  Modify  Tools   10:22:36 pm
```

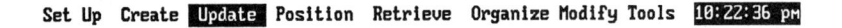

```
Record#  NAME                                      ADDRESS
         CITY              STATE  ZIP    PHONE     MONEY  DATE      PAID  NOTES
      5 *Jeannie Iams                              1234 Fox Lane
         Berkeley          CA     94708  415-456-7890  100.00  12/25/89  .F.  Memo

ASSIST              <C:> NAD                    Rec: 5/20
              Press any key to continue work in ASSIST._
```

FIGURE 7-4.	Results of displaying a marked record

You can also recall a marked record by using the command Recall on the Update menu. First, make sure the marked record number is current and shows on the status bar.

a. Highlight Recall and press [Enter]. This opens the Search/Scope menu for the command Recall.

b. Press [Enter] to select "Execute the command." If dBASE successfully recalls the record, it will report back as shown in the screen in Figure 7-5.

c. Press any key to continue working in the Assist.

You can recall only a record marked for deletion. If you try to recall a record that's not marked for deletion, dBASE will tell you "No records recalled."

Examples

1. Since deleting records is a two-step process, you can continue to mark records and then recall them without actually deleting the

```
Set Up  Create  Update  Position  Retrieve  Organize  Modify  Tools    10:22:56 pm
```

```
       1 record recalled
ASSIST         |<C:>|NAD              |Rec: 5/20
              Press any key to continue work in ASSIST._
```

| FIGURE 7-5. | dBASE reporting a marked record recalled |

records. For example, mark record 1 for deletion by using the Delete command.

First make the record current. Press [P] to open the Position menu, select Goto Record and press [Enter], and then select TOP and press [Enter]. Make sure the number for record 1 appears on the status bar.

Now mark the record for deletion. Press [U] to open the Update menu, highlight Delete, and press [Enter] twice. You should see the message "1 record deleted" and then return to the Assist.

2. When you use the Delete command, you should double-check your work since dBASE doesn't display the record you marked. You can check your work by displaying the marked record on your screen or by opening either the Edit or Browse screen to view the marked record. You'll use the Display command in this example.

Make sure the record you marked remains the current record number. Press [U] to open the Update menu, highlight Display, and press [Enter]. Information in the current record, along with the asterisk, will appear on your screen.

3. Recall the marked record 1 by using the Recall command on the Update menu. Press [U], highlight Recall, and press [Enter] twice. dBASE will report that it recalled one record. If record 1 is the only marked record in the database, you can be sure it was recalled. Otherwise, you might want to check your work.

Exercises

1. When you mark a record for deletion, has the record actually been deleted from the database?

2. When dBASE displays the message "1 record deleted" in Assist screen, has a record been deleted?

3. Has a record been recalled when dBASE reports "1 record recalled"?

4. Use the command Goto Record to make record 10 in NAD.DBF current. Mark that record for deletion by using the command Delete, and then return to Assist.

5. Display the contents of record 10 on screen. Make sure it has been successfully marked, and then return to Assist.

6. Recall record 10.

7. Use the command Goto Record to make record 11 in NAD.DBF current. Mark the record for deletion, and display the contents to double-check. Recall the record and return to Assist.

MARK AND RECALL A GROUP OF RECORDS 7.2

Deleting records one by one gives you the closest control over deleting records, but it's not always the most efficient way to mark records for deletion. You'll find, as your databases grow in size, that you'll want to delete several records that share similar characteristics but are sprinkled throughout the database. For example, if you're using a database to keep track of your business customers, you might want to delete all those who haven't bought from you in the past year. It would be tedious to search through the entire database for the records that fit this criterion.

Use the Search/Scope menu attached to the command Delete to mark records in a group for deletion. You select a group to be marked in the same way that you've used the Search/Scope menu to locate records. You build search conditions (and scope conditions if you're working with a very large database).

You can use the Search/Scope menu attached to the command Recall to recall records marked in a group, but this is a tricky procedure. The best way to recall marked records is to specify a scope for all records and then recall all marked records. If you want to recall a subgroup of a group of records marked for deletion, you will have to be very careful about the precise criteria you use when you build search conditions. Otherwise, you might end up recalling only some of the records in the subgroup. Unless you become very adept at specifying search-and-scope conditions, it's better to recall all records first and then reselect the group you want to mark for deletion.

When you mark or recall a group of records, always view the results. It would be tedious to display each record one by one to see if it has been marked successfully for deletion. You can use the command List on the Retrieve menu to list all records in the current database.

a. Press [R] to open the Retrieve menu.

b. Highlight List and press [Enter]. This opens the Search/Scope menu for the command List.

c. Press [Enter] to select "Execute the command." dBASE asks "Send output to printer? Y/N."

d. Press [N] to accept the default answer No. Information for each record will begin to scroll upwards on your screen.

e. If this scrolling moves more quickly than you're able to perceive the information, press [Ctrl]-[S] to stop the scrolling. Once the records freeze on your screen, you can read the field information and look for the asterisks, which show a record is marked for deletion.
f. To resume, press any key.
g. To stop the scrolling before the end, press [Esc].

If you try to recall a large group of marked records by building search or scope conditions and you notice that some records were not recalled, you might want to run the command List and stop the scrolling each time you see an asterisk, write down the record number, and continue scrolling until you see the next asterisk. When you're finished checking, you can open the Browse screen, go to each marked record you want to recall, and press [Ctrl]-[U] to recall the record. This can be tedious, but it is thorough.

Examples

1. In NAD, mark a group of records for deletion of people who owe you less than $100. Begin by making sure NAD.DBF is the current database. Press [U] to open the Update menu, highlight Delete, and press [Enter]. This opens the Search/Scope menu. Highlight "Build a search condition" and press [Enter]. This opens the two boxes you use to select a field to search on, as shown in Figure 7-6. Highlight MONEY and press [Enter]. Highlight "< Less Than" and then press [Enter]. Type 100 and press [Enter] twice. Highlight "Execute the command" and press [Enter]. dBASE tells you how many records are marked this way. Press any key to return to Assist.

2. To list the records that have been marked for deletion, press [R] to open the Retrieve menu, highlight List, and press [Enter]. This opens the Search/Scope menu for the command List. Press [Enter] to select "Execute the command." dBASE asks "Send output to printer? Y/N." Press [N] to accept the default answer No.

    Information for each record in NAD.DBF will begin to scroll upward on your screen, as shown in Figure 7-7. Notice the asterisks for record numbers 6, 7, and 8. All three of those records show less than 100 in the MONEY field. If you want to check records more

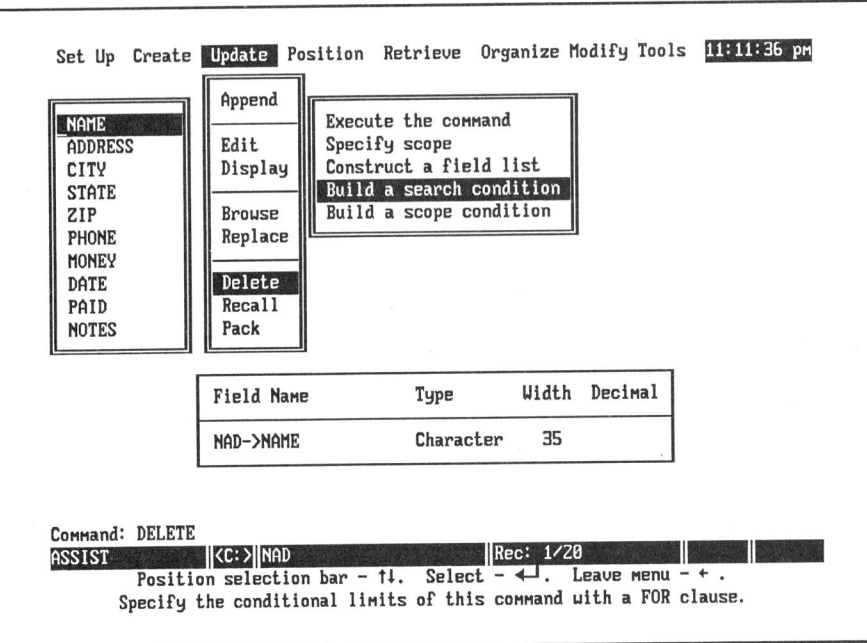

FIGURE 7-6. Field list boxes to build a search condition

closely, press Ctrl-S to stop the scrolling. If all the records scrolled by before you had a chance to stop the scrolling, repeat the preceding commands to repeat the command List, but keep your fingers hovering over Ctrl-S.

Press any key to continue scrolling, in case other records not yet displayed have been deleted. Press Esc to bail out of scrolling and return to the Assist.

3. To mark all the records in a database for deletion, press U, highlight Delete, and press Enter. This opens the Search/Scope menu. Highlight "Specify scope" and press Enter. Highlight ALL and press Enter. (You might remember that the ALL command was disabled when you used the Locate command. You can't locate all the records in a database.)

Highlight "Execute the command" and press Enter. dBASE will tell you it has deleted a number of records in the database that equals the total number of records. Press any key to return to the Assist.

Chapter 7 Deleting Records **151**

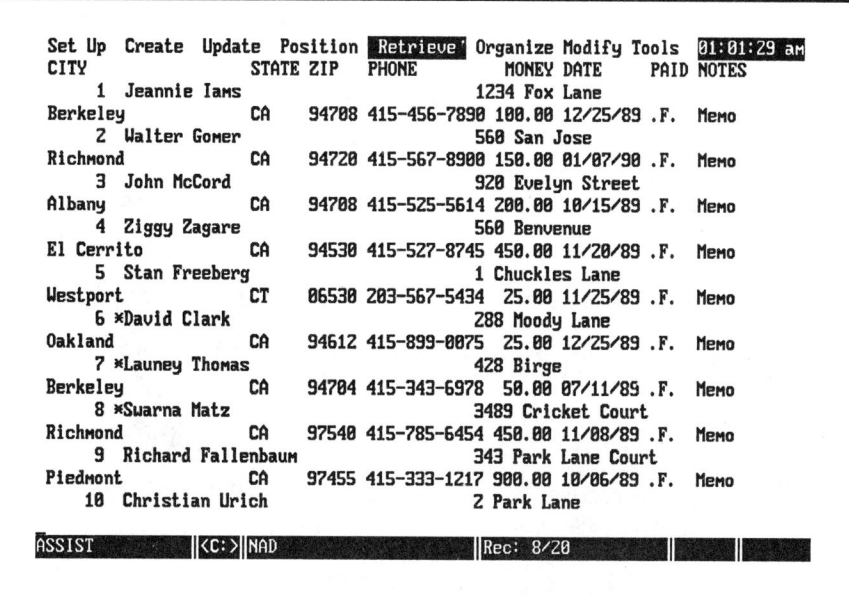

```
Set Up  Create  Update  Position  Retrieve  Organize  Modify  Tools   01:01:29 am
CITY              STATE  ZIP    PHONE          MONEY  DATE    PAID  NOTES
      1 Jeannie Iams                  1234 Fox Lane
Berkeley           CA    94708  415-456-7890  100.00 12/25/89  .F.  Memo
      2 Walter Gomer                  560 San Jose
Richmond           CA    94720  415-567-8900  150.00 01/07/90  .F.  Memo
      3 John McCord                   920 Evelyn Street
Albany             CA    94708  415-525-5614  200.00 10/15/89  .F.  Memo
      4 Ziggy Zagare                  560 Benvenue
El Cerrito         CA    94530  415-527-8745  450.00 11/20/89  .F.  Memo
      5 Stan Freeberg                 1 Chuckles Lane
Westport           CT    06530  203-567-5434   25.00 11/25/89  .F.  Memo
      6 *David Clark                  288 Moody Lane
Oakland            CA    94612  415-899-0075   25.00 12/25/89  .F.  Memo
      7 *Launey Thomas                428 Birge
Berkeley           CA    94704  415-343-6978   50.00 07/11/89  .F.  Memo
      8 *Swarna Matz                  3489 Cricket Court
Richmond           CA    97540  415-785-6454  450.00 11/08/89  .F.  Memo
      9 Richard Fallenbaum            343 Park Lane Court
Piedmont           CA    97455  415-333-1217  900.00 10/06/89  .F.  Memo
     10 Christian Urich               2 Park Lane

ASSIST         <C:>  NAD            Rec: 8/20
```

FIGURE 7-7. Records scrolling up from the command List

4. You can recall all records marked for deletion by using the same command, "Specify scope," attached to the Search/Scope menu for Recall. Press (U), highlight Recall, and press (Enter). Highlight "Specify scope" and press (Enter). Highlight ALL and press (Enter). Highlight "Execute the command" and press (Enter). To double-check your work, press (R) and then (Enter). After viewing the results, press any key.

5. You can recall a subgroup of marked records by building the proper search condition. To delete all records of people who owe you $200 or more, you need only recall records for people who owe you less than $200.

   Press (U) to open the Update menu, highlight Recall, and press (Enter). Highlight "Build a search condition" and press (Enter). Highlight MONEY and press (Enter). Highlight "< Equal To or Less Than" and press (Enter). Type **200** and press (Enter) twice. Highlight

"Execute the command" and press [Enter]. dBASE will report back the number of records recalled. Press any key to continue working in Assist.

Exercises

1. What are the three ways you can tell that dBASE has marked a record for deletion?

2. Can you delete all records in a database at once?

3. How do you display a scrolling list of all records in the current database?

4. How can you stop and then restart the scrolling?

5. Mark all records for deletion in NAD.DBF for people who owe you more than $500.

6. How do you recall these marked records?

7.3 PACK A DATABASE

Once you've marked one or more records for deletion—and you're sure they're the records you want to delete—you remove them from the database permanently by running the command Pack on the Update menu. This is the command that actually removes the marked records from the database and packs the remaining records into a smaller disk file. The procedure is the same whether you're deleting one marked record or many marked records.

When dBASE is told to pack a database, it automatically makes a backup copy of the database to the same directory, using the same name as the database but adding the extension .BAK. This preserves your original database in case you change your mind and want to keep records you've permanently deleted.

To delete all marked records:

a. Press [U] to open the Update menu.

b. Press [↓] to highlight the command Pack at the bottom of the menu.

c. Press [Enter]. dBASE will report back how many records it copies into the new version of the database. These are all the records that have not been deleted.

d. Press any key to return to the Assist.

dBASE has now deleted all marked records and copied the remaining records back into NAD.DBF. dBASE has also created a separate file called NAD.BAK, which is a backup file of the original database.

Even though deleting records is a two-step process designed to protect you against mistakes, mistakes will occur. If you pack a database with records marked for deletion that you want to keep, you can still access the data by using the backup file created automatically by dBASE when you pack the file. For example, when you packed NAD.DBF, dBASE created a backup file called NAD.BAK. This backup file contains all the records that were in NAD.DBF before you packed the database.

You can't load a backup database using the Assist because the Assist lets you load only database files that end in .DBF. However, you can find the file name by using the Directory command, and you can rename the file by using the command Rename on the Tools pull-down menu. You'll learn how to do this in Chapter 15.

If you pack a database that has no records marked for deletion, all the records will be recopied to the database. This is a good way to create a backup version of your current database; dBASE always creates a backup copy of the current database when it packs the database, regardless of whether it removes any records.

To delete records regularly and successfully, you need to know how to navigate around records in a database, how to select a group of records based upon similar characteristics, and how to display and list records so that you can see whether they have been marked for deletion.

These procedures require good skills in working with records in the Browse screen as well as in the Assist screen. It's useful to compare the advantages and disadvantages of working in each screen to delete records. You can move around records in both screens with the same facility. The Browse screen displays record contents all the time, which can be helpful. It also shows which files have been marked for deletion.

You can toggle the mark on or off easily. Your efficiency in working in the Browse screen begins to drop off when you work with large databases.

In the Assist screen, you have to take extra steps to display record contents. However, you can select a group of records by using the Scope/Search menu as part of the command Delete. You can also scroll all record contents on your screen and observe which records have been marked for deletion. You can't do either of these things when you use the Browse screen.

To make sure the right number of records has been deleted, remember how many records you intended to delete and then subtract that number from the total records in the database. The result should match the figure dBASE reports back after it packs the database.

Exercises

1. Does packing a database remove all records marked for deletion?

2. Does packing a database remove all records previously recalled?

3. Does dBASE create a backup file of the original database when you pack it?

4. If you mark one record for deletion and then pack the database, how many records will remain?

5. How do you pack a database and return to the Assist?

EXERCISES

MASTERY SKILLS CHECK

1. What are the two steps for deleting a record?

2. If you want to recall a record, where does this procedure fit into the two-step process?

3. Mark the top record in NAD.DBF for deletion, display the contents of the record, recall it, and then return to Assist.

4. Mark the top record in NAD.DBF, pack the database, and return to Assist.

INTEGRATING SKILLS CHECK

1. Make VALUE.DBF current. Go to the bottom record and mark it for deletion. Then go to the top record and mark that record for deletion. Display the results by using the command List and check for asterisks next to the records you've marked. Finally, recall the records and return to Assist.

2. Make NAD.DBF current. Open the Browse screen and mark the first three records for deletion. Then recall them. Make sure record 3 is current, or highlighted. Exit the Browse screen and enter the Edit screen. Mark the record for deletion. Return to the Assist screen. Display the contents of record 3. Recall the record using the command Recall, and return to the Assist.

3. Make VALUE.DBF current. Mark all records for deletion, and then pack the database.

Modifying a Database

►8◄

CHAPTER OBJECTIVES

In this chapter you will learn how to

▶ **Insert fields**   8.1

▶ **Change existing fields**   8.2

▶ **Delete fields**   8.3

You'll probably want to modify the structure of a database after you use it for a while. Modifying a database lets you make changes in the way you keep track of information. You won't update the structure of a database as often as you update the contents, but you will have to make changes periodically.

This chapter describes how you make fundamental changes to the structure of a database by building onto the information you learned in Chapter 3. That's where you first designed and then created the structure for NAD.DBF, using all five of the field types. There are three types of changes you can make to the structure of an existing database: You can insert new fields, rename existing fields, and delete fields for which you no longer have any use.

Modifying a database is almost as easy as creating one. You begin with an existing structure and will probably keep most of the structure intact. The most frequent change you'll make will be to insert new fields to hold new types of information. In other cases, you'll want to change the nature of a field—its name, width, or type—to accommodate changes in the information the field will hold. In some cases, you'll want to delete a field completely and either lose the information the field contained or copy the information to another field.

Before you begin making changes to the structure of a database, you have to be clear about the type of changes you want to make. You run the risk of losing part or all of the information in your database if you don't make your changes correctly. This can happen when you change the name or type of a field without taking precautions beforehand, and it most certainly will happen when you delete a field unless you copy the information to another field.

Fortunately, dBASE creates a backup copy of the database file when you give the command to modify a database. If you lose information inadvertently, you can always start over again with an original version of the database.

Chapter 8   Modifying a Database   **159**

Exercises

1. Load dBASE into your computer and make NAD the current database.

2. List the current structure of NAD.DBF and familiarize yourself with the details of the various fields in this database. Return to the Assist screen.

3. View the contents of NAD.DBF in the Browse screen and scan through the various records to refresh your memory of its structure. Return to the Assist screen.

SKILLS CHECK

INSERT FIELDS

8.1

The most common type of modification you'll make to a database is to insert new fields. Just as you expand an active database by adding more records, so will you want to expand the structure of your database periodically as you find you need to save and analyze more types of information.

To change the structure of a database, you first need to make the database current. You can change the structure of the current database only. You do this by working in what is called the Modify screen for database files. This screen is practically identical to the Create screen you used in Chapter 3. The only difference is that the words MODIFY STRUCTURE appear on the status bar instead of the word CREATE.

To open the Modify Structure screen, begin in the Assist screen. Then

a. Press [M] to open the Modify pull-down menu.

b. Press [Enter] to accept the top command, "Database file," which is highlighted by default. (If you haven't yet opened a database, the command "Database file" will be disabled.)

The screen in Figure 8-1 shows what the Modify Structure screen looks like with NAD.DBF as the current database. The structure of NAD.DBF is exactly like the one in Figure 3-6, which shows the structure for NAD.DBF just after you finished creating it. Whenever you enter the Modify Structure screen, the cursor will be blinking under the first character in the first field.

When you plan to insert new fields, you need to decide beforehand the types of fields you want to insert and their names, sizes, and positions in the database. These are the same questions you have to answer when you first create a database.

The position of fields in the structure of a database can be important. You want fields to appear in logical groups. For example,

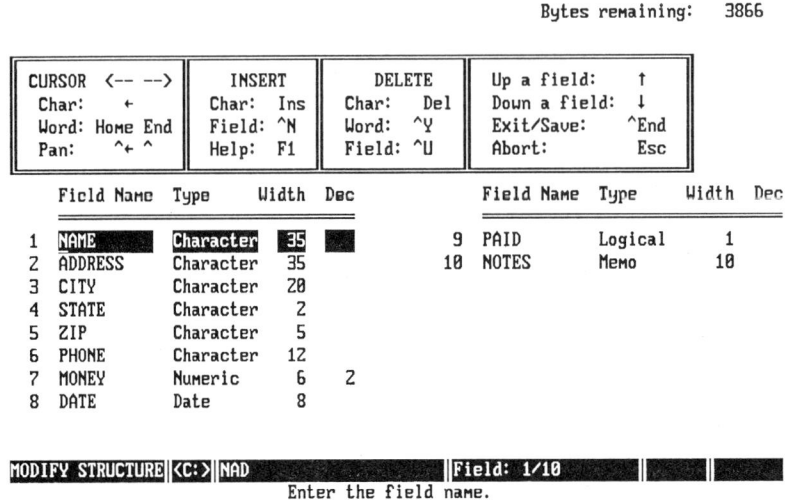

```
                                                    Bytes remaining:    3866

   CURSOR  <-- -->     INSERT          DELETE      Up a field:     ↑
   Char:      ←        Char:  Ins      Char:  Del  Down a field:   ↓
   Word: Home End      Field: ^N       Word:  ^Y   Exit/Save:      ^End
   Pan:     ^← ^→      Help:  F1       Field: ^U   Abort:          Esc

        Field Name   Type      Width  Dec          Field Name  Type      Width  Dec

     1  NAME         Character   35           9    PAID        Logical     1
     2  ADDRESS      Character   35          10    NOTES       Memo       10
     3  CITY         Character   20
     4  STATE        Character    2
     5  ZIP          Character    5
     6  PHONE        Character   12
     7  MONEY        Numeric      6    2
     8  DATE         Date         8

 MODIFY STRUCTURE |<C:>| NAD              | Field: 1/10 |
                        Enter the field name.
        Field names begin with a letter and may contain letters, digits and underscores
```

FIGURE 8-1. | The Modify Structure screen for NAD.DBF

when you enter the name and address of new contacts into NAD.DBF, it's easiest to enter the name on one line, press [Enter] and insert the street address on the next line, press [Enter] and fill in the city, and then alternatively press [Enter] and fill in the state, zip code, and phone information for each succeeding field. If you inserted the fields in random order, you'd have to jump around the structure each time you wanted to insert information for a new record.

NOTE: You can change the way fields are displayed in the Append and Edit screens by designing format files. You'll learn how to do this in Chapter 11. Since you're not yet designing format files, you should pay close attention to where you want to insert new fields.

Inserting fields is very easy:

a. Place the highlight bar in the position where you want to insert the new field.

b. Press [Ctrl]-[N]. Remember that "N" stands for "new field". This inserts a blank field and pushes all subsequent fields down one position.

c. Define the characteristics of the new field. Type the new field name, press [Enter], select the field type you want to use, press [Enter], and type the field size, if one applies. This is the same way you insert fields when you create a database.

All the rules for creating field names apply to the Modify Structure screen. You can use a maximum of 11 characters for a field name. You can use only letter and number characters and the underscore symbol (_). A database can't contain two fields with the same name, even if they're different types of fields. If you try to insert a new field by using the name of an existing field, dBASE will warn you and ask that you use a different name.

While working in the Modify Structure screen, you can escape all changes made to the current database since the last save:

a. Press [Esc]. dBASE asks you to confirm your move to abandon all changes.

b. Press ⟦Y⟧ or press ⟦Esc⟧ a second time. dBASE returns you to the Assist screen. The Modify menu remains open, and the command "Database file" highlighted. Just press ⟦Enter⟧ to go back into the Modify Structure screen. The original structure will be displayed.

When you're finished inserting and defining all your new fields and you're satisfied with your work, save the new structure to disk:

a. Press ⟦Ctrl⟧-⟦End⟧ to save the new structure. dBASE asks you to confirm the save.

b. Press ⟦Enter⟧. You'll return to the Assist screen. The database you modified is saved to disk and all records from the backup file are copied into it.

c. Double-check your results. List the new structure using the command "List database structure" on the Tools menu or view the database contents in the Browse screen.

Before you begin inserting your first field, you should understand the process dBASE follows when you attempt to modify the structure of a database. Whenever you enter the Modify Structure screen for database files, dBASE automatically creates a backup copy of the database. This backup file is actually the original database file with the extension changed from .DBF to .BAK. For example, when you enter the Modify screen for NAD.DBF, dBASE changes NAD.DBF to NAD.BAK.

dBASE then copies the structure of NAD.BAK to a file with the .DBF extension. You make all your changes to this empty structure. When you save the new structure to disk, dBASE copies all records from the .BAK file into the new structure with the .DBF extension. This is how you end up with the newly redesigned .DBF file and a .BAK file of the original database. If all this sounds a bit complicated, just realize that dBASE makes a backup of the current database each time you enter the Modify Structure screen for database files.

You don't risk losing data when you insert fields. You only run this risk when you change characteristics of existing fields or delete fields.

Examples

1. Insert a new character field into NAD.DBF called COUNTRY. This will let you keep track of international addresses. Make sure NAD.DBF is current. Press [M], and then [Enter] to move into the Modify screen for database files. Once the structure appears, press [↓] five times. This should highlight the PHONE field. When you press [Ctrl]-[N] to insert a new field, the highlighted field and all subsequent existing fields will move down one position.

    The reason you want to insert the COUNTRY field after the ZIP field is because most of your records will still be for people in your own country. Most of the time you won't want to insert a country name. Placing the COUNTRY field after the ZIP field lets you enter all the information for domestic records and then press [PgDn] to go to the next record.

    Press [Ctrl]-[N] to insert room for the new field. Notice that the field PHONE, which you had highlighted, moves down one notch. Type **COUNTRY** and press [Enter] twice. This inserts the field name, accepts the default field type of character, and moves the cursor to the Width column. Type **20** and press [Enter]. (Most country names will not exceed 20 characters.) Press [Enter] to set the new field. This moves the cursor down to the next field. Your screen should change to look like the one in Figure 8-2.

    Press [Ctrl]-[End] to save the change to disk. dBASE will ask you to "Press ENTER to confirm. Any other key to resume." Press [Enter]. If you press any other key, you'll cancel the the save and continue working in the Modify Structure screen for database files.

2. Continue viewing NAD.DBF in the Modify Structure screen and insert a new numeric field into NAD.DBF called CHARGES. This field will contain the monthly charges you incur for communicating with the person in each record. This can be a considerable expense with foreign contacts. Where should this field go? The most logical position is just after the PHONE field, since it applies to phone charges.

164 Teach Yourself dBASE III PLUS

```
                                        Bytes remaining:   3846

┌─────────────────┬──────────────┬──────────────┬──────────────────────┐
│ CURSOR  <-- --> │ INSERT       │ DELETE       │ Up a field:     ↑    │
│ Char:     ← →   │ Char:    Ins │ Char:    Del │ Down a field:   ↓    │
│ Word: Home End  │ Field:   ^N  │ Word:    ^Y  │ Exit/Save:     ^End  │
│ Pan:     ^← ^→  │ Help:    F1  │ Field:   ^U  │ Abort:         Esc   │
└─────────────────┴──────────────┴──────────────┴──────────────────────┘

     Field Name   Type      Width  Dec         Field Name  Type      Width  Dec

  1  NAME         Character    35           9  DATE        Character    8
  2  ADDRESS      Character    35          10  PAID        Logical      1
  3  CITY         Character    20          11  NOTES       Memo        10
  4  STATE        Character     2
  5  ZIP          Character     5
  6  COUNTRY      Character    20
  7  PHONE        Character    12
  8  MONEY        Numeric       6    2

 MODIFY STRUCTURE  <C:>  NAD              Field: 7/11
                          Enter the field name.
 Field names begin with a letter and may contain letters, digits and underscores
```

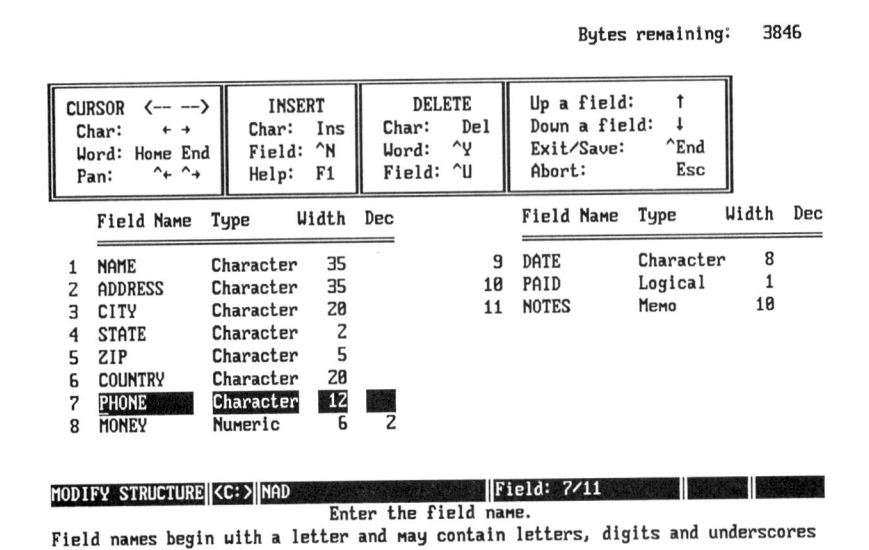

FIGURE 8-2. The COUNTRY field defined

Highlight the MONEY field and press [Ctrl]-[N]. This opens room for the new field and bumps the MONEY field down one notch. Type **CHARGES** and press [Enter]. Now press SPACEBAR to switch the field type to numeric. Press [Enter] and type **6** in the Width column. Press [Enter] and type **2** for the Dec column. Press [Enter] a final time to move the cursor down one field. Your screen should now look like the one in Figure 8-3.

3. Save these changes and exit the Modify Structure screen. Press [Ctrl]-[End] to prepare the save. Notice the message on the bottom line of your screen: "Database records will be APPENDED from backup fields of the same name only!!" This means dBASE will copy information from each field in the backup file into fields in the new structure with the same name. You'll learn the significance of this message when you change the characteristics of an existing field in the next section.

Chapter 8   Modifying a Database   **165**

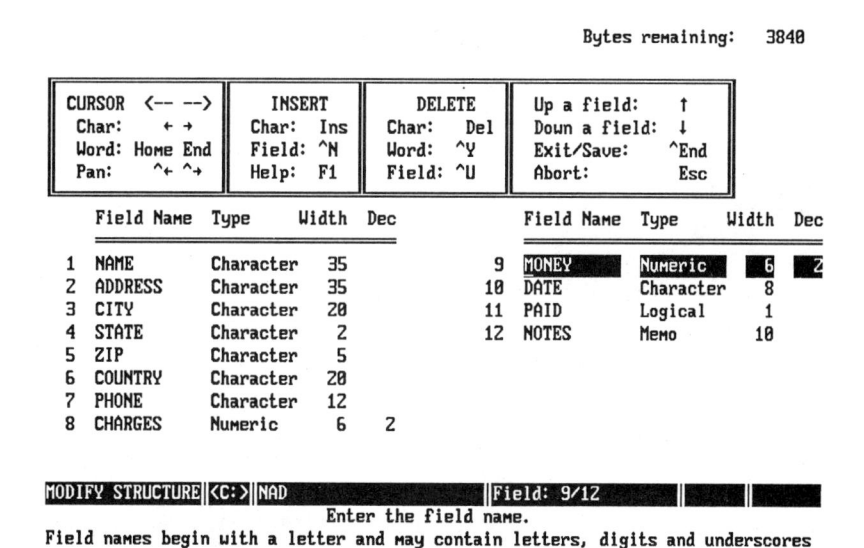

```
                                                 Bytes remaining:    3840

    CURSOR   <-- -->    INSERT          DELETE       Up a field:    ↑
    Char:     ← →       Char:   Ins     Char:   Del  Down a field:  ↓
    Word: Home End      Field:  ^N      Word:   ^Y   Exit/Save:     ^End
    Pan:      ^← ^→     Help:   F1      Field:  ^U   Abort:         Esc

          Field Name  Type       Width Dec          Field Name  Type       Width Dec
       1  NAME        Character    35            9  MONEY       Numeric      6    2
       2  ADDRESS     Character    35           10  DATE        Character    8
       3  CITY        Character    20           11  PAID        Logical      1
       4  STATE       Character     2           12  NOTES       Memo        10
       5  ZIP         Character     5
       6  COUNTRY     Character    20
       7  PHONE       Character    12
       8  CHARGES     Numeric       6    2

   MODIFY STRUCTURE |<C:>| NAD                     |Field: 9/12 |
                        Enter the field name.
   Field names begin with a letter and may contain letters, digits and underscores
```

FIGURE 8-3.   NAD.DBF list with new field CHARGES

Press [Enter] to confirm the save. dBASE will take a moment to copy all information back to the newly redesigned structure and then return you to the Assist screen.

4. Double-check your work. First, list the new structure to your screen. Press [T] to open the Tools menu, highlight the command "List structure," and press [Enter] twice. dBASE will display a structure that looks like the one shown in Figure 8-4.

5. Learn how to escape changes you've made in the Modify Structure screen. Reenter the Modify screen for the current database, which should be NAD.DBF. Press [M] and then [Enter]. Press [Ctrl]-[N] to insert a new blank field in the first position of the structure. Type **TEST** and press [Enter] twice, and then type **10** and press [Enter]. This inserts a new character field called TEST, ten spaces wide.

To cancel this change, press [Esc]. dBASE asks you to confirm this move. Press [Y] to confirm the cancel. If you press any key

```
         Set Up  Create  Update  Position  Retrieve  Organize  Modify Tools  03:12:18 am


     Structure for database: C:NAD.dbf
     Number of data records:     20
     Date of last update   : 06/27/90
     Field  Field Name  Type       Width    Dec
         1  NAME        Character     35
         2  ADDRESS     Character     35
         3  CITY        Character     20
         4  STATE       Character      2
         5  ZIP         Character      5
         6  COUNTRY     Character     20
         7  PHONE       Character     12
         8  CHARGES     Numeric        6      2
         9  MONEY       Numeric        6      2
        10  DATE        Character      8
        11  PAID        Logical        1
        12  NOTES       Memo          10
     ** Total **                     161
     ASSIST          |<C:>|NAD              |Rec: 1/20
                Press any key to continue work in ASSIST._
```

FIGURE 8-4. | The structure of NAD.DBF listed on screen

other than [Esc] or [Y], you'll remain working in the Modify Structure screen, and the change will not be cancelled. When you cancel a modification, you'll return to the Assist screen.

Exercises

1. Are there any differences between inserting new fields when you create a database and inserting new fields when you modify a database?

2. Do you have to insert new fields over existing fields?

3. Are new fields saved as soon as you insert them?

4. How do you save new fields you've inserted into the structure?

5. If you want to insert a new field for a fax telephone number, what would you call the field, where would you insert it most logically in NAD.DBF, what field type would you use, and how wide would you make it?

Chapter 8 Modifying a Database **167**

```
                                            Bytes remaining:    3808

    CURSOR   <-- -->    INSERT         DELETE       Up a field:     ↑
    Char:     ← →       Char:  Ins     Char:  Del   Down a field:   ↓
    Word: Home End      Field: ^N      Word:  ^Y    Exit/Save:      ^End
    Pan:    ^← ^→       Help:  F1      Field: ^U    Abort:          Esc

       Field Name  Type       Width  Dec        Field Name  Type       Width  Dec

    1  NAME        Character    35           9   CHARGES     Numeric      6     2
    2  ADDRESS     Character    35          10   MONEY       Numeric      6     2
    3  CITY        Character    20          11   DATE        Date         8
    4  STATE       Character     2          12   PAID        Logical      1
    5  ZIP         Character     5          13   NOTES       Memo        10
    6  COUNTRY     Character    20          14   FIELD1      Character   10
    7  PHONE       Character    12          15   FIELD2      Character   10
    8  FAX         Character    12          16               Character

    MODIFY STRUCTURE |<C:>| NAD              |Field: 16/16|
                            Enter the field name.
    Field names begin with a letter and may contain letters, digits and underscores
```

| FIGURE 8-5. | FAX, FIELD1, and FIELD2 defined in NAD.DBF |

6. Insert the new FAX field into NAD.DBF, using the answers given for the previous exercise. Begin in the Assist screen, make the change, save the change, and return to the Assist screen. (You can view the results after the next exercise.)

7. Insert two new fields, FIELD1 and FIELD2, both character type fields of ten spaces each, at the bottom of the structure for NAD.DBF. Your screen should look like the one in Figure 8-5. Save the structure.

CHANGE EXISTING FIELDS   8.2

When you modify the structure of a database, you can also change the three basic characteristics of a field: the name, the type, and the width. You should pay close attention when you change existing fields because you run the risk of losing part or all of the information contained within the fields you change. You always have the original information saved in a backup file, but you shouldn't rely on the backup file. With care, you can change characteristics of existing fields and not lose any information.

Changing the name, type, or width of a field is a little trickier than inserting or deleting fields.

   a. Highlight the field you want to change.

   b. Place the cursor in the column you want to change and make the change. For example, to change the field name, just start typing the new name. To change the field type, press [Enter] to move the cursor to the column Type, and then press SPACEBAR to select the type you want to use.

   c. Continue moving to other fields you want to change and make the changes.

   d. Press [Ctrl]-[End] to save the changes, and then press [Enter] to confirm the save and return to the Assist screen.

When you enter the Modify screen for database files, typeover mode is always on. This means you'll always type over existing characters, which is the easiest way to make your changes to the way fields are defined. You can always press [Ctrl]-[Y] to delete all the field information at once, but this is optional. You would then type all the new information.

When you change the characteristics of an existing field, such as the name, type, or width, you run the risk of losing information in several ways. Until you become more familiar with the various hazards, you should probably change one field at a time and then save each change. There's a hazard to saving frequently as well, but you'll learn these hazards in order.

You risk losing data when you save the newly redesigned structure to disk, and dBASE tries to copy all field information back to the original fields. dBASE warns you when you press [Ctrl]-[End] that records will be appended to fields of the same name only. This is almost, but not quite, true.

When you save a new structure to disk, dBASE tries to copy all field information for each record back to the original records and fields. If you insert a new field, nothing is copied to the new field, since it doesn't exist in the original database. If you change the name of a field, dBASE searches for the field in the original database that doesn't exist in the new structure. If only one field name was changed, dBASE is smart enough to figure out that the information in the old field name should be copied to the new field name. But if you change the names of two or more fields, dBASE can't figure out where you want the information contained in the old fields, so it doesn't copy that information over.

There is a way to circumvent this problem. You can change one field name and save the change. You can then return to the Modify screen, change the second field name, and then save that change. Proceed this way through all the field names you want to change. You probably won't want to change multiple field names very often, but when you do, be aware of the hazards you face.

Saving your changes frequently during a single modification carries with it its own hazard. Even though dBASE automatically creates a backup of the original file, it saves only the most recent version. Each backup copy overwrites the preceding backup copy. If you start modifying a database in steps, such as changing a series of field names and saving each change, checking your work, and then going back to insert or delete fields, information that existed a few minutes ago might no longer exist, not even in the backup file.

To protect against this, you can give unique names to the various backup files that are created, such as NAD1.BAK, NAD2.BAK, and so on. Use a scheme that makes sense to you and indicates the order of backups, such as the date or time you made the backup. You can give a file a date name, such as 09-19-90.NAD, or a time name, such as 10:30AM.NAD. You'll learn how to rename files in Chapter 15.

You run the the greatest danger of inadvertently losing information when you change the name of a field, but you also face a danger when you try to change the type of an existing field. The degree of danger depends upon the type of field you're trying to change. You can convert a numeric, date, or logical field to a character-type field without much danger because character-type fields accept all characters and have the least demanding format. Decimal numbers, date formats such as 08/08/90, and the four possible entries for logical fields, T, F, Y, and N, are all acceptable to character fields. Any special symbols that are part of a more specific field, such as the decimal point in a numeric field and the two slash marks in a date field, will be saved and displayed in the character field.

You can change a character field to a numeric, date, or logical field successfully only if the information in the character field is suitable for the more specific field you're trying to convert the character field to. For example, if you want to change a character field to a numeric field, the character field must contain numbers only. dBASE will not append any data from a character field to a numeric field if one or more of the characters is not a number.

When you change a character field to numeric, you must also specify the decimal width if you want to use one. If a decimal already exists in the character field numbers, dBASE will retain the decimal character, but it will drop whatever numbers extend beyond the width you declare in the Dec column. That is, if you forget to define a decimal width in the converted field and the character field information contains four numbers after the decimal point, all four decimal numbers will be dropped. Also, remember that you can't create numeric fields wider than 19 spaces.

When you change the width of a character or numeric field, you run the risk of losing data only if you shortened the field width. dBASE will try to squeeze in as much information as it can when it copies records to the new structure, but all information in excess of the new field widths will be dropped. For example, if you shorten the NAME field from 35 to 20 characters, you'll lose all information that exceeds 20 characters in the NAME field for each record.

Converting character fields to date fields follows the same rules as converting to numeric fields, with two exceptions. Date fields are limited to the established format of eight spaces, and the slash marks must exist in the character field information in the right sequence (mm/dd/yy), or no information will be carried over.

Memo fields can't be converted in either direction. Because memo field information is contained in a separate file, you can't change a memo field to any other type of field, nor can you change another field type to a memo field and retain the previous field's information.

Examples

1. Change the DATE field from date type to character. Make sure NAD.DBF is current. Press [M] and then [Enter] to open the Modify

Database screen. Highlight DATE and press [End], and then press SPACEBAR four times to switch the field type to Character. dBASE should retain 8 in the Width column. If it doesn't, change the width figure to 8. Press [Ctrl]-[End] and then [Enter] to save the change and return to the Assist screen.

List the new structure. Press [T], highlight "List structure," and press [Enter] twice. Scan the structure. Your screen should look something like the one in Figure 8-6. Press any key to return to the Assist screen.

View the record information to make sure the correct data was copied back into the new field type for DATE correctly. Press [U], highlight Browse, and press [Enter]. If the date characters still appear, the change was successful. Press [Esc] to return to Assist.

2. Change the DATE field back to date type. Repeat the steps for the previous example through the step of highlighting the DATE field. Now press [Enter] and press SPACEBAR twice to switch the field type to date. There's no need to specify a field width, since all date type

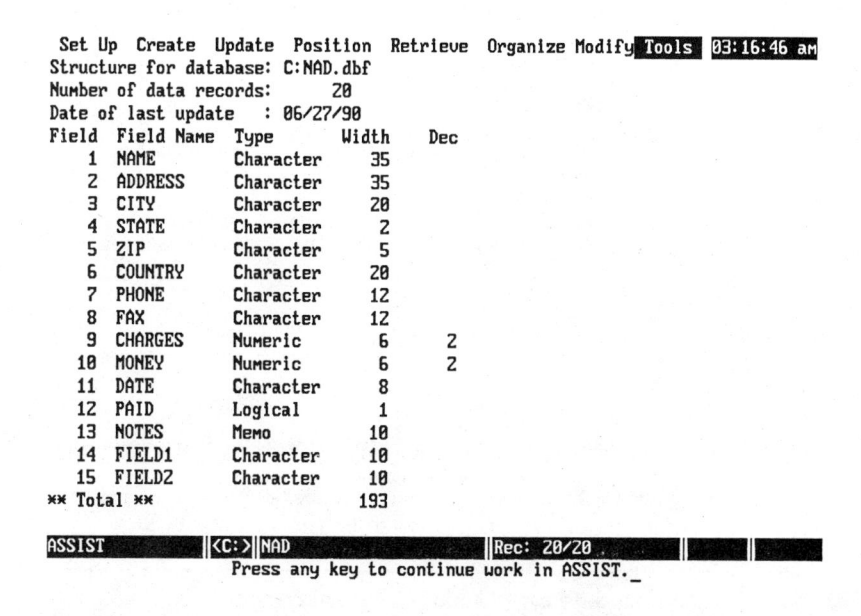

```
   Set Up  Create  Update  Position  Retrieve  Organize  Modify Tools  03:16:46 am
   Structure for database: C:NAD.dbf
   Number of data records:      20
   Date of last update   : 06/27/90
   Field  Field Name  Type        Width   Dec
       1  NAME        Character     35
       2  ADDRESS     Character     35
       3  CITY        Character     20
       4  STATE       Character      2
       5  ZIP         Character      5
       6  COUNTRY     Character     20
       7  PHONE       Character     12
       8  FAX         Character     12
       9  CHARGES     Numeric        6     2
      10  MONEY       Numeric        6     2
      11  DATE        Character      8
      12  PAID        Logical        1
      13  NOTES       Memo          10
      14  FIELD1      Character     10
      15  FIELD2      Character     10
   ** Total **                     193
ASSIST          |<C:>|NAD                    |Rec: 20/20
              Press any key to continue work in ASSIST._
```

FIGURE 8-6.   NAD.DBF listed with a character-type DATE field

fields are eight characters wide. Press Ctrl-End and then Enter to save the structure. List the new structure. Press T, highlight "List structure," and press Enter. View the results then press any key to return to Assist.

3. Change the numeric field in NAD.DBF called MONEY to a character-type field. Make sure NAD.DBF is the current database. Press M and then Enter. Highlight the MONEY field and press Enter to move your cursor from the Field Name column. Press SPACEBAR four times to switch the field type from numeric to character, and then press Enter to fix the change and move the cursor to the Width column.

Type 6 to retain the same width as the previous field type, and press Enter to fix the change. Your screen should now look like the one in Figure 8-7, with DATE changed back to date type and MONEY changed to character type.

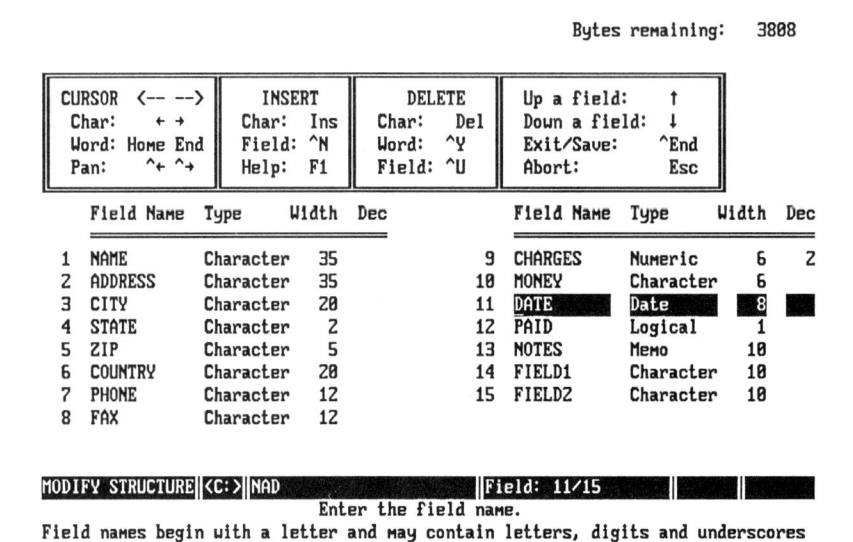

```
                                              Bytes remaining:    3808

 ┌─────────────────┬─────────────┬─────────────┬──────────────────┐
 │ CURSOR  <-- --> │ INSERT      │ DELETE      │ Up a field:   ↑  │
 │ Char:    ← →    │ Char:   Ins │ Char:   Del │ Down a field: ↓  │
 │ Word: Home End  │ Field:   ^N │ Word:    ^Y │ Exit/Save:  ^End │
 │ Pan:    ^← ^→   │ Help:    F1 │ Field:   ^U │ Abort:       Esc │
 └─────────────────┴─────────────┴─────────────┴──────────────────┘

     Field Name  Type       Width  Dec        Field Name  Type       Width  Dec

  1  NAME        Character   35            9  CHARGES     Numeric      6     2
  2  ADDRESS     Character   35           10  MONEY       Character    6
  3  CITY        Character   20           11  DATE        Date         8
  4  STATE       Character    2           12  PAID        Logical      1
  5  ZIP         Character    5           13  NOTES       Memo        10
  6  COUNTRY     Character   20           14  FIELD1      Character   10
  7  PHONE       Character   12           15  FIELD2      Character   10
  8  FAX         Character   12
```

`MODIFY STRUCTURE` `<C:>` `NAD`   `Field: 11/15`
Enter the field name.
Field names begin with a letter and may contain letters, digits and underscores

---

FIGURE 8-7. | DATE to date type, MONEY to character type

Chapter 8   Modifying a Database   **173**

Press [Ctrl]-[End] to save the change and [End] to confirm the save. This saves the changed field type, copies back all the record information, and returns you to the Assist screen.

4. Now check whether the information in the DATE field was saved correctly. Press [U], highlight Browse and press [Enter]. To obtain the exact screen shown in Figure 8-8, press [F1] to turn off help, lock the first field, and pan to the right. To lock the NAME field, press [Ctrl]-[Home] to open the menu bar, press [L], type 1, and press [Enter]. Then press [Ctrl]-[→] six times to pan to the right. You can see that the numbers for the MONEY field, including the decimal points have been saved. Retain the Browse screen for the following example.

5. Now convert the character field MONEY back to numeric with a minor change. Highlight record 1. You'll first change the decimal amount in the MONEY field. Press [Enter] four times to move the

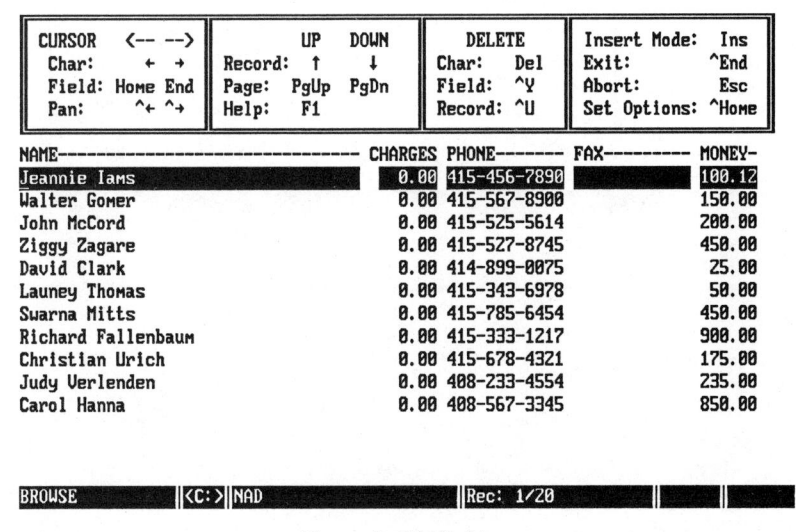

```
┌─────────────────────┬─────────────────────┬─────────────────┬─────────────────────┐
│ CURSOR    <-- -->   │          UP   DOWN  │     DELETE      │ Insert Mode:   Ins  │
│ Char:      ← →      │ Record:  ↑    ↓     │ Char:     Del   │ Exit:         ^End  │
│ Field: Home End     │ Page:   PgUp  PgDn  │ Field:     ^Y   │ Abort:         Esc  │
│ Pan:      ^← ^→     │ Help:    F1         │ Record:    ^U   │ Set Options: ^Home  │
└─────────────────────┴─────────────────────┴─────────────────┴─────────────────────┘
NAME─────────────────────────────── CHARGES PHONE─────── FAX──────── MONEY─
Jeannie Iams                          0.00 415-456-7890              100.12
Walter Gomer                          0.00 415-567-8900              150.00
John McCord                           0.00 415-525-5614              200.00
Ziggy Zagare                          0.00 415-527-8745              450.00
David Clark                           0.00 414-899-0075               25.00
Launey Thomas                         0.00 415-343-6978               50.00
Suarna Mitts                          0.00 415-785-6454              450.00
Richard Fallenbaum                    0.00 415-333-1217              900.00
Christian Urich                       0.00 415-678-4321              175.00
Judy Verlenden                        0.00 408-233-4554              235.00
Carol Hanna                           0.00 408-567-3345              850.00



BROWSE       |<C:>|NAD            |Rec: 1/20    |        |
                       View and edit fields.
```

FIGURE 8-8.   The MONEY field retains its numbers in the Browse screen

cursor over the MONEY field. Type **92.123** and press [Enter]. You can type over the existing characters or delete them first and then add the new ones. When you're finished, your screen should look like the ones in Figure 8-9. Press [Ctrl]-[End] to save this new information and return to the Assist screen.

Now you can convert the MONEY field back to a numeric field and see what happens to the fifth digit you just inserted, the number 3. Press [M] and then [Enter]. Highlight the MONEY field and press [End]. This moves your cursor to the Type column. Press SPACEBAR once to switch from character to numeric, and then press [Enter] to fix the change and move the cursor to the Width column. Type **6** and press [Enter]. This fixes the change and moves your cursor to the Dec column. Type **2** and press [Enter]. This and the previous step define the numeric field width as a total of 6 spaces wide with two of the spaces reserved for decimal numbers. Your screen should look like the one in Figure 8-10. Press [Ctrl]-[End] to

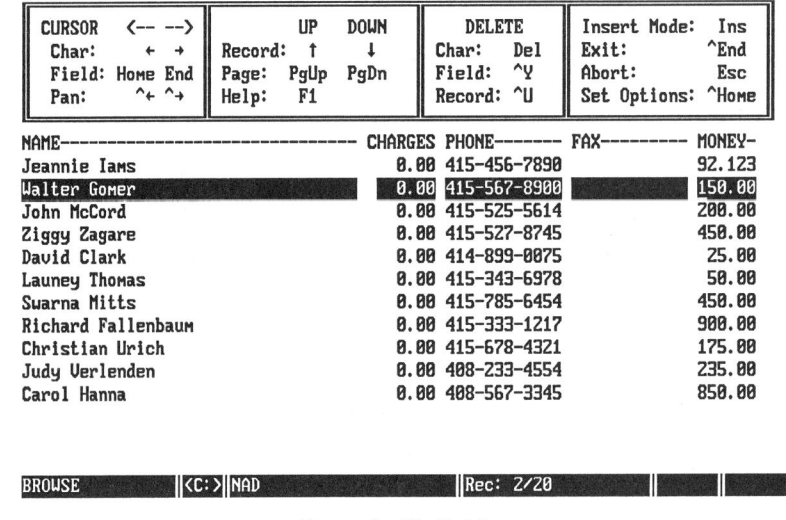

```
┌─────────────────────────┬──────────────────┬─────────────────┬────────────────────────┐
│ CURSOR    <-- -->       │      UP   DOWN   │    DELETE       │ Insert Mode:    Ins    │
│ Char:      ←   →        │ Record:  ↑   ↓   │ Char:    Del    │ Exit:          ^End    │
│ Field: Home End         │ Page: PgUp PgDn  │ Field:    ^Y    │ Abort:          Esc    │
│ Pan:       ^← ^→        │ Help:    F1      │ Record:   ^U    │ Set Options:  ^Home    │
└─────────────────────────┴──────────────────┴─────────────────┴────────────────────────┘
NAME------------------------ CHARGES PHONE-------- FAX--------- MONEY-
Jeannie Iams                    0.00 415-456-7890              92.123
Walter Gomer                    0.00 415-567-8900             150.00
John McCord                     0.00 415-525-5614             200.00
Ziggy Zagare                    0.00 415-527-8745             450.00
David Clark                     0.00 414-899-0075              25.00
Launey Thomas                   0.00 415-343-6978              50.00
Swarna Mitts                    0.00 415-785-6454             450.00
Richard Fallenbaum              0.00 415-333-1217             900.00
Christian Urich                 0.00 415-678-4321             175.00
Judy Verlenden                  0.00 408-233-4554             235.00
Carol Hanna                     0.00 408-567-3345             850.00


BROWSE      |<C:>|NAD              |Rec: 2/20  |
                          View and edit fields.
```

FIGURE 8-9. | Numbers changed in the MONEY field for record 1

Chapter 8   Modifying a Database

```
                                          Bytes remaining:  3808

 ┌──────────────────┬──────────────┬──────────────┬────────────────────┐
 │ CURSOR  <-- -->  │ INSERT       │ DELETE       │ Up a field:    ↑   │
 │ Char:     ← →    │ Char:   Ins  │ Char:   Del  │ Down a field:  ↓   │
 │ Word: Home End   │ Field:  ^N   │ Word:   ^Y   │ Exit/Save:   ^End  │
 │ Pan:    ^← ^→    │ Help:   F1   │ Field:  ^U   │ Abort:        Esc  │
 └──────────────────┴──────────────┴──────────────┴────────────────────┘

      Field Name   Type      Width  Dec            Field Name   Type      Width  Dec
   1  NAME         Character   35           9      CHARGES      Numeric     6     2
   2  ADDRESS      Character   35          10      MONEY        Numeric     6     2
   3  CITY         Character   20          11      DATE         Date        8
   4  STATE        Character    2          12      PAID         Logical     1
   5  ZIP          Character    5          13      NOTES        Memo       10
   6  COUNTRY      Character   20          14      FIELD1       Character  10
   7  PHONE        Character   12          15      FIELD2       Character  10
   8  FAX          Character   12

 │MODIFY STRUCTURE│<C:>│NAD                 │Field: 11/15│
                    Enter the field name.
 Field names begin with a letter and may contain letters, digits and underscores
```

| FIGURE 8-10. | Changing MONEY back to numeric type field |

save the change and then [Enter] to confirm the save and return to the Assist screen.

View the results in the Browse window. Press [U], highlight Browse, and then press [Enter]. Press [Ctrl]-[Home] and then [T] to highlight the first record. Your screen should look like the one in Figure 8-11. Remember to turn off help, lock the first field, and press [Ctrl]-[→] six times to pan to the right. Notice that the fifth digit you entered as part of the change, the number 3, no longer appears in the MONEY field. It doesn't fit into the two spaces you created for the decimal width, so dBASE dropped the number off. You can see that the two integers and first two decimal numbers have been saved.

Exercises

1. Is there any danger of losing information when you change existing fields?

```
CURSOR    <-- -->              UP    DOWN    DELETE          Insert Mode:  Ins
Char:      ←  →    Record:      ↑     ↓      Char:    Del    Exit:        ^End
Field: Home End    Page:      PgUp  PgDn     Field:    ^Y    Abort:        Esc
Pan:       ^← ^→   Help:       F1            Record:   ^U    Set Options: ^Home

NAME--------------------------------- PHONE-------- FAX--------- CHARGES MONEY-
Jeannie Iams                          415-456-7890                 0.00   92.12
Walter Gomer                          415-567-8900                 0.00  150.00
John McCord                           415-525-5614                 0.00  200.00
Ziggy Zagare                          415-527-8745                 0.00  450.00
Stan Freeburg                         203-567-5434                 0.00   25.00
David Clark                           415-899-0075                 0.00   25.00
Launey Thomas                         415-343-6978                 0.00   50.00
Swarna Mitts                          415-785-6454                 0.00  450.00
Richard Fallenbaum                    415-333-1217                 0.00  900.00
Christian Smith                       415-678-4321                 0.00  175.00
Judy Verlenden                        408-233-4554                 0.00  235.00

BROWSE          |<C:>|NAD              |Rec: 1/20|
                         View and edit fields.
```

FIGURE 8-11. The first record showing changed MONEY numbers

2. What are the three characteristics you can change in an existing field?

3. What precaution do you follow to prevent losing field information when you change the name of the field?

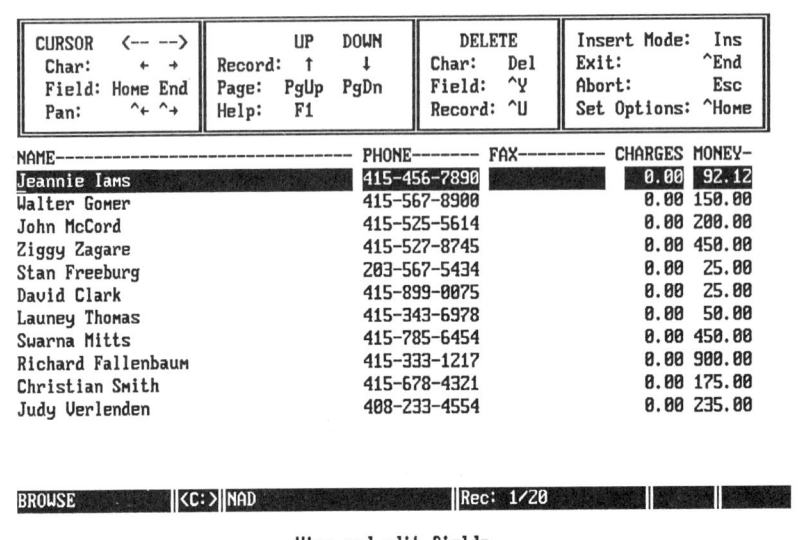

4. Begin in the Assist screen and change the PAID field in NAD.DBF from logical to character. List the structure on screen, then return to the Assist.

5. Change the PAID field back to logical type and then see if any field information has been lost.

6. Change the width of the NAME and ADDRESS field widths to 25 spaces each. Do not save these changes.

7. Change the width of the NAME and ADDRESS fields back to 35 spaces. Then save the changes, list the structure on screen, and return to the Assist screen.

DELETE FIELDS

|8.3|

Deleting a field means removing the field from the database. This is the easiest change to make to a database, but it's also the one change where you're assured of losing all the data, at least in the field you delete.

You can delete fields as easily as you can insert them. First, make sure the database in which you want to delete one or more fields is current.

a. Press [M] and then [Enter] to open the Modify screen.

b. Highlight the field you want to delete.

c. Press [Ctrl]-[U]. The highlighted field will disappear, and the subsequent fields will move up one position.

d. Press [Ctrl]-[End] to save, and then press [Enter] to confirm the save. You'll return to the Assist screen.

Once you delete a field and then save the new structure, all information in the deleted field for every record will be lost. You should only delete a field when you're sure you no longer need the data contained in the field.

However, when you delete a field and then save the new structure, the old field information remains in the backup copy until the next time dBASE makes a backup copy. You can refer to the backup copy if you change your mind and decide you want to keep the deleted field's data.

NOTE: You can copy information from one field to another by using dBASE commands at the dot prompt, but you can't do this while working in the Assist screen. If you're going to delete a field, you might want to insert a new field that will hold the old field information. You'll have to swap the information from one field to the other at the dot prompt.

You'll probably want to abandon your changes more often when you delete fields than when you make any other change to a database structure. If you delete one or more fields from a structure and then decide you want to retain some or all of the fields, before you save the new structure press [Esc] twice and then [Enter] to return to the Modify screen and use the original structure.

If you try to delete every field in a database and press [Ctrl]-[End] to save the new structure of no fields, dBASE warns you that no fields will be saved. If you press [Enter] to confirm this, you'll erase the modified database from your disk. The backup file will exist, but not the current structure. When you return to the Assist screen, no database will be current.

Examples

1. Delete a field and then cancel the change. Do this with the COUNTRY field you inserted earlier in this chapter. Make sure NAD.DBF is current. Press [M] and then [Enter]. Highlight COUNTRY, and press [Ctrl]-[U].

   Now cancel the change. Press [Esc]. dBASE asks on the navigation line if you want to abandon the change. It asks for a Y or N answer. Press [Y] or [Esc] to abandon the cancel. dBASE returns you to the Assist screen. The Modify menu is still open, and the command "Database file" still highlighted. Press [Enter] to return to the Modify screen for NAD.DBF. The deleted field COUNTRY remains in the structure.

2. Now delete COUNTRY for good. Make sure NAD.DBF is current. Press [M] and then [Enter]. Highlight COUNTRY, press [Ctrl]-[U] and press [Enter]. Press [Ctrl]-[End] to save the new structure and then [Enter] to confirm the save and return to the Assist screen.

   Double-check the results. Press [T], highlight "List structure" and then press [Enter] twice. It should look like the one in Figure 8-12. Press any key to return in the Assist screen.

3. Delete the FAX field you inserted earlier. Press [M] and then [Enter]. Highlight FAX, press [Ctrl]-[U] and then press [Enter]. Press [Ctrl]-[End] to save, and [Enter] to confirm the save.

Chapter 8 Modifying a Database **179**

```
  Set Up  Create  Update  Position  Retrieve  Organize  Modify  Tools   03:21:47 am
Structure for database: C:NAD.dbf
Number of data records:      20
Date of last update     : 06/27/90
Field  Field Name   Type        Width    Dec
    1  NAME         Character     35
    2  ADDRESS      Character     35
    3  CITY         Character     20
    4  STATE        Character      2
    5  ZIP          Character      5
    6  PHONE        Character     12
    7  FAX          Character     12
    8  CHARGES      Numeric        6       2
    9  MONEY        Character      6
   10  DATE         Date           8
   11  PAID         Logical        1
   12  NOTES        Memo          10
   13  FIELD1       Character     10
   14  FIELD2       Character     10
** Total **                      173

ASSIST          <C:> NAD              Rec: 20/20
              Press any key to continue work in ASSIST._
```

FIGURE 8-12. NAD.DBF with COUNTRY deleted

Double check the results. Press [T], highlight "List structure" and then press [Enter] twice. It should look like the one in Figure 8-13. Press any key to return to the Assist screen.

Exercises

1. When you delete a field and then save the change, is the field gone for good?

2. When you delete a field and then save the change, is the information gone for good?

3. Begin in Assist and delete FIELD1 from NAD.DBF, making the change permanent. Return to Assist.

4. Delete FIELD2 from NAD.DBF. Check your results by listing the new structure of NAD.DBF to your screen. The structure of NAD.DBF should now look like it did when you started this chapter. Return to Assist.

```
          Set Up  Create  Update  Position  Retrieve  Organize  Modify Tools  03:22:30 am

     Structure for database: C:NAD.dbf
     Number of data records:      20
     Date of last update    : 06/27/90
     Field  Field Name   Type        Width    Dec
         1  NAME         Character      35
         2  ADDRESS      Character      35
         3  CITY         Character      20
         4  STATE        Character       2
         5  ZIP          Character       5
         6  PHONE        Character      12
         7  CHARGES      Numeric         6      2
         8  MONEY        Character       6
         9  DATE         Date            8
        10  PAID         Logical         1
        11  NOTES        Memo           10
        12  FIELD1       Character      10
        13  FIELD2       Character      10
     ** Total **                       161

     ASSIST        <C:> NAD                   Rec: 20/20
                Press any key to continue work in ASSIST._
```

FIGURE 8-13. NAD.DBF with FAX deleted

EXERCISES

MASTERY SKILLS CHECK

1. Make VALUE.DBF current. (You created this database in Chapter 6.) Insert a new character-type field called NEWFIELD, ten spaces wide. Save this change and return to the Assist screen.

2. Change the name of the QUANTITY field in VALUE.DBF to NUMBER, and then save the change.

3. Delete the field PRICE in VALUE.DBF, and then abandon the change.

4. Change the name of the NUMBER field in VALUE.DBF back to QUANTITY, and then save the change.

5. List the new structure of VALUE.DBF on your screen, and then return to Assist.

Chapter 8   Modifying a Database   **181**

1. Begin in the Assist screen and create a database called SAMPLE.DBF
   with three fields: NAME, a character field, width = 10; NUMBER, a
   numeric field, Width = 1, Dec = 0; and DATE, a date field. Save this
   structure and proceed directly to enter the following information:

	NAME	NUMBER	DATE
Rec 1:	Record 1	1	01/01/90
Rec 2:	Record 2	2	01/02/90
Rec 3:	Record 3	3	01/03/90

   INTEGRATING SKILLS CHECK

   Once you've entered this information, save the file to disk and
   return to the Assist screen.

2. Display the structure of SAMPLE.DBF in the Modify screen. Delete
   the NAME field but do not save the change. List the structure of
   SAMPLE.DBF, and then return to the Assist.

3. Change the NUMBER and DATE fields to character type. List the
   new structure on screen. View the contents in the Browse screen.
   Return to Assist.

4. Delete all three fields in SAMPLE.DBF and save the new structure.
   Notice the warning at the bottom of your screen: "Empty structure
   will not be saved." Return to Assist. Notice in your status bar that
   SAMPLE.DBF is no longer current. In fact, the database no longer
   exists.

Organizing a Database

▶9◀

CHAPTER OBJECTIVES

In this chapter you will learn how to

▶ Index a database 9.1
▶ Use the Seek command 9.2
▶ Sort a database 9.3
▶ Copy database files 9.4

Information must be organized before you can make much sense of it. The elements of a database structure—field names, types, and sizes—are all intended to organize information within each record. You obtain a higher level of organization by organizing all the records within a single database.

In this chapter, you'll learn how to create index files, sort databases, and copy databases to new files. Each of these three techniques provides a different approach to organizing individual records within a database file.

You'll also learn how to use the command Seek. You can use this command only after you've attached an appropriate index to the database where you want to locate records.

Organizing a database means arranging individual records so they appear in a sequence that makes sense to you, a sequence that helps you understand and work with the database information efficiently and intelligently. The way you organize records depends upon what you want to do with the information.

There are three ways to organize records in dBASE databases, and each has its matching command on the Organize pull-down menu. Press [O] now from the Assist screen to open this menu and view the commands:

Index	Lets you build a separate file, called an index file, based on fields in the current database. The index file controls the organization of records within the database
Sort	Lets you reorganize the order of records in a database. You can reorganize records in the original database, or you can reorganize the records and save them to a new database
Copy	Lets you copy records in one database to another database by using the Search/Scope menu, which lets you select the records that go into the new database

Chapter 9 — Organizing a Database — 185

Exercises

1. Load dBASE and make NAD.DBF the current database. View the contents of this database in the Browse screen. Return to Assist.

2. Make record 10 in NAD.DBF current. Make sure the right record number is current. View the contents of this record in the Edit screen. Return to Assist.

3. Go to the top record in NAD.DBF. List all records in NAD.DBF on your screen. Be sure that no records have been marked for deletion. Return to Assist.

SKILLS CHECK

INDEX A DATABASE

9.1

When you index a database, you ask dBASE to create a separate and smaller disk file based upon designated fields in the database. You index a database on a specific field or fields that control the order in which records are displayed. For example, if you index NAD.DBF on the NAME field, the records in NAD.DBF will be displayed in alphabetical order in the NAME fields. Since the records were entered in first name, last name order, the index will alphabetize beginning with first names. The screen in Figure 9-1 shows the record in NAD.DBF indexed according to the alphabetical order of the NAME field entries. You can index on all field types except memo and logical fields.

There are two steps to working with indexes. First you create the index, and then you attach the index to the database it's based upon. To create an index, first make sure the database you want to index is current. Then

a. Press [O] to open the Organize pull-down menu. The top command, Index, is highlighted.

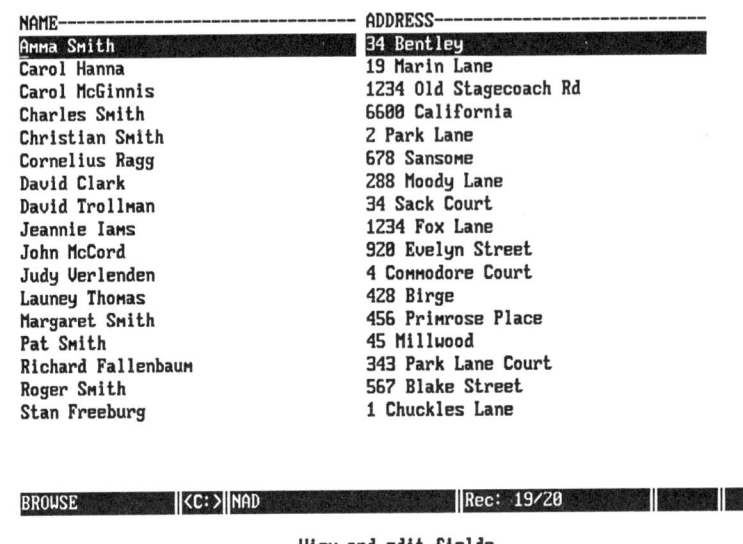

```
NAME----------------------------- ADDRESS---------------------------
Amma Smith                        34 Bentley
Carol Hanna                       19 Marin Lane
Carol McGinnis                    1234 Old Stagecoach Rd
Charles Smith                     6600 California
Christian Smith                   2 Park Lane
Cornelius Ragg                    678 Sansome
David Clark                       288 Moody Lane
David Trollman                    34 Sack Court
Jeannie Iams                      1234 Fox Lane
John McCord                       920 Evelyn Street
Judy Verlenden                    4 Commodore Court
Launey Thomas                     428 Birge
Margaret Smith                    456 Primrose Place
Pat Smith                         45 Millwood
Richard Fallenbaum                343 Park Lane Court
Roger Smith                       567 Blake Street
Stan Freeburg                     1 Chuckles Lane


BROWSE           |<C:>|NAD                    |Rec: 19/20
                        View and edit fields.
```

FIGURE 9-1. NAD.DBF indexed on the NAME field

b. Press [Enter] to start the indexing process. dBASE asks for the field or fields you want to base the index on:

   The index key can be any character, numeric, or
   date expression involving one or more fields in
   the database file. It is usually a single field.
   Enter an index key expression:

   In this case, an *index key expression* is a field name.

c. You can enter the field name or names you want to use in two ways: You can type the field name on screen or you can open a list of available fields.

d. Press [F10] to open the field list for the current database. Highlight the field name you want to use and press [Enter]. You can select multiple field names if you want to. Just make sure you insert a + sign (press [+]) between each field name. The field names you select will appear on the command line, or the line just above the status bar. dBASE separates field names with a comma.

Once you've selected the field or fields you want to use, press ⇨ or ⇦ to close the field list window.

e. Press [Enter]. dBASE asks which drive you want to save the index file to.

f. Highlight the drive letter you want to use and press [Enter]. dBASE displays this prompt:

```
Enter a file name (consisting of up to 8
letters or digits) followed by a period and
a file name extension (consisting of up to 3
letters or digits.)
Enter the name of the file:
```

dBASE is asking you to declare the name you want to give the index file. Selecting the proper index file name can be important. You'll learn how to do this in just a moment.

g. Type the file name you want to use and press [Enter]. dBASE will automatically add the extension .NDX, which stands for "index." dBASE proceeds to build the index and report on its progress, and then it tells you when it's finished.

h. Press any key to return to the Assist.

The larger the database, or the more fields you add to the index, the longer it takes to build the index file. For very large databases of many thousands of records, you should probably plan to do something else while the index is being built.

When you first create an index, dBASE automatically attaches it to the current database. When you make another database current, the link between the previous database and the index is broken. Whenever you make the previous database current again and want to view the records in the indexed order, you have to attach the index. This is the purpose of a dBASE request that you have not responded to up to this point in the book, the prompt that asks if the database is indexed or not. You see the request after selecting the drive and name of the database file you want to make current; "Is the file indexed? [Y/N]." Up to this point, you've been pressing [N] for no or pressing [Enter] to insert the default answer N.

Once you create an index file and want to use it, press [Y] when dBASE asks for an index file. The screen in Figure 9-2 shows how

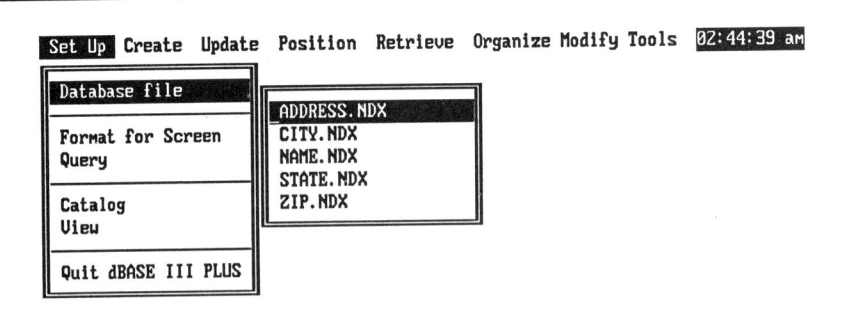

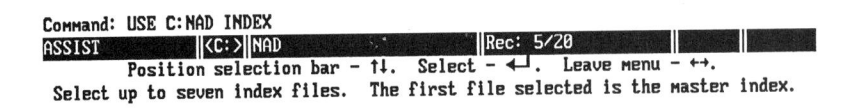

```
  Set Up  Create  Update  Position  Retrieve  Organize Modify Tools   02:44:39 am
 ┌─Database file──┐
 │                │┌─────────────────┐
 │ Format for Screen│ ADDRESS.NDX   │
 │ Query          ││ CITY.NDX        │
 │                ││ NAME.NDX        │
 │ Catalog        ││ STATE.NDX       │
 │ View           ││ ZIP.NDX         │
 │                │└─────────────────┘
 │ Quit dBASE III PLUS │
 └────────────────┘


Command: USE C:NAD INDEX
ASSIST              <C:>  NAD                  Rec: 5/20
              Position selection bar - ↑↓.  Select - ↵.  Leave menu - ←→.
      Select up to seven index files.  The first file selected is the master index.
```

FIGURE 9-2. | List of available index files

dBASE displays the list of available index file names for NAD.DBF, where an index has been built for each field in the database. You select one or more index names from this list and press [Enter]. You must make sure you attach indexes built from the current database only, or you'll end up with strange displays of records on your screen when you use the Edit, Append, or Browse screen—or perhaps no displays at all. dBASE can't double-check whether the index you're selecting is built from the current database.

Once you attach an index to a database, it remains attached until you make another database current. As long as an index is attached to a database, it controls the order of records in the database. The most demonstrable evidence of this control is when you work in the Edit, Browse, or Append screens. You'll find your progress slowed down noticeably as you move from one record to another. When an index is attached to a database, the two files work hand in hand, and this cooperation can slow your progress. Each time you move from one record to another in the Edit or Append screen, or when you move from one screenful to another in the Browse screen, dBASE must refer to the index to find out which record or group of records should be displayed next. The larger the database, the slower the performance. Although indexing a database might slow down its performance, the gain in organization usually outweighs the slowdown in speed.

The question of names for index files can become a problem when you start creating a lot of indexes, particularly different indexes for the same database. When you start out, you can give the index the same name as the database file you attach it to. As you create more than one index file for the same database, you'll have to differentiate each index by using names that signify the effect of the index. For example, NAME.NDX organizes records in NAD.DBF by name, and ZIP.NDX organizes the records by ZIP code.

As you begin to use more databases, you'll have to pay close attention to picking out appropriate names for your index files. You can't have two files named NAME.NDX, even if they're designed around records in different databases. DOS doesn't allow duplicate file names in the same directory. You could store index files with the same name in different directories, but working with directories in dBASE III PLUS is difficult. As a solution, you could call one of the index files NADNAME.NDX and the second index file VENDNAME.NDX (for vendor name index).

If you try to create an index file by using the name of an index file that already exists, dBASE will warn you and ask what you want to do. For example, if you try to create a file called NAME.NDX in the current directory when one already exists there, dBASE will ask, "C:name.ndx already exists, overwrite it? (Y/N)." Press [Y] to overwrite the old index file or [N] to cancel the index. If you press [Enter], the default answer N will be entered, and the index file will not be created. Instead, you'll return to the Assist screen.

You can use two separate index files and load them in sequence. When you do this, the order of precedence is determined by the order in which you loaded them. The first index is called the *master index*; it controls the overall organization of the database. The second index controls the organization of records within groups determined by the master index.

As mentioned, you can also build a single index based on more than one field in a database. The first field you use in an index based on multiple fields serves as the master, or controlling, field. If you type the field names instead of selecting them from the list of fields, make sure you insert a plus sign between the field names you want to use.

When you begin to build various indexes, including both single-field and multiple-field indexes and then attach several of these indexes to a database, you have to make sure you aren't selecting indexes that will conflict with each other. For example, if you attach one index based on the NAME field, a second index based on the STATE field, and a third index based on the NAME and ADDRESS fields, the third index is useless, since the first two indexes already create the same effect. Pay close attention to the indexes you attach to a database and try to keep the number of active indexes to a minimum.

Viewing a database such as NAD.DBF organized by the NAME field opens a new dimension to your understanding of how to design a database structure and how to use different fields. As you saw in Figure 9-1, the records are alphabetized starting with the first letter of the first names. This is the best way to organize NAD.DBF if you're trying to distinguish the record for John McCord from Walter Gomer, but it's not the most professional way to organize names. It would probably be better to break the names into two fields, one called FIRSTNAME for the first name, the other called LASTNAME for the last name. This way you could create an index based on the LASTNAME field that would make it easier to locate records by name.

When you create indexes, dBASE arranges alphabetical characters in alphabetical order: A, B, C, followed by a, b, c. This is the ASCII alphabetical order, not strict alphabetical order. It arranges numbers in numerical order: 1, 2, 3. You can't create indexes based on reverse alphabetical or numerical order in the Assist, but you can create such indexes at the dot prompt.

When an index is attached to a database and you update the database by appending new records or editing information in old records, dBASE automatically updates the indexes. All indexes that aren't attached when you update the database will have to be rebuilt. Remember, an index is a separate file, and it has no way of knowing you've made changes to the database or what the changes are unless the index is attached to the database when you make the changes. If you attach an out-of-date index to an updated database, records that have been added since the old index was last built will not be displayed in the Edit or Browse screens. Always make sure your indexes are current.

Examples

1. Create an index for NAD.DBF based on the NAME field. Make sure NAD.DBF is current. Press [O], and then [Enter]. When dBASE asks you which field you want to use for the index, press [F10]. This opens the list of field names. The top field, NAME, is highlighted by default. (Notice that the NOTES field name is dimmed. You can't build indexes on memo fields.) Press [Enter] to accept the NAME field. Press [→] to close the field list, and then press [Enter] again. dBASE asks for the name of the index. Type **NAME** and press [Enter]. dBASE proceeds to build an index called NAME.NDX and reports back "100% completed   20 records indexed." Press any key to return to the Assist screen.

2. Practice attaching NAME.NDX to NAD.DBF. First quit dBASE, then reload the program. Press [S], press [Enter] twice, highlight NAD, and press [Enter] again. When dBASE asks if the file is indexed, press [Y]. dBASE opens a window of available index names. In this example, NAME.NDX is the only index file name available. Highlight that name and press [Enter]. You'll see the label "Master" appear next to the index name. This means that NAME.NDX is the first index you've selected, the one that provides overall control of the records. You can attach multiple indexes to a single database, but only one index can serve as the master file. You'll see how this works in a moment when you begin to work with multiple indexes.

    Once you've selected NAME.NDX as an index, press [→] to close the list of index file names. This returns you to the Assist screen.

    At this point, you have attached the index file NAME.NDX to the database NAD.DBF. To see the effects, open the Browse screen. Press [U], highlight Browse, and press [Enter]. When the screen appears, you should see the contents of NAD.DBF with the records organized according to the alphabetical order of the NAME field, as shown in Figure 9-1.

3. To see how NAME.NDX slows down the performance of dBASE, press [Esc] to return to the Assist screen. Highlight Edit and press [Enter]. Now press [PgDn] to go to the next record. Press [PgDn] several times quickly. You should notice a slight delay in response time. If

you don't, you can compare the performance to an unindexed NAD.DBF in the next example.

4. You can detach the index NAME.NDX from NAD.DBF by closing NAD.DBF and then opening it again without attaching the index. Press [S], press [Enter] twice, highlight NAD, and press [Enter] two more times. Now when you view NAD.DBF in the Browse screen, the records will be disorganized, or organized in the original order in which you entered them.
   Now that NAD.DBF is unindexed, check its performance. Press [U], highlight Edit, and press [Enter]. Now press [PgDn] several times and then [PgUp], to see how dBASE speeds up when an index isn't attached to the database.

5. Create a second index, based on the STATE field. Make sure NAD.DBF is current. Press [O], press [Enter], and press [F10]. When the list of field names appears, press [↓] three times to highlight STATE. Then press [Enter] to accept this field name as the basis for the index. Press [→] to close the list. Press [Enter] twice to accept the current drive and open the file name request, type **STATE**, and press [Enter]. dBASE now creates an index file called STATE.NDX based upon the alphabetical order of entries in the STATE field of NAD.DBF. Press any key to return to Assist.

6. Now attach STATE.NDX to NAD.DBF. Then press [S], press [Enter] twice, highlight NAD, press [Enter], and press [Y]. This opens the list of index file names, which should contain NAME and STATE. Highlight STATE and press [Enter]. This makes the STATE index the master index. Now see what effect this has. Press [U], highlight Browse, and press [Enter]. Lock the first field and pan twice to the right: press [Ctrl]-[Home], press [L], type **1**, and press [Enter]. Then press [Ctrl]-[→] twice. The records in NAD.DBF should be organized as shown in the screen in Figure 9-3. Almost all the state entries are for California (STATE = CA), but there are two other states, Arizona (AZ) and Connecticut (CT). The Arizona entry comes first, followed by the entries for California.

Chapter 9 — Organizing a Database

```
NAME------------------------------ CITY-------------- STATE ZIP--
Carol McGinnis                    Tucson              AZ    80560
Jeannie Iams                      Berkeley            CA    94708
Walter Gomer                      Kensington          CA    94720
John McCord                       Albany              CA    94708
Ziggy Zagare                      El Cerrito          CA    94530
David Clark                       Oakland             CA    94612
Launey Thomas                     Berkeley            CA    94704
Swarna Mitts                      Richmond            CA    97540
Richard Fallenbaum                Piedmont            CA    97455
Christian Smith                   San Francisco       CA    94017
Judy Verlenden                    Carmel Valley       CA    93924
Carol Hanna                       Aptos               CA    95003
David Trollman                    Redwood City        CA    94723
Margaret Smith                    Redwood City        CA    94565
Roger Smith                       Berkeley            CA    94710
Cornelius Ragg                    San Francisco       CA    94710
Charles Smith                     San Francisco       CA    94601


BROWSE        <C:> NAD              Rec: 14/20
                      View and edit fields.
```

FIGURE 9-3. NAD.DBF indexed on the STATE field

7. You could achieve the same effect as that shown in the screen in Figure 9-3 by creating a single index based on both the STATE and NAME fields. To do this, make sure NAD.DBF is current. Press [O], press [Enter], and press [F10]. Highlight STATE and press [Enter], then highlight NAME and press [Enter]. You should see these field names added on the action line on your screen, just above the status bar. In this case, the first field name becomes the master field name, although no indication of this will show on your screen.

Press [→] to close the list of field names, and then press [Enter] twice. Type **STATNAME** and press [Enter]. (You can use up to eight characters for a dBASE index name.) dBASE proceeds to build the index called STATNAME.NDX. Press any key to return to Assist. If you attach STATNAME.NDX to NAD.DBF and view the results in the Browse screen, your screen should look like the one in Figure 9-3.

Exercises

1. Is an index part of a database file or a separate disk file?

2. Is an index the only way you can organize records in a database?

3. Can you create several indexes for the same database?

4. Do indexes for the same database have a precedence for controlling the organization of records?

5. What fields can't you base an index upon?

6. What is a master index?

7. How many fields can you index NAD.DBF on?

8. Create an index called MONEY.NDX based on the MONEY field in NAD.DBF.

9. Attach MONEY.NDX to NAD.DBF and view the results in the Browse screen. Then return to Assist.

9.2 USE THE SEEK COMMAND

You were introduced to the command Seek on the Position menu in Chapter 6. You can't use this command until you've attached an index to the current database. The command Seek relies on information in the index to seek or locate the record you're looking for.

To use the Seek command, you must first make sure of two conditions:

- The database you want to seek records in must be active.

- An index that is built on the field which you want to search is attached to the database.

Chapter 9   Organizing a Database   **195**

Once you've opened the database and index you want to use, follow these steps:

a. Press [P] to open the Position menu.

b. Press [Enter] to execute the command Seek, which is highlighted by default. dBASE asks you to "Enter an expression." This means information in the attached indexed field for the record you want to seek. This information must be accurate to the letter, including uppercase and lowercase spellings, and the information must be preceded and followed with quotation marks. You can use single or double quotes.

c. Press [Enter]. dBASE looks for the first record matching the expression you've declared. If it finds a record, the record number appears on the status bar. dBASE reports back if it doesn't find a record containing the information you've specified as an expression.

d. Press any key to return to the Assist.

Once dBASE has found the record you're seeking, you can view it in the Edit or Browse screen. The Edit screen is best since it displays more information for a single record.

The only information you can search on is information in the indexed field. dBASE calls this the *key field*. Although you have to take several extra steps to use the command Seek, it's a quicker way to locate records than the command Locate.

Examples

1. Seek the record in NAD.DBF with the name Walter Gomer. First make sure NAD.DBF is current and you've attached the index NAME.NDX to NAD.DBF. Press [P], and then [Enter]. Type **'Walter Gomer'** (or **"Walter Gomer"**) and press [Enter]. dBASE shows Rec: 2/20 on the status bar. Press any key to return to the Assist.

   Now view the record. Press [←], then [↓], and then [Enter]. This should display the information for Walter Gomer's record in the Edit screen. Press [Esc] to return to the Assist.

2. Seek the record in NAD.DBF for Judy Verlenden. First make sure NAD.DBF and NAME.NDX are current. Press (P), and then (Enter). Type '**Judy Verlenden**' and press (Enter). To view this record in the Edit screen, press (←), then (↓), and then (Enter), and view the record. Press (Esc) to return to the Assist screen.

Exercises

1. What two conditions are necessary for the command Seek to work?

2. What is the purpose of using the command Seek?

3. Use the command Seek to find the record Carol McGinnis, and then return to the Assist.

9.3 SORT A DATABASE

Sorting a database means reorganizing the actual records in a database and saving them to a disk file in the sorted order. When you index a database, you create a separate index file that controls the way records are displayed in the original database. When you sort a database, you create a duplicate copy of the original database in which the records are saved in the sorted order.

To sort a database, first make sure that the database you want to sort is current. The procedure you follow is similar but not identical to the steps you followed to create an index.

a. Press (O) to open the Organize menu.

b. Press (↓) to highlight the command Sort, and then press (Enter). dBASE displays a list of fields in the current database. The screen in Figure 9-4 shows the field list for NAD.DBF. The top field is highlighted by default. Information about the highlighted field is displayed in the center of the screen.

Chapter 9 Organizing a Database **197**

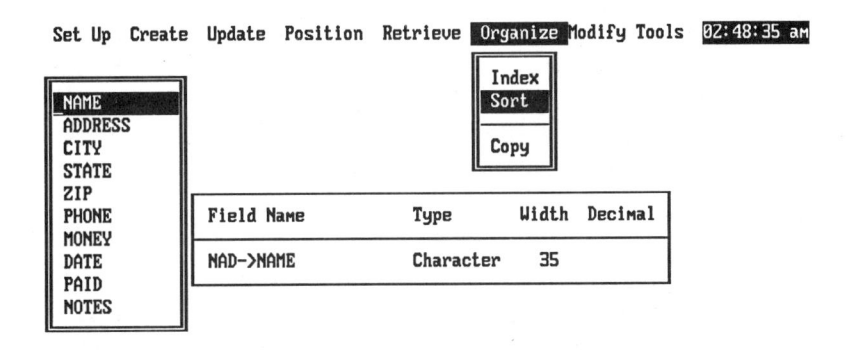

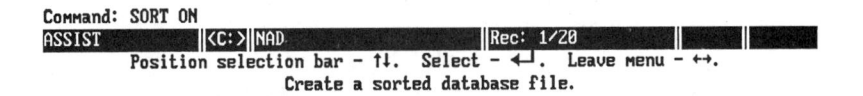

```
    Set Up   Create   Update  Position  Retrieve  Organize Modify  Tools  02:48:35 am
                                          Index
   NAME                                   Sort
   ADDRESS
   CITY                                   Copy
   STATE
   ZIP
   PHONE        Field Name      Type       Width  Decimal
   MONEY
   DATE         NAD->NAME       Character    35
   PAID
   NOTES



Command: SORT ON
ASSIST          |<C:>|NAD              |Rec: 1/20
              Position selection bar - ↑↓.  Select - ↵.  Leave menu - ↔.
                         Create a sorted database file.
```

| FIGURE 9-4. | Field list for NAD.DBF when sorting |

   c. Highlight the field you want to sort on and press [Enter]. This moves the highlight bar to the next field down in the list of fields. You can select more than one field to sort on.

   d. Press [←] or [→] when you've selected all the fields you want to base the sort on. This closes the field list and opens the list of available drive letters. dBASE is asking you which drive you want to save the sorted database on.

   e. Highlight the drive you want to use and press [Enter]. dBASE then asks what name you want to give the sorted database file by displaying the following prompt:

```
Enter a file name (consisting of up to 8
letters or digits) followed by a period and
a file name extension (consisting of up to 3
letters or digits.)
Enter the name of the file:
```

f. Type the name you want to use for the newly sorted database file and press [Enter]. You must use a name different from the current database file name. dBASE sorts the records into the new order, and then records them to the new database file. dBASE reports back how many records it has sorted, how many records it's copying, and finally when it's finished.

g. Press any key to return to the Assist.

Whenever you sort a database, you create a new disk file of the same size, with the name you specified. It takes longer to sort a database than to create an index. It also uses up considerably more disk space when you create separate sorted database files.

Only sort a database that will retain the sorted order for some time. Don't go to the trouble of resorting a database each time you want to view the records in a new order; you should use an index for that. When you append new records to any database, dBASE automatically adds them to the end of the database. Therefore, as soon as you begin adding or updating records to a sorted database, the newer records will appear at the end, regardless of what information they contain. Updated records also might not appear in the proper sorted order. You can see that if you change information in a database frequently, it's better to use an index to organize the records than to resort the database.

You are not excluded from using indexes when you work with a sorted database; you can sort a database and then build an index for the sorted database. The index order does not make a fundamental change to the order of records in the database. The index controls the way records are handled, such as when they are displayed or printed.

Whenever you sort a database, make sure the sorted database is the current database and view the results of the sort in the Browse screen.

a. Press [S] to open the Set Up menu, and then press [Enter] twice to accept the command "Database file" and the default drive letter.

b. Highlight the new database file name and press [Enter] twice—first to load the database, second to skip over the request for an index. The new file name will appear on the status bar.

c. Press [U] to open the Update menu, highlight Browse, and press [Enter].

You can sort a database on several fields, just as you can index a database on several fields. The order in which you select the fields will determine their precedence in controlling the sorted order. You can select fields from the fields list, or you can type in the field names, separated by plus signs. As with index files, you cannot sort a database on a logical or memo field.

If you're working with a dual floppy disk computer, you probably won't want to sort databases. You won't be able to create databases large enough to warrant resorting, and you certainly won't have the extra disk space it requires to hold the duplicate database files.

Examples

1. Sort NAD.DBF on the NAME field. First make sure NAD.DBF is the current database, then press [O] to open the Organize menu, press [↓] to highlight the command Sort, and press [Enter]. Then press [F10] to open the field list. Since the NAME field is highlighted by default, press [Enter] again. The field name appears on the action line. Press [→] to close the field list, and then press [Enter] to accept the current drive. Type **NADNAME** to name the sorted database, and press [Enter]. dBASE creates the sorted database file name and displays the following message: "100% Sorted 20 Records sorted . . . Copying text file." Press any key to return to the Assist screen.

2. Double-check the results of the sort. Press [U], highlight Browse, and press [Enter]. The results should look just like the screen in Figure 9-1. Sorting and indexing a database on the same field or fields yield the same results.
   Press [↓] and [↑] to check response time. A database responds more quickly without an index attached.

3. Sort NAD.DBF on the STATE field. Make sure NAD.DBF is the current database. Press [O] to open the Organize menu, press [↓] to highlight the command Sort, and then press [Enter]. Press [↓] three times to highlight STATE, and then press [Enter]. Press [→] to close the field list, and then press [Enter] to accept the current drive.

Type **STATE** to name the sorted database and press Enter. dBASE goes to work creating the sorted database. When you see the message showing that it's finished, press any key to return to the Assist screen.

4. Double-check the results of the latest sort. Press U, highlight Browse, and press Enter. The results should look just like the screen in Figure 9-3.

Exercises

1. When you sort a database, do you create a separate file?

2. Is it called a sort file?

3. What is the separate file?

4. What are the major differences between using a sorted database and an indexed database?

5. Sort NAD.DBF on the MONEY field to a file called NADMONEY .DBF. View the results in the Browse screen, and then return to Assist. (Remember to make NADMONEY.DBF current after you create it, or you'll view the contents of NAD.DBF in the Browse screen.)

9.4 COPY DATABASE FILES

The third command on the Organize pull-down menu, called Copy, lets you copy the contents of the current database file to another database file of a different name. This lets you build other database files based upon information in existing database files.

You can copy files in four ways:

- You can create an exact copy of the database file.

Chapter 9   Organizing a Database

- You can create another database containing selected fields in the current database.
- You can create another database containing selected records in the current database.
- You can create another database containing both selected fields and records in the current database.

Copying a database file is a fairly straightforward process. To copy a database file, make sure the database is current. Then

a. Press [O] to open the Organize pull-down menu.

b. Press [↑] to highlight the command Copy and press [Enter]. dBASE asks you for the name of the file copy you want to create.

c. Type the file name and press [Enter]. dBASE presents you with the Search/Scope menu. You learned how to work with this menu in Chapter 6.

d. Highlight the command you want to use. If you select "Execute the command," dBASE will build a duplicate database file with the name you specify. If you select any other command, follow the steps for completing the command, and then select "Execute the command."

e. Press [Enter] to copy the new file. dBASE will keep you posted on its progress.

f. Press any key when the copy has been created to return to the Assist screen.

Whenever you copy records that contain memo fields to a new file, dBASE creates two new files: the database copy file and the memo field copy file. The memo field copy file is given the same name as the database copy file, with a different extension. For example, when you copy records from NAD.DBF to COPY.DBF, a second file is also created, called COPY.DBT, that contains memo field entries for the records in COPY.DBF.

To make an exact duplicate of the current database, simply press [Enter] when the Search/Scope menu appears. The top command,

"Execute the command," is highlighted by default. This command builds a duplicate of the current file to a file of the name you specify. This procedure works the same as the command "Copy file" on the Tools menu, which you'll learn about in Chapter 15.

The procedure is trickier when you want to select a group of fields or records for the new database file by using the Search/Scope menu. The ways you specify a scope or build a search or scope condition are identical to the techniques you learned in Chapter 6, when you first worked with this menu to locate records within a database.

You must always give the copy file a name that doesn't exist in the current directory. dBASE will warn you if the copy file name you want to use is already taken. You can then either overwrite the previous file or pick another file name. You'll learn how to find file names in the current directory in Chapter 15.

Examples

1. Make a duplicate copy of NAD.DBF, giving it the file name NADCOPY. First, make sure NAD.DBF is current. Then press [O] to open the Organize menu, press [↑] to highlight the command Copy, and press [Enter]. dBASE opens the Search/Scope menu with the top command, "Execute the command," highlighted. Press [Enter]. dBASE asks you for the name of the file copy. Type **NADCOPY** and press [Enter]. dBASE will report on its progress, and then write the new file to disk and automatically add the extension .DBF to the copy file name.

2. Whenever you make a new file, check its integrity by viewing the contents. First, make NADCOPY current. Press [S], and then [Enter] twice. Highlight NADCOPY and press [Enter] twice. Now press [U], highlight Browse, and then press [Enter]. NADCOPY should contain the same records as NAD, in the same order. Press [Esc] to return to the Assist screen.

3. Make a copy of the first ten records in NAD.DBF. You'll specify a scope condition to do this. Make sure NAD.DBF is current. Then press [O], [↑], and then [Enter]. Type **NADTEN** and press [Enter].

Chapter 9 Organizing a Database 203

When the Search/Scope menu appears, highlight the command "Specify scope" and press [Enter]. Highlight NEXT and press [Enter], then type **10** and press [Enter]. When the Search/Scope menu reappears, highlight the command "Execute the command" and press [Enter]. dBASE proceeds to copy the first ten records in NAD.DBF to the file called NADTEN.DBF. When dBASE reports that the copying is complete, press any key to return to the Assist screen.

Double-check your work. Press [U], highlight Browse, and press [Enter]. Only the first ten records should appear, as shown in the screen in Figure 9-5.

4. Make a copy of all records in NAD.DBF for the five fields NAME, ADDRESS, CITY, STATE, and ZIP. You'll build a field list for this copy. Make sure NAD.DBF is current. Then press [O], [↑], and then [Enter]. Type **NADTRUE** and press [Enter]. (After all, the true name-

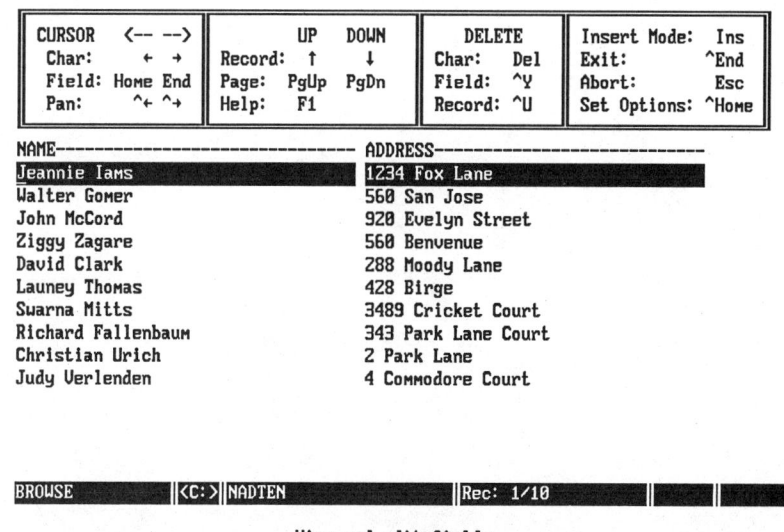

```
┌─────────────────────┬──────────────────┬──────────────────┬──────────────────────┐
│ CURSOR    <-- -->   │      UP   DOWN   │    DELETE        │ Insert Mode:   Ins   │
│ Char:      ← →      │ Record:  ↑   ↓   │ Char:     Del    │ Exit:          ^End  │
│ Field: Home End     │ Page:  PgUp PgDn │ Field:    ^Y     │ Abort:         Esc   │
│ Pan:       ^← ^→    │ Help:   F1       │ Record:   ^U     │ Set Options:   ^Home │
└─────────────────────┴──────────────────┴──────────────────┴──────────────────────┘
 NAME─────────────────────────── ADDRESS───────────────────────
 Jeannie Iams                    1234 Fox Lane
 Walter Gomer                    560 San Jose
 John McCord                     920 Evelyn Street
 Ziggy Zagare                    560 Benvenue
 David Clark                     288 Moody Lane
 Launey Thomas                   428 Birge
 Swarna Mitts                    3489 Cricket Court
 Richard Fallenbaum              343 Park Lane Court
 Christian Urich                 2 Park Lane
 Judy Verlenden                  4 Commodore Court


 ▐BROWSE      ▌▐<C:>▌▐NADTEN        ▌▐Rec: 1/10  ▌▐     ▌▐  ▌
                     View and edit fields.
```

FIGURE 9-5. Records copied to NADTEN.DBF and viewed in the Browse screen

and-address database contains only names and addresses.) When the Search/Scope menu appears, highlight the command "Build a field list" and press [Enter]. When the list of field names appears, press [Enter] five times. This should select the five fields NAME, ADDRESS, CITY, STATE, and ZIP. You can see them stack up on the action line.

Press [←] to close the list of field names. When the Search/Scope menu reappears, highlight the command "Execute the command" and press [Enter]. When dBASE has finished copying the new file, view the results in the Edit screen. This is the best way to view the list of fields in each record. Press [U], highlight Edit, and press [Enter]. The results should look like the screen in Figure 9-6.

5. Make a copy of all the records in NAD.DBF that contain entries in California. You'll build a search condition for this copy. Make sure NAD.DBF is current. Then press [O], [↑], then [Enter]. Type **NADCA**

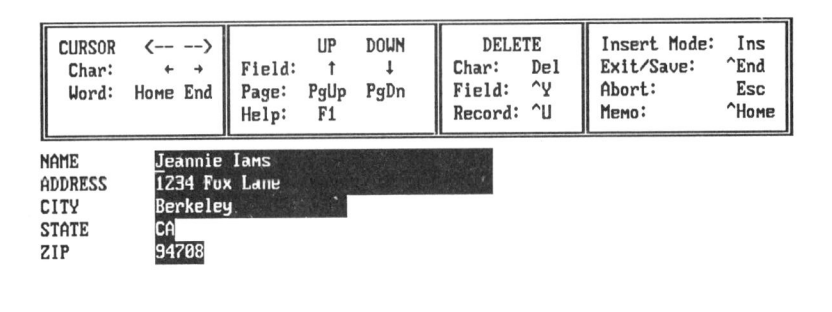

FIGURE 9-6. Records copied to NADTRUE.DBF viewed in Edit screen

Chapter 9   Organizing a Database   **205**

and press [Enter]. When the Search/Scope menu appears, highlight the command "Build a search condition" and press [Enter]. When the list of field names appears, highlight STATE and press [Enter]. dBASE asks for the field information you want to base the search and selection on. Type **CA** and press [Enter]. Make sure you use all uppercase letters.

When the Search/Scope menu reappears, highlight the command "Execute the command" and press [Enter]. When dBASE has finished copying the new file, it should show that 18 records were copied to NADCA.DBF.

Exercises

1. How many different ways can you copy database files by using the command Copy on the Organize menu?

2. Describe the different ways you can copy database files.

3. How do you select fields and records to copy?

4. Make a copy of NAD.DBF to a copy called MONEY.DBF, selecting only the NAME, PHONE, and MONEY fields. Return to the Assist.

5. Make a copy of NAD.DBF to a copy called OWES.DBF, selecting only those fields in which the amounts in the MONEY field are greater than $499. Then return to the Assist.

EXERCISES

1. Index NAD.DBF on the DATE field to DATE.NDX. Display the results in the Browse screen. Return to the Assist.

    MASTERY SKILLS CHECK

2. Index NAD.DBF on both the DATE and PAID fields, in that order, to DATEPAID.NDX. Display the results in the Browse screen. Return to the Assist.

3. Sort NAD.DBF on the ZIP field. Display the results in the Browse screen. Return to the Assist.

4. Sort NAD.DBF on the ZIP and NAME fields, in that order to a file called ZIPNAME. Display the results in the Browse screen. Return to the Assist.

5. Make a copy of NAD.DBF to UPDATE.DBF, selecting the NAME, PHONE, and MONEY fields and only those records that owe you more than $499. Then return to the Assist.

INTEGRATING SKILLS CHECK

1. Find out what dBASE help has to say about the Index command on the Organize menu, and then close help.

2. Find out what dBASE help has to say about the Sort command on the Organize menu, and then close help.

3. Begin in the Assist screen and create the database NAME.DBF with one field called NAME, and make it a character type field of 30 spaces. Insert the following three entries into the database:

   Record 1   Walrus
   Record 2   Minnow
   Record 3   Anteater

   Index the database on the NAME field to NAME.NDX. View the results in the Browse screen. (They should appear in alphabetical order, with Anteater at the top.) Return to the Assist.

4. Close NAD.DBF by exiting dBASE, and then reload the program and make NAD.DBF current without attaching an index.

5. Append a new record to NAME.DBF, using the name Aardvark. Do not update the index NAME.NDX. Instead, attach the now out-of-date index to NAME.DBF and view the results in the Browse screen.

6. Explain why the record for Aardvark doesn't show. Return to the Assist.

7. Sort NAME.DBF on the NAME field to NEWNAME.DBF. View the results in the Browse screen. Return to the Assist.

8. Copy all the contents of NAD.DBF to a file called DEBTS.DBF, and then return to the Assist.

Simple Printing
▶10◀

CHAPTER OBJECTIVES

In this chapter you will learn how to

▶ Print a single screen 10.1

▶ Use the List command 10.2

▶ Use the Display command 10.3

Viewing and studying database information printed on paper is crucial to every database manager's job. You can manipulate records and fields on your computer screen to compare and contrast information, but periodically you have to set the facts down on paper.

Sometimes you'll want to print information about selected records on the spot so you can check records for errors, or keep a paper copy of the record information handy. At other times, usually after a period of time such as at the beginning or end of each month, you need to print out all the records in a database using a standard form. These are historical records of the database information showing all changes made during the month. Managers use this information to track trends and changes over longer periods of time, such as calendar quarters, selling seasons, and even years.

There are many ways you can print information while working in dBASE III PLUS. Your choices run the gamut from printing a single screen to printing sophisticated reports that include information from several databases.

Most of the time, when you want to print database information, you'll use one of the four commands at the top of the Retrieve menu:

List   Displays a continuous list of the contents of records in the current database that meet the criteria you specify in the Search/Scope menu

Display   Displays the contents of 1 to 15 records in the current database that meet the criteria you specify, and then pauses. Press any key to see the next screenful if there are more records to display

Report   Prints records by using the report file you select. The report file must already have been created and designed by using the Create Report screen and then saved to disk

Label   Prints records using the label file you select. The label file must already have been created and designed by using the Create Label screen and then saved to disk

Whenever you select one of the commands List, Report, or Label, dBASE presents two features in sequence before you can actually begin any printing. The first feature is the Search/Scope menu. You learned how to use the commands on this menu in Chapter 6, when you learned about the command Locate. You've since used it for other commands as well. You use this menu to select the group of records you want to print.

The second feature dBASE presents is a prompt that asks whether you want to print the information to your screen or to a printer. The prompt looks like this: "Direct the output to the printer? Y/N." If you press [Enter], dBASE accepts N as the default answer and directs the printed output to your screen. To print the information on a paper printer, you must press [Y]. In this chapter, you'll learn how to print both to your screen and to the printer.

NOTE: To print successfully, be sure you have a printer attached to your computer, that the printer is turned on, and that it is filled with paper. These are obvious conditions, but ones that are often overlooked by eager students.

There's a fifth command in Assist that can give you printed output. This is the command "List structure" on the Tools pull-down menu. Whenever you select this command, dBASE asks where you want to send the output, and then prints the field names, types, and widths to the device you select.

In this chapter, you'll learn how to print database information in three ways: to a single screen, by using the command List, and by using the command Display. Printing dBASE information by using reports and labels is covered in separate chapters devoted to creating and printing reports (Chapter 12) and creating and printing labels (Chapter 13).

You should realize that dBASE doesn't have much capacity to print attractive formats. At best, you're limited to selecting fields and records to print. When you work with reports, you can add headers, footers, and other incidental text. And you can add boxes and lines. But don't expect fancy page formatting.

Exercises

SKILLS CHECK

1. Make NAD.DBF current. View the records in the Edit screen, and then return to the Assist screen.

2. View the contents in the Browse screen. Highlight the last record in the database. Highlight record 10. Highlight the first record. Return to the Assist screen.

3. When you work in the Assist, where does dBASE display the current record number?

4. Go to several records while remaining in the Assist screen. First go to the bottom of the database. Check the status bar to make sure. Go to record 10. Check the status bar. Go to the top record. Check the status bar.

5. Attach NAME.NDX to NAD.DBF.

6. Unattach NAME.NDX from NAD.DBF.

10.1 PRINT A SINGLE SCREEN

Printing database information to a single screen uses a print function built into DOS, not into dBASE. This is called the DOS *print screen function,* and it's available in all programs that run in DOS. This function sends the screen image you're looking at to the printer. To print the screen you're viewing, press [Shift]-[PrtSc]. On some keyboards, the second key is marked [PrtSc].

The printout in Figure 10-1 shows the result of printing a dBASE screen to a printer by using this method. The figure shows the Browse screen displaying the first screenful of records in NAD.DBF. The printed details vary widely depending upon the quality of your printer. In some cases, particularly with dot-matrix printers, graphic features on the screen, such as pull-down menus and other boxed-in

```
NAME-------------------------------    ADDRESS--------------------------
Jeannie Iams                           1234 Fox Lane
Walter Gomer                           560 San Jose
John McCord                            920 Evelyn Street
Ziggy Zagare                           560 Benvenue
Stan Freeburg                          1 Chuckles Lane
David Clark                            288 Moody Lane
Launey Thomas                          428 Birge
Swarna Mitts                           3489 Cricket Court
Richard Fallenbaum                     343 Park Lane Court
Christian Urich                        2 Park Lane
Judy Verlenden                         4 Commodore Court
Carol Hanne                            19 Marin Lane
Dave Trollman                          34 Sack Court
Carol McGinnis                         1234 Old Stagecoach Rd
Margaret Smith                         456 Primrose Rd
Roger Smith                            567 Blake Street
Roger Stewart                          567 Blake Street
Cornelius Ragg                         678 Sansome


BROWSE              <C:>  NAD                    Rec:  1/20
                            View and edit fields.
```

FIGURE 10-1. The Browse screen printed by using the DOS print screen command

features, will appear as letter characters and not the graphic line characters you were expecting. In most cases, you'll get an imperfect representation of what you see on the screen.

You can improve the quality of these single printings by loading the DOS TSR program GRAPHICS.COM when you first boot your computer. You can also improve the quality with other utility programs. These programs are not worth the trouble unless you find yourself printing a lot of screens by using the DOS print screen command. You should not view the DOS print screen function as something you'll use for most of your printing. It is designed for quick, and rudimentary, printings of screen information that you want to save for reference before your screen image changes.

Printing a single screen means that you print only what you see on your screen. If you're looking at database information displayed in the Browse screen, position the records in the database so the ones you want to print are displayed on screen. This might take a bit of maneuvering. If you want a series of records, you might have to print multiple screens, one after the other. To do this, press [Shift]-[PrtSc], press [PgDn] to display the next screen, press [Shift]-[PrtSc] a second time, and so on, until you've printed all the records.

Printing single screens by using record information displayed in the Edit screen can be a quick and helpful way to double-check individual record information.

When dBASE displays the contents of a single record, you will see the message "Press any key to return to the Assist." If you press the key-combination [Shift]-[PrtSc] instead, you'll print the current screen to the printer. When the printing is complete, the displayed record will remain on screen. You have to press another key to return to the Assist.

Examples

1. Use the DOS print screen command to print the contents of record 1 in NAD.DBF while it's displayed in the Edit screen. First make sure NAD.DBF is current. If record 1 isn't the current record, press [P] to open the Position menu, press [↑] to highlight Goto Record, and press [Enter] twice, the second time to execute the command TOP.

    Now open the Edit screen: Press [U], highlight Edit, and press [Enter]. Once the contents for record 1 are displayed in the Edit screen, print the screen: Press [Shift]-[PrtSc].

2. Use the DOS print screen command to print the contents of the first screenful of records in NAD.DBF, as shown in Figure 10-1. First press [Esc] to close the Edit screen. Highlight Browse and press [Enter]. Now press [Shift]-[PrtSc].

Exercises

1. Is the DOS print screen function available in dBASE only?

2. Make a DOS print of the Assist interface.

3. Make a DOS print of record 8 displayed in the Edit screen, and then return to the Assist screen.

USE THE LIST COMMAND   10.2

You can print information in a database by using the command List. Printing all or part of the information in a database this way results in a more attractive printout.

The command List is designed to print information from a group of similar records. You select the group by using commands on the Search/Scope menu attached to the command List. The easiest way to start out printing database information with the command List is to print all of the fields and records in a database. First make sure the database you want to print is current. Then

a. Press [R] to open the Retrieve menu.

b. Press [Enter] to accept the command List at the top of the menu. This opens the Search/Scope menu for the command List.

c. Press [Enter] to accept the command "Execute the command" at the top of the menu.

d. Press [Enter] to accept the default answer N. This sends a listed output of all records in every field to your screen. The list will

```
      Set Up  Create  Update  Position  Retrieve  Organize Modify Tools  12:13:33 pm
   Record# NAME                              ADDRESS
   CITY                    STATE ZIP   PHONE    MONEY DATE      PAID NOTES
        1 Jeannie Iams                  1234 Fox Lane
   Berkeley                CA    94708 415-456-7890  92.12 12/25/89 .F. Memo
        2 Walter Gomer                  560 San Jose
   Kensington              CA    94720 415-567-8900 150.00 01/07/90 .F. Memo
        3 John McCord                   920 Evelyn Street
   Albany                  CA    94708 415-525-5614 200.00 10/15/89 .F. Memo
        4 Ziggy Zagare                  560 Benvenue
   El Cerrito              CA    94530 415-527-8745 450.00 11/20/89 .F. Memo
        5 Stan Freeburg                 1 Chuckles Lane
   Westport                CT    06530 203-567-5434  25.00 11/25/89 .F. Memo
        6 David Clark                   288 Moody Lane
   Oakland                 CA    94612 415-899-0075  25.00 12/25/89 .F. Memo
        7 Launey Thomas                 428 Birge
   Berkeley                CA    94704 415-343-6978  50.00 07/11/89 .F. Memo
        8 Swarna Mitts                  3489 Cricket Court
   Richmond                CA    97540 415-785-6454 450.00 11/08/89 .F. Memo
        9 Richard Fallenbaum            343 Park Lane Court
   Piedmont
   ASSIST        |<C:>|NAD              |Rec: 1/20
```

FIGURE 10-2. Listing NAD.DBF to screen

scroll from the bottom to the top and then disappear off the top of your screen. The screen in Figure 10-2 shows the result of running the command List when NAD.DBF is current.

If you print the output to the printer, the result will look something like the printout in Figure 10-3. The information is displayed in a different format than when the information is printed to screen. This is because different margins have probably been set for your screen than for the printer. You can't change the screen margins by using any settings in dBASE. They are controlled by your screen display hardware and the setup in the printer.

NOTE: You can change the printed effects by changing the settings in the printer. If you want to experiment with different printer settings, refer to your printer manual.

Jeannie Iams Berkeley	1234 Fox Lane
Walter Gomer Kensington	560 San Jose
John McCord Albany	920 Evelyn Street
Ziggy Zagare El Cerrito	560 Behrens
Stan Freeberg Westport	1 Chuckles Lane
David Clark Oakland	288 Moody Lane
Launey Thomas Berkeley	428 Birge
Swarna Mitts Richmond	3489 Cricket Court
Richard Fallenbaum Piedmont	343 Park Lane Court
Christian Urich San Francisco	2 Park Lane
Judy Verlenden Carmel Valley	4 Commodore Court
Carol Hanna Aptos	19 Marin Lane
Dave Trollman Redwood City	34 Sack Court
Carol McGinnis Tucson	1234 Old Stagecoach Rd
Margaret Smith Redwood City	456 Primrose Place
Roger Smith Berkeley	567 Blake Street
Cornelius Ragg San Francisco	678 Sansome Street
Charles Vernon San Francisco	6600 California
Ahma Price-Smith El Sobrante	34 Bentley
Pat Smith Mill Valley	45 Millwood

FIGURE 10-3. Listing NAD.DBF to paper

When you display the scrolling list of information on your screen, you can freeze the scrolling at any point by pressing (Ctrl)-(S). You unfreeze the scrolling by pressing any key. Whenever you freeze the screen, you can print the current screenful of information to your printer by using (Shift)-(PrtSc). This does not turn scrolling back on again. You have to press any other key to restart scrolling.

You can list records in an indexed database to your screen or printer in the index order by attaching the index to the database first, and then running the List command.

You can narrow down the group of records that will be printed by specifying a scope or by building scope or search conditions. You can also narrow down the fields that are displayed for each record by building a list of fields that will be printed. This latter method is perhaps the best and quickest way to adjust the amount of information printed on each line.

You might have to juggle the fields you select to print. When you use the command List, dBASE prints records according to the width defined for each field. This means that sometimes field information appears too far apart, at other times too close together. You shouldn't modify the structure of a database by adjusting field widths to make your listed information look better. Listing database information is a quick way to get a clean printout. If you want something that looks more attractive, you should design and create reports. These provide much better control over the format and appearance of printed database information.

When you construct a list of fields to print, you might want to view the result on screen first. Although the format isn't the same as on paper, it will give you an idea of how much space the selected fields will occupy on each line.

Examples

1. List all the records of people in NAD.DBF who owe you $100 or more. First, make sure NAD.DBF is current. Press (R) to open the Retrieve menu. Highlight List and press (Enter). Highlight "Build a

search condition" and press [Enter]. Highlight MONEY and press [Enter]. Highlight > = Greater Than or Equal To and press [Enter]. Type **100** and press [Enter] twice, once to enter the number, the second time to select "No more conditions." Highlight "Execute the command" and press [Enter] twice. Your screen should change to look something like the one in Figure 10-4. Press any key to return to the Assist.

2. Narrow down the number of displayed fields to three: NAME, PHONE, and MONEY. First, make sure NAD.DBF is current. Then press [R] to open the Retrieve menu, highlight List, and press [Enter]. Highlight "Construct a field list" and press [Enter]. The first field, NAME, is highlighted, so press [Enter]. Highlight PHONE and press

```
      Set Up  Create  Update  Position  Retrieve  Organize Modify Tools   12:15:23 pm


        Record#  NAME                          ADDRESS
        CITY              STATE ZIP   PHONE       MONEY DATE      PAID NOTES
             2  Walter Gomer                     560 San Jose
        Kensington         CA   94720 415-567-8900 150.00 01/07/90 .F.  Memo
             3  John McCord                      920 Evelyn Street
        Albany             CA   94708 415-525-5614 200.00 10/15/89 .F.  Memo
             4  Ziggy Zagare                     560 Benvenue
        El Cerrito         CA   94530 415-527-8745 450.00 11/20/89 .F.  Memo
             8  Swarna Mitts                     3489 Cricket Court
        Richmond           CA   97540 415-785-6454 450.00 11/08/89 .F.  Memo
             9  Richard Fallenbaum               343 Park Lane Court
        Piedmont           CA   97455 415-333-1217 900.00 12/06/89 .F.  Memo
            10  Christian Smith                  2 Park Lane
        San Francisco      CA   94017 415-678-4321 175.00 08/13/89 .F.  Memo
            11  Judy Verlenden                   4 Commodore Court
        Carmel Valley      CA   93924 408-233-4554 235.00 07/10/89 .F.  Memo
            12  Carol Hanna                      19 Marin Lane
        Aptos              CA   95003 408-56
        ASSIST         |<C:>|NAD              |Rec: 10/20
```

FIGURE 10-4. Listing records who owe $100 or more

⏎. Highlight MONEY and press ⏎. The three field names you've selected, NAME, PHONE, and MONEY, should appear on the action line.

Press ← to close the "Construct a field list" menu. Highlight "Execute the command" and press ⏎ twice. The screen on Figure 10-5 shows the result when the scrolling is frozen at the start.

3. List the three fields NAME, PHONE, and MONEY for all records in which people owe you more than $500. First, make sure NAD.DBF is current. Then press R, highlight List, and press ⏎. Highlight "Construct a field list" and press ⏎. Highlight NAME and press ⏎, highlight PHONE and press ⏎, and then highlight MONEY and press ⏎. Press ← to close the list.

Now build the search condition. Highlight "Build a search condition" and press ⏎. Highlight MONEY and press ⏎.

```
 Set Up   Create   Update   Position   Retrieve   Organize Modify Tools    12:17:53 pm
 Record#  NAME                              PHONE           MONEY
       1  Jeannie Iams                      415-456-7890     92.12
       2  Walter Gomer                      415-567-8900    150.00
       3  John McCord                       415-525-5614    200.00
       4  Ziggy Zagare                      415-527-8745    450.00
       5  Stan Freeburg                     203-567-5434     25.00
       6  David Clark                       415-899-0075     25.00
       7  Launey Thomas                     415-343-6978     50.00
       8  Swarna Mitts                      415-785-6454    450.00
       9  Richard Fallenbaum                415-333-1217    900.00
      10  Christian Smith                   415-678-4321    175.00
      11  Judy Verlenden                    408-233-4554    235.00
      12  Carol Hanna                       408-567-3345    850.00
      13  David Trollman                    415-865-9090    600.00
      14  Carol McGinnis                    602-873-4457    500.00
      15  Margaret Smith                    415-645-9034    250.00
      16  Roger Smith                       415-896-7534    150.00
      17  Cornelius Ragg                    415-743-6520    200.00
      18  Charles Smith                     415-875-4567    340.00
      19  Amma Smith
 ASSIST          |<C:>|NAD           |Rec: EOF/20
```

FIGURE 10-5.   Listing the three fields NAME, PHONE, and MONEY

Highlight > Greater Than and press [Enter]. Type 500 and press [Enter] twice, first to insert the value, second to accept the command "No more conditions." Highlight "Execute the command" and press [Enter]. The result will look like the screen in Figure 10-6.

4. List the contents of NAD.DBF in the indexed order of NAME.NDX. First, attach the index. Press [S], press [Enter] twice, highlight NAD, press [Enter], and press [Y]. Highlight NAME and press [→].

Now list the records in the index order. Press [R], and then [Enter] three times. Watch the scrolling result. Press any key to return to the Assist.

```
Set Up  Create  Update  Position  Retrieve  Organize Modify Tools   12:19:06 pm




                     Record#  NAME                  PHONE          MONEY
                          9   Richard Fallenbaum    415-333-1217   900.00
                         12   Carol Hanna           408-567-3345   850.00
                         13   David Trollman        415-865-9090   600.00
                   ASSIST       |<C:>|NAD              |Rec: 1/20
                          Press any key to continue work in ASSIST._
```

FIGURE 10-6. Listing selected fields and records

Exercises

1. Print to paper a list of the names and addresses (including city, state, and ZIP Code) for all people in NAD.DBF.

2. Print on screen the records for everyone who owes you more than $500, and then return to the Assist.

3. Print on screen the name of everyone who owes you more than $500, and then return to the Assist.

10.3 USE THE DISPLAY COMMAND

The command Display is used to display the contents of records in screenfuls. If you don't specify any conditions by using the Search/Scope menu, you'll print the current record to your screen. You used the command Display first in Chapter 6 to display the contents of a single record.

When you select a group of records to display and the group contains more than a screenful of records, dBASE asks you after each screenful if you want to see the next screenful. dBASE says that if you do, "Press any key." Actually, pressing [Esc] stops the display. Pressing any key other than [Esc] at the dBASE question displays the next screenful. If you press [Esc] to stop the display, pressing any key returns you to the Assist screen. The command Display won't print any information to your printer, although you can print the screen by using the DOS print screen function.

The command Display differs from the command List in two ways. First, while the command Display can display more than one record on the screen, it can't display more than a screenful at a time. The command List can scroll a list of records on screen or print the records to your printer. Second, when you use the command Display, you can't print records to paper. You can only display records on your screen.

Chapter 10 Simple Printing

To display the current record:

a. Make sure the record you want to display is current.

b. Press [R] to open the Retrieve menu.

c. Highlight the command Display and press [Enter]. dBASE presents the Search/Scope menu, highlighting the command "Execute the command."

d. Press [Enter]. dBASE displays the contents of the current record on your screen, as shown by the screen in Figure 10-7.

```
  Set Up  Create  Update  Position  Retrieve  Organize Modify Tools   12:19:58 pm
```

```
  Record#  NAME                            ADDRESS
           CITY           STATE ZIP  PHONE      MONEY DATE       PAID NOTES
       1   Jeannie Iams                    1234 Fox Lane
           Berkeley       CA    94708 415-456-7890 92.12 12/25/89 .F.  Memo

  ASSIST          <C:> NAD                  Rec: 1/20
                    Press any key to continue work in ASSIST._
```

| FIGURE 10-7. | Displaying the current record |

You can display a series of up to 15 records by constructing search-and-scope conditions, and you can narrow down the fields that are displayed for each record by constructing a field list.

If an index is attached to the current database and you select to display (print to screen) all the records in the database, they will appear in the indexed order.

Examples

1. To display the first record in NAD.DBF, first make sure NAD.DBF is current. Then press (R), highlight Display, and press (Enter). Highlight "Specify scope" and press (Enter). Highlight RECORD, press (Enter), and then type 1 and press (Enter). Now highlight the command "Execute the command" and press (Enter). The contents of record 1 will be displayed on screen. Press any key to return to the Assist.

2. To display the NAME, PHONE, and MONEY field contents for the first record in NAD.DBF, press (R), highlight Display, and press (Enter). (The first record should still be the current record from the previous example, but double-check this on the status bar.) Highlight "Construct a field list" and press (Enter) twice, first to execute the command, second to select the NAME field. Highlight PHONE and press (Enter). Highlight MONEY and press (Enter). Press (←) to close the field list. Highlight "Execute the command" and press (Enter). Your screen should look like the one in Figure 10-8.

3. To display the NAME, PHONE, and MONEY field contents for all records in NAD.DBF that owe you more than $500, make sure you start at the beginning of the database. Press (P), highlight Goto Record, and press (Enter) twice.

    Now select the fields you want to display. Press (R), highlight Display, then press (Enter). Highlight "Construct a field list" and

```
          Set Up  Create  Update  Position  Retrieve  Organize Modify Tools  12:20:34 pm




                    Record#  NAME                          PHONE        MONEY
                         1   Jeannie Iams                  415-456-7890 92.12
                    ASSIST         |<C:>|NAD              |Rec: 1/20
                               Press any key to continue work in ASSIST._
```

| FIGURE 10-8. | Displaying NAME, PHONE, and MONEY fields in the current record |

press (Enter) twice, the second time to select the NAME field. Highlight PHONE and press (Enter). Highlight MONEY to select that field and select (Enter). Press (←) to close the field list.

Now construct the search condition. Highlight "Build a search condition" and press (Enter). Highlight MONEY and press (Enter). Highlight > Greater Than and press (Enter). Type **500** and press (Enter) twice, once to insert that value, a second time to accept "No more conditions." Highlight "Execute the command" and press (Enter).

4. To display all the records in NAD.DBF according to the indexed order of NAME.NDX, first make sure NAD.DBF is current and NAME.NDX is attached. Press (S), press (Enter) twice, highlight NAD, and press (Enter). Press (Y), highlight NAME, and press (→).

Now begin the display. Press R, highlight Display, and press (Enter). Highlight "Specify scope" and press (Enter), and then highlight ALL and press (Enter). Now highlight "Execute the command" and press (Enter). It will take two screenfuls to display all the records in NAD.DBF. Then press any key to return to the Assist screen.

Exercises

1. Display the bottom record in NAD.DBF, and then return to the Assist.

2. Display the NAME and PHONE field information for record 1.

3. Display the contents of the next three records (records 2, 3, and 4), and then return to the Assist.

4. Display the names and amounts for people in NAD.DBF who owe you more than $500.

5. What are the two differences between the commands Display and List?

EXERCISES

MASTERY SKILLS CHECK

1. Make sure NAD.DBF is current. List all records in NAD.DBF to the screen. Then display the first record to the screen. Do not return to the Assist.

2. Print a copy of the record displayed on screen to the printer. Once you have a successful print, return to the Assist.

3. List all records in NAD.DBF to your printer, using the NAME, ADDRESS, CITY, STATE, and ZIP fields only.

4. Display the last record in NAD.DBF, and then return to the Assist.

1. Begin in Assist and find out what dBASE on-line help has to say about the commands List and Display on the Retrieve menu.

2. Make VALUE.DBF current and list all records to the screen. Then list all records to the printer.

3. Attach NAME.NDX to NAD.DBF. Display the first 15 records, and then return to the Assist.

INTEGRATING SKILLS CHECK

Creating and Using Formats
▶11◀

CHAPTER OBJECTIVES

Completing this chapter will help you to

▶ Become familiar with the Create Format screen   11.1

▶ Select a database   11.2

▶ Design and use format files   11.3

▶ Modify and enhance format files   11.4

▶ Create more complex features   11.5

Format files are entry forms you use to append information to and edit information in records in a database. You create, design, and use format files to change the way database fields appear on your screen when you append and update records in a database. This lets you arrange the fields in a more convenient or appealing format on your screen, display only those fields you want to use, and lock out those fields you don't want to enter information into.

Up to this point, you've used the default features dBASE III PLUS provides when you want to append new records to a database or to edit information that already exists in a database. These are the Append screen, which you learned how to use in Chapter 4, and the Edit and Browse screens, which you learned about in Chapter 5.

In this chapter, you'll learn how to customize the way field names appear on the screen so you can add new records and update existing information in a database by using only the fields you want to use and in the order you want to use them. You do this by creating and designing what are called *format files,* or files that control the formatted appearance of the screen while working in dBASE.

You'll follow these five steps when you create, design, and use format files while working in dBASE III PLUS:

a. Select the database you want to base your format file upon.

b. Design the format file, using fields in the database you've selected or created by using the Create screen for format files.

c. Return to dBASE and load the format file so it controls your screen.

d. Enter information into and edit information in a database through the customized format file by using the commands Append and Edit.

e. Modify the format file and refine it for your continued use by using the Modify screen for format files.

These steps require that you use five commands in the Assist: the command Format on the Create pull-down menu, the command Format for Screen on the Set Up pull-down menu, the command

Format on the Modify menu, and the commands Append and Edit on the Update menu. You'll also use other commands within the Create and Modify screens for format files.

Exercises

1. Begin in the Assist screen and make NAD.DBF current. List the structure of NAD.DBF on screen.

2. Display the list of field names, types, and widths.

3. Return to the Assist screen.

SKILLS CHECK

BECOME FAMILIAR WITH THE CREATE FORMAT SCREEN

11.1

You use the command Format on the Create pull-down menu to create format files. This moves you into a full-screen component of the dBASE program called the Create screen for format files. This screen contains its own pull-down menu structure.

To see the commands on these menus:

a. Press [C] to open the Create menu.

b. Press [↓] to highlight the command Format and press [Enter].

c. Press [Enter] to accept the default disk drive.

d. Type **TEST** and press [Enter].

Your screen will change to display the Create screen for format files, as shown in Figure 11-1.

You can find four pull-down menu names on the top line of this screen. The Set Up menu is displayed each time you enter this screen. The upper-right corner displays a clock showing the current time. You'll use the broad middle area of the screen to position the fields you want to use for your format file.

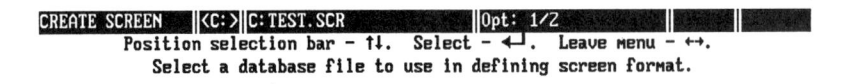

```
 Set Up            Modify         Options          Exit  12:30:36 pm
┌─────────────────────────────┐
│ Select Database File        │
│ Create New Database File    │
├─────────────────────────────┤
│ Load Fields                 │
└─────────────────────────────┘
```

```
CREATE SCREEN   |<C:>|C:TEST.SCR          |Opt: 1/2
             Position selection bar - ↑↓.  Select - ↵.  Leave menu - ↔.
             Select a database file to use in defining screen format.
```

FIGURE 11-1. The Create screen for format files

The bottom of this screen contains the three lines standard to most dBASE III PLUS screens: a status bar, a navigation line, and a message line. The status bar shows the name of the screen you're working in (CREATE SCREEN), the current drive letter (most likely C), the name of the format file you're designing (in Figure 11-1, it's called TEST.SCR).

dBASE assigns the extension .SCR to all format files you design in the Create screen. The extension stands for "Screen," which reminds you that format files control the way your screen displays field names and information.

You might be interested in knowing how dBASE implements format files. When you're finished designing a .SCR file and you save it to disk, dBASE automatically generates a matching .FMT file (which stands for "format") that actually controls the way field information appears on screen. The screen file you designed just controls the way dBASE designs the format file. dBASE gives the format file the same name as your screen file. For example, if you create a format for TEST.SCR and save it to disk, dBASE will generate a second file called TEST.FMT that actually formats the screen the way you designed TEST.SCR.

There are four pull-down menus you can use in the Create screen for format files:

Set Up	Three commands that let you select a database file to work with, create a new database file, or load specific fields from the database you've selected into your format file
Modify	Nine ways you can define the fields you want to use in your format file. You'll usually use this menu only for complex activities. It is described in the "Modifying and Enhancing Format Files" section of this chapter
Options	Three commands that allow you to generate a file containing all the commands in the screen file as well as to draw single or double lines on screen
Exit	Two commands that return you to the Assist screen. One lets you save your work, the other abandons any changes you've made to the current format file since you last saved it to disk

Table 11-1 shows a layout of these four menus.

The only help you can find in the Create screen for format files will be on the navigation and message lines. When you press [F1], nothing happens. dBASE will provide you with instructions on the message and navigation lines for all situations as you design and modify format files.

You work with pull-down menus and their commands in the Create screen for format files in the same way that you work with menus in the Assist screen. That is, you can press [→] or [←] to scroll

| TABLE 11-1. | Layout for Pull-down Menus |

Set Up	Modify	Options	Exit
Select Database File	*Screen Field Definition	Generate text file image	Save
Create New Database File	Action: Display/SAY		Abandon
Load Fields	Source:	*Draw a window or line	
	Content:	Single bar	
	Type:	Double bar	
	Width:		
	Decimal:		
	Picture Function:		
	Picture Template:		
	Range:		

*These features are not commands, but instructions that describe what you can do with the commands beneath them.

through the menus. You can press the first letter of the menu name to open a menu, for example, [M] to open the Modify menu. And you can press [Ctrl]-[F] to open the Exit menu or [Ctrl]-[A] to open the Set Up menu.

NOTE: There are two features in these menus that can never be accessed because they are instructions rather than commands. The first is the "Screen Field Definition" on the Modify menu and the second is "Draw a window or line" on the Options menu.

Repeatedly press [→] slowly to view the contents of the Modify, Options, and Exit pull-down menus. As you can see, most of the menu commands are disabled. This is because you haven't yet opened a database to work with. Make sure you return to the Set Up menu.

Once you begin selecting fields, you can use the Modify pull-down menu to modify and define each field precisely the way you want it to appear on the screen. You're given nine ways to define fields.

Once you've selected the fields you want to use and have defined and located them precisely where you want them to appear, you can use the Options menu to generate a text file that contains all the commands you've inserted into the screen file. This file contains all the dBASE commands that are necessary to generate the matching format file. You'll see an example of this file in the last section of this chapter.

You can also use the Options menu to draw single and double lines around features in the format file. Lines and boxes help set off fields or groups of fields from each other, as well as organize field information displayed on the screen.

At any point while you're working in the Create screen for format files, you can save your work to that point or you can abandon all the work you've done since your last save. If you haven't saved the file at all, nothing will remain on disk.

The easiest way to abandon your work is to press [Esc]. Since you haven't yet created anything for TEST.SCR:

a. Press [Esc]. dBASE asks "Are you sure you want to abandon operation? (Y/N)."

b. Press [Y]. This returns you to the Assist screen. No disk file TEST.SCR exists on disk because you never saved it.

Examples

1. Begin in the Assist screen and open the Create screen for a format file called SAMPLE. Press [C] to open the Create menu, [↓] to highlight the command Format, and then [Enter] twice. Type **SAMPLE** and press [Enter].

2. Become familiar with pull-down menus and commands in the Create screen for format files. Press [Ctrl]-[F] to open the Exit menu directly. Press [O] to open the Options menu, and then press [M] to open the Modify menu. Press [Ctrl]-[A] to open the Set Up menu directly. Press [↓] to highlight the command Create New

Database File. Press Ctrl-E to highlight the top command on this menu. Press E to open the Exit menu. Press Ctrl-C to highlight the bottom command, Abandon. Press Enter to execute this command. Press Y to confirm that you want to abandon all changes.

Exercises

1. Working in the Assist screen, how do you open the Create screen for format files?

2. What are the default extensions dBASE gives to the two files that make up format files, and what do they stand for?

3. Do you have to make a database current before you open the Create screen for format files?

4. Name two commands you can use to open the Exit menu directly in the Create screen for format files.

5. Name two commands you can use to open the Set Up menu directly in the Create screen for format files.

11.2 SELECT A DATABASE

When you design a format file, you select field names from a database file that you want to display and insert them into the format file. You can pick the position where the field names and information will appear, and you can adjust the amount of information that will be shown. You can also insert certain graphic features, such as single and double lines, and text characters. But until you select a database to use, you can't design a format file.

You can select a database to use in three different ways:

Chapter 11　　　　　　　　　　　　　　　　Creating and Using Formats　**237**

- Select an existing database file first, and then enter the Create screen for format files.
- Open the Create screen first, and then select an existing database file. This is the easiest method.
- Open the Create screen first, create the database file you want to use, and then select it. This is a complex procedure and is described in the last section of this chapter.

The database file you base your format file upon doesn't have to contain any information in it. You work only with the structure of a database, not the data itself.

If you select a database before entering the Create screen for format files, make sure that the correct database name appears on the status bar of the Assist screen. Once you enter the Create screen, you can double-check the current database file name by checking the Source field in the Modify menu. Just press [M] to open the Modify menu. The name of the current database will show in the field for Source. You'll see how this works shortly, with the first example.

If you want to select the database after you enter the Create screen:

a. Press [S] to open the Setup menu if it is not already showing.

b. Press [Enter] to execute the top command, Select Database File. dBASE displays a list of available database file names.

c. Highlight the database name you want to use and press [Enter].

Selecting a database while working in the Create screen lets you change your mind about which database to use without having to exit the Create screen.

Once you've selected a database to work with, most of the pull-down menu commands will be enabled.

Examples

1. Begin in the Assist screen and create a format file called NAD.SCR based on NAD.DBF. First, make sure NAD.DBF is current. Next, open the Create screen for format files: press [C], [↓], and [Enter]

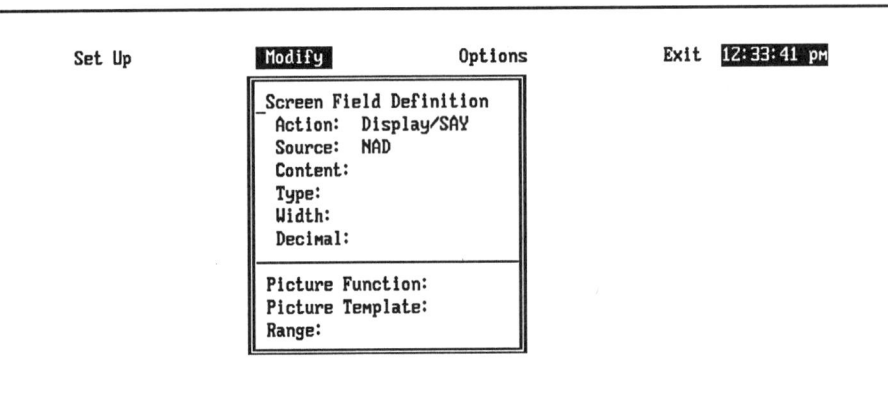

```
       Set Up           Modify          Options        Exit  12:33:41 pm
                       ┌─────────────────────────┐
                       │_Screen Field Definition │
                       │ Action:   Display/SAY   │
                       │ Source:   NAD           │
                       │ Content:                │
                       │ Type:                   │
                       │ Width:                  │
                       │ Decimal:                │
                       │                         │
                       │ Picture Function:       │
                       │ Picture Template:       │
                       │ Range:                  │
                       └─────────────────────────┘




CREATE SCREEN    |<C:>||C:NAD.SCR           |Opt: None    |     |
      Position selection bar - ↑↓. Select - ↵. Leave menu - ↔. Blackboard - F10.
```

FIGURE 11-2.	The Modify menu showing NAD as the source file

twice, type **NAD**, and press (Enter) once again. Until you become comfortable with format files, you should probably use the same name as the database you're going to base the format file upon.

You can tell right away that a database has been selected. The bottom command on the Set Up menu, called Load Fields, suddenly becomes enabled. You can scroll through the other menus if you want to see the other commands that are now enabled.

Check to make sure NAD is the source database: Press (M) to open the Modify pull-down menu. Your screen should look like the one in Figure 11-2. Notice the database name NAD in the Source field.

2. Select another database while you're working in the Create screen. With the Set Up menu displayed in the Create screen, highlight the command Select Database File and press (Enter). A box will open and display database files available in the current directory.

Select SAMPLE, which you created in Chapter 5: press (↓) once to highlight the file name, and then press [Enter]. Once again, the command Load Fields should appear enabled.

Whenever you start designing a format file based upon a database, you should double-check that the correct database has been selected. Press [→] and check the file name in the Source field.

Exercises

1. Do you have to select a database file before you design a format file?

2. Do you have to select a database file before you enter the Create screen for format files?

3. Can you build a database while you are designing a format file?

4. What is the easiest way to select a database?

5. Select NAD.DBF while working in the Create screen for format files.

6. How do you check which database file you've selected?

DESIGN AND USE FORMAT FILES — 11.3

Once you've entered the Create screen for format files and selected a database to use, follow these five steps to design a format file:

a. Select field names from the database you want to use.

b. Insert the appropriate field names into the current format file.

c. Define each field in a special way if you want to.

d. Add additional features such as text, lines, and boxes to the file if you want to.

e. Save the format file to disk.

The third and fourth steps are optional; you might not want to make more complex changes to the format.

To select fields from the current database, insert the fields, save the file, and view the effect:

a. Press [S] to open the Set Up menu if it is not already open.

b. Press [↑] to highlight the bottom command, Load Fields. This opens a box of field names in the selected database. The top field is highlighted. Select fields from this box in the same way you selected fields while working in the Search/Scope menu. Highlight the field name and press [Enter].

c. Once you've selected all the fields you want to load, press [F10]. This inserts the selected fields in a group onto the screen. You're now working in a feature called the blackboard. Once you've inserted field names onto the blackboard, you can then work with the fields in various ways, changing their names and moving them around until you've created the design you want to use.

d. Press [E] to open the Exit menu, and then press [Enter] to execute the command Save, which saves the .SCR file and automatically creates the matching .FMT file. You can now use the format file to see how it positions fields on your screen.

e. Open the Edit or Append screen on the Update menu to view the effect of the new format file on your screen. Whenever you create a format file, it becomes the default method for displaying information from this database.

When you use a format file to display database information, remember that it has been built for the current database. As soon as you make another database current, the display format for the Edit and Append screens will revert to the default. This displays all fields along the left side of your screen.

When you build several different format files that apply to the same database, you can switch back and forth between format files by using the command Format for Screen on the Set Up menu in the Assist screen.

When designing a format file, you want to load only those fields that will be displayed on your screen. For example, if you want to create a format file that lets you load only the name, address, and phone number for new records in NAD.DBF, you would select the six fields NAME, ADDRESS, CITY, STATE, ZIP, and PHONE. Although NAD.DBF has grown to contain many more fields, there are times when you might only want to enter the names, addresses, and phone numbers of new people.

Before you begin the examples, you should understand the concept of the blackboard. This is the space underneath the pull-down menus. You might notice the message on the navigation line: "Blackboard - F10." This means that you press [F10] to work in the blackboard. Your screen will change to look like the one in Figure 11-3. In this case, no fields have been inserted. But you can see that the displayed menu has disappeared and that the cursor appears in the upper-left corner, on the second line from the top. Notice also that three position indicators, for page, row, and column, appear on the right side of the status bar. These change to reflect the current position of your cursor while you are working in the blackboard.

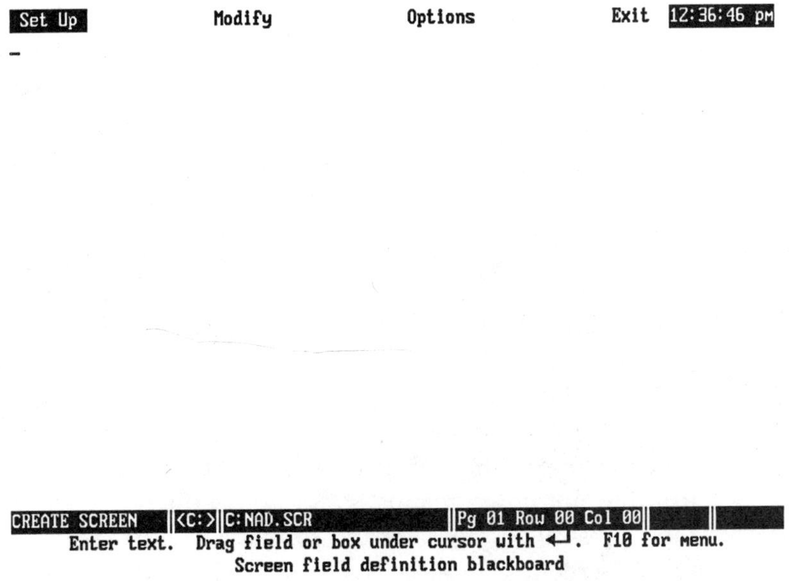

```
  Set Up           Modify           Options          Exit  12:36:46 pm
```

```
CREATE SCREEN  |<C:>|C:NAD.SCR        |Pg 01 Row 00 Col 00|
        Enter text.  Drag field or box under cursor with ←. F10 for menu.
                       Screen field definition blackboard
```

FIGURE 11-3. The blackboard

Notice the message on the navigation line: "F10 for menu." When working in the blackboard, you press [F10] to regain the use of the pull-down menus. Pressing [F10] repeatedly toggles you between using the blackboard and the pull-down menus.

Exit the Create screen for format files before you move on to the examples. Press [Esc] twice to return to the Assist screen.

Examples

1. Create a simple and clean format file you'll use to enter names, addresses, and phone numbers into records in NAD.DBF. Call the file NAD.SCR.

    Begin in the Assist screen, press [C] to open the Create menu, press [↓] to highlight the command Format, press [Enter] twice, type NAD, and press [Enter] once again. (Since you didn't save the format file with the same name that you viewed earlier, the file NAD.SCR doesn't exist on disk.)

    Now begin loading fields into the format file. Press [S] to open the Set Up menu, if it is not already showing. Highlight the command Load Fields and press [Enter]. A box listing all the fields in NAD.DBF will appear. Press [Enter] to select the top field, NAME, which is already highlighted. Notice that an arrow appears next to the selected field name. To select the ADDRESS field, press [↓] and then [Enter]. Another arrow will appear next to the field name. Continue to select the next four field names by pressing [↓], then [Enter] four more times.

    When the six fields NAME, ADDRESS, CITY, STATE, ZIP, and PHONE have been selected, press [F10] to insert them into the blackboard of NAD.SCR. Your screen should change to look like the one in Figure 11-4. The field names will appear on the left margin, and the field widths will extend to the right, filled with Xs displaying the number of spaces in each field width.

    Once the group of selected fields has been inserted, press [F10] to use the pull-down menus. Press [E] to open the Exit menu, and then press [Enter] to save the format file NAD.SCR and exit the Create screen.

    Now view the new format on screen. Press [U] to open the Update menu, highlight the command Edit, and press [Enter]. Your

Chapter 11   Creating and Using Formats **243**

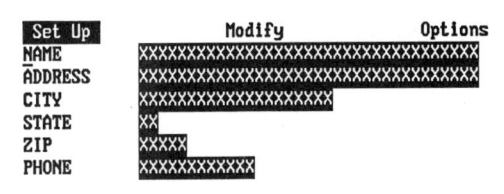

```
        Set Up        Modify          Options        Exit  12:41:30 pm
        NAME       XXXXXXXXXXXXXXXXXXXXXXXXXX
        ADDRESS    XXXXXXXXXXXXXXXXXXXXXXXXXX
        CITY       XXXXXXXXXXXXXXXX
        STATE      XX
        ZIP        XXXXX
        PHONE      XXXXXXXXXX
```

```
CREATE SCREEN   <C:>  C:NAD.SCR        Pg 01 Row 00 Col 00
          Enter text.  Drag field or box under cursor with ⏎.  F10 for menu.
                        Screen field definition blackboard
```

FIGURE 11-4.   The contents of NAD.SCR

screen will change to display the format shown in Figure 11-5. Notice that all fields you didn't insert into the format file are now excluded from your screen. Press [Esc] to return to the Assist screen.

2. You could use all the fields in NAD.DBF and separate the group of fields you want to use often from the group you rarely use. Move to the Create screen for format files by pressing [C], [↓], and then [Enter] twice. Type **FULL** and press [Enter]. This opens the Create screen for the file FULL.SCR. With the Set Up menu open, press [↑] to highlight the command Load Fields, and press [Enter]. This displays the fields for NAD.DBF, which remains the current database.

   Select the first six fields by pressing [Enter], then [↓], and repeating these two keystrokes five more times. Then press [F10] to load the six selected fields—NAME, ADDRESS, CITY, STATE, ZIP, and PHONE—into the blackboard.

```
NAME     Jeannie Iams
ADDRESS  1234 Fox Lane
CITY     Berkeley
STATE    CA
ZIP      94708
PHONE    415-456-7890
```

```
EDIT          <C:> NAD          Rec: 1/20
```

FIGURE 11-5. Effects of NAD.SCR

Press [↓] ten times to move the cursor four lines below the bottom field, PHONE. The counter on the left side of the status bar should show the cursor in position Pg 01 Row 10 Col 00. (From now on, only the row and column indicators will be referred to; you'll work only on the first page for these examples.)

Now select a second group of fields. Press [F10] to return to working with the pull-down menus. Press [S] to open the Set Up menu, highlight Load Fields, and press [Enter] to open the list of fields. Highlight MONEY and press [Enter] to select it. Select each of the remaining fields by pressing [↓] and then [Enter] three more times. When you have selected the bottom four fields, press [F10] to insert them into the format file.

Save this work by pressing [F10], then [E] to open the Exit menu, and then [Enter] to execute the Save command. When you return to the Assist screen, press [U] to open the Update menu, [↓] twice to highlight the Edit command, and then [Enter] to open the Edit screen. Your screen should look like the one in Figure 11-6.

Chapter 11   Creating and Using Formats   **245**

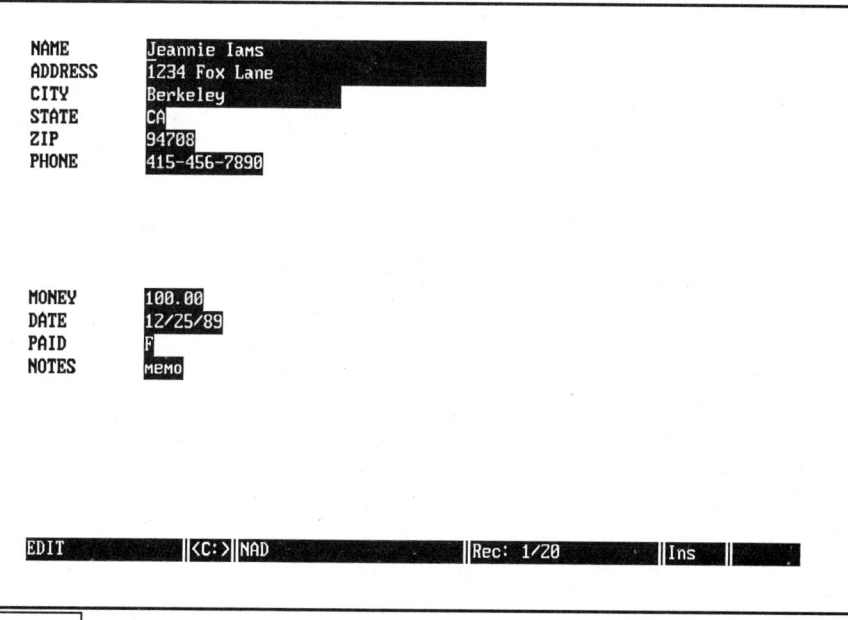

```
NAME      Jeannie Iams
ADDRESS   1234 Fox Lane
CITY      Berkeley
STATE     CA
ZIP       94708
PHONE     415-456-7890




MONEY     100.00
DATE      12/25/89
PAID      F
NOTES     MEMO








EDIT         <C:> NAD                    Rec: 1/20       Ins
```

FIGURE 11-6.	Effects of FULL.SCR

3. Once you've created more than one format file, you can switch between them easily. Press [Esc] to return to the Assist screen, press [S] to open the Set Up menu, press [↓] to select the command Format for Screen, and then press [Enter] twice. This moves you through the list of drive letters and opens a box listing available format files.

   Notice that the two format files are displayed as NAD.FMT and FULL.FMT. These are the files created by dBASE from the matching .SCR files. You use the .SCR file to create and modify a screen format. dBASE uses the matching .FMT file to determine the new display. Make sure NAD.FMT is highlighted, and then press [Enter]. Now open the Edit screen: Press [U] to open the Update menu, highlight the command Edit, and then press [Enter].

Exercises

1. What is the difference between a .SCR file and the matching .FMT file?

2. Can you load a field into a format file that isn't available in the selected database?

3. What is the name of the broad area in the Create screen where you insert fields?

4. What key do you press in the Create screen for format files to switch between working with pull-down menus and working in the blackboard?

5. Begin in the Assist screen and create the format file QUICK.SCR, select NAD.DBF, and load into the format file the three fields NAME, PHONE, and MONEY. Then save this file, view the results in the Edit screen, and return to the Assist screen.

6. Does a format file become effective as soon as you exit the Create screen for format files?

11.4 MODIFY AND ENHANCE FORMAT FILES

Once you've created a format file and seen its effects, you'll probably want to change certain aspects of the displayed format. Don't worry. You can modify format files as easily as you modified database files. You'll work in the Modify screen for format files to do this.

To modify a format file, begin in the Assist screen. Then

a. Press [M] to open the Modify pull-down menu.

b. Highlight the command Format and press [Enter] twice. dBASE displays a list of format screen files you can modify. Notice that all these file names end with .SCR.

c. Highlight the format file you want to modify and press [Enter]. This moves you into the Modify screen for format files. This screen is identical to the Create screen for format files in every way except that the name MODIFY SCREEN shows instead of CREATE SCREEN.

Designing your first few format files will take a bit of going back and forth between the Edit or Append screen, where you use the format file, and the Modify screen, where you readjust fields in the format file, until you have everything just as you want it. After designing and modifying a few format files, you'll find you can design whatever format you want.

There are all sorts of ways you change the appearance of format files beyond inserting fields. You can change the names of the fields, such as NAME and ADDRESS, to Name and Address. You can remove field names completely from the formatted display if you don't want to see them on screen. You can reposition field names so field information appears in more appropriate locations on your screen. You can also increase or decrease the field widths displayed on your screen.

In addition, you can insert text at various places in the display, such as the instructions "Enter first name here ->." You can also enter warnings, such as "Do not enter the area code for local telephone numbers." This is handy if you use a communications program that dials phone numbers displayed in a dBASE field. You can also insert single or double lines and boxes to separate various sections of the screen into discrete areas.

You shouldn't view the blackboard as a word processor, but you are given editing controls, which are listed in Table 11-2.

There are other more complicated design elements that you'll use in only the most sophisticated format files. The last section of this chapter gives you an introduction to these elements.

All these design elements might sound complicated, particularly if you've never used them before. dBASE will display instructions on the navigation line that tell you what you can do at each point in the process. You can also find all the information you need to know about a field by placing the cursor anywhere on the field name or width and pressing F10. This opens the Modify pull-down menu, which displays information about the field.

The Modify menu also lets you change aspects of fields, but you'll learn more about this in the next section. Inserting and moving fields on a screen and inserting text and graphic features are not at all difficult. The only difficult part is making the resulting format look attractive on your screen. This takes a graphic sense that you will gain from experience.

| Table 11-2. | Editing Controls for Format Files |

Keys	Action
↓	Move cursor down one row
↑	Move cursor up one row
→	Move cursor right one column
←	Move cursor left one column
Home	Move cursor back one item
End	Move cursor ahead one item
Type character key	Insert character
Del	Delete character
Ctrl-Y	Delete line from form
Load Fields	Insert field into form
Ctrl-U	Delete field from form
(Cursor on field) Ins *	Increase field form width
(Cursor on field) Del *	Decrease field form width
(Cursor on field) F10-↑	Increase database field width
(Cursor on field) F10-↓	Decrease database field width

*Changing the size of a field within a format file is not recommended because decreasing the field width possibly truncates data, and increasing the field width wastes screen space.

Examples

1. You'll now remove one field from the format file NAD.SCR, center the remaining five fields, and change the representation of their field names. Begin in the Assist screen and press M to open the Modify pull-down menu, highlight the command Format and press Enter twice, highlight NAD.SCR, and press Enter.

    Make sure the database NAD.DBF is current. Assuming that the Set Up menu is displayed and the command Select Database File is highlighted, press Enter, highlight NAD.DBF, and press Enter again. Now press F10 to begin working in the blackboard.

Chapter 11 Creating and Using Formats **249**

Place the cursor on the line containing the PHONE field and press [Ctrl]-[Y]. This deletes the line.

2. Now you can change the representation of field names and the location of the remaining five fields. Move the cursor under the first letter of NAME. Notice the information displayed on the message line. It's a bit cryptic, but the part that interests you at this point says that you should enter the text you want to and then drag the field to its new position by placing the cursor at the new position and pressing [Enter].

Press SPACEBAR four times to erase the four letters of the name. You could press [Del] to delete characters but this will move up anything to the right of your cursor. When you press SPACEBAR, you're just entering blank characters. Then press [→] eight more times to move the cursor under the field area for NAME marked with Xs. As soon as the cursor enters the field area, new information appears on your message line: "Field: NAD − >NAME Type: Character Width: 35." This identifies the field area you're going to move.

Press [Enter] to select this field width. Now press [↓] seven times. Only the cursor will move. The field area will remain where it was. Next press [→] 15 times. You're in the the correct position when the indicators show Row 07 Col 27.

Press [Enter] and the NAME field width will appear beginning in the current cursor position. You have now fixed the field in a new position. Press [←] six times and type **Name:**. You've now moved the first field to the middle of your screen, and you've also changed the field description.

If you reposition a field and then decide you want to move it again, just place the cursor in the field width, press [Enter], and move it to the new position. If you want to move the field to the left or right on the current line, you might find it easier to move the field to a new line first, fix it there, and then move the field back to the original line and fix it in the correct position.

Now move the other four fields and rename them the same way. Press [Home] twice. The cursor moves to the beginning of Name: the first time, and to the left margin the second time. Press [↑] five times to place the cursor on the first character of ADDRESS. Press SPACEBAR seven times to erase those characters, press [End] to move the cursor under the matching field width, and then press [Enter]. Move the cursor to Row 08 Col 27, which is the position directly underneath the NAME field (or Name: field, if you prefer).

Press [Enter] to fix the field. Press [←] nine times, type **Address:** and press [Home] five times. This moves the cursor back to the left margin. Now move the remaining three fields by using the same techniques. Remember to relabel the field names **City:**, **State:**, and **Zip:**.

Now make sure the new design is what you want. Press [F10] to access pull-down menus, press [E], and press [Enter]. When you return to the Assist screen, press [U], highlight Edit, and press [Enter]. View the results, and then press [Esc] to return to the Assist.

3. The next step is to enhance NAD.SCR by inserting a double-line box around the six fields. Press [M], highlight the command Format, press [Enter] twice, highlight NAD.SCR, and press [Enter]. Press [O] to open the Options menu, highlight the command "Double bar," and press [Enter]. Selecting the single or double bar command moves you immediately to the blackboard.

Notice that the message line changes to tell you how to control the cursor while drawing a box. Move the cursor to Row 6 Col 14 and press [Enter]. Now move the cursor to Row 14 Col 65 and press [Enter]. The box will appear as you have just drawn it.

4. Now you'll reinsert the PHONE field in a new location and insert text that warns you about handling local and long-distance phone numbers differently. First, while working in the blackboard, move the cursor to Row 18 Col 25.

Press [F10] to gain use of the menus and press [S] to open the Set Up menu. Highlight Load Fields and press [Enter]. Highlight the PHONE field and press [Enter]. Now press [F10] to work in the blackboard. The PHONE field name and width will appear in the new position. Press SPACEBAR five times to erase the letters for the PHONE field name, and then back up and type **Phone:** in the same location.

Now press [↑] twice and [Backspace] five times to reposition the cursor. Type **Don't insert area codes for local calls:** Your screen should now look like the one in Figure 11-7.

Save this changed design. Press [F10], then [E], and then [Enter]. Check the results of your new design by viewing its effects in the Edit screen.

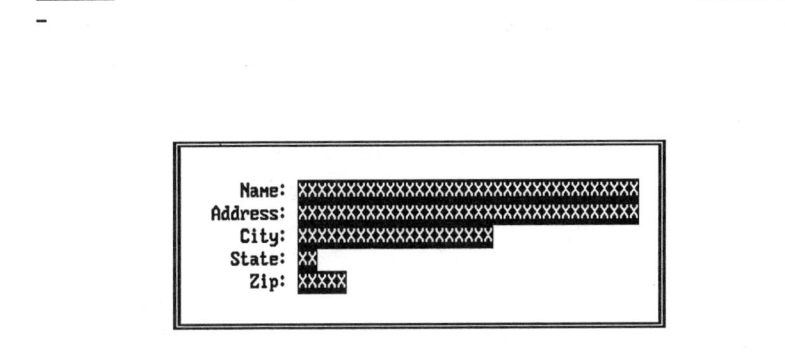

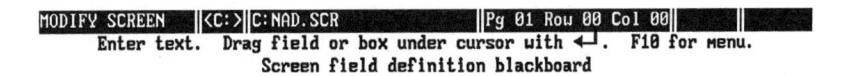

Chapter 11 Creating and Using Formats 251

```
    Set Up         Modify          Options       Exit  01:04:34 pm
     -
```

```
                    Name: XXXXXXXXXXXXXXXXXXXXXXXXXXXXXX
                 Address: XXXXXXXXXXXXXXXXXXXXXXXXXXXXXX
                    City: XXXXXXXXXXXXXXXXXXX
                   State: XX
                     Zip: XXXXX
```

Don't insert area codes for local calls:

Phone: XXXXXXXXXXX

```
MODIFY SCREEN   |<C:>|C:NAD.SCR         |Pg 01 Row 00 Col 00|
        Enter text.  Drag field or box under cursor with ⏎.  F10 for menu.
                        Screen field definition blackboard
```

| FIGURE 11-7. | NAD.SCR completely redesigned |

Exercises

1. Is there any difference between the Create and Modify screens for format files?

2. Can you change the names of fields in a format file?

3. What features can you insert into format files?

4. How do you move a field in a format file?

5. Where does dBASE display instructions for working with each procedure in the Create and Modify screens for format files?

11.5 CREATE MORE COMPLEX FEATURES

You can create and redesign complex format files by using all of the controls described so far. dBASE also provides, for more experienced users, the ability to perform the following modifications:

- Generate a text file containing all the commands dBASE needs to create the format file from your screen file instructions. This shows the field names and their positions in the format file. Use the command "Generate text file image" on the Options menu to do this.
- Change the type of characters you can put into a field, as well as change the display of the characters in the format file when you use it. Use the commands Picture Template and Picture Function on the Modify menu to do this.
- Change the widths of fields in the current database structure. Use the command Width on the Modify menu to do this.
- Insert new fields into the current database and set their widths. Use the command Content on the Modify menu to do this.
- Build a database while you design the format file. Use the Create a New Database File command on the Set Up menu to do this.

The first feature, a text file of all commands in a format file, is a handy record of the fields and design elements that create a format file. To create the text file of commands for a format file, begin in the format file you want to document.

    a. Press [O] to open the Options menu.

    b. Press [Enter] to execute the command "Generate a text file image."

dBASE will generate the file so quickly that it might look as if nothing has happened. The file is saved to disk in the current directory, using the name of the format file and the extension .TXT. You can view the contents by using any word processor or text editor.

You use various commands on the Modify menu to change the type of characters you can put into a field, the way characters are displayed when the format file is used, and the widths of existing fields, and to insert new fields into the current database.

To use any of these commands while working in the Modify screen for format files:

a. Press [F10] to work in the blackboard.

b. Place the cursor on the field you want to change.

c. Press [F10] again.

d. Press [M] to open the Modify menu.

e. Highlight the command you want to use and make the necessary changes.

f. Press [F10], then [E], and then [Enter] to save the changes and return to the Assist screen.

Table 11-3 describes the nine fields in the Modify pull-down menu. You'll work with each of them in the upcoming examples.

To create a database file while you work within a format file, you first need to name the database. Then you can name a new field and define the characteristics of the new field.

Begin by creating a new format file or modifying an existing format file. Once you've entered the Create or Modify screen:

a. Press [S] to open the Set Up menu, if it's not already open.

b. Highlight the command Create a New Database and press [Enter].

c. Type the name of the new database and press [Enter].

d. Now that you've created the database, at least in name, you must still select it for use. Press [Enter] to execute the command Select a Database. dBASE will display the name of the database you just declared among other possible choices.

e. Highlight the new database name and press [Enter].

Now that you've selected the new database, you have to insert fields into it. After all, you can't create a format file without loading one or more fields from the selected database into the format file.

a. Press [F10] to work in the blackboard.

b. Press [F10] a second time. This opens the Modify menu.

Table 11-3. Command Definitions for the Modify Pull-down Menu

Field	Definition
Action	Toggles between Display/SAY and Edit/GET, which are dBASE programming language terms. The first displays text, the second edits a field
Source	Displays the name of the active database, or the database from which you will load fields
Content	Displays the name of the field name currently selected on the blackboard. If no field name has been selected, this remains blank
Type	Defines the type of field currently selected, such as character, numeric, date, logical, or memo
Width	Displays the width of the currently selected field
Decimal	Displays the decimal component of a numeric field width
Picture Function	Lets you select a different way to display existing characters when you use the format file. The function you select converts existing characters to another form of display, such as the date from American (mm/dd/yy) to European (dd/mm/yy)
Picture Template	Lets you select the type of characters you can insert into a database when you use the format file. This restricts the types of characters you can enter
Range	Lets you specify a range of maximum and minimum values for numbers displayed in numeric and date fields only

c. Press ⬇ to highlight the command Content and press [Enter]. dBASE will then display a small box containing the notation <NewField>, which is highlighted.

d. Press [Enter] to define the name of the new field. dBASE asks for the name of the new field.

e. Type the new name and press [Enter]. The Modify menu reappears, and the Content field, which contains the new field name, is highlighted. The character type is accepted by default.

f. Press ⬇ to highlight the Type field. Press [Enter] repeatedly to scroll through the five field types. Display the type you want to use for the new field.

g. Press ⬇ to embed the field type and highlight the Width field. Press [Enter] to activate the field. An arrow will appear in the field name. Type in the field width value and press [Enter]. You can also press ⬆ to increase the field width or ⬇ to decrease the field width.

h. Press ⬇ to highlight the Decimal field if you want to change that setting. You can increase and decrease the value the same way you did the Width setting. Press [Enter] to confirm any changes you make.

You can continue inserting new fields in this way. As soon as you finish defining one field, highlight Content and press [Enter]. dBASE will display a list of the fields you've created so far, along with a single <NewField> name. Highlight this name and continue.

Be aware that when you create a database while working with a format file, fields are inserted in a special order. When you create a database structure while working with a format file, the first field you insert becomes field 1 until you insert the next field. Then field 1 becomes field 2. Each existing field is pushed down one number in the structure to make room for the next field, which always enters the structure as field 1.

This is the opposite of the way fields are inserted when you create a database by using the Create screen for databases. In this screen, you insert field 1, field 2, and so on, and the fields retain these positions until you modify the structure.

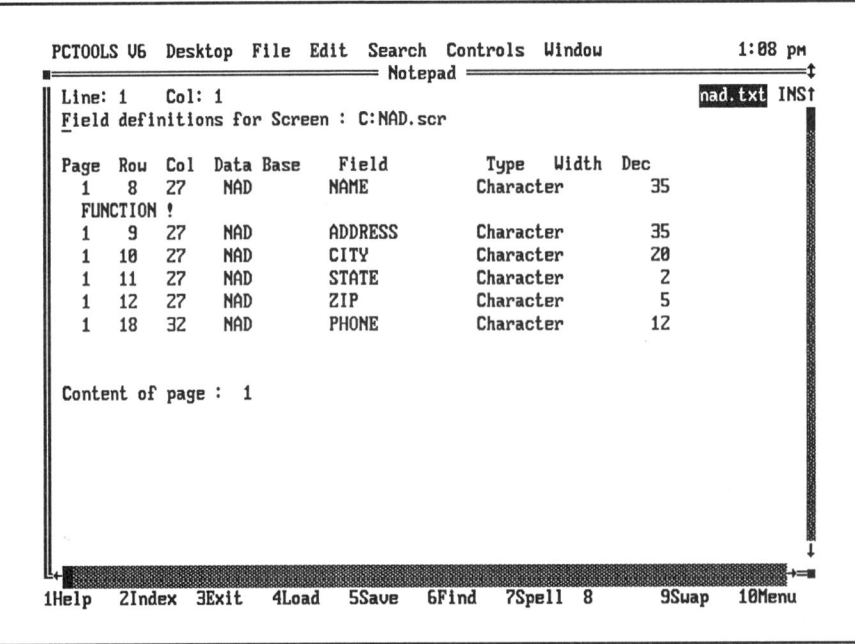

```
PCTOOLS V6  Desktop  File  Edit  Search  Controls  Window        1:08 pm
═══════════════════════════════ Notepad ═══════════════════════════════
Line: 1    Col: 1                                          nad.txt INSt
Field definitions for Screen : C:NAD.scr

Page  Row  Col  Data Base    Field          Type    Width  Dec
  1    8   27   NAD          NAME           Character  35
  FUNCTION !
  1    9   27   NAD          ADDRESS        Character  35
  1   10   27   NAD          CITY           Character  20
  1   11   27   NAD          STATE          Character   2
  1   12   27   NAD          ZIP            Character   5
  1   18   32   NAD          PHONE          Character  12


Content of page : 1




1Help  2Index  3Exit  4Load  5Save  6Find  7Spell  8      9Swap  10Menu
```

FIGURE 11-8. The contents of NAD.TXT

Examples

1. For those who would like to explore the internal structure of screen files, write the contents of NAD.SCR to a text file. Begin in the Assist screen and open the Modify screen for the file NAD.SCR. Press [M], highlight Format, press [Enter] twice, highlight NAD.SCR, and then press [Enter]. In the Modify screen, press [O], and then [Enter]. dBASE writes the commands for NAD.SCR to a disk file called NAD.TXT. Exit the Modify screen by pressing [Esc] twice. Figure 11-8 shows the contents of NAD.TXT in the PC Tools Desktop editor.

2. Change the type of characters for the NAME field of NAD.DBF from mixed case to all uppercase. Begin by working in the blackboard of NAD.SCR. Make sure NAD appears in the Source field. Place the cursor under the NAME field width, and press [F10] to open the Modify menu. Highlight the command Picture Template and press [Enter]. dBASE displays the list of character input symbols you can use, as shown by the screen in Figure 11-9. You will find the cursor

Chapter 11   Creating and Using Formats   **257**

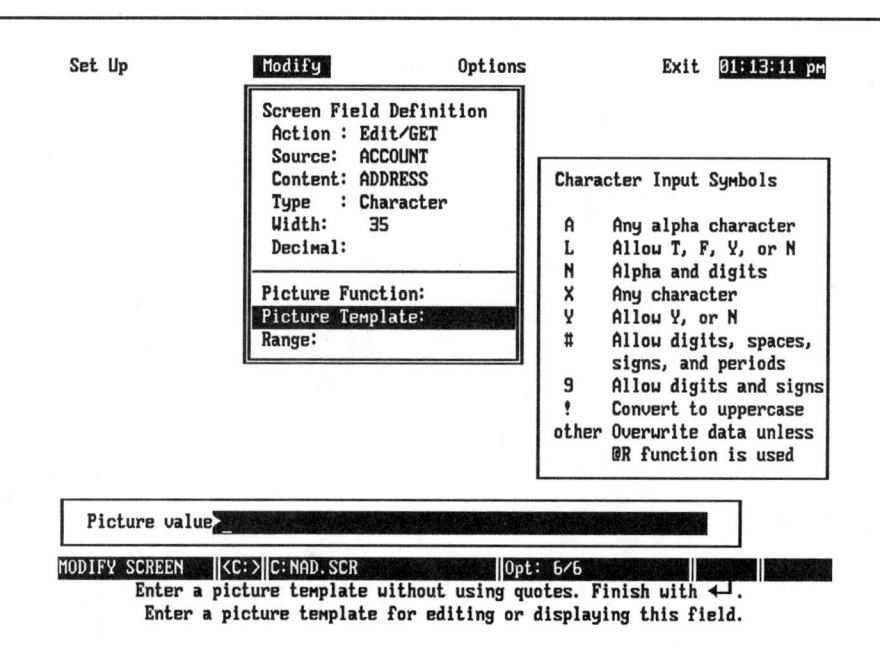

```
       Set Up          Modify        Options              Exit  01:13:11 pm
                  ┌─────────────────────────┐
                  │ Screen Field Definition │
                  │ Action : Edit/GET       │
                  │ Source:  ACCOUNT        │
                  │ Content: ADDRESS        │   ┌──────────────────────────────┐
                  │ Type   : Character      │   │ Character Input Symbols      │
                  │ Width:   35             │   │                              │
                  │ Decimal:                │   │ A     Any alpha character    │
                  │                         │   │ L     Allow T, F, Y, or N    │
                  │ Picture Function:       │   │ N     Alpha and digits       │
                  │ Picture Template:       │   │ X     Any character          │
                  │ Range:                  │   │ Y     Allow Y, or N          │
                  └─────────────────────────┘   │ #     Allow digits, spaces,  │
                                                │         signs, and periods   │
                                                │ 9     Allow digits and signs │
                                                │ !     Convert to uppercase   │
                                                │ other Overwrite data unless  │
                                                │         @R function is used  │
                                                └──────────────────────────────┘
  ┌──────────────────────────────────────────────────────────────────┐
  │  Picture value▸                                                  │
  └──────────────────────────────────────────────────────────────────┘
  MODIFY SCREEN   <C:>  C:NAD.SCR            Opt: 6/6
           Enter a picture template without using quotes. Finish with ↵.
           Enter a picture template for editing or displaying this field.
```

| FIGURE 11-9. | List of Character Input Symbols |

in the lower-left box. Type ! 35 times and then press [Enter]. This symbol, as defined in Figure 11-9, converts all characters that appear in the NAME field into uppercase. You must insert the symbol for as many characters as you want displayed in the field width. Entering 35 symbols makes sure all possible characters will be converted.

Now save the format file and test it. Press [E], and then [Enter]. Press [U], then highlight Edit, and press [Enter]. After viewing the results, press [Esc].

3. To change the date display from American to European style in FULL.FMT, begin working in the blackboard for FULL.FMT. Make sure NAD appears in the Source field. Place the cursor under the DATE field width and press [Enter]. Now press [F10] to open the Modify menu. Highlight the field Picture Function and press [Enter]. dBASE displays the list of date functions you can use, as shown by the screen in Figure 11-10. Type E and press [Enter]. (You can also

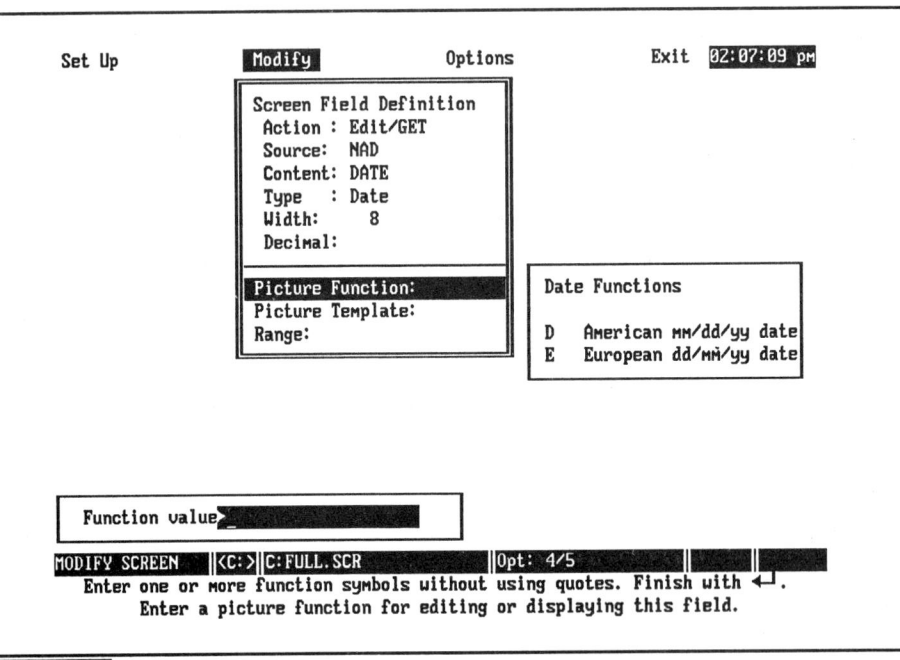

```
    Set Up         Modify         Options         Exit  02:07:09 pm
                  ┌─────────────────────────────┐
                  │ Screen Field Definition     │
                  │   Action : Edit/GET         │
                  │   Source:  NAD              │
                  │   Content: DATE             │
                  │   Type   : Date             │
                  │   Width:      8             │
                  │   Decimal:                  │
                  │                             │ ┌─────────────────────────────┐
                  │   Picture Function:         │ │ Date Functions              │
                  │   Picture Template:         │ │                             │
                  │   Range:                    │ │   D   American mm/dd/yy date│
                  └─────────────────────────────┘ │   E   European dd/mm/yy date│
                                                  └─────────────────────────────┘




              ┌──────────────────────────────────────┐
              │ Function value                       │
              └──────────────────────────────────────┘
   MODIFY SCREEN   |<C:>|C:FULL.SCR          |Opt: 4/5
         Enter one or more function symbols without using quotes. Finish with ↵.
         Enter a picture function for editing or displaying this field.
```

FIGURE 11-10. Date functions you can use

use **e**.) You need to enter only one character, either a **D** or an **E**. You don't have to enter eight Ds or eight Es.

Save the format file and test it. Press (E) and then (Enter). Press (U), highlight Edit, and press (Enter). View the results and press (Esc).

4. To change the width of fields for the selected database while working in the Create or Modify screen for format files, place the cursor on the field whose width you want to change. Press (F10) to open the Modify menu. Highlight the Width field and press (Enter). An arrow should appear in the Width field. Type in the new width value, or press (↑) to increase the field width or (↓) to decrease the field width. Press (Enter) to set the new width. Be careful when you decrease the width of a field. When you save the format file, you'll also save the new width size to the database. You might lose some characters that were stored in the original field width.

5. Create a new database at the same time you work in the format file

NAD.SCR. While working in the Create or Modify screen for format files, press [S] to open the Set Up menu, press [↓] to highlight the command Create New Database File, and then press [Enter]. dBASE asks you for the name of the file. Type **QUICK** and press [Enter]. Now make the new database current. The command Select a Database File should be highlighted automatically. Press [Enter], highlight QUICK, and press [Enter].

Press [→]. This opens the Modify menu with QUICK in the Source field. Press [↓] to highlight Content, and then press [Enter]. dBASE displays the <NewField> box highlighted. Press [Enter], type **FIELD1**, and press [Enter]. Press [↓] twice to highlight the Width field. Press [Enter], type **10**, and press [Enter] a second time.

Highlight the field Content and press [Enter]. dBASE opens the field box, displaying FIELD1 below <NewField>, which is highlighted. Press [Enter], type **FIELD2** to name the new field, and press [Enter]. This second field is inserted with the previous field type and size.

To create an identical third field, press [Enter] twice and type **FIELD3**. You need to highlight the Type and Width fields only when you want to change field types or widths.

With the list of new fields still open, notice that FIELD2 has moved down to make room for FIELD3, which is now the top field in the database structure.

You can't enter any information into a database created while you are working in a format file, but you don't need to. You only need to use a database with defined fields to create a format file. You can add records later by using the Append screen.

Exercises

1. What are the contents of the text file generated by the command "Generate a text file image" on the Options menu?

2. Where is this file printed and stored?

3. What type of file is it?

4. What does the Character Input Symbols list let you do?

5. What does the Character Input Functions list let you do?

6. What menu do you use to make changes to the current database?

7. What is the danger of changing a field width in the selected database?

8. Do you have to insert information into a database that you create while working with a format file?

EXERCISES

MASTERY SKILLS CHECK

1. Begin in the Assist screen and create a format file called CHECK.SCR for NAD.DBF that contains the three fields NAME, PHONE, and MONEY in the upper-left corner of the format file.

2. Change the NAME field name to Name. Erase the PHONE field name. Move the PHONE field width to the right side of the top line so it begins at position Row 00 Col 57. Precede it with the name Phone.

3. Erase the MONEY field name. Move the MONEY field to position Row 04 Col 20. Draw a single-line box around the field.

4. Save the format file, view the results, and then return to the Assist screen.

5. Modify CHECK.SCR by adding this line of text beginning in position Row 07 Col 10: **Call if this amount passes $500.** Then save the change.

INTEGRATING SKILLS CHECK

1. Begin in the Assist screen and create a format file called VALUE.SCR. Use VALUE.DBF as the source file. You created this database in Chapter 6. Erase the original field names. Place all four fields— ITEM, QUANTITY, PRICE, and COST—in the center of the format

file, one below the other, with the top field ITEM beginning in Row 00 Col 20. Precede each field with a new name: Item, Quantity, Price, Cost. Save the format file, test it, and return to the Assist screen.

2. Create a format file called MY.SCR. Create the database MY.DBF with these six character fields: NAME (30 spaces), ADDRESS (30 spaces), CITY (20 spaces), STATE (2 spaces), ZIP (5 spaces), and PHONE (12 spaces). Insert only the NAME and PHONE fields in MY.SCR. You can use it to make quick calls to friends whose names you store in MY.DBF. Save the format file.

Creating and Using Reports
▶12◀

CHAPTER OBJECTIVES

In this chapter you will

- ▶ Become familiar with the Create Report screen — 12.1
- ▶ Design reports — 12.2
- ▶ Print reports — 12.3
- ▶ Modify reports — 12.4

Printing database information clearly is crucial for professional database managers. You can always view your own information on screen. But as soon as you want to communicate data and its implications to other people, professional-looking reports become indispensable.

Creating the visual display of information on paper or the screen can seem complicated at first, but designing, creating, and modifying reports is really only a bit more difficult than the work you performed in Chapter 10, where you learned how to make simple printings of database information.

In this chapter you'll learn how to create and modify reports by using the Create and Modify Report screens and print them by using the Retrieve Report screen. By using reports, you can place database information into columns, add text and titles to clarify the information, and calculate and display totals based upon numeric field information.

Exercises

SKILLS CHECK

1. Make NAD.DBF current, and then see what dBASE on-line help has to say about the Report command on the Create menu.

2. List the structure of NAD.DBF on screen so you can refamiliarize yourself with its contents. Return to the Assist screen.

3. See what dBASE on-line help has to say about the Report command on the Modify menu.

4. Make NAD.DBF current and attach the index NAME.NDX to it.

5. List the contents of NAD.DBF in the indexed order of NAME.NDX on your screen, and then return to the Assist screen.

6. See what dBASE on-line help has to say about the Report command on the Retrieve menu.

BECOME FAMILIAR WITH THE CREATE REPORT SCREEN

12.1

You create a report in dBASE III PLUS by using the Create screen for report files. This is a full-screen component of the program, a variation of the Create screen that you've used for database and format files. You use the commands in this screen to insert fields from the current database into a report file. You then design, insert, and edit text and other features in the report. Finally, you print the report file.

Before you can open the Create screen for report files, you must open, or make current, the database you want to design the report around. The essential elements of a report are field names, which you select from a specific database. You can open a database in two ways: before you open the Create screen for report files, or after you specify the name of the report file you want to create.

a. Make current the database you want to design the report around.

b. Press [C] to open the Create menu.

c. Highlight the command Report. The easiest way to to this is to press [↑] twice. Then, press [Enter]. dBASE opens a prompt box that asks you what name you want to give the report.

d. Type the report file name and press [Enter]. If you haven't yet opened a database, dBASE will say "No database is in USE. Enter file name:."

e. Type the database file name you want to use and press [Enter]. dBASE presents you with the Create screen for report files. Figure 12-1 shows this screen for a report called NAD.FRM. The extension .FRM stands for "form," or the design format of the report.

Notice the name CREATE REPORT on the left side of the status bar. The Create screen for reports is given the name of the feature you can

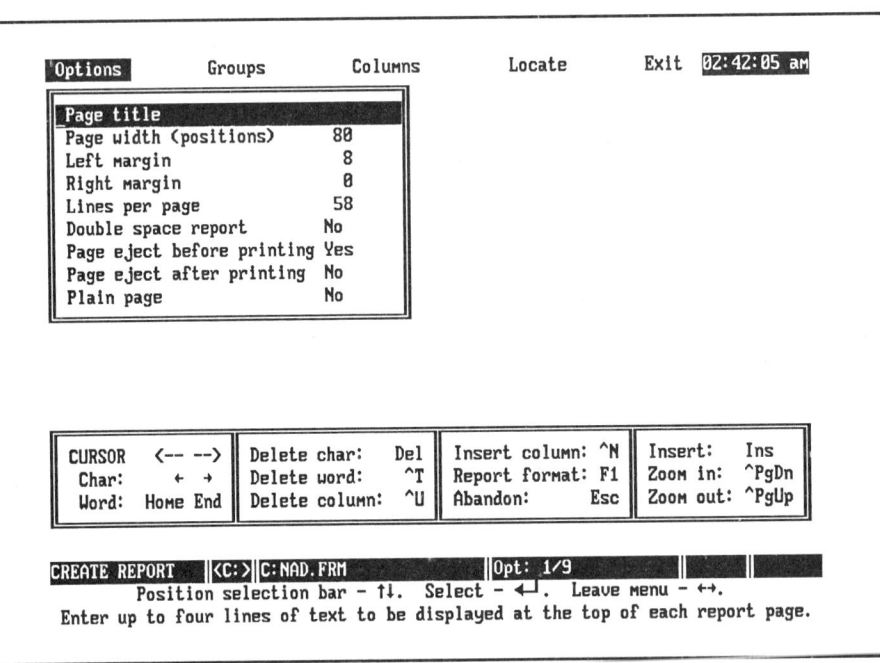

```
 Options        Groups      Columns      Locate      Exit  02:42:05 am
┌─────────────────────────────────────┐
│ Page title                          │
│ Page width (positions)       80     │
│ Left margin                   8     │
│ Right margin                  0     │
│ Lines per page               58     │
│ Double space report          No     │
│ Page eject before printing   Yes    │
│ Page eject after printing    No     │
│ Plain page                   No     │
└─────────────────────────────────────┘


┌──────────────────┬───────────────────┬────────────────────┬───────────────────┐
│ CURSOR   <-- -->│ Delete char:   Del│ Insert column:  ^N │ Insert:      Ins  │
│ Char:     ← →   │ Delete word:   ^T │ Report format:  F1 │ Zoom in:    ^PgDn │
│ Word: Home End  │ Delete column: ^U │ Abandon:       Esc │ Zoom out:   ^PgUp │
└──────────────────┴───────────────────┴────────────────────┴───────────────────┘
 CREATE REPORT   |<C:>|C:NAD.FRM            |Opt: 1/9
         Position selection bar - ↑↓.  Select - ↵.  Leave menu - ←→.
    Enter up to four lines of text to be displayed at the top of each report page.
```

FIGURE 12-1. The Create Report screen

create in it, that is, REPORT, whereas Create screens you've looked at previously, such as those for database and format files, just say CREATE. Most of this screen should look familiar to you by now.

You can find a table of help information in the lower half of your screen. The status bar and navigation and messages lines are at the bottom of the screen. There's a menu bar at the top of the screen with the names of five pull-down menus. And the leftmost pull-down menu, the Options menu, is open by default.

Become familiar with all the commands you can use in the Create Report screen. The five pull-down menus are defined here.

Options	Nine options that let you change basic formatting features of a report page, including two commands that let you determine whether pages are ejected before and after printing the report

Groups	Six commands that let you determine the way groups of commands will be handled during printing
Columns	Five commands that let you create columns and adjust their settings, as well as insert field names into columns
Locate	Lets you locate specific field names in columns
Exit	Lets you save the report file you've created and return to the Assist screen or exit the current report and abandon all changes since the last save

There's a minimum of 22 commands on the five pull-down menus in the Create Report screen. The Locate menu doesn't contain any selections when you first create a report file. After you begin inserting columns into the current report file, however, this menu will display the names of columns that you insert.

Figure 12-2 shows a map of all five pull-down menus and their commands. The menus and commands are identical in the Create Report and Modify Report screens. You work with these menus, and the commands on these menus, in the same way that you work with all other pull-down commands in the Assist and other dBASE screens. Press [→] or [←] to scroll through the menus in sequence. To open a menu directly, press the key that matches the first letter of the menu name. Press [↑] and [↓] to highlight different commands. Press [Enter] to execute the highlighted command. You can also use the [Ctrl]-key-combinations shown in Table 2-1 to open menus and highlight commands.

Usually, when you highlight commands on a pull-down menu, the number of the command appears on the right side of the status bar followed by the number of commands in the menu. For example, when you open the Options menu, the top command is highlighted by default. The indicator on the right side of the status line shows "Opt: 1/9," which means the top command is the first of nine commands. Press [↓] once and the indicator changes to "Opt: 2/9."

Options		Groups	Columns	Locate	Exit
Page title		Group on expression	Contents		Save
Page width (positions)	80	Group heading	Heading		Abandon
Left margin	8	Summary report only No	Width 0		
Right margin	0	Page eject after group	Decimal places		
Lines per page	58	Sub-group on expression	Total this column		
Double space report	No	Sub-group heading			
Page eject before printing	Yes				
Page eject after printing	No				
Plain page	No				

FIGURE 12-2. Menu map for the Create and Modify Report screen

TABLE 12-1. Help Instructions Defined

Keys	Action
→	Move cursor right one space
Home	Move cursor left one word
←	Move cursor left one space
End	Move cursor right one word
↑	Move cursor up one line
↓	Move cursor down one line
F1	Toggle Report Format/Help
Ins	Toggle insert/typeover mode
Press character key	Insert character
Ctrl-N	Insert column
Del	Delete character
Ctrl-T	Delete word
Ctrl-U	Delete column
Ctrl-PgDn	Zoom in
Ctrl-PgUp	Zoom out
Esc	Abandon changes

This indicator changes, however, when you open the Columns pull-down menu; it shows which column number you're working with.

There is another difference between pull-down menu selections in the Create Report screen and other menu commands in dBASE. The menu selections in the Create Report screen are not really commands. They are formatting features that you can insert into or change in the report. In fact, there are three types of menu selections in the Create Report screen; they can be distinguished by the way each one lets you change the current setting.

- You can insert text strings or field names after the menu selection.
- You can increase or decrease the current numeric value for the format setting.
- You can toggle a format setting on or off.

To insert text strings and field names in such options as the "Page Title" setting on the Option menu

a. Highlight the setting and press [Enter]. dBASE displays an arrow in the field area.

b. Type the text, or, to insert field names, press [F10] to open a list of field names in the current database and then select the fields you want to use.

c. Press [Enter] to set the new text.

The top option on the Groups pull-down menu lets you insert text strings or field names directly after selecting the Groups menu.

Some of these settings let you insert more text than others. With these settings, dBASE opens a box called an *entry area*, which lets you insert up to four lines of text. When you're finished inserting text into the entry area, you press [Ctrl]-[End] to close the box and insert the text, or as much of it as can fit, right after the menu selection.

For those settings that don't open an entry area, you can still expand your work area for entering characters. This applies specifically to three settings: "Group on expression" (Groups), "Group heading" (Groups), and "Contents" (Columns). Once you've activated one of these settings, press [Ctrl]-[PgDn] to *zoom* into the setting. This opens a line to work with just above the status bar. This line lets you view more text, as you insert it, than will fit in the space after the setting. You can zoom out of this line by pressing [Ctrl]-[PgDn], or you can just press [Enter] to close the zoom line and insert the text into the setting.

To increase or decrease a numeric value:

a. Highlight the setting containing the numeric value.

b. Press [Enter].

c. Type the numeric value you want to use and press [Enter]. The new value will appear next to the setting.

With some numeric settings, you're limited to minimum and maximum values. dBASE will warn you on the message line if your value violates these limits. If it does, press SPACEBAR and enter a new value.

You can also change values within numeric settings by pressing [Enter], and then pressing [↑] to raise the number or [↓] to lower the number. Press [Enter] to set the new value.

The sixth through ninth commands on the Options menu contain settings you can toggle on or off.

To toggle a setting on or off:

a. Highlight the setting.

b. Press [Enter]. dBASE displays the alternative setting. (These are all Yes/No settings.)

Pressing [F1] toggles help on and off. Table 12-1 defines the commands in the help table.

There are two differences between help in the Create Report screen and help in most other dBASE screens. The first difference is that the help table appears in the lower half of the Create Report screen, while it appears at the top of most other dBASE screens.

The second difference is that when the help table is toggled off, a new feature is toggled on. This is called the report format area, and you'll see it each time help is turned off. This area provides a graphic depiction of the layout of the current report as you design it. Two symbols appear in a single line in this area when you first start working with a report. The line looks like this:

```
>>>>>>>>----------------------------------------------------------------------
```

There are eight right brackets followed by 70 dashes. The right angle brackets stand for the default left margin setting of 8 spaces. The dashes stand for the rest of the current page width. You can change these graphic features to depict different margin and page width settings as well as to view text that you want to insert in the report. You'll see how these features work when you begin to change some of these settings in the examples for this section.

When you toggle the report format area on, you can use various commands on the pull-down menus to define information that you then insert into this area. When the help table is showing, you can use some of the commands to change page settings, such as margins, but you cannot insert features into the report format. The report format area must be showing if you want to insert features into the report.

You can abandon your work in the Create Report screen at any point by using the command Abandon on the Exit menu or by following one of these two procedures. The first is as follows:

a. Press (Esc). dBASE will ask you, "Are you sure you want to abandon operation? [Y/N]." A message on the navigation line tells you to "Enter Y or N."

b. Press (Y). You'll return to the Assist screen and none of your work in the Create Report screen will be saved to disk.

The other procedure is to abandon your work by pressing (Esc) twice.

Examples

1. Start designing a report for NAD.DBF called NAD.FRM. You'll open NAD.DBF as you create the report. First make sure no database file is current. If one is current, exit dBASE and then reload the program.

    Now start to open the Create Report screen for NAD.FRM. Press (C), (↑) twice, and then (Enter). To name the report, type **NAD** and press (Enter). dBASE tells you that no database is in use and asks you to specify a database name. Type **NAD** and press (Enter). Your screen should change to look like the one in Figure 12-1.

2. Scroll through the pull-down menus in the Create Report screen. Make sure the Options menu is showing. Press (Ctrl)-(A) to open the Options menu if it isn't open. Press (→) four times to scroll through all five pull-down menus. Press (L) to open the Locate menu. This menu contains no selections when you open it for a new report file. Selections will appear on this menu only after you create columns.

3. On the Options menu, toggle the setting "Double space report" from double to single space: Highlight the "Double space" report setting, which should read Yes, and press [Enter]. Notice that it switches to No. Press [↓] to highlight "Page eject before printing." Press [Enter] to toggle this to No.

4. On the Options pull-down menu, change the "Page width" setting from 80 to 65: Make sure that the Options pull-down menu is showing. (Press O if it isn't.) Press [↓] to highlight the setting "Page width." Press [Enter], type 65 and press [Enter]. Press [F1] to turn on the report format area if it is not already showing. Notice that the line of dashes in the report format area has shortened considerably. This reflects the new page width you've just declared. Counting the brackets and dashes, there should be a total of 65 symbols on the line, showing that you have a current page width setting of 65 positions (or spaces).

5. Experiment with the "Left margin" and "Right margin" settings: Highlight "Left margin" and press [Enter]. Press [↓] seven times to set the number to 0. Press [Enter], and watch all the left brackets on the symbols line disappear. You've removed the left margin.

   Highlight "Right margin" and press [Enter]. Type 20 and press [Enter]. Notice that 20 left angle brackets (<) appear on the right side of the symbols line. They show the current setting for the right margin of the report.

6. Experiment with the way you enter text and field names into a report: On the Options menu, highlight the setting "Page title," and then press [Enter]. An arrow will appear. Notice that the entry area, or editing box, opens on the right side of your screen, as shown in Figure 12-3. You type text into this box that will serve as the page title for your report. Type **List of People Who Owe Me Money** and press [Ctrl]-[End]. Notice how the box disappears and that the first part of this text appears after the "Page title" setting on the Options pull-down menu.

   Now press [G] to open the Groups menu. The top setting, "Group on expression," should be highlighted by default. Press [Enter]. Notice the arrow dBASE inserts after the setting. This means

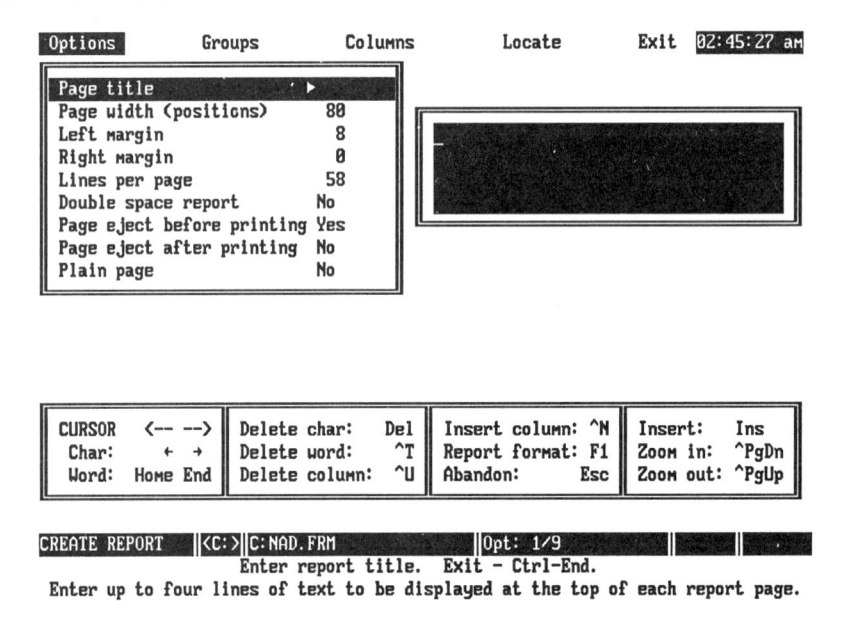

```
Options          Groups          Columns          Locate          Exit  02:45:27 am
Page title                    ▸
Page width (positions)       80
Left margin                   8
Right margin                  0
Lines per page               58
Double space report          No
Page eject before printing   Yes
Page eject after printing    No
Plain page                   No
```

```
CURSOR   <-- -->   Delete char:    Del    Insert column: ^N    Insert:   Ins
Char:      ← →     Delete word:    ^T     Report format: F1    Zoom in:  ^PgDn
Word:   Home End   Delete column:  ^U     Abandon:       Esc   Zoom out: ^PgUp
```

```
CREATE REPORT  |<C:>|C:NAD.FRM              |Opt: 1/9|
              Enter report title.  Exit - Ctrl-End.
Enter up to four lines of text to be displayed at the top of each report page.
```

| FIGURE 12-3. | The editing box |

the setting is ready to receive information. Press [F10]. dBASE opens two boxes, one a list of field names in NAD.DBF, the other identifying the currently highlighted command, which is NAME. Press [Enter], and NAME appears after the setting "Group on expression." Press [Enter] again to set this entry.

7. You can zoom in and out of certain settings in the Create Report screen. This means you can expand the area where you enter text. Refer back to Table 12-1, and you'll notice two commands you might not recognize—Zoom in and Zoom out.

Practice zooming in and out of certain settings. Make sure the Groups menu is still open. Press [↓] to highlight the setting "Group heading," and then press [Enter] to activate the setting. Now press [Ctrl]-[PgDn] to zoom into a larger work area. This area appears highlighted above the status bar, where the action line sometimes appears. You can find the cursor blinking in the first position of this area.

Type some text into this work area: **This is the expanded work**

area. Press `Enter`. This closes the work area and inserts the text after the setting Group heading on the Groups menu, but you can't see all of the text next to the setting. The zoom area is designed to let you view a much longer string of text than can be displayed after a menu setting.

8. Don't save the changes you've made to NAD.FRM. Press `Esc` twice to abandon the changes you've just made and to return to the Assist screen.

Exercises

1. How many pull-down menus are there in the Create Report screen?

2. What is different about the commands on these menus and the commands on other dBASE pull-down menus?

3. What feature replaces the help table when you press `F1` to toggle help off?

4. A line of symbols appears when you turn help off, including right angle brackets and dashes. What do these symbols indicate?

5. Enter the Create Report screen for a report called TEST. Open the Groups pull-down menu and toggle the setting "Summary report only" to Yes.

6. Change the "Left margin" setting on the Options menu from 8 to 10.

7. Quit the Create Report screen without saving any changes.

DESIGN REPORTS — 12.2

Designing report files successfully requires that you have a clear understanding of the fields and information that you're basing the report upon. It also helps to have what is called a graphic eye, or the ability to conceive of the way information can be best presented in a report. If you don't have such a graphic eye, you can develop it over time by working in the Create Report screen and experimenting with various features that you might want to use. That is what you'll do in the rest of this chapter.

Once you select the report format settings that you want to use on the Options menu, you open the Columns menu and insert field names into the columns you want to use. To insert a field name in a column, highlight the Contents setting and press (Enter) and then (F10). This opens a list of field names for the current database. Highlight the field name you want to insert and press (Enter). The field name will appear after the Contents setting. If you want to insert more than one field name, make sure you insert a plus sign (+) between field names.

In the following examples, you'll create a report called NAD.FRM that lists information in NAD.DBF in a two-column format. The screen in Figure 12-4 shows what the first part of the report looks like printed to the screen. The left column contains the names of the people who owe you money. The right column contains the amounts they owe. The screen in Figure 12-5 shows what the end of the report looks like. This is more appealing and informative than the list you created in Chapter 10 because it arranges field information in columns that are aligned and it calculates the total of numerical information.

Since creating reports is a highly individual task, you'll learn the basic steps when you work with the examples that follow this section. In the rest of this section, you'll learn about the definitions of the various settings in the Create and Modify Report screens, which are defined in Table 12-2. If you enter a value that dBASE cannot accept, dBASE will beep and display on the message line the range of minimum and maximum values for the setting.

Examples

1. Begin creating NAD.FRM by opening the Create Report screen: Make sure NAD.DBF is current. Press (C), press (↑) twice, and press (Enter). Type **NAD** and press (Enter). Your screen should change to look like the one in Figure 12-1.

Chapter 12 Creating and Using Reports **277**

```
Set Up  Create  Update  Position  Retrieve  Organize Modify Tools   12:13:28 pm

        Page No.      1
        07/22/90
                             Update of Debtors

        Debtors                    Money Owed


        Jeannie Iams                 92.12
        Walter Gomer                150.00
        John McCord                 200.00
        Ziggy Zagare                450.00
        Stan Freeburg                25.00
        David Clark                  25.00
        Launey Thomas                50.00
        Swarna Mitts                450.00
        Richard Fallenbaum          900.00
        Christian Smith             175.00
        Judy Verlenden              235.00
        Carol Hanna                 850.00
ASSIST          |<C:>|NAD                |Rec: 1/20
```

FIGURE 12-4. The results of printing a report

```
Set Up  Create  Update  Position  Retrieve  Organize Modify Tools   12:13:28 pm
        John McCord                 200.00
        Ziggy Zagare                450.00
        Stan Freeburg                25.00
        David Clark                  25.00
        Launey Thomas                50.00
        Swarna Mitts                450.00
        Richard Fallenbaum          900.00
        Christian Smith             175.00
        Judy Verlenden              235.00
        Carol Hanna                 850.00
        David Trollman              600.00
        Carol McGinnis              500.00
        Margaret Smith              250.00
        Roger Smith                 150.00
        Cornelius Ragg              200.00
        Charles Smith               340.00
        Amma Smith                  250.00
        Pat Smith                   500.00
        *** Total ***
                                   6392.12
ASSIST          |<C:>|NAD                |Rec: 1/20
              Press any key to continue work in ASSIST.
```

FIGURE 12-5. The end of the report

TABLE 12-2. Definitions of All Menu Settings *(continued on next page)*

Options Menu

Page title	Inserts the text at the top of every page in the report
Page width	Sets the width of each page in the report, in positions or spaces. Default value is 80. The "Left margin" and "Right margin" values are subtracted from this figure to get the printed width of the page
Left margin	Sets the left margin for each page beginning at the left edge of the paper. Default value is 8
Right margin	Sets the right margin for each page beginning at the right position set by the "Page width" setting. Default values is 0, or no right margin
Lines per page	Sets the number of lines printed on each page. Default value is 58 lines
Double space report	Toggles between printing double spaced or printing single spaced. Default is No. This means that single spacing is set
Page eject before printing	Toggles eject on or off. Default is Yes. This means that your printer will eject a blank page at the beginning of printing the report
Page eject after printing	Toggles eject on or off. Default is No. This means that your printer will not eject a blank page at the end of printing the report
Plain page	Toggles page numbers and system date on and off. Default is No

TABLE 12-2. Definitions of All Menu Settings (*continued on next page*)

Groups Menu

Group on expression	Groups records according to an index field or expression you declare here
Group heading	Inserts the text before a group when printing
Summary report only	Toggles the printing of a summary report on or off. A summary report is a list of all groups and subtotals if they contain numeric field information. Default is No. This means that a summary report is not printed
Page eject after group	Toggles eject of a page for each group. Default is No. This means that your printer will not start a new page for each group of fields
Sub-group on expression	Lets you define a subgroup of records based upon an indexed field. A subgroup is a group below the main group
Sub-group heading	Inserts the text as the heading that will be printed before the sub-group

Columns Menu

Contents	Lets you define the contents of the current column using valid dBASE expressions, or field names in the current database. If you use multiple fields for the contents, make sure you separate each field name with a plus sign
Heading	Lets you define the text that will appear as the heading for the current column

TABLE 12-2. Definitions of All Menu Settings

Columns Menu (*continued*)

Width	Lets you define the width for the current column. The default setting is the width of the current field. If no field has been inserted, the width is 0, which is also the minimum value
Decimal places	Lets you define the decimal places for the current column if you're inserting numeric fields in the column. This setting is highlighted only when you've inserted a numeric field. The default value is the width of the current field
Total this column	Toggles column total calculation on or off. The default setting is Yes

Exit Menu

Save	Saves the report as designed to disk and returns you to the Assist screen
Abandon	Abandons all changes made to the current report since the last save to disk and returns you to the Assist screen. Pressing [Esc] twice, or [Esc] and then [Y], does the same thing

2. The first element you'll insert into the report is the text that will appear on the top line of each page of the report. Make sure the Options menu is open and the selection "Page title" highlighted, and then press [Enter]. This opens the entry area, where you can find the cursor. This box lets you enter up to four lines of text.

Type **Update of Debtors** and then press [Ctrl]-[End]. This closes the entry area and inserts the sentence you just typed after the "Page title" setting. You can see the first part of the entry in the menu setting.

Chapter 12   Creating and Using Reports   **281**

3. Create the first column and insert the first field into it: Press [C] to open the Columns menu. The indicator on the right side of the status bar should say "Column 1." Press [Enter] to activate the top setting, called Contents. This lets you enter the fields that will serve as the contents of the columns. An arrow will appear after the setting name indicating that you can now change the setting. The navigation line now tells you to enter an expression, press [F10] for a field menu, and then finish by pressing [Enter].

Press [F10] to open the list of fields in NAD.DBF, as shown in Figure 12-6. The NAME field should be highlighted. Press [Enter]. NAME will appear in the field following the Contents setting, and the field list will close. Notice that the number 30 appears in the Width column. This reflects the width of the NAME field in NAD.DBF, which is the first field you entered into the Contents setting. Change the number now: Highlight the Width setting and press [Enter]. Type 40 and press [Enter] twice.

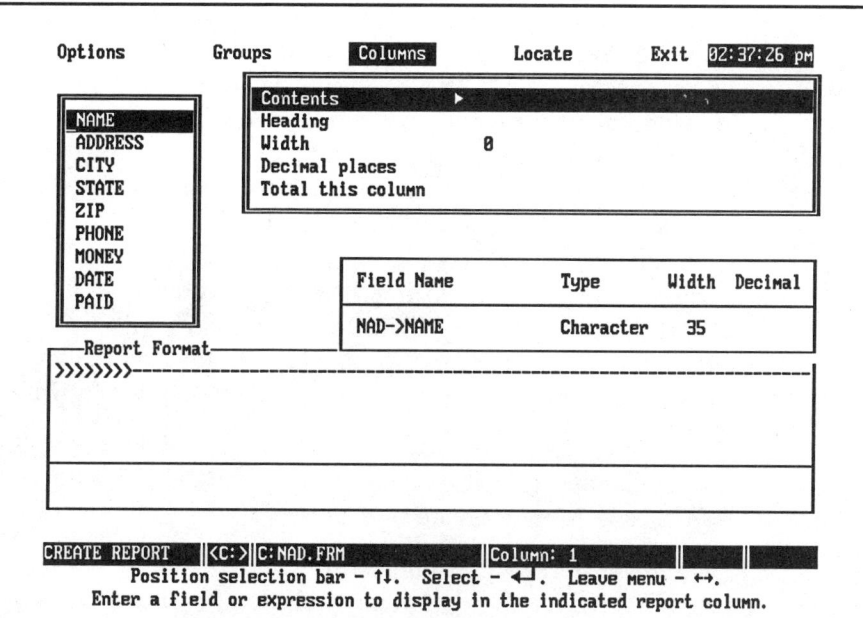

FIGURE 12-6.   The field list in the Create Report screen

4. Now that you've created your first column, see how the Locate menu has changed. Press [→] and you'll see that the field name you just entered into column 1 shows as the only option on the Locate menu. (Earlier the Locate menu contained no options.) The Locate menu helps you locate specific columns in a report. Once you create multiple columns in reports, you'll use the Locate menu to go to specific columns quickly so that you can change and edit their contents.

5. Go back to the Columns menu and insert some text that will describe the information in column 1. Press [↓] to highlight the Heading setting. Press [Enter] to open the entry area. Then type **Debtors** and press [Ctrl]-[End]. The text should appear in the Heading field on the pull-down menu.

   Notice that the text appears in the report format area. dBASE won't insert the field information into the report until you save the report and print it to screen or paper, but the report format area will show you many of the features you've inserted in the report.

6. Now create a second column. This will contain the amount of money each person owes you. Notice the information on the right side of the navigation line: "Prev/Next column - PgUp/PgDn." This information always appears when you work with the Columns menu, except when you make a setting current. Press [PgDn] to move to the second column. Notice that the indicator on the right side of the status bar changes to show column 2.

   Insert the MONEY field for the second column: Press [↑] to highlight the Contents setting. Press [Enter] and then [F10]. Highlight MONEY and press [Enter] twice, the second time to fix the setting. Notice that the Width setting changes to 6 and the "Decimal places" setting changes to 2. These reflect the field settings for MONEY in NAD.DBF.

7. Insert text that identifies column 2: Highlight Heading and press [Enter]. Type **Money Owed** and press [Ctrl]-[End].

8. Save this report so that you can print it to your screen and test it: Press [E] to open the Exit menu and then [Enter] to execute the Save command. dBASE will save NAD.FRM to disk and return you to the Assist screen.

Exercises

1. What does the "Page title" setting let you do?

2. How do you create a column?

3. How do you know which column you're working with?

4. How do you insert a field name into a column?

5. Open the Create Report screen for a report called TEST. You can base this report on NAD.DBF. Insert the NAME field into column 1.

6. Create a heading for column 1 called "Name of Debtors."

7. Insert the PHONE field into column 2. Create a heading for this column called "Phone Number."

8. Save this report.

PRINT REPORTS 12.3

Printing a report is as easy as printing any other information. You'll use the Report command on the Retrieve menu to print a report. You can print a report to the screen or to the printer. You can select a range, or group, of records to print by using the Search/Scope menu.

Before you can print a report, make sure that the database that supplies field information to the report is current. If no database is current, none of the commands on the Retrieve menu are enabled. Once you've opened the database for the report form, you can then proceed to print the report file.

To print NAD.FRM, first make sure NAD.DBF is current. Then

a. Press [R] to open the Retrieve menu.

b. Highlight the command Report by pressing [↓] twice. Then press [Enter]. dBASE opens a list of drive letters.

c. Press [Enter] to accept the current drive, or highlight the drive that you want to use and press [Enter]. dBASE opens a list of report file names you can use.

d. Highlight the name of the report file that you want to print and press [Enter]. dBASE displays the Search/Scope menu. You can work in this menu to select records to print, or you can proceed to print the report to include all records in the database.

e. Press [Enter] to select "Execute the command," which is highlighted by default. dBASE asks where you want to send the report.

f. Press [Enter] to send the report to the screen. Press [Y] to send it to the printer.

When you print a report, dBASE displays information for the fields you've specified in the space you've declared for the report field widths. dBASE also calculates the totals of all entries in numeric fields. It calculates subtotals as well if you define them on the Groups menu when you design the report.

If you attach an index file or files to the database that you're using as the source of information for the report, the indexes will control the order in which field information appears in the report.

If you've marked any records for deletion in the database but have not yet packed the database, information from the marked records will appear in the report. No asterisks will appear next to the record information, however, as they do when you use the command List.

If you don't make the appropriate database current before you print a report, no information will appear in the report, or the wrong information will appear. When you print a report, dBASE reads the fields in the report format and extracts the corresponding information from the matching database. If you print NAD.FRM when another database is current, only information for fields that match those by name in the report file will be printed. Most likely, this will be the wrong information.

You should have little problem using the Search/Scope menu to select a group of records to print in the report. As long as you're using the correct database, the fields in the report and database will match up. The command "Construct a field list" is disabled in the version of the Search/Scope menu that is attached to the Report command. This prevents you from either conflicting with the report design and trying to print fields that aren't in the report file or excluding fields that are in the report.

Examples

1. Print the report NAD.FRM to the screen. First make sure NAD.DBF is current. Then press [R], highlight Report, and press [Enter] twice. dBASE displays a list of the report file names that you can use. Highlight NAD.FRM and press [Enter]. dBASE displays the Search/Scope menu. Press [Enter] twice.

   As soon as the report starts printing on the screen, press [Ctrl]-[S] to freeze the printing. Your screen should change to look like Figure 12-4. When you press any key to resume printing, your screen will change to look like Figure 12-5. Press any key to unfreeze the report and let it run through the end of its printing to the screen. When you reach the end of the report, you'll notice a total value for the amounts printed in the MONEY field. To return to the Assist screen, press any key.

2. Print the report NAD.FRM to the screen, displaying information only for the first ten records in NAD.DBF. You'll use the "Specify scope" command to do this.

   First make sure NAD.DBF is current. Press [R], highlight Report, and then press [Enter] twice. Highlight NAD.FRM and press [Enter]. Highlight "Specify scope" and press [Enter]. Highlight NEXT, press [Enter], type 10, and press [Enter]. Highlight "Execute the command" and press [Enter] twice. Your screen should look something like the one in Figure 12-7.

```
Set Up  Create  Update  Position  Retrieve  Organize Modify Tools   04:15:18 pm

        Page No.    1
        08/22/90
                              Update of Debtors



        Jeannie Iams              92.12
        Walter Gomer             150.00
        John McCord              200.00
        Ziggy Zagare             450.00
        Stan Freeburg             25.00
        David Clark               25.00
        Launey Thomas             50.00
        Swarna Mitts             450.00
        Richard Fallenbaum       900.00
        Christian Smith          175.00


ASSIST            <C:> NAD               Rec: 16/20
```

FIGURE 12-7. Printing the first ten records

3. Print the report NAD.FRM to the screen displaying only information for people who live in Arizona. You'll build a search condition to do this.

   Press (R), highlight Report, and press (Enter). Highlight NAD .FRM and press (Enter) twice. Highlight "Build a search condition" and press (Enter). Highlight STATE and press (Enter), highlight = Equal To and press (Enter), type **AZ**, and press (Enter) twice to confirm "No more conditions." Highlight "Execute the command" and press (Enter) twice. Your screen should change to look something like the one in Figure 12-8.

4. Print NAD.FRM to the screen in the order created by the index NAD.NDX. First, attach the index to NAD.DBF: Press (S), press (Enter) twice, highlight NAD, and press (Enter) again. Now press (Y), highlight NAME.NDX, press (Enter), and press (→).

   Once NAD.DBF is current and NAME.NDX is attached to it, print the report: Press (R), highlight Report, and press (Enter) twice. Highlight NAD.FRM and press (Enter) three times. You'll see the

Chapter 12　　　　　　　　　　　　　　　　　　　Creating and Using Reports　**287**

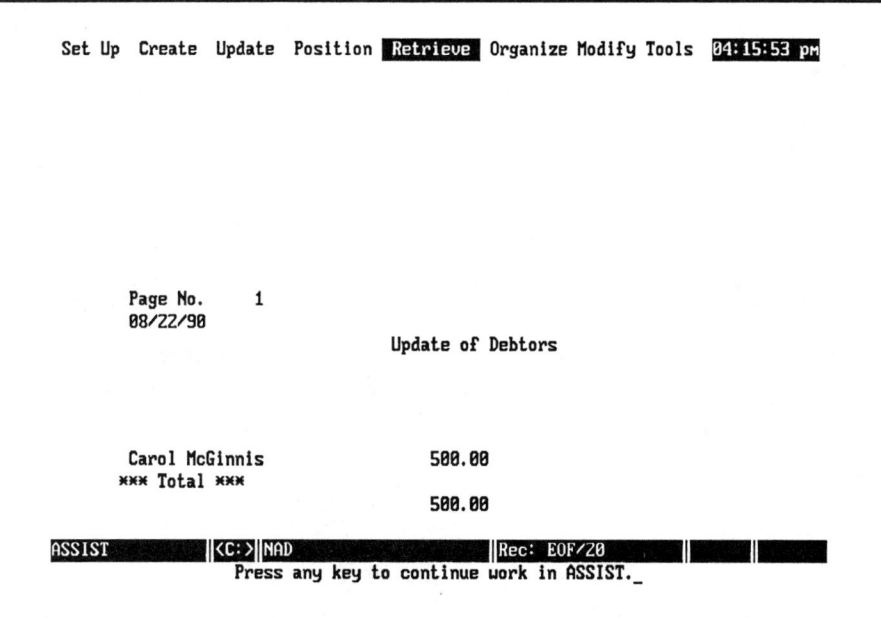

```
        Set Up  Create  Update  Position  Retrieve  Organize Modify Tools  04:15:53 pm




                  Page No.    1
                  08/22/90
                                         Update of Debtors



                  Carol McGinnis         500.00
                  *** Total ***
                                         500.00
        ASSIST           <C:> NAD                    Rec: EOF/20
                          Press any key to continue work in ASSIST._
```

FIGURE 12-8.　Printing records for STATE = AZ only

report printed to your screen. If you want to freeze the scrolling to check the order of records in the NAME field, press [Ctrl]-[S]. Press any key to resume the printing.

Exercises

1. When you print a report, do you have the option of printing either to the screen or the printer?

2. Can you select a group of records to print in the report by using the Search/Scope menu?

3. Select all the records in NAD.DBF for the state of Connecticut (STATE = CT) to print in NAD.FRM, print the report to the screen, and then return to the Assist screen.

4. Can you select a group of fields to print in a report after you have created the report form?

5. Why?

12.4 MODIFY REPORTS

Once you've created a report, you can modify it by using the Modify Report screen. To open this screen, make current the database the report is based on, and then use the Report command on the Modify menu:

a. Press [M] to open the Modify menu.

b. Highlight Report. The best way to do this is to press [↑] twice.

c. Press [Enter] twice. dBASE displays a list of the names of available report forms.

d. Highlight the name of the report form that you want to modify, and then press [Enter]. dBASE will move you into the Modify Report screen, as shown in Figure 12-9. The only difference between this screen and the Create Report screen is the label on the left side of the status bar, MODIFY REPORT.

All commands in the Modify Report screen are identical to the commands in the Create Report screen. You can make all changes by using the same setting commands. When you're finished making changes, press [E] to open the Exit menu, and then press [Enter] to save your changes and return to the Assist screen.

Make sure that the database you've made current is the correct database. You can open the Modify Report screen for a report form regardless of which database is current, even if the database has no relation to the report form that you want to modify.

If you're working in a report form when the wrong database is current, you can still change report settings by toggling them on or off,

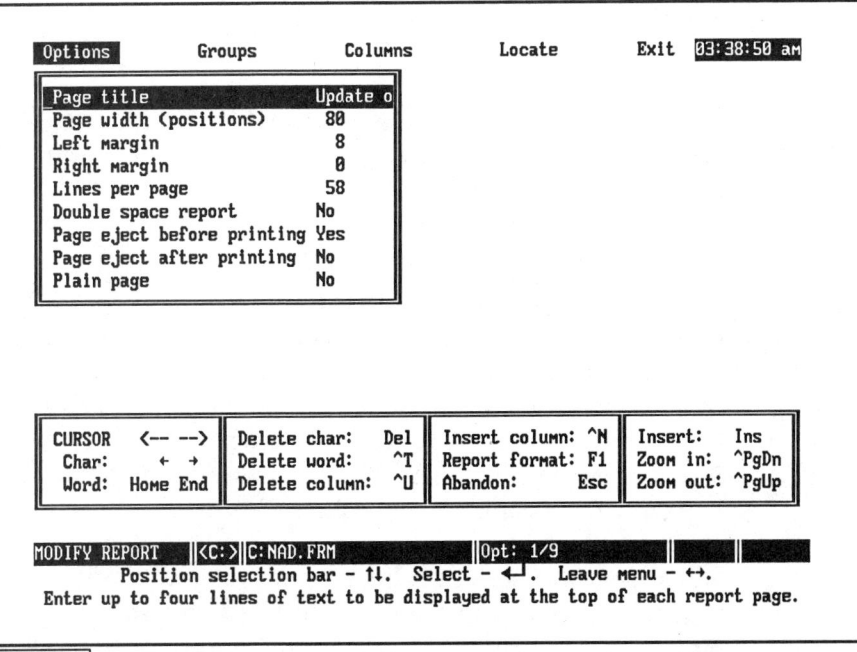

```
 Options       Groups      Columns      Locate      Exit  03:38:50 am
┌─────────────────────────────────────┐
│ Page title                 Update o │
│ Page width (positions)     80       │
│ Left margin                 8       │
│ Right margin                0       │
│ Lines per page             58       │
│ Double space report        No       │
│ Page eject before printing Yes      │
│ Page eject after printing  No       │
│ Plain page                 No       │
└─────────────────────────────────────┘
```

```
CURSOR   <-- -->  | Delete char:   Del | Insert column: ^N | Insert:    Ins
Char:      ← →    | Delete word:   ^T  | Report format: F1 | Zoom in:  ^PgDn
Word:   Home End  | Delete column: ^U  | Abandon:      Esc | Zoom out: ^PgUp
```

```
MODIFY REPORT  |<C:>|C:NAD.FRM        |Opt: 1/9
           Position selection bar - ↑↓. Select - ↵. Leave menu - ←→.
       Enter up to four lines of text to be displayed at the top of each report page.
```

FIGURE 12-9. The Modify Report screen

raising and lowering their numeric values, and typing in new text. The only thing that you can't do is insert fields from the right database. Whenever you're working with a report setting that will accept field names and you press F10, field names from the current database will appear on screen. If you want to insert fields from the right database, you should save the changes you've made so far, exit the Modify Report screen, and make the right database current. Then reenter the Modify Report screen for the same report file name and continue your work. You can also abandon any changes you've made while working in the Modify Report screen by pressing Esc twice.

Summary reports are reports where information is summarized for each group you create using the Groups menu. Only the summarized information is printed. A summary report takes less time to print, but it also prints less information.

You can switch back and forth easily between modifying a report file and printing it. This helps you fine-tune your adjustments.

Examples

1. Open the Modify Report screen for NAD.FRM. First make sure NAD.DBF is current. Then press [M] to open the Modify menu. Press [↑] twice to highlight the command Report and press [Enter] twice. dBASE displays a list of the names of available report forms. Highlight NAD.FRM and press [Enter].

2. Change NAD.FRM so that it contains three columns instead of two, with different information in the columns. You'll add the address, city, and state names to column 1. You'll replace the MONEY field in column 2 with the PHONE field. And you'll create a new column 3 containing the MONEY field. This way information about each person will appear in the left column, his or her phone number will appear in the middle column, and the amount of money each owes will appear in the right column.

    Begin by changing column 1. Press [C], and then [Enter]. You will find the cursor blinking after NAME. Type + (the plus key). This is the way to link multiple field names. The setting for Contents now contains NAME+.

3. Insert the second, third, and fourth fields in the Contents setting: Press [F10] to open the field list, press [↓] to highlight ADDRESS, and press [Enter]. This inserts the second field. Type +, press [F10], press [↓] twice to highlight CITY, and then press [Enter]. This inserts the third field. Type +, press [F10], press [↓] three times to highlight STATE, and then press [Enter]. This inserts the fourth field. The setting for Contents should now read NAME+ADDRESS+CITY+STATE. Press [Enter] to fix these field names in the Contents selection. The arrow that first appeared when you activated this setting disappears.

4. Move to column 2 by pressing [PgDn]. Then press [Enter] to activate the Contents setting. Press [Backspace] five times to erase MONEY, and then press [Enter] to fix the change. Press [Enter] again, press [F10] to open the field list, highlight PHONE, and press [Enter].

5. Press [PgDn] to move to column 3. Press [Enter], then [F10], highlight MONEY, and press [Enter] twice to fix the field into the third column.

6. Save this modification and print it to the screen to test the results: Press [E], and then [Enter] to save the report. Press [R], highlight Report, and then press [Enter] five times.

You can switch back and forth between modifying a report and printing it rather easily. When you start out and have created only one report, you can move even more quickly since only one report name appears when dBASE asks you to select a report file name to print or modify.

Exercises

1. Is there any difference between the commands you use in the Modify Report screen and those in the Create Report screen?

2. Can you modify a report that hasn't yet been created?

3. Do you have to open the right database to modify a report form?

4. What risks are there when you make changes to a report form without making the right database current?

5. Begin in the Assist screen. Change the "Left margin" setting on the Options menu to 0.

6. On the Groups menu, change the "Summary report only" command to Yes, and then save the setting.

7. Print NAD.FRM to the screen, and then return to the Assist screen.

8. What happens when "Summary report only" is switched to Yes?

EXERCISES

MASTERY SKILLS CHECK

1. Why would you want to create a report rather than print database information by using the command List or Display?

2. Create a report called NAD1.FRM that displays two fields of information in NAD.DBF, the NAME field and the MONEY field. Save the report.

3. Print NAD1.FRM to the screen for all records in NAD.DBF.

4. Reprint NAD1.FRM to the screen for records in which MONEY > $100.

5. Modify NAD1.FRM so that the phone number appears in a third column.

6. Print the revised version of NAD1.FRM to the screen for all records in NAD.DBF.

INTEGRATING SKILLS CHECK

1. To create a report based on VALUE.DBF, what is the first step you take?

2. Make VALUE.DBF current.

3. Create a report called VALUE. Place each of the four fields in a column of its own. Save the report.

4. Print the report VALUE to the screen. View the results and return to the Assist screen.

5. Begin in the Assist screen and modify the report VALUE so that it contains this line of text at the top: "Report on All Items in VALUE.DBF." Save the report.

Creating and Using Labels
▶13◀

CHAPTER OBJECTIVES

In this chapter you will

▶ **Become familiar with the Create Label screen**   13.1

▶ **Create labels**   13.2

▶ **Print labels**   13.3

▶ **Modify labels**   13.4

Printing labels requires a specific type of report format. Creating, designing, and printing labels let you produce physical tags that you can affix to all sorts of items. These items include letters, boxes, other containers, and anything else that needs to be identified with information from a database.

Labels are such a frequently used report format that dBASE provides separate Create Label and Modify Label screens where you can create and design labels exclusively. These screen components behave similarly to the Create and Modify Report screens that you learned to use in Chapter 12.

In this chapter, you'll explore the Create Label, Modify Label, and Retrieve Label screens, become familiar with their menu commands, and learn how to use them to design, modify, and print labels.

Exercises

SKILLS CHECK

1. Make NAD.DBF current. See what dBASE on-line help has to say about the Label command on the Create menu.

2. See what dBASE on-line help has to say about the Label command on the Modify menu.

3. See what dBASE on-line help has to say about the Label command on the Retrieve menu.

4. Attach the NAME.NDX index to NAD.DBF.

5. List the contents of NAD.DBF on the screen in the indexed order, and then return to the Assist screen.

6. Display the structure of NAD.DBF on screen, and then return to the Assist screen.

BECOME FAMILIAR WITH THE CREATE LABEL SCREEN — 13.1

You create labels in dBASE III PLUS using the Create Label screen. This is a smaller version of the Create Report screen, designed exclusively for creating label formats. You use settings in this screen to design the format that you want to use and to insert fields from a database into the label.

Before you can open the Create screen for label files, you must make current the database that will provide information for the labels. The only elements you can insert into a label are field names. For example, if you want to print mailing labels to people in NAD.DBF, you need to insert the NAME, ADDRESS, CITY, STATE, and ZIP fields into a label format.

You can set up a database for designing labels in two ways: before you open the Create Label screen or after you specify the name of the label file you want create.

a. Make current the database you want to use to supply information for the labels you're going to design.

b. Press [C] to open the Create menu.

c. Highlight the Label command. The easiest way to do this is to press [↑]. Press [Enter] twice. dBASE asks you what name you want to give the label file.

d. Type the label file name and press [Enter]. If you haven't yet opened a database, dBASE will say "No database is in USE. Enter file name:."

e. Type the database file name that you want to use and press [Enter]. dBASE presents you with the Create Label screen. Figure 13-1 shows this screen for a label file called NAD.LBL. The extension stands for "Label."

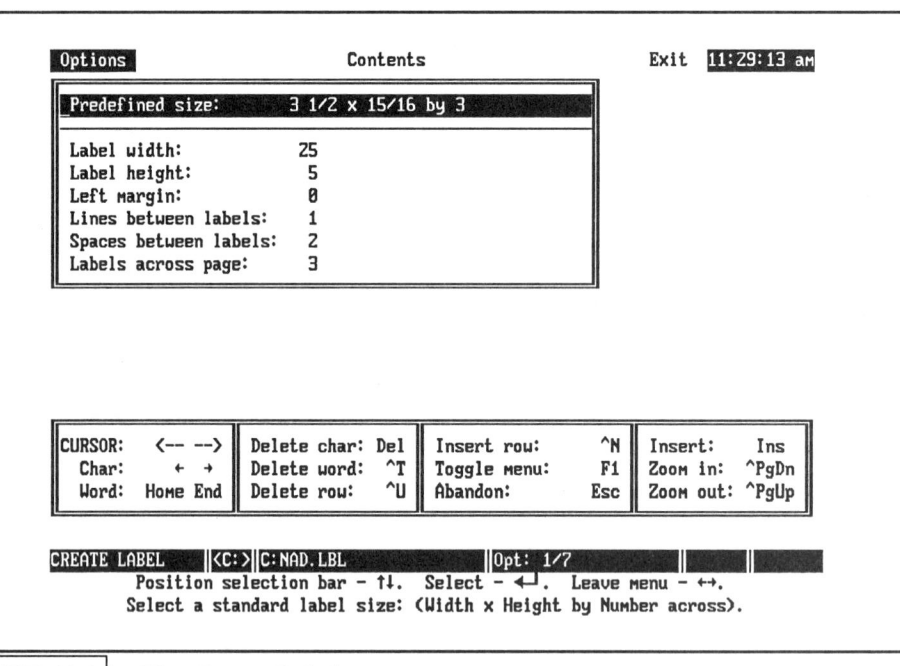

```
 Options              Contents              Exit  11:29:13 am
┌─────────────────────────────────────────┐
│ Predefined size:    3 1/2 x 15/16 by 3  │
│                                         │
│ Label width:        25                  │
│ Label height:       5                   │
│ Left margin:        0                   │
│ Lines between labels:  1                │
│ Spaces between labels: 2                │
│ Labels across page:    3                │
└─────────────────────────────────────────┘
```

```
┌─────────────────┬──────────────────┬──────────────────┬──────────────────┐
│ CURSOR: <-- -->  │ Delete char: Del │ Insert row:   ^N │ Insert:     Ins  │
│ Char:   ← →      │ Delete word: ^T  │ Toggle menu:  F1 │ Zoom in:   ^PgDn │
│ Word:   Home End │ Delete row:  ^U  │ Abandon:     Esc │ Zoom out:  ^PgUp │
└─────────────────┴──────────────────┴──────────────────┴──────────────────┘
 CREATE LABEL    |<C:>|C:NAD.LBL         |Opt: 1/7
         Position selection bar - ↑↓.  Select - ↵.  Leave menu - ↔.
         Select a standard label size: (Width x Height by Number across).
```

FIGURE 13-1. The Create Label screen

Most of this screen should look familiar to you, not only from your work with other versions of the Create screen, but because of your work in Chapter 12, where you learned how to create and design reports. The status bar and navigation and message lines are at the bottom of the screen. A menu bar is at the top. In this screen, there are only three menu names. The leftmost pull-down menu, the Options menu, is open by default.

Become familiar with all the commands in the Create Label screen. The three pull-down menus are defined here:

    Options   Seven settings that let you select a specific label format and fine-tune the printed characteristics of the labels

Contents   Five lines that let you enter specific fields into each line of each label that you want to print. The number of lines that appears in this menu is determined by the setting for "Label height" on the Options menu. A value of 5 is the default

Exit   Lets you either save the label file you've created and return to the Assist screen or exit the current label file and abandon all changes since the last save.

You can also abandon all your work in the Create screen for label files in either of these two ways:

- Press [Esc]. dBASE will ask you to confirm the abandon. Press [Y].

- Press [Esc] twice.

Figure 13-2 shows a map of the three pull-down menus in the Create Label screen. Technically, there are only nine commands on the menus: the seven on the Options menu and the two on the Exit menu. The menus and commands are identical in the Create Label and Modify Label screens. You work with these menus, and the commands on these menus, in the same way that you work with all other pull-down commands in dBASE. Press [→] or [←] to scroll through the menus in sequence. To open a menu directly, press the key that matches the first letter of the menu name. Press [↑] and [↓] to highlight different commands. Press [Enter] to execute the highlighted command. You can also use the [Ctrl]-key-combinations shown in Table 2-1 to open menus and highlight commands.

Most of the menu selections in the Create Label screen are really not commands but settings. They don't do anything except store values that control the format of the label and insert text and field information into the label. The Options menu lets you change format settings, and the Contents menu lets you insert field names into lines

```
        Options                          Contents              Exit

Predefined size:   3 1/2 x 15/16 by 1   Label contents 1:     Save
-----------------------------------                     2:     Abandon
Label width:       35                                   3:
Label height:      5                                    4:
Left margin:       0                                    5:
Lines between labels:  1
Spaces between labels: 0
Labels across page:    1
```

FIGURE 13-2. Menu map of commands in the Create Label screen

on each label. In the Contents menu, you can zoom into a larger work area for each label contents line by pressing [Ctrl]-[PgDn]. You zoom out of this work area by pressing [Ctrl]-[PgUp].

To increase or decrease a numeric value within the Options menu:

a. Highlight the setting containing the numeric value.

b. Press [Enter].

c. Type the numeric value that you want to use and press [Enter]. The new value will appear next to the setting.

With some numeric settings, you're limited to minimum and maximum values. dBASE will warn you on the message line if your selection violates these limits. If it does, press SPACEBAR and enter a new value.

You can also change numeric values by pressing [Enter], pressing [↑] to raise the number or pressing [↓] to lower the number, and then pressing [Enter] to set the new value.

Pressing [F1] toggles help on and off. Table 13-1 defines the commands in the help table.

Examples

1. Scroll through the pull-down menus in the Create Label screen. Make sure that the Options menu is showing. If it isn't, press [Ctrl]-[A]. Press [→] twice to scroll through all three pull-down menus. Press [O] to reopen the Options menu.

2. On the Options pull-down menu, check the various types of default label settings that you can use. Highlight "Predefined size" and press [Enter] five times. You'll cycle through all five basic types of label formats that you can use and return to the original setting. You'll learn more about the details for these formats in the next section.

TABLE 13-1.	Help Instructions Defined
Key	**Action**
→	Move cursor right one space
Home	Move cursor right one word
←	Move cursor left one space
End	Move cursor left one word
↑	Move cursor up one line
↓	Move cursor down one line
F1	Toggle Report Format/Help
Ins	Toggle insert/typeover mode
Press character key	Insert character
Ctrl-N	Insert column
Del	Delete character
Ctrl-T	Delete word
Ctrl-U	Delete column
Ctrl-PgDn	Zoom in
Ctrl-PgUp	Zoom out
Esc	Abandon changes

3. Change the numeric value for the "Label width" setting from 35 to 25. Make sure that the Options pull-down menu is showing. Press O if it isn't. Press ↓ to highlight the "Label width" setting. Press Enter, type 25, and press Enter.

4. Experiment with the way you enter field names into lines on a label. Press C to open the Contents menu. The "Label contents 1" line is highlighted. Press Enter, and then F10 to open the field list window. The NAME field should be highlighted. Press Enter twice to insert this field name into "Label contents 1" and to fix the contents.

5. Practice zooming in and out of lines in the Contents menu. Press ↓ to highlight "2." Press Enter to activate the setting. Now press Ctrl-PgDn to zoom into a larger work area. You work with this area in the same way that you work with the unzoomed setting. Press Enter to close the zoomed area.

Exercises

1. How many pull-down menus are there in the Create Label screen?

2. Make sure NAD.DBF is current. Open the Create Label screen by creating a label file called NAD.LBL.

3. Open the Options pull-down menu and change the "Label height" setting to 10.

4. Open the Contents menu.

5. How many lines are present? Why?

6. Change the "Left margin" setting on the Options menu from 0 to 5.

7. Quit the Create Label screen without saving any changes.

CREATE LABELS   13.2

Designing labels requires only that you know how the various predefined labels should look when printed and that you know what fields you want to print on different lines of the label. You don't need a graphic eye to create labels, although you will probably want to go back and modify label files the first few times that you create them.

Once you select the label settings on the Options menu that you want to use, you open the Contents menu and insert field names into the various lines that you want to use. To insert a field name on a "Label contents" line:

a. Highlight the line and press [Enter]

b. Press [F10]. This opens a list of field names for the current database.

c. Highlight the field name that you want to insert and press [Enter]. The field name will appear on the current line. If you want to insert more than one field name, make sure that you insert a plus sign (+) between field names.

d. Press [Enter] to fix the contents of the setting.

TABLE 13-2.	Definitions of All Settings

Options

Predefined size	Lets you select one of five different types of label formats. These are the most popular types of labels and correspond to label paper you can buy at most stationery stores: 3 1/2 x 15/16 by 1 3 1/2 x 15/16 by 2 3 1/2 x 15/16 by 3 4 x 1 7/16 by 1 3 2/10 x 11/12 by 3 (Cheshire)
Label width	Lets you adjust the width of a label and override the predefined label value for this setting
Label height	Lets you adjust the height of a label and override the predefined label value for this setting
Left margin	Lets you adjust the width of the left margin (the distance between the left side of the label and the first column of characters for the label text). This width will occur in all columns you use. Default value is 0
Lines between labels	Lets you adjust the number of blank lines that will be printed between labels. Default value is 1
Spaces between labels	Lets you adjust the number of horizontal spaces between labels
Labels across page	Lets you change the number of labels that will be printed across a single page and override the predefined label value for this setting

Exit

Save	Saves the label file as designed to disk and returns you to the Assist screen
Abandon	Abandons all changes made to the current label file since the last save to disk and returns you to the Assist. Pressing (Esc) twice, or (Esc) and then (Y) does the same thing.

The best way to learn about labels is to start creating them. Table 13-2 describes the settings that you can select for various types of labels. The default value for many of these settings is determined by the current setting of the "Predefined size" field. If you try to change a setting and enter a value that dBASE cannot accept, dBASE will beep and display the range of minimum and maximum values for the current setting on the message line.

When you start designing your first labels, you should probably stick with the values you're given for the predefined size you're using. Once you print labels and find that they aren't quite lining up with the edges of the actual labels, you can use the "Lines between labels" setting to adjust label text so that it's centered on each label. You might also have to juggle with other settings to make the label look just right. (You'll make some adjustments later in this chapter, after you print NAD.LBL.)

In the following examples, you'll create a label file called NAD.LBL. The format you'll use will print 33 labels to a page—11 labels in 3 columns. Each label will contain 3 lines of information from NAD.DBF. Information from the NAME field will appear on the top line. Information from the ADDRESS field will appear on the second line. And information from the CITY, STATE, and ZIP fields will appear on the third line.

Examples

1. Begin creating NAD.LBL by opening the Create Label screen. Make sure that NAD.DBF is current. Then press [C], press [↑], and then press [Enter]. Type **NAD** and press [Enter] twice. Your screen should change to look like the one in Figure 13-1.

2. The first thing you need to do is select the predefined label that you want to use. Highlight "Predefined size" and press [Enter] until the size "3 1/2 x 15/16 by 3" appears after this selection. As you cycle through the various predefined sizes, notice how the values in settings change. Press [Enter] to fix the setting.

3. Accept all settings except the "Label width" setting. Change the "Label width" setting to 30: Highlight "Label width," press [Enter], type **30**, and press [Enter] again.

304   Teach Yourself dBASE III PLUS

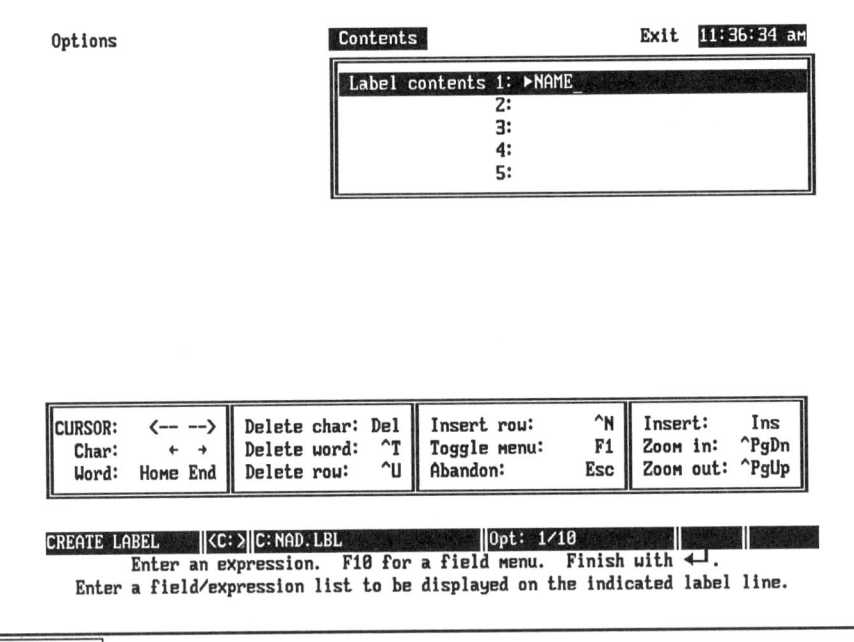

```
   Options                    Contents              Exit  11:36:34 am
                      ┌─────────────────────────────────┐
                      │ Label contents 1: ▶NAME_        │
                      │                2:               │
                      │                3:               │
                      │                4:               │
                      │                5:               │
                      └─────────────────────────────────┘




 ┌─────────────────────┬─────────────────────┬──────────────────────┐
 │CURSOR:    <-- -->   │Delete char: Del     │Insert row:      ^N   │Insert:     Ins │
 │Char:      ←   →     │Delete word: ^T      │Toggle menu:     F1   │Zoom in:   ^PgDn│
 │Word:    Home End    │Delete row:  ^U      │Abandon:        Esc   │Zoom out:  ^PgUp│
 └─────────────────────┴─────────────────────┴──────────────────────┘
 CREATE LABEL    |<C:>|C:NAD.LBL              |Opt: 1/10|
        Enter an expression.  F10 for a field menu.  Finish with ↵.
        Enter a field/expression list to be displayed on the indicated label line.
```

FIGURE 13-3.   NAME inserted in Line 1

4. Now insert the first field in the label. Press [→] to open the Contents menu. "Label contents 1" should be highlighted. Press [Enter] and then [F10] to open the list of field names in NAD.DBF. The NAME field should be highlighted. Press [Enter]. The field NAME will appear after "Label contents 1," as shown in Figure 13-3. Press [Enter].

5. Now insert the second field. Press [↓] to highlight "2.". Press [Enter], then [F10], highlight ADDRESS, and press [Enter] twice to fix this field name.

6. Insert the third, fourth, and fifth fields in "Label contents 3." Press [↓] to highlight "3." Press [Enter] and then [F10] to open the field list. Highlight CITY and press [Enter]. Type +. Press [F10], highlight STATE, and press [Enter]. Type +. Press [F10] one more time, highlight ZIP, and press [Enter]. The three lines of your label should look like this:

```
Line 1: NAME
Line 2: ADDRESS
Line 3: CITY+STATE+ZIP
```

7. Save this label file so that you can print it to your screen and test it. Press [E] to open the Exit menu and then [Enter] to execute the Save command. dBASE will save NAD.LBL to disk and return you to the Assist screen.

Exercises

1. What does the "Predefined size" setting let you do?

2. Where do you insert field names?

3. How do you insert a field name into a line?

4. How do you insert multiple field names?

5. How do you save a label file?

PRINT LABELS — 13.3

Printing a label file is as easy as printing a report. You'll use the command Label on the Retrieve menu to print the labels. You can print labels to the screen or to the printer. You can also use the Search/Scope menu to select a range or a group of records to print as labels.

Before you can print labels, make sure that the proper database for supplying record information to the labels is current. If no database is current, none of the commands on the Retrieve menu are enabled. Once you've opened the database for the label file, you can proceed to print the labels.

To print NAD.LBL, first make sure NAD.DBF is current. Then

a. Press [R] to open the Retrieve menu.

b. Highlight the Label command by pressing [↓] three times. Then press [Enter]. dBASE opens a list of available drive letters.

c. Press [Enter] to use the current drive, or highlight the drive that you want to use and press [Enter]. dBASE presents a list of label file names that you can use.

d. Highlight the name of the label file that you want to print and press [Enter]. dBASE displays the Search/Scope menu. You can work in this menu to select records to print, or you can proceed to print all the records as labels.

e. Press [Enter] to select "Execute the command," which is highlighted by default. dBASE asks where you want to send the labels.

f. Press [Enter] to send the labels to the screen. Press [Y] to send them to the printer.

If you attach an index file or files to the database that you're using as the source of information for the labels, the indexes will control the order in which record information appears on the labels. This is particularly handy when you want to print mailing labels in ZIP code order.

If you've marked any records for deletion in the database, but have not yet packed the database, the marked records will be printed as labels. However, no asterisks will appear next to the record information.

If you don't make the appropriate database current before you print labels, no information will appear in the labels, or the wrong information will appear. When you print labels, dBASE reads the fields in the label file and extracts the information from the matching database. If you print NAD.LBL when another database is current, only information for fields that match those in the label file by name will be printed. Most likely, this will be the wrong information.

You shouldn't have much trouble using the Search/Scope menu to select a group of records to print in the labels. As long as you're using the correct database, the fields in the label file and the database should match up. The command "Construct a field list" is disabled in the

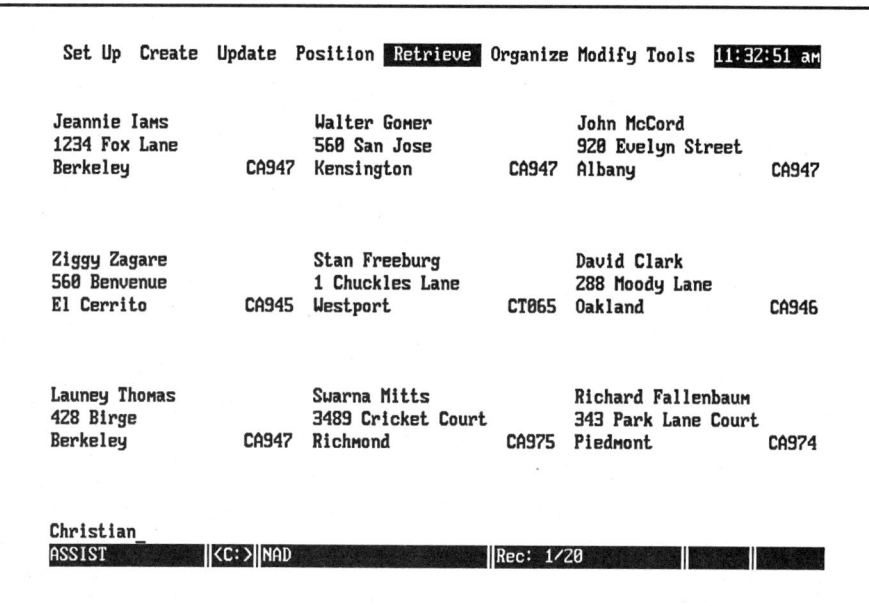

```
    Set Up  Create  Update  Position  Retrieve  Organize  Modify  Tools   11:32:51 am

         Jeannie Iams              Walter Gomer            John McCord
         1234 Fox Lane             560 San Jose            920 Evelyn Street
         Berkeley         CA947    Kensington     CA947    Albany             CA947


         Ziggy Zagare              Stan Freeburg           David Clark
         560 Benvenue              1 Chuckles Lane         288 Moody Lane
         El Cerrito       CA945    Westport       CT065    Oakland            CA946


         Launey Thomas             Swarna Mitts            Richard Fallenbaum
         428 Birge                 3489 Cricket Court      343 Park Lane Court
         Berkeley         CA947    Richmond       CA975    Piedmont           CA974


         Christian_
    ASSIST              |<C:>|NAD             |Rec: 1/20
```

FIGURE 13-4. NAD.LBL printed to screen

version of the Search/Scope menu that's attached to the Label command. This prevents you from either conflicting with the label design and trying to print fields that aren't in the label file or excluding fields that are in the label file.

Examples

1. Print the label file NAD.LBL to your screen. First make sure NAD.DBF is current. Then press [R], highlight Label, and press [Enter] twice. dBASE displays a list of the label file names you can use. Highlight NAD.LBL and press [Enter]. dBASE displays the Search/Scope menu. Press [Enter] two more times.

    As soon as the labels start printing on your screen, press [Ctrl]-[S] to freeze the printing. Your screen should look something like the one in Figure 13-4. Take a close look at the labels. The third line isn't quite right. There's too much room for the CITY information, and there's not enough room for the STATE and ZIP information. In fact, the last two digits of the ZIP code may not even appear. You'll change this in the next section, where you learn how to modify label files.

2. Presuming that you can adjust the third line so it works correctly, practice working with the Search/Scope menu. Print the labels NAD.LBL and display information for only the first five records in NAD.DBF.

First make sure NAD.DBF is current. Press (R), then (↓) three times, and then (Enter) twice. Highlight NAD.LBL and press (Enter). Highlight "Specify scope" and press (Enter). Highlight NEXT, press (Enter), type 10, and press (Enter). Highlight "Execute the command" and press (Enter) twice. Your screen should look something like the one in Figure 13-5.

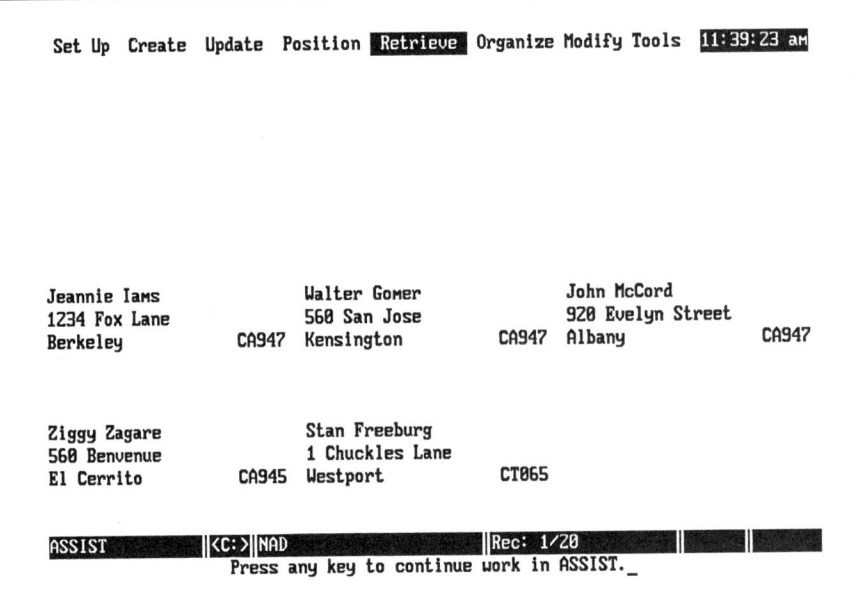

```
Set Up  Create  Update  Position  Retrieve  Organize  Modify  Tools    11:39:23 am




              Jeannie Iams              Walter Gomer              John McCord
              1234 Fox Lane             560 San Jose              920 Evelyn Street
              Berkeley         CA947    Kensington       CA947    Albany            CA947



              Ziggy Zagare              Stan Freeburg
              560 Benvenue              1 Chuckles Lane
              El Cerrito       CA945    Westport         CT065


ASSIST              |<C:>|NAD              |Rec: 1/20
              Press any key to continue work in ASSIST._
```

FIGURE 13-5. First five records printed as labels

3. Print NAD.LBL in the order created by the index NAD.NDX. First, attach the index to NAD.DBF: Press [S], press [Enter] twice, highlight NAD, and press [Enter] again. Now press [Y], highlight NAME, press [Enter], and press [→].

Once NAD.DBF is current and NAME.NDX is attached to it, print the labels: Press [R], highlight Label, and then press [Enter] five times. You'll see the labels printed to the screen in alphabetical order according to the NAME field.

Exercises

1. When you print labels, do you have the option of printing to either the screen or the printer?

2. Can you use the Search/Scope menu to select a group of records to print as labels?

3. Select all the records in NAD.DBF for the state of California (STATE = CA) to print as labels, print the labels to the screen, then return to the Assist screen.

4. Can you select a group of fields to print in labels after you've created the label format?

5. Why?

MODIFY LABELS   13.4

Once you've created a label file, you can modify it by using the Modify Label screen. To open this screen, make sure the proper database is current, and then use the Label command on the Modify menu.

a. Press [M] to open the Modify menu.

b. Highlight Label. The best way to do this is to press ⬆.

c. Press [Enter] twice. dBASE displays a list of the names of available label file names.

d. Highlight the name of the label file that you want to modify, and then press [Enter]. dBASE will move you into the Modify Label screen, as shown in Figure 13-6. The only difference between this screen and the Create Label screen is the label on the left side of the status bar, MODIFY LABEL.

All commands in the Modify Label screen are identical to the commands in the Create Label screen. You can make all changes by using the same setting commands. When you're finished making changes, press [E] to open the Exit menu, and then press [Enter] to save your changes and return to the Assist screen.

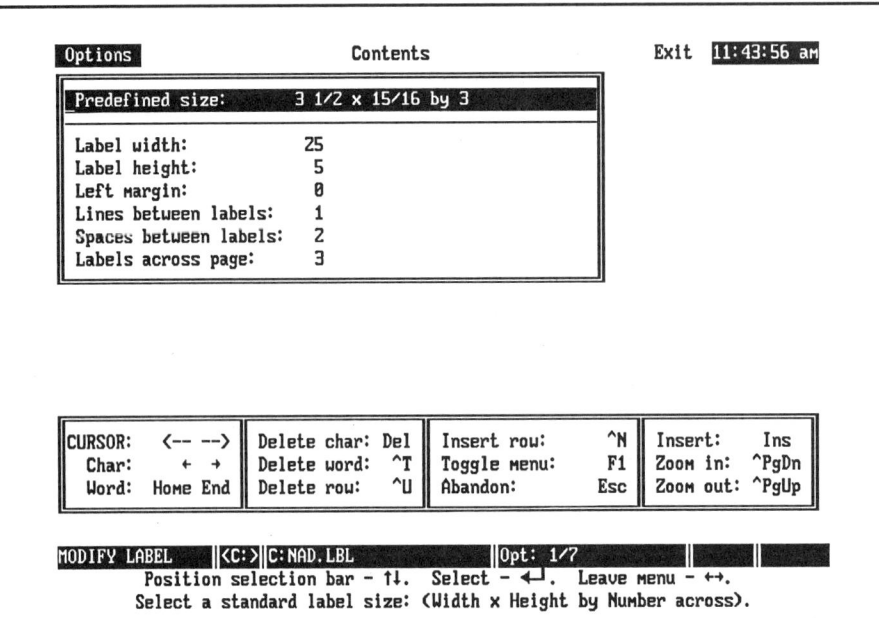

FIGURE 13-6. The Modify Label screen

Make sure that the database you've made current is the correct database. You can open the Modify Report screen for a label file regardless of which database is current, even one that has no relation to the label file you want to modify.

Once you're working in a label file with the wrong database current, you can still change label file settings. The only thing that you can't do is insert fields from the right database. Whenever you're working with one of the lines in the Contents menu, when you press [F10], field names from the current database will appear on screen. If you want to insert fields from the right database, you should save the changes you've made so far to the label file, exit the Modify Label screen, make the right database current, and then reenter the Modify Label screen and continue you work.

You can escape any changes you've made while working in the Modify Label screen by pressing [Esc] twice.

You can switch back and forth easily between modifying a label file and printing it. This helps you fine-tune your adjustments.

Examples

1. Open the Modify Label screen for NAD.LBL. First make sure NAD.DBF is current. Then press [M] to open the Modify menu. Press [↑] to highlight the command Label, and then press [Enter] twice. dBASE displays a list of the names of available label forms. Highlight NAD.LBL and press [Enter].

2. Change NAD.LBL so that the information on the third line is easier to read. You can't change the size of fields as they are displayed in a label. The size is controlled by the type of label you have selected.

    You have to move the ZIP code down to the fourth line. Press [C] to open the Contents menu. Press [↓] twice to highlight "3." Press [Enter]. The cursor appears at the end of the line. Press [Backspace] four times to erase +ZIP. Press [Enter] to fix this change.

3. Now insert the ZIP field on the fourth line. Press [↓] to highlight "4," and then press [Enter]. Press [F10], highlight ZIP, and press [Enter] twice.

4. Print the new label file to see what it looks like. Press E, and then Enter. When you return to the Assist screen, press R, press ↓ three times, and press Enter five times. This prints the labels to the screen. In a moment, the screen will change to look something like the one in Figure 13-7. Notice that all the CITY and STATE information appears on line 3 and that the ZIP information appears on line 4.

Exercises

1. Is there any difference between the commands you use in the Modify Label screen and in the Create Label screen?

2. Do you have to open the correct database to modify a label form?

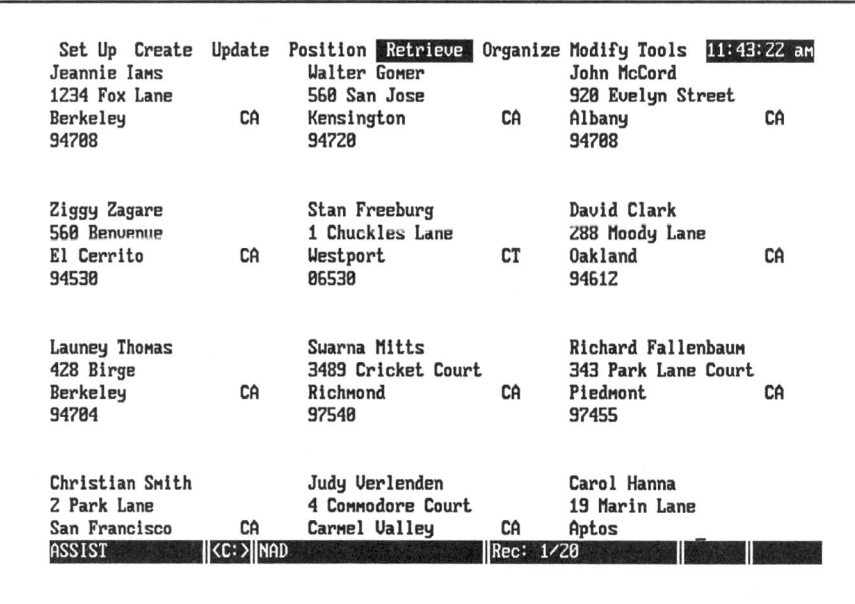

```
     Set Up  Create  Update  Position  Retrieve  Organize  Modify  Tools   11:43:22 am
  Jeannie Iams                  Walter Gomer              John McCord
  1234 Fox Lane                 560 San Jose              920 Evelyn Street
  Berkeley          CA          Kensington       CA       Albany               CA
  94708                         94720                     94708

  Ziggy Zagare                  Stan Freeburg             David Clark
  560 Benvenue                  1 Chuckles Lane           288 Moody Lane
  El Cerrito        CA          Westport         CT       Oakland              CA
  94530                         06530                     94612

  Launey Thomas                 Swarna Mitts              Richard Fallenbaum
  428 Birge                     3489 Cricket Court        343 Park Lane Court
  Berkeley          CA          Richmond         CA       Piedmont             CA
  94704                         97540                     97455

  Christian Smith               Judy Verlenden            Carol Hanna
  2 Park Lane                   4 Commodore Court         19 Marin Lane
  San Francisco     CA          Carmel Valley    CA       Aptos
  ASSIST           |<C:>|NAD                     |Rec: 1/20
```

FIGURE 13-7. Modified NAD.LBL printed to screen

3. Begin in the Assist screen. Open the Modify Label screen, change the "Predefined size" to "3 1/2 x 15/16 x 2," save the change, and return to the Assist screen.

4. Print the modified label file to your screen, and then return to the Assist screen.

5. What is the major difference between the label layout that you just printed and the previous label layout?

EXERCISES

1. What is the difference between creating a report and creating labels?

   MASTERY SKILLS CHECK

2. When would you want to create labels?

3. Create a label format for NAD.DBF called AMOUNT that prints information from the NAME, MONEY, and DATE fields. Use the "3 1/2 x 15/16 by 3" label format.

4. Check the results of these labels by printing them to the screen, and then return to the Assist screen.

5. Now print the labels to the printer.

1. Create a label format for VALUE.DBF called ITEM.LBL that displays information from the ITEM and PRICE fields. Use the predefined size of 3 1/2 x 15/16 by 1.

   INTEGRATING SKILLS CHECK

2. Print the labels to the screen, and then return to the Assist screen.

3. Create two indexes for VALUE.DBF, one based on the ITEM field and called ITEMNAME.NDX (to distinguish it from the NAME .NDX created for NAD.DBF), the other based on the PRICE field and called PRICE.NDX.

4. Print the labels for ITEM.LBL, making sure that the items are listed in alphabetical order.

5. Print the labels for ITEM.LBL a second time, making sure that the items are listed in order of price.

Creating and Using Queries
▶14◀

CHAPTER OBJECTIVES

In this chapter you will

▶ Become familiar with the Create Query screen   14.1

▶ Design and use query files   14.2

▶ Modify query files   14.3

Query files let you select which records you can work with in the current database. This means that query files control which records will appear when you use the Edit or Browse screen, as well as which records you can work with when you delete records and replace information in fields.

You'll design query files in a manner that is similar to building search conditions, but you won't use the Search/Scope menu. Instead, you'll use two full-screen components of dBASE called the Create Query and Modify Query screens.

Exercises

SKILLS CHECK

1. Make sure record 1 in NAD.DBF is current. Locate the first record with an address in California, then return to the Assist screen.

2. Continue to find the next record with an address in California, then return to the Assist screen.

3. List all records in NAD.DBF with addresses in California, then return to the Assist screen.

4. List all records in NAD.DBF that owe you $500 or more, then return to the Assist screen.

5. List all records in NAD.DBF with addresses in California that owe you $500 or more, then return to the Assist screen.

14.1 BECOME FAMILIAR WITH THE CREATE QUERY SCREEN

You'll work in the Create Query screen to create queries in dBASE. This is a variation of the Create screen you've used to design other dBASE files, such as databases, formats, and labels. You have to make a database file current before you can open the Create Query screen, and you can design a query file only around the current database.

Chapter 14 Creating and Using Queries **317**

```
 Set Filter          Nest         Display        Exit  06:24:20 pm
┌─────────────────────────────────┐
│ Field Name                      │
│ Operator                        │
│ Constant/Expression             │
│ Connect                         │
├─────────────────────────────────┤
│ Line Number     1               │
└─────────────────────────────────┘
```

Line	Field	Operator	Constant/Expression	Connect
1				
2				
3				
4				
5				
6				
7				

```
CREATE QUERY  |<C:>|C:TEST.QRY         |Opt: 1/2
              Position selection bar - ↑↓.  Select - ↵.  Leave menu - ↔.
              Select a field name for the filter condition.
```

FIGURE 14-1. The Create Query screen

To open the Create Query screen:

a. Press [C] to open the Create pull-down menu.

b. Highlight the command Query and press [Enter] twice. This selects the command and the current drive. dBASE asks you to give the query file you want to create a name.

c. Type the name you want to give the query file and press [Enter]. If you haven't yet made a database file current, dBASE will now ask you to do so now. dBASE will then move you into the Create Query screen, as shown in Figure 14-1. This screen was created for a query file called TEST.QRY. The extension .QRY stands for "query."

The Create Query screen is similar to other full-screen components of the dBASE program that you've already worked with. You can see the status bar at the bottom of your screen, along with the navigation and message lines. The top line shows four options you can use, three of which are attached to pull-down menus (the Display command does not open a menu):

Set Filter	Lets you set the conditions dBASE uses to select and organize records when you use the query file.
Nest	Lets you specify the precedence of filter conditions that you insert in the query file.
Display	Lets you view records in the current database that match the filter condition for the current query file. This allows you to check the conditions you've built into the query file to make sure they behave as you want them to.
Exit	Lets you exit the Create Query screen and either save all the changes you've made to the current query file or abandon all changes made since the last save.

The first two commands open the pull-down menus that you'll use most often to design query files. These two menus let you insert the conditions that control which records will appear in the database when you use the Browse or Edit screen. You'll insert field names, operators, text strings, and other valid dBASE terms to design the query file.

The Display option, rather than opening a pull-down menu, activates the display of records that match the filter conditions in the current query file.

The middle section of the Create Query screen is unique to this screen. It is called the *query form.* It displays the various filter conditions that you create for the current query file. You can enter up to seven different filter conditions in a single query file, one on each line of the query form. Studying the columns in this form gives you a good overview of the anatomy of a filter condition. For each condition, you enter a field name, an operator, and a constant value or dBASE expression that the operator acts on. You can also connect conditions so they act in concert. You'll see how this works when you begin to create your first query filter conditions in the next section.

You can abandon all your work in the Create Query screen using the following procedure:

a. Press [Esc]. dBASE will ask you to confirm the abandon.

b. Press [Y] (or [Esc]). Pressing any other key will leave you working in the Create Query screen.

Figure 14-2 shows a map of the menus and their commands. These menus and commands are identical in the Create Query and Modify Query screens. You work with these menus, and the commands on these menus, in the same way that you work with all other pull-down commands in dBASE. Press [→] or [←] to scroll through the menus in sequence. To open a menu directly, press the key that matches the first letter of the menu name. Press [↑] and [↓] to highlight different commands. Press [Enter] to execute the highlighted command. You can also use the [Ctrl]-key combinations shown in Table 2-1 to open menus and highlight commands.

As with Create screens for reports and labels, the menu commands in the Create Query screen are really settings that store values that control the query conditions. dBASE calls this *building filter conditions,* or building the conditions that filter the records you can view and work with.

```
Set Filter              Nest        Display     Exit

Field Name              Add                     Save
Operator                  Start:0               Abandon
Constant/Expression       End:  0
Connect                 Remove
                          Start:0
Line Number    1          End:  0
```

FIGURE 14-2. Menu map for the Create and Modify Query screens

Examples

1. Begin creating a query file called TEST.QRY based on information in NAD.DBF. First make sure NAD.DBF is current. Then press [C] to open the Create pull-down menu, highlight Query, and press [Enter] twice. Type **TEST** and press [Enter]. Your screen should change to look like the one in Figure 14-1.

2. Scroll through the pull-down menus in the Create Query screen. Press [E] to open the Exit menu if it isn't already showing. Press [→] several times to scroll through the pull-down menus.

3. Press [Esc] twice to abandon all the work you've done so far. This returns you to the Assist screen.

Exercises

1. How many pull-down menus are there in the Create Query screen and what are their names?

2. Make sure that NAD.DBF is current. Open the Create Query screen by creating a query file called NAD.QRY.

3. How do you execute the Display command?

4. After displaying a record, how do you open the pull-down menu to the right of the Display command?

5. Quit the Create Query screen without saving any changes.

14.2 CREATING AND USING QUERY FILES

To design query files, you need to know the structure of the database you're working with, and you need to have a good idea of which records in the database you want to use. Once you have this information, you can begin to build conditions that collect the records that you want to work with and exclude those records that you don't want to work with.

Follow these steps to build a query file:

a. Use the Set Filter menu to declare one or more filter conditions.

b. Use the Nest menu if you want to override the way dBASE handles filter conditions or the order of precedence it follows when processing conditional operators. You will use this menu only when you start using complex filter conditions.

c. Use the Display menu to see the effects of the current query file on the current database.

d. Use the Exit menu to exit the current file and save or abandon changes.

You'll use the Set Filter menu to insert the filter conditions for the query file. The menu includes these options:

Field Name	Lets you select the field name you want to use as a filter condition.
Operator	Lets you select a conditional operator that filters the contents of the field name.
Constant/Expression	Lets you insert a constant expression, such as a text string, or a dBASE expression, such as a field name, that the operator acts upon. Table 14-1 defines the three types of operators you can use when designing query files.
Connect	Lets you connect filter conditions in various ways so they act together. Table 14-2 defines the connecting operators you can use.
Line Number	Lets you select the line number where you want to place the filter condition. An order of precedence is created according to the number of the line where the filter condition is saved.

TABLE 14-1.	List of Operators for Different Field Types *(continued on next page)*
Character Fields	
= Matches	Must make a perfect match, including uppercase and lowercase, between contents of text string (or string of characters) field and constant/expression.
< > Does Not Match	Must not make a perfect match between contents of text string and constant/expression.
Begins with	Contents of text string must begin with characters in constant/expression.
Does Not Begin with	Contents of text string must not begin with characters in constant/expression.
Ends with	Contents of text string must end with characters in constant/expression.
Does Not End with	Contents of text string must not end with characters in constant/expression.
$ Contains	The characters must exist somewhere in the text string. They don't have to be the only characters in the field name, but they must occur in the same sequence.
Does Not Contain	Contents of text string must not contain the characters in the constant/expression in the same sequence.
Is Contained in	Inverse of the $ Contains operator. The text string must contain some of the characters.
Is Not Contained in	Inverse of the "Does not contain" operator. The text string must not contain some of the characters.
> Comes After	Text string must follow in the alphabet; for example, "pet" comes after "pat." Usually one letter or at most a few letters are involved.
> = Comes After or Matches	Text string must match or follow in the alphabet (usually involves one letter or at most a few letters).

TABLE 14-1. List of Operators for Different Field Types

Character Fields (*continued*)

< Comes Before	Text string must precede in the alphabet; for example, "pat" comes before "pet" (usually involves one letter or at most a few letters).
< = Comes Before or Matches	Text string must match or precede in the alphabet (usually involves one letter or at most a few letters).

Numeric and Date Fields

= Equals	The numbers or date in the constant/expression must make an exact match with the contents of the named field.
> More Than	The numbers or date in the constant/expression must be more than the contents of the named field.
> = More Than or Equal to	The numbers or date in the constant/expression must be equal to or more than the contents of the named field.
< Less Than	The numbers or date in the constant/expression must be less than the contents of the named field.
< = Less Than or Equal to	The numbers or date in the constant/expression must be less than or equal to the contents of the named field.
< > Not Equal to	The numbers or date in the constant/expression must not be equal to the contents of the named field.

Logical Fields

Is True	The logical field contents must be true (T or Y).
Is False	The logical field contents must be false (F or N).

TABLE 14-2. Connecting Operators

No combination	Creates no combination. Same as not inserting a connecting operator. Use this connection to cancel a previous connection.
Combine with .AND.	Requires that all the connected filter conditions be true.
Combine with .OR.	Requires that one of the connected filter conditions be true.
Combine with .AND..NOT.	Opposite of the "Combine with .AND." operator. This requires that all connected filter conditions not be true.
Combine with .OR..NOT.	Opposite of the "Combine with .OR." operator. This requires that one of the connected filter conditions not be true.

You have to insert the first three items—field name, operator, and constant expression—to create a valid filter condition. You can connect filter conditions by using a variety of connecting operators, but this is an optional setting. You can arrange the order in which dBASE will process the filter conditions by placing them on specific lines of the query form. If you don't select specific lines, dBASE will put the first condition on line 1, the second condition on line 2, and so on.

To insert a field name in the Field Name setting, highlight the setting, press (Enter), and then press (F10). This opens a list of field names for the current database. Highlight the field name that you want to base your filter condition upon and press (Enter). Three things happen when you do this. First, the field name you've selected appears after the Field Name setting on the Set Filter menu. Second, the field name also appears in the query form, in the first column, marked Field, for line 1. Third, the highlight bar moves down to the next setting, Operator.

To declare an operator, highlight the Operator setting (if it is not already highlighted) and press (Enter). This opens a list of operators that you can use for the type of field name you selected. Highlight the operator that you want to use and press (Enter). The operator name appears after the Operator setting in the Set Filter menu and in the second column, marked Operator, in the query form for line 1. The highlight bar moves down to the next setting.

There are three different groups of operators that you can use: one each for character fields, numeric and date fields, and logical fields. Table 14-1 defines the three groups of operators.

The Constant/Expression setting lets you define the data that the operator will use—much like the data you specify when building a search condition.

The Connect setting lets you connect adjacent filter conditions according to various connecting operators. To insert a connecting operator, highlight the Connect setting and press (Enter). Highlight the operator that you want to use and press (Enter). This inserts the operator name after the Connect setting and in the rightmost column of the query form. Table 14-2 defines the connect operators you can use.

The Nest menu lets you change the way filter conditions are handled by the query file. You'll learn more about filter conditions and how they work when you use the Modify Query screen later in this chapter.

The Display menu lets you display the contents of records in the current database that match the filter conditions you've created in the current query file. Figure 14-3 shows an example of a displayed record. Each record is displayed in the same format as in the Edit screen, with field names running down the left side of your screen. If the record contains more fields than can show above the query form, you can press (PgDn) to see the next group of fields that can fit. You can expand the room provided for fields by toggling the query form off. Just press (F1). The query form will disappear, and the displayed fields for the current record will expand. Press (F1) to toggle the query form back on. This works only when you've built a valid filter condition for the current database file and you're working with the Display command.

```
     Set Filter          Nest          Display          Exit  06:32:34 pm
     NAME      Jeannie Iams
     ADDRESS   1234 Fox Lane
     CITY      Berkeley
     STATE     CA
     ZIP       94708
     PHONE     415-456-7890
     MONEY        92.12
     DATE      12/25/89
    ┌──────┬─────────┬───────────┬─────────────────────┬─────────┐
    │ Line │ Field   │ Operator  │ Constant/Expression │ Connect │
    ├──────┼─────────┼───────────┼─────────────────────┼─────────┤
    │  1   │ STATE   │ Matches   │ 'CA'                │         │
    │  2   │         │           │                     │         │
    │  3   │         │           │                     │         │
    │  4   │         │           │                     │         │
    │  5   │         │           │                     │         │
    │  6   │         │           │                     │         │
    │  7   │         │           │                     │         │
    └──────┴─────────┴───────────┴─────────────────────┴─────────┘
   CREATE QUERY    |<C:>|C:TEST.QRY          |Rec: 1/20     |
     Next/Previous record - PgDn/PgUp.  Toggle query form - F1.  Leave option - ↔.
           Display records in the database that meet the query condition.
```

FIGURE 14-3. A displayed record

Once you've created a query, it's easy to put the file to use. Beginning in the Assist screen:

a. Make sure the database you want to work with is current.

b. Press [S] to open the Set Up pull-down menu.

c. Highlight the command Query and press [Enter] twice. dBASE displays a list of query files in the current drive.

d. Highlight the query file you want to use and press [Enter].

Now you can work in the Edit or Browse screen to view, edit, or delete only those records that match the filter conditions you've placed in the query file. If you're working with an indexed database, the records will be arranged in the indexed order.

Once you use a query file, it remains current until you use another query file or quit dBASE. To use another query file:

a. Press [S] to open the Set Up pull-down menu.

b. Highlight the command Query and press [Enter] twice. dBASE displays a list of query files in the current drive.

c. Highlight the query file you want to use and press [Enter].

The new query file will now control the records that you can work with.

If you try to use a query file for the wrong database—that is, one in which the query file doesn't contain the same field names as the database—dBASE will tell you the query file is invalid.

Examples

1. Build a query file called 200PLUS.QRY that shows only those records in NAD.DBF where people owe you $200 or more. First, make sure that NAD.DBF is current. Then press [C] to open the Create menu, highlight Query, and press [Enter] twice. Type **200PLUS** and press [Enter]. This opens the Create Query screen for a file called 200PLUS.QRY. The Set Filter menu should be displayed.

   Press [Enter] to activate the Field Name setting. Highlight MONEY and press [Enter]. This inserts the field name MONEY in the Field Name setting and in the Field column of the query form. It also moves the highlight bar down to the Operator setting. Press [Enter] to open the list of operators you can use for the numeric field MONEY. Highlight "> More Than" and press [Enter]. This inserts that operator and moves the highlight bar down to the Constant/Expression setting. Press [Enter], type "200", and press [Enter] again. Whenever you enter text as a dBASE expression, you must surround it with quotation marks (either single or double quotes).

2. Preview the query file 200PLUS.QRY, and then save the file if it looks like what you want. Press [D] to activate the Display command. The first record in NAD.DBF that contains an entry in the MONEY field of over 200 will be displayed.

To save the file, press [E] to open the Exit menu and then [Enter]. This returns you to the Assist screen.

3. Use the query file 200PLUS.QRY. Begin in the Assist screen. Press [S], highlight Query, and press the [Enter] key twice. Highlight 200PLUS.QRY and press [Enter]. Now view the effect. Press [U], highlight Edit, and press [Enter]. Once the first record is displayed, press [PgDn] and then [PgUp] several times to see which records you can view. Press [Esc] to exit the Edit screen.

Highlight Browse and press [Enter]. Notice that only a few of the records in NAD.DBF show in this screen. Press [Esc] to return to the Assist screen.

4. Build a query file called 200CA.QRY that shows only those records in NAD.DBF where people owe you $200 or more and live in California. First make sure NAD.DBF is current. Then press [C], highlight Query, and press [Enter] twice. Type **200CA** and press [Enter].

With the Create Query screen showing, press [Enter] to activate the Field Name setting. Highlight STATE and press [Enter] three times. This fixes STATE in the Field Name setting and inserts Matches in the Operator setting. Press [Enter] again to activate the Constant/Expression setting, type **"CA"**, and press [Enter]. With the Connect setting highlighted, press [Enter], highlight Combine with .AND., and press [Enter]. This moves you to an empty Set Filter menu for line 2.

Now that you've defined the first filter condition, build the second: Press [Enter], highlight MONEY, and press [Enter] twice. Highlight "> More Than" and press [Enter] twice. Type **"200"** and press [Enter].

5. Test the effects of 200CA.QRY. Press [→] twice, and then press [Enter] to activate the Display command. The first record in NAD.DBF that meets the filter conditions built into 200CA.QRY will be shown. You can press [PgDn] to see the rest of the fields in the first record and to move to the next record that meets the filter conditions.

Once you're satisfied with the effects, save the file. Press [E], and then [Enter]. This returns you to the Assist screen.

Chapter 14   Creating and Using Queries   **329**

6. Change the order that dBASE uses to process the filter conditions in 200CA.QRY. Press [N] to open the Nest menu. Highlight the Start command under Remove and press [Enter]. Type **2** and press [Enter]. This should remove the left parenthesis from line 2. Highlight Start under Add. Type **1** and press [Enter]. The left parenthesis should now appear on line 1. Press [E], then [Enter] to save this change. This should return you to the Assist screen.

Exercises

1. What two things do you need to know to design a query file?

2. Can you view the effects of the current query file without leaving the Create Query screen?

3. Create a query file called 200-400.QRY, using NAD.DBF, that shows only those records for people who owe you more than $200 and less than $400.

4. Display the results of the file.

5. Save the file to disk.

6. View the results in the Browse screen.

MODIFYING QUERIES   14.3

You can modify a query file as easily as you created it. Just use the Modify Query screen instead of the Create Query screen to do this.

a. Make sure that the database you used as the source of fields for the query file is current.

b. Press [M] to open the Modify pull-down menu.

c. Highlight Query and press [Enter] twice. dBASE displays a list of query file names on the current drive.

d. Highlight the name of the query file you want to modify and press [Enter]. Your screen will change to look like the one in Figure 14-4 (which displays the contents for 200CA.QRY).

All commands in this screen, including the pull-down menu structure, are identical to those in the Create Query screen.

In most cases, you'll modify field names, operators, and constants and expressions. To do this, begin in the Modify Query screen:

a. Press [S] to open the Set Filter menu, if it's not already open.

b. Highlight the Line Number setting and press [Enter].

c. Type the line number that matches the filter condition in the query form you want to change. Each filter condition must exist on a line number of its own. dBASE will display the information for the filter condition in the Set Filter menu.

d. Highlight the setting you want to change, press [Enter], make the change, and then press [Enter] to fix the change.

e. Once you've made all the changes you want to, press [E] and then [Enter] to save the changes and return to the Assist screen.

One of the more common modifications you'll make is to reorder the sequence of operators when you start building complex filter conditions. dBASE normally processes the operators you've selected for filter conditions according to this order:

.NOT.
.AND.
.OR.

You can override this sequence by surrounding with parentheses the conditions you want processed first. You do this by opening the

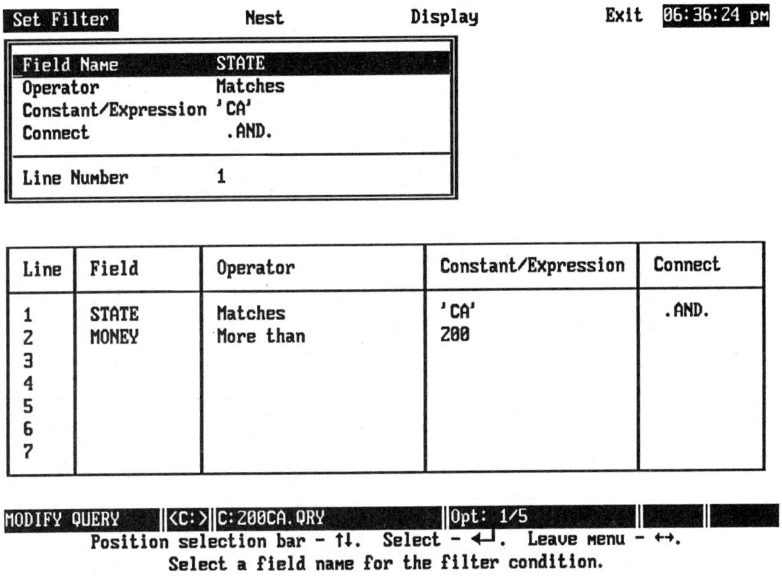

Chapter 14   Creating and Using Queries

```
 Set Filter            Nest         Display        Exit  06:36:24 pm
┌─────────────────────────────────────┐
│ Field Name          STATE           │
│ Operator            Matches         │
│ Constant/Expression 'CA'            │
│ Connect             .AND.           │
│                                     │
│ Line Number         1               │
└─────────────────────────────────────┘
```

Line	Field	Operator	Constant/Expression	Connect
1	STATE	Matches	'CA'	.AND.
2	MONEY	More than	200	
3				
4				
5				
6				
7				

```
MODIFY QUERY    |<C:>|C:200CA.QRY    |Opt: 1/5
         Position selection bar - ↑↓.  Select - ↵.  Leave menu - ↔.
                 Select a field name for the filter condition.
```

FIGURE 14-4.   Modify Query screen

Nest menu and inserting numbers in the Start and End settings for Add. You can change these settings, or remove them completely, by entering Start and End values for the Remove settings.

Since a query file remains current until you use a different query file, pay close attention when you modify the current query file. You should probably use the Display command to make sure that you haven't made a drastic change that prevents all records from being displayed.

Examples

1. Modify 200CA.QRY so it contains two more filter conditions, as shown by the screen in Figure 14-5. Beginning in the Assist screen, press (M), highlight Query, and press (Enter) twice. Highlight 200CA.QRY and press (Enter). With the Set Filter menu showing,

highlight the Line Number setting and press (Enter). Type **2** and press (Enter). This displays the filter conditions entered on the second line of the query form.

Highlight the Connect setting and press (Enter). Highlight Combine with .OR. and press (Enter). This moves you to an empty Set Filter menu for line 3. Press (Enter), highlight MONEY, and press (Enter) twice. Highlight "> More Than" and press (Enter) twice. Type **400** and press (Enter) twice. Highlight Combine with .AND. and press (Enter) twice. This moves you to an empty Set Filter menu for line 4 and opens the field list. Highlight MONEY and press (Enter) twice. Highlight "< Less Than" and press (Enter) twice. Type **600** and press (Enter).

Now save this file and view its effects in the Browse screen. Press **E** and then (Enter) to save the file and return to the Assist screen. Now make the query active. Press **S**, highlight Query, press (Enter) twice, highlight 200CA.QRY, and press (Enter) again.

FIGURE 14-5. Defining four filter conditions

Now view its effects on the range of records. Press [U], highlight Browse, and press [Enter] to open the Browse screen. Press [F1] to turn off help and [PgUp] to see the top of the file. Your screen should look something like the one in Figure 14-6. This has narrowed down the range of records to those that match the filter conditions in the query file. Press [Esc] to return to the Assist screen.

2. Modify 200CA.QRY and change the order of two of the operators. Press [M], highlight Query, press [Enter] twice, highlight 200CA.QRY, and press [Enter]. Press [N] to open the Nest menu. Highlight the Start setting for Add and press [Enter], type 2, and press [Enter] again. Notice that an opening parenthesis appears before the filter conditions on line 2. This shows that you're asking dBASE to process everything following this parenthesis before the other operators.

Now mark the end of the group you want processed first. Highlight the End setting for Add, press [Enter], type 3, and press

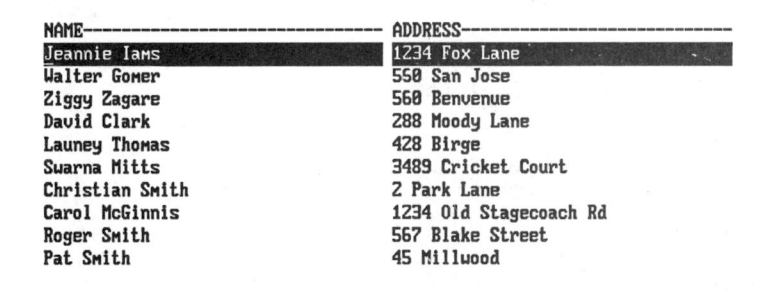

```
NAME----------------------------- ADDRESS---------------------------------
Jeannie Iams                      1234 Fox Lane
Walter Gomer                      550 San Jose
Ziggy Zagare                      560 Benvenue
David Clark                       288 Moody Lane
Launey Thomas                     428 Birge
Swarna Mitts                      3489 Cricket Court
Christian Smith                   2 Park Lane
Carol McGinnis                    1234 Old Stagecoach Rd
Roger Smith                       567 Blake Street
Pat Smith                         45 Millwood
```

BROWSE |<C:>|NAD |Rec: 1/20

View and edit fields.

FIGURE 14-6. Effects of four filter conditions

[Enter]. Notice that a closing parenthesis appears after the filter conditions on line 3. Your screen should now look like the one in Figure 14-7.

Save this change and view the results in the Browse screen. Press [E] and then [Enter] to save the file. This returns you to the Assist screen. The query file 200CA.QRY is still active because you haven't yet loaded another query file or quit dBASE. Press [U], highlight Browse, press [Enter], and press [PgUp]. The screen in Figure 14-8 shows the approximate results.

You've lost one record by processing the .OR. condition before the .AND. condition. The .AND. would normally be processed before the .OR. condition. The record for Carol McGinnis, which showed in the screen in Figure 14-6, no longer shows in the screen in Figure 14-8. Two of the MONEY conditions are processed before the STATE condition, which becomes an exclusive and not inclusive condition. Therefore, only records where STATE = CA are included.

Line	Field	Operator	Constant/Expression	Connect
1	STATE	Matches	'CA'	.AND.
2	(MONEY	Less than	200	.OR.
3	MONEY	More than	400)	.AND.
4	MONEY	Less than	600	
5				
6				
7				

FIGURE 14-7. Order of precedence changed

Chapter 14   Creating and Using Queries   **335**

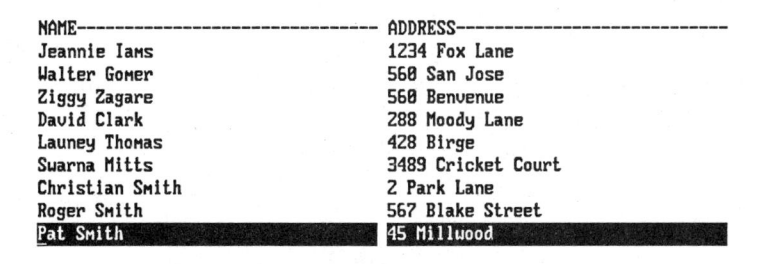

```
NAME-------------------------------- ADDRESS---------------------------
Jeannie Iams                         1234 Fox Lane
Walter Gomer                         560 San Jose
Ziggy Zagare                         560 Benvenue
David Clark                          288 Moody Lane
Launey Thomas                        428 Birge
Swarna Mitts                         3489 Cricket Court
Christian Smith                      2 Park Lane
Roger Smith                          567 Blake Street
Pat Smith                            45 Millwood
```

```
BROWSE        |<C:>|NAD              |Rec: 20/20
```

View and edit fields.

FIGURE 14-8.   Effects of changed precedence

Exercises

1. Are there any differences between the Modify Query screen and the Create Query screen, other than the name of the screen?

2. How do you change a specific filter condition?

3. Modify the query file 200CA.QRY, change the state name in the Constant/Expression field to Arizona, then save this change.

4. What is the normal order of precedence for handling operators in dBASE?

EXERCISES

MASTERY SKILLS CHECK

1. Create a query file called SAMPLE.QRY for NAD.DBF that shows only those records for people who owe you more than $500.

2. Display the effects of this query file.

3. Save the query file.

4. View the results in the Browse screen.

5. Modify the query file so it shows only records for people who owe you more than $200 but less than $800.

6. Save the file and view its effects in the Browse screen, and then return to the Assist screen.

INTEGRATING SKILLS CHECK

1. Prepare to create a query file for VALUE.DBF. First, make VALUE.DBF current. Then display the structure of this database, so you can refamiliarize yourself with the field definitions.

2. Create a query file called VALUE.QRY. Create a filter condition in which only those records where UNITS exceeds 500 are shown.

3. Display the effects of this file. Then save it and view the results in the Browse screen.

4. Try to view the contents of NAD.DBF by using VALUE.QRY.

Managing Files
▶15◀

CHAPTER OBJECTIVES

In this chapter you will learn how to

▶ Change drives and list directories   15.1

▶ Copy, rename, and erase files   15.2

▶ Import and export information   15.3

dBASE lets you change drives and access your disk files by using the Tools pull-down menu. You'll use commands on this menu to change your current drive, to copy, rename, and erase files, to list file names on screen, to list the structure of the current database, and to import and export database files.

Managing your files by using these commands is important since you can create many different types of files while working with dBASE and can store them on different drives. These files include databases, indexes, reports, and format files, just to name a few.

You might also want to import information from PFS:File data files to dBASE databases or export dBASE information to PFS:File data files.

Exercises

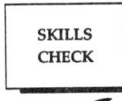

SKILLS CHECK

1. Make NAD.DBF current, then list the structure on your screen. List the structure of VALUE.DBF on screen. Return to the Assist screen.

2. Find out how dBASE on-line help defines the seven commands on the Tools menu.

3. Make sure no database is current. Quit dBASE, then reload the program. Which command on the Tools menu is disabled?

15.1 CHANGE DRIVES AND LIST DIRECTORIES

Changing drives and listing directories are routine activities you'll want to perform from time to time and in conjunction with each other. Changing drives lets you make another drive current. Listing directories lets you display the names of files that exist on the current drive.

The current drive letter always shows in the middle of the status bar. To change the current drive:

a. Press ⓣ to open the Tools pull-down menu.

b. Press [Enter] to select the command "Set Drive." dBASE opens a window listing drive letters, with the current drive highlighted.

c. Highlight the drive you want to switch to and press [Enter]. If you're switching to a floppy disk drive, dBASE may ask you to insert a disk into the drive you're trying to switch to. The new drive letter should appear on the status bar.

Be aware of an anomaly that can occur when you use the drive selection box. The list of displayed drive letters are suggested choices and might not reflect the drives available on your computer. The letters A through E are always displayed by default. If your computer has more drives available, the additional drive letters might or might not show on the list, depending upon how you've configured the disk drives. If your computer has fewer than five drives, the letters A through E will still show, but you'll find that you can't access files on a drive that doesn't exist.

Different situations develop when you try to switch to a nonexistent drive letter, depending upon which command you use to open the drive selection window. When you open the Tools menu and select the "Set drive" command, dBASE displays drive letters that make it look as if you can change to another drive. The new drive letter appears on the status bar. When you try to access or create a file on the new current drive, however, dBASE reports back "File is not accessible."

When you open the drive selection window by using any other command, such as the command "Database file" on the Set Up menu, dBASE simply won't let you switch to an uninstalled drive. Make sure you are always working with a valid drive letter.

To list a directory of files on the current drive:

a. Press ⓣ to open the Tools pull-down menu.

b. Highlight the command Directory and press [Enter] twice. This opens a list of ten types of file names you can display, as shown by the screen in Figure 15-1.

c. Highlight the type of file you want to list and press [Enter]. dBASE will then list on the screen the files you've selected.

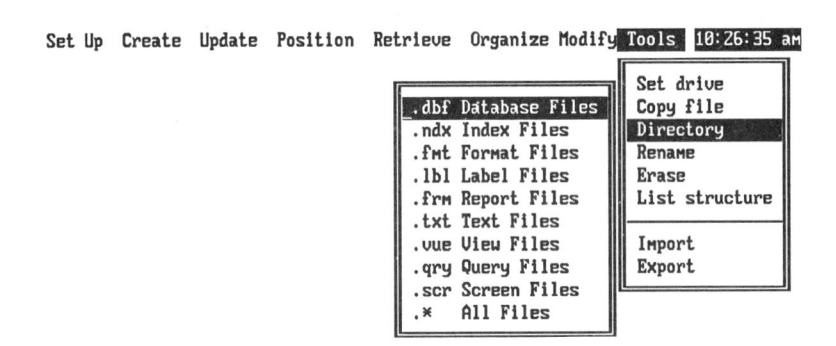

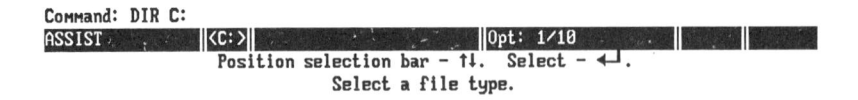

```
Set Up  Create  Update  Position  Retrieve  Organize  Modify  Tools  10:26:35 am
                                                      ┌──────────────┐
                                      ┌──────────────┐│ Set drive    │
                                      │.dbf Database Files│ Copy file │
                                      │.ndx Index Files  ││ Directory │
                                      │.fmt Format Files ││ Rename    │
                                      │.lbl Label Files  ││ Erase     │
                                      │.frm Report Files ││ List structure│
                                      │.txt Text Files   │├──────────────┤
                                      │.vue View Files   ││ Import    │
                                      │.qry Query Files  ││ Export    │
                                      │.scr Screen Files │└──────────────┘
                                      │.*   All Files    │
                                      └──────────────────┘

Command: DIR C:
ASSIST          |<C:>|                    |Opt: 1/10
                 Position selection bar - ↑↓.  Select - ↵.
                          Select a file type.
```

FIGURE 15-1.   The Directory menu

The only type of file shown in Figure 15-1 that you haven't used so far in this book is View files. These are files that let you link information from multiple databases, which is an advanced technique.

You cannot change directories while working in the Assist interface. You have to exit to DOS or switch to the dot prompt to change directories on the current drive.

Examples

1. Change the current drive from C to A. Press [T] to open the Tools pull-down menu. Then press [Enter] to execute the top command, "Set drive." This opens the list of disk drive letters. Highlight the letter A and press [Enter]. The letter A should appear on the status bar.

Chapter 15   Managing Files   **341**

2. List all files on the disk in the A drive. Press [T], highlight Directory, and press [Enter] twice. Highlight .* All Files and press [Enter]. Scan the list of files, and then press any key to return to the Assist screen.

3. Change the current drive back to C. Press [T], press [Enter], highlight C, and press [Enter]. Make sure C: appears in the middle of the status bar.

4. List all database files on your C drive. Press [T], highlight Directory, and then press [Enter] twice. Highlight *.DBF Database Files and press [Enter]. (*.DBF means all files that end with the extension .DBF.) View the results, and then press any key to return to the Assist screen.

Exercises

1. How can you tell which drive is current?

2. Can you change directories by using the Tools menu?

3. List all format files on your C drive, and then return to the Assist screen.

COPYING, RENAMING, AND ERASING FILES | 15.2 |

You can use three commands on the Tools menu to perform the routine DOS housekeeping procedures:

Copy file	Copies one file to another
Rename	Lets you give an existing file a different name
Erase	Erases a file completely from the disk drive

You work with all three of these commands in a similar way:

a. Highlight the command you want to use and press (Enter). dBASE opens the box of disk drives.

b. Highlight the drive you want to use and press (Enter). dBASE opens a list of file names on the selected drive.

c. Highlight the file name you want to handle and press (Enter). dBASE proceeds to rename or erase the file you've selected and return you to the Assist screen. If you want to copy the file, dBASE opens the box of disk drives, letting you select which drive you want to copy the file to.

d. Highlight the drive you want to copy the file to and press (Enter). dBASE asks you what name you want to give the copied file.

e. Type the file name you want to use and press (Enter). dBASE copies the file.

You'll use the first three steps for renaming and erasing files. You'll use all five steps to copy a file.

If you try to copy a file by using a file name that already exists in the selected drive or rename a file by using a name that already exists in the current drive, dBASE will warn you that a file of the same name already exists. You can overwrite the existing file or select a new and unique file name.

You cannot rename a dBASE database file while it is current. You need to make another database file current first or quit dBASE and then reload the program.

If you erase a file inadvertently, you cannot recover it by using dBASE. You can use any of the popular DOS utilities, such as the Norton Undelete or Quick Undelete program or the PC Tools Undelete

Chapter 15   Managing Files   **343**

file command, to recover the erased file. Just make sure you recover the file before you continue with any other work. If you write over the deleted file before you recover it, you probably will lose part or all of the information.

Examples

1. Copy NAD.DBF to a file called COPY.DBF in the current drive. First, press [T] to open the Tools pull-down menu, press [↓] to highlight the command "Copy file," and press [Enter] twice. dBASE displays a list of file names in the current drive, as shown by the screen in Figure 15-2. Unfortunately, the file names are not arranged in alphabetical order. (Your list of files will probably differ from the list shown in this figure.)

    Press [↓] or [PgDn] as often as it takes to highlight NAD.DBF, and then press [Enter] twice. dBASE asks you to give the file a new name. Type **COPY.DBF** and press [Enter]. dBASE reports its progress in copying the file. When dBASE is finished, press any key to return to the Assist screen.

2. Rename COPY.DBF as RENAME.FIL. Notice that the command you just used remains highlighted. Press [↓] twice to highlight the command Rename, and then press [Enter] twice. When dBASE displays the list of file names, press [↓] as many times as it takes to highlight COPY.DBF. Press [Enter] twice, and when dBASE asks for the new file name, type **RENAME.FIL** and press [Enter]. dBASE reports the number of bytes it has copied. When the count is finished, press any key to return to the Assist screen.

3. Now erase RENAME.FIL. Press [T], press [↓] to highlight the command Erase, and then press [Enter] twice. When dBASE displays the list of file names, press [↓] as many times as it takes to highlight RENAME.FIL. Press [Enter] once. When dBASE reports back "File has been deleted," press any key to return to the Assist screen.

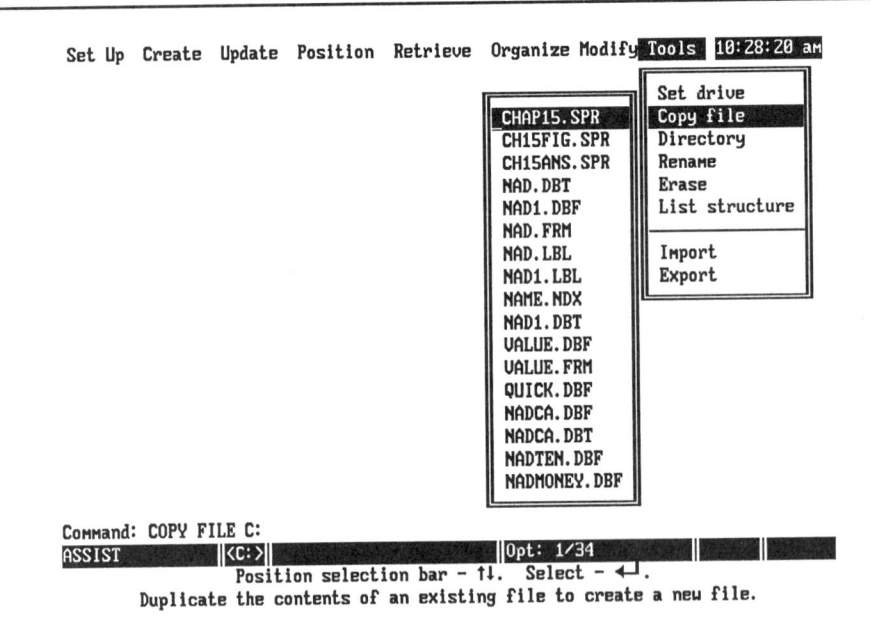

```
Set Up  Create  Update  Position  Retrieve  Organize  Modify Tools  10:28:20 am
                                                         ┌─────────────┐
                                          ┌─────────────┐│ Set drive   │
                                          │CHAP15.SPR   ││ Copy file   │
                                          │CH15FIG.SPR  ││ Directory   │
                                          │CH15ANS.SPR  ││ Rename      │
                                          │NAD.DBT      ││ Erase       │
                                          │NAD1.DBF     ││ List structure│
                                          │NAD.FRM      │└─────────────┘
                                          │NAD.LBL      ││ Import      │
                                          │NAD1.LBL     ││ Export      │
                                          │NAME.NDX     │└─────────────┘
                                          │NAD1.DBT     │
                                          │VALUE.DBF    │
                                          │VALUE.FRM    │
                                          │QUICK.DBF    │
                                          │NADCA.DBF    │
                                          │NADCA.DBT    │
                                          │NADTEN.DBF   │
                                          │NADMONEY.DBF │
                                          └─────────────┘
Command: COPY FILE C:
ASSIST         |<C:>|                      |Opt: 1/34  |
            Position selection bar - ↑↓.  Select - ↵.
         Duplicate the contents of an existing file to create a new file.
```

FIGURE 15-2. List of file names

Exercises

1. Do you follow the same basic steps for using the commands "Copy file," Rename, and Erase on the Tools pull-down menu?

2. Copy VALUE.DBF to a file called BACKUP.DBF and then return to the Assist screen.

3. Rename BACKUP.DBF as a file called OTHER.DBF and then return to the Assist screen.

4. Erase OTHER.DBF and then return to the Assist screen.

IMPORTING AND EXPORTING INFORMATION   15.3

You can only import data files from PFS:File into dBASE using menu commands in the Assist. To do this, you use the command Import on the Tools menu. You can export dBASE data to PFS:File data files by using the command Export.

You use these commands in a similar but not identical way. To import a PFS:File:

a. Press [T] to open the Tools menu.

b. Highlight the command Import and press [Enter]. dBASE asks you to specify the name of the file you want to import.

c. Type the name of the file you want to import and press [Enter]. PFS:File data files usually don't have an extension, but you always have to type all characters in the file name that you want to convert.

d. When the conversion is complete, press any key to return to the Assist screen.

When you execute the Import command, dBASE takes the file you've specified and copies it to a dBASE file, using the same file name as the PFS:File data file but with the .DBF extension. dBASE identifies the structure of the PFS:File data file and creates the necessary fields for dBASE. dBASE also creates default view and format files for the new database.

The new field names in the dBASE structure are given the names FIELD1, FIELD2, and so on. You'll probably want to modify this structure and change the field names to something more appropriate to the database. Remember to change only one field name at a time, save the change, make sure the field information was copied correctly to the new field name, and then change the next field name and repeat the process. You don't want to change more than one field name between saves.

Be aware of the limitations in dBASE and PFS:File data files when you convert files from one format to the other. When you convert a PFS:File data file to a dBASE database, the most important limitations to keep in mind are a maximum of 4000 bytes or characters in each record, 128 fields in a record, and 254 characters in a field. If the PFS:File data file exceeds these limits, the extra information will not be converted to dBASE format.

When you want to export a dBASE database file to a PFS:File data file, you must make the dBASE database file current. You can do this before or after you select the command Export.

To export a dBASE database file to a PFS:File data file:

a. Press [T] to open the Tools menu.

b. Highlight the command Export and press [Enter]. dBASE asks you to specify the name of the PFS:File data file you want to create.

c. Type the name of the file you want to create, and then press [Enter]. If you haven't yet made a database current, dBASE asks for the name of the file you want to export.

d. Type the name of the dBASE database you want to export and press [Enter]. dBASE will show its progress in converting the file.

e. When the conversion is complete, press any key to return to the Assist screen.

This converts the dBASE database to a matching PFS:File data file. If the dBASE database file you export has an index attached to it, the records will be exported in the indexed order. If you have activated a format file, that format file will also be copied for use in PFS:File. You'll need to use the PFS:File program to ascertain the success of the conversion and to make changes to the new PFS:File data file. If the dBASE database file you're exporting contains memo fields, the memo field information will be copied along with the other field information.

dBASE will tell you if it can't find the name of the file you have specified. If you try to create a file by using a name that already exists, dBASE will warn you.

Examples

1. Export the file NAD.DBF to a PFS:File data file. First, make sure NAD.DBF is current. Press [T], then [↑] once to highlight the command Export, and then press [Enter]. Highlight the drive you want to export the file to and press [Enter]. dBASE will ask you what name you want to give the PFS:File file. Type **TEST.FIL** and press [Enter]. dBASE will proceed to copy NAD.DBF to a PFS:File data file with the name TEST and show you its progress. Press any key to return to the Assist screen.

   Check the results of this work. Highlight the command Directory and press [Enter] twice. Highlight .* All Files and press [Enter]. You should see the file TEST.FIL in the list of file names. Press any key to return to the Assist screen.

2. Import the PFS:File data file called TEST.FIL to a dBASE database file. Highlight the command Import and press [Enter] twice. Type **TEST.FIL** and press [Enter]. dBASE will proceed to create a file called TEST.DBF and show you its progress. When dBASE is finished, press any key to return to the Assist screen.

   Check the results of this work. Highlight the command Directory and press [Enter] three times. You should see the file TEST.DBF in the list of database file names. Press any key to return to the Assist screen.

3. Now check the structure of the new file. Make TEST.DBF current, and then list its structure. Press [S], then [Enter] twice, highlight TEST.DBF, and then press [Enter] twice. Press [T] to open the Tools menu, highlight the command "List structure," and press [Enter]. Your screen should look something like the one in Figure 15-3. Press any key to return to the Assist screen.

```
           Set Up  Create  Update  Position  Retrieve  Organize  Modify Tools  10:29:20 am




           Structure for database: C:TEST.dbf
           Number of data records:     20
           Date of last update   : 07/13/90
           Field  Field Name  Type       Width   Dec
              1   FIELD01     Character    75
              2   FIELD02     Character    72
              3   FIELD03     Character    75
              4   FIELD04     Character    74
              5   FIELD05     Character    76
              6   FIELD06     Character    74
              7   FIELD07     Character    74
              8   FIELD08     Character    75
              9   FIELD09     Character   254
           ** Total **                    850
          ASSIST           <C:> TEST                 Rec: 1/20
                        Press any key to continue work in ASSIST._
```

FIGURE 15-3. The structure of TEST.DBF

Exercises

1. What type of file can you import from and export to while working in the Assist screen?

2. Will all data be imported or exported automatically?

EXERCISES

MASTERY SKILLS CHECK

1. Change the current drive to A and then back to C.

2. Copy VALUE.DBF to a file called TEST.DBF on the C drive.

3. List all database files in the current directory and locate TEST.DBF.

Chapter 15   Managing Files

4. Rename TEST.DBF to MY.DBF.

5. Export MY.DBF to NEW.TXT, a PFS:File data file.

6. Import NEW.TXT to dBASE format.

7. Erase TEST.DBF, MY.DBF, and NEW.DBF from the current drive. List all files and make sure you've deleted these files.

1. Make a copy of NAD.DBF and call it EXAMPLE.DBF.

2. Make EXAMPLE.DBF current, list the structure, then return to the Assist screen.

3. Modify the contents of EXAMPLE.DBF and insert a new field called ACCT_NU, five spaces wide, as the first field (before NAME). This will stand for account number, but make it a character-type field. Then return to the Assist screen.

4. Prepare to insert account numbers into the first five records in EXAMPLE.DBF. First make sure the first record in EXAMPLE.DBF is current. Then open the Edit screen.

5. Insert account numbers in the first five records in EXAMPLE.DBF. Begin by inserting the number 1 in the ACCT_NU field of the first record. Then move to record number 2 and insert the number 2 in ACCT_NU. Continue adding the record number to records number 3, 4 and 5. Save this new data and return to the Assist screen.

6. Check the results of adding new data using the Browse screen. Then return to the Assist screen.

7. List the first screenful of records in EXAMPLE.DBF to your screen. Remember to press [Ctrl]-[S] to stop the scrolling, so you can look more closely at the first screenful of listed records. Then return to the Assist screen.

8. Display those records in EXAMPLE.DBF that contain an account number. (Hint: Base your search condition on the criteria where the ACCT_NU field contains values higher than 0). Return to the Assist screen.

9. Change the name EXAMPLE.DBF to ACCOUNTS.DBF. Make sure EXAMPLE.DBF is not current when you change its name (the best way to do this is exit dBASE, then reload the program). Then return to the Assist screen.

10. Change the name of EXAMPLE.DBT to ACCOUNTS.DBT. This is the file that provides memo field information for ACCOUNTS.DBF. Return to the Assist screen.

11. Exit dBASE.

Installing dBASE III PLUS
▶A◀

This appendix describes the complete contents of the dBASE III PLUS package for version 1.1 and the minimum system requirements you need to run dBASE. It also describes how you install the program for computers that have hard disks, as well as for dual floppy disk computers.

STEPPING THROUGH THE INSTALLATION

To install dBASE III PLUS on your computer, you should first make sure you have all the package contents available. Then you copy all the program disk files to backup copies. Finally, you copy a set of program files to your hard disk or a set of working floppy disks, if your computer does not have a hard disk.

Installing dBASE III PLUS is easy once you follow some preliminary steps. Follow these eight steps, of which installing the program is number six, and you complete the process.

1. Check package contents.

2. Make backup copies.

3. Read the README.TXT file.

4. Ascertain your system configuration.

5. Run the ID program.

6. Run the Install program.

7. Optionally place dBASE on your path.

8. Test run the program.

The following sections explain each of these steps in greater detail.

CHECKING THE PACKAGE CONTENTS

If you're working with a new package of dBASE III PLUS, or if the program has not yet been used, you must first install the program on

Appendix A Installing dBASE III PLUS **353**

a working disk. The only items that are absolutely crucial to installing the basic version of dBASE III PLUS are System Disk #1 and System Disk #2. If you bought the program, however, you'll want to make sure that you received everything you paid for.

The documentation consists of the two loose-leaf binders called *Learning and Using dBASE III PLUS* and *Programming with dBASE III PLUS*. These two binders contain all the documentation and program disks.

Here is a description of the seven disks:

System Disk #1	The first of a two-part collection of program files that must be copied to your working disk and blended with other files from System Disk #2 before you can use dBASE III PLUS
System Disk #2	The second of a two-part collection of program files that must be copied to your working disk and blended with other files from System Disk #1 before you can use dBASE III PLUS
Sample Programs & Utilities	A collection of 79 sample program files you can use to experiment with activities in dBASE III PLUS
On-Disk Tutorial	A menu-driven tutorial program that walks you through a tour of the dBASE III PLUS program. You can take the entire tour, take a look at parts of the tour, or exit the tutorial at any time
Application Generator	A program written in the dBASE programming language that creates dBASE III PLUS applications. It is designed to serve as a shortcut and to reduce your program development time. First-time users might want to take a look at this program, but it has been designed for users who want to move directly into dBASE programming

Administrator #1   The first half of a set of files that enables dBASE III PLUS to be used on a network

Administrator #2   The second half of a set of files that enables dBASE III PLUS to be used on a network

The only disks you need in order to use this book are System Disk #1 and System Disk #2.

The rest of the package supplies documentation and additional information in leaflets detailing Ashton-Tate support and services, warranty registration, and other products they supply.

MAKING BACKUP COPIES

Always make backup copies of all disks you buy that contain software programs. This protects your purchases. The software copyright law allows you to do this. These backup copies are called *archival copies* and are intended to store your program software files in case you lose your working copies.

Making Backup Copies on a Dual Floppy Disk System

To make copies of the dBASE III PLUS program disk files on a dual floppy disk drive, place the first original disk in drive A and a blank disk in drive B. (Make sure the program disk is in drive A.) Then follow these steps:

1. Type **A:** to log onto the A drive, and then press [Enter].

2. When the A:\> shows on the DOS command line, you can run the DOS program DISKCOPY: Type **DISKCOPY A: B:** and press [Enter]. The program will ask you to insert the disk you want to copy from

Appendix A   Installing dBASE III PLUS   **355**

into drive A and the disk you want to copy to into drive B and then press [Enter] when you're ready. You should have already done this, but you might want to double-check now.

3. When the disks are as they should be, press [Enter]. This begins the disk-copying process. When the first disk is copied, the program will ask if you want to copy another.

4. Press [Y] and then [Enter]. Then replace the first original disk with the second original disk in drive A, and insert a new blank disk in drive B to receive the copied files.

5. Press [Enter]. Continue in this way until all the disks have been copied. You might want to make several sets of copies, just for your own protection.

Making Backup Copies on a Hard Disk System

To make backup copies with a hard disk, first create a temporary directory that can hold each disk's worth of files. This directory should allow for a minimum of 360K of disk space. Next, copy the original disk files to the directory.

Begin in the root directory, the one that appears each time you boot your computer. You should see the C:> or C:\> prompt.

1. Type **MD TEMP** and press [Enter].

2. Now log into this temporary directory: Type **CD TEMP** and press [Enter]. Once the DOS prompt reads C:\TEMP>, you're ready to begin the copying.

3. Place the first original disk in your floppy drive, presumably the A drive. Type **COPY A: *.*** and press [Enter]. (The space between the colon and the first asterisk is optional.) This copies all the disk files

to the hard disk. dBASE will tell you when the copying is complete. Remove the original disk and replace it with a blank formatted floppy.

4. Type **COPY *.* A:** and press [Enter]. (This time you should make sure there is a space before and after the asterisks.) This copies the files to a new floppy disk.

5. When this copying is complete, delete the first set of files on the hard drive. First make sure you're still working in the TEMP subdirectory on your hard drive. Then type **DEL *.*** and press [Enter]. dBASE will ask if you're sure of what you're doing. Press [Y]. Repeat the procedure for the second original disk and each subsequent original disk. If you want to make several copies of disk sets, don't delete the hard-disk files after the first copy. Instead, make your second and third copies, and then delete the hard-disk files and move on to the next original disk.

Remember to label clearly all disks, including the names of the files they contain. Once you've installed the programs, place the original disks and copies in a safe location, preferably in two different locations. Some people put their most important disks in a fire safe box, or even in their bank security box.

READING THE README.TXT FILE

You should read the contents of the file README.TXT before you do anything further. This is a short text file that describes how you install the dBASE III PLUS program for a PC that contains only 256K of memory available for dBASE. You can load README.TXT into any editor or word processor for viewing. It is also reprinted here.

Appendix A   Installing dBASE III PLUS   **357**

IMPORTANT INFORMATION

Before using your dBASE III PLUS disks, please note the following information before installing dBASE III PLUS:

For 256K dBASE III PLUS Operation:

dBASE III PLUS runs with DOS version 2.xx if you have 256K installed memory in your computer. If you have a minimum of 384K of installed memory, dBASE III PLUS runs with DOS version 3.xx as well as version 2.xx.

For 256K operation, we provide two files, CONFI256.SYS and CONFI256.DB, on System Disk #1. These two files set system parameters for maximum overall performance of dBASE III PLUS in a 256K environment. Save the original CONFIG.SYS and CONFIG.DB files (also on System Disk #1) to another disk, and then use the DOS COPY command to copy CONFI256.SYS and CONFI256.DB to CONFIG.SYS and CONFIG.DB, respectively.

Copyright© 1984, 1985, 1986, Ashton-Tate Corporation. Reprinted by permission. All rights reserved.

MINIMUM SYSTEM REQUIREMENTS

To work with dBASE III PLUS version 1.1, you need to use an IBM PC or compatible computer. If you're using MS-DOS or PC-DOS version 2.x (2.0, 2.10, 2.11), you need only 256K RAM. If you're using DOS 3.x, you'll need a minimum of 384K RAM.

There are no special video requirements. This low need for RAM, combined with the versatility of the program, are what make dBASE III PLUS the most popular database manager.

RUNNING THE ID PROGRAM

Before you can install dBASE III PLUS on a working disk, either hard or floppy, you must run the ID program. You need to know some of the information printed on the warranty card, a folded-over brochure labeled "FREE! 90 days of technical support." The front page of this brochure displays the product name, serial number, and part number for the program you're trying to install. You're only interested in the serial number.

Begin at the DOS prompt:

1. Type **ID** and press [Enter].

2. Type your name and press [Enter].

3. Type your company name and press [Enter]. If you are an individual and want to leave this blank, press [Enter] twice.

4. Type the serial number displayed on the front page of the warranty brochure, and then press [Enter]. The ID program will ask if you want to edit any of your entries.

5. Check the three entries you've just made. The first two are up to you, but the serial number you enter must match the one for the program you want to install. If you enter an incorrect number, the ID program will tell you this. If you want to edit, press [Y]. If you want to continue, press [N]. You'll have to enter the correct ID number before you can proceed to use dBASE III PLUS.

6. The ID program will take a few moments to double-check the serial number you've entered, and then it will encode the information on the system disk. This information will be transferred to any working disk you now make, including a hard disk.

7. The ID program is complete when you hear a beep and see the message "Identification completed".

Once System Disk #1 has been ID'd, you can run the install program.

INSTALLING ON A HARD DISK

To install the program on a hard disk:

1. Place System Disk #1 in a floppy disk drive.

2. Type **INSTALL C:\DBASE** to install the program on your hard disk, using a directory called DBASE. The syntax is

   INSTALL <drive>: <directory>

   which means you can select any active drive and use any existing DOS directory name. Just insert the parameters you want to use after INSTALL. Make sure to place a colon after the drive letter.

3. Replace System Disk #1 with System Disk #2 when the install program asks you to.

4. When the install program is finished, you'll return to the DOS prompt, or the DOS shell if you're using one.

When the dBASE program is fully installed, you should end up with these seven files:

ASSIST.HLP	A text file containing help information that you can access while working in dBASE III PLUS
CONFIG.DB	A small configuration file that customizes the environment for dBASE III PLUS. In its default version, this file contains the following two commands: STATUS=ON COMMAND=ASSIST You can view and edit this file by using an editor or word processor that displays ASCII text files. For your work in this book, leave the contents of this file as they are
DBASE.EXE	The main dBASE program
DBASE.MSG	A file of various help messages that can appear on your screen

DBASE.OVL   An overlay file called by DBASE.EXE when necessary (these Overlay (OVL) files contain extra program information and are called by dBASE automatically for special functions)

DBASEINL.OVL   A second overlay file called by DBASE.EXE when necessary

HELP.DBS   A file that contains additional help information

These are the only files you need to run dBASE III PLUS. There are other files on the other five package disks that can help you with other features of the program that aren't described in this book.

INSTALLING ON A FLOPPY DISK

To install the program on a floppy disk, make sure you're working with a 5 1/4-inch disk formatted for 1.2MB or a 3 1/2-inch disk formatted for 720K.

To begin the install:

1. Place System Disk #1 in a floppy disk drive.

2. Type **INSTALL A:** to install the program on a disk in your A drive. The syntax is

   INSTALL <drive>: <directory>

   but you don't need to use a directory on a floppy disk.

3. Replace System Disk #1 with System Disk #2 when the install program asks you to.

4. When all the files have been copied from both system disks, the install program will be complete, and you'll return to the DOS prompt, or the DOS shell if you're using one.

The seven files you need to install occupy 524K of disk space.

PLACING DBASE IN YOUR DOS PATH STATEMENT

If you plan to use dBASE III PLUS a lot, you should place the DBASE directory on your path statement. You can find the path statement—if one exists—in the AUTOEXEC.BAT file that tells DOS where to search for program names you want to load.

The contents of a sample AUTOEXEC.BAT file look like this:

```
prompt=$p$g
path=c:\dos;c:\pctools;c:\word;c:\dbase;
cls
```

The middle line displays the path statement, which contains the directory names you want DOS to look through for program names. Whenever you enter a program name such as DBASE, DOS looks for the appropriate executable file first in the root directory, then in the DOS directory, then in the PCTOOLS directory, then in the WORD directory, and finally in the DBASE directory.

Placing the DBASE directory on your path lets you load dBASE from other directories and use files in those directories. Otherwise, you'll be restricted to using files only in the DBASE directory or root directories of other disks.

Once you've placed the DBASE directory on your path, you must reboot the system for it to become effective. If you don't want to reboot, you can create a temporary path from your DOS prompt this way:

1. Type **PATH=C:\DBASE;**

2. Press [Enter].

RUNNING THE TUTORIAL PROGRAM

One of the seven dBASE program disks is called On-Disk Tutorial. This contains a tutorial program built from 72 files that walks you through a menu-driven tour of the dBASE III PLUS program.

To run the tutorial:

1. Place the TUTORIAL disk in a floppy disk drive.

2. Log onto that drive (for example, if you're using the A drive, type **A:** and press [Enter]).

3. Type **INTRO** and press [Enter].

4. When the program has loaded into your computer, type the letter key that matches your system video mode (C for a color monitor with a color card, M for a monochrome monitor with a monochrome card, B for a color monitor with a monochrome card).

5. You can now traverse the tutorial, or bail out anytime you want to, by pressing [Esc].

That's all there is to it. You can now turn back to Chapter 1 and begin your self-education.

Answer Section

▶B◀

EXERCISES 1.1

1. Phone book, directory of employees at work, restaurant menu, classified advertisements at the back of a newspaper

2. Telephone utility, gas and electric utility, water utility, state and federal tax records, social security records, car registration, house mortgage, driving record

EXERCISES 1.2

1. Assist and the dot prompt

2. dBASE II, dBASE III, dBASE III PLUS, dBASE IV

3. dBASE IV

4. dBASE III PLUS

1.3 EXERCISES

1. No

2. The dBASE program loads and operates more quickly

3. You need less memory, and you can protect your program and data files from damage or prying eyes

2 EXERCISES

1. DBASE ENTER (if the Set Up menu appears, you're at the Assist; if the dot prompt appears, F2)

2. (Highlight Quit dBASE III PLUS) ENTER

2.1 EXERCISES

1. The way you communicate with a program

2. Keeps you advised as to the status of your current activity, such as current drive and highlighted menu option

3. The third line from the bottom of your screen

Appendix B Answer Section 365

4. Gives you instructions for working in the Assist interface

5. Describes the currently highlighted command in more detail

EXERCISES 2.2

1. Eight

2. RIGHT ARROW seven times

3. M

4. CTRL-F

5. CTRL-A

6. DOWN ARROW

7. CTRL-C

8. DOWN ARROW

EXERCISES 2.3

1. ASSIST ENTER

2. ESC

3. F2

2.4 EXERCISES

1. C (to open the Create menu), F1 (read help window), ESC, DOWN ARROW, F1 (read help window), ESC, DOWN ARROW, F1 (read help window), ESC, DOWN ARROW, F1 (read help window), ESC, DOWN ARROW, F1 (read help window), ESC, DOWN ARROW, F1 (read help window), ESC

2. S (to open the Set Up menu), DOWN ARROW, DOWN ARROW, F1 (read help window), ESC, DOWN ARROW, DOWN ARROW, F1 (read help window), ESC

3. ESC, F1, **2**

4. **7**

5. ESC

6. **HEP** ENTER, Y (read help screen), ESC

7. F2

3 SKILLS CHECK

1. **DBASE** ENTER, ENTER

2. RIGHT ARROW

3. F1

Appendix B   Answer Section   367

EXERCISES 3.1

1. Name, street address, city, state, ZIP code, and phone number

2. INVOICE, COMPANY, TITLE, and TYPE are character. QUANT and PRICE are numerical. IMPORT is logical. ORDERED is date

3. Character type

EXERCISES 3.2

1. The Create pull-down menu lets you create any one of six different dBASE file types. Only one of these types is a database file. The Create Database screen is the screen you use to actually design and create the structure of fields that will contain database information

2. Alphabetic characters, numbers, and the underline symbol

3. The minimum is one character and the maximum is 254

4. **STATE** ENTER, ENTER, **2** ENTER

5. **ZIP** ENTER, ENTER, **5** ENTER

6. **PHONE** ENTER, ENTER, **15** ENTER

EXERCISES 3.3

1. Any number that isn't going to be calculated, such as a ZIP code, an invoice number, street address, or telephone number

2. Quantity, price, cost, invoice amount, tax, freight, degrees, years, weight, height

3. Minimum of 1, maximum of 19

4. Seven (5+2=7)

5. Eight (10−2=8)

3.4 EXERCISES

1. Eight

2. One

3. T, F, Y, or N

4. To contain text information that doesn't fit into a character field, including text that can be formatted with carriage returns and tab marks

3.5 EXERCISES

1. No

2. Yes

3. Yes

4. No

Appendix B	Answer Section	369

MASTERY SKILLS CHECK

1. RIGHT ARROW, ENTER, ENTER, **TEST** ENTER

2. **ITEM** ENTER, ENTER, 30 ENTER

3. **DATE** ENTER, SPACEBAR, SPACEBAR, ENTER

4. **PAID** ENTER, SPACEBAR three times, ENTER

5. **QUANTITY** ENTER, SPACEBAR, ENTER, 5 ENTER, ENTER

6. **COMMENTS** ENTER, SPACEBAR four times, ENTER

7. CTRL-END, ENTER, N

8. CTRL-F, DOWN ARROW five times (highlight the command "List structure"), ENTER, N (observe the structure), any key

INTEGRATING SKILLS CHECK

1. CTRL-A, CTRL-C, (highlight the command Quit dBASE III Plus), ENTER (view the DOS prompt), **DBASE** ENTER, ENTER, RIGHT ARROW, F1 (read the help window), ESC

2. Character fields for customer name, number, street address, mailing address, city, state, country, mail code, phone number, FAX number, buyer contact, and billing contact. Numerical fields for monthly purchase total and annual purchase total. Date field for date last paid. Logical field for paid this month, paid within 60 days, and paid within 90 days

3. To keep track of cents

4. CTRL-F, DOWN ARROW five times (highlight the command "List structure"), F1 (read the help window), ESC

4 SKILLS CHECK

1. CTRL-A (to open the Set Up menu), CTRL-C (to highlight the command Quit DBASE III PLUS), ENTER

2. (At the DOS prompt) **DBASE** ENTER, (at the copyright screen) ENTER, F1

3. Ten fields: NAME, ADDRESS, CITY, STATE, ZIP, PHONE, MONEY, DATE, PAID, and NOTES

4. NAME, ADDRESS, CITY, STATE, ZIP, and PHONE are character fields. MONEY is a numerical field. DATE is a date field. PAID is a logical field. NOTES is a memo field

4.1 EXERCISES

1. (Open the Set Up menu, highlight "Database file") ENTER, ENTER, **TEST** ENTER, N (view status line) ENTER, ENTER, **NAD** ENTER, N (view status line)

2. (In the Assist screen) U, F1 (see definition of command Edit), ESC, DOWN ARROW, F1 (see definition of command Browse), ESC

Appendix B   Answer Section   **371**

EXERCISES 4.2

1. Yes

2. (Make sure NAD shows on the status line) CTRL-A, ENTER, ENTER, (highlight TEST) ENTER, N, U, ENTER

3. CTRL-A, ENTER, ENTER (highlight NAD), ENTER, N, U, ENTER

4. 10

5. Character type: 6, numeric type: 1, date type: 1, logical type: 1, memo type: 1

EXERCISES 4.3

1. No

2. No

3. (Make sure NAD.DBF is current) U, ENTER, (press PGDN to move to new record; EOF should show on status bar) **Walter Gomer** ENTER, **560 San Jose** ENTER, **Kensington** ENTER, **CA, 94708, 415-456-7890, 150** ENTER, ENTER, **010790, F**

4. **John McCord** ENTER, **920 Evelyn** ENTER, **Albany** ENTER, **CA, 94706, 415-525-5614, 200** ENTER, ENTER, **101589, F**

5. **Izzy Zagare** ENTER, **350 Benvenue** ENTER, **El Cerrito** ENTER, **CA, 94530, 415-527-8745, 450** ENTER, ENTER, **112089, F**

6. ENTER, ESC

4.4 EXERCISES

1. No

2. Yes

3. 5000

4. Yes

5. Yes

6. (Make sure NAD.DBF is current) U, ENTER, (press PGDN until record 3 shows on status bar) DOWN ARROW nine times (placing cursor in NOTES field width), CTRL-HOME, **Said he'd pay me back in two weeks.** CTRL-W, ESC

MASTERY SKILLS CHECK

1. None

2. Database file

3. U, F1 (read the description), ESC

4. CTRL-A, ENTER, ENTER, (highlight TEST) ENTER, N, U, ENTER, F1, F1, ESC

5. CTRL-A, ENTER, ENTER, (highlight NAD) ENTER, N, U, ENTER, (press DOWN ARROW nine times), CTRL-HOME, F1, F1, CTRL-W, ESC

6. Database text file

Appendix B

Answer Section 373

7. dBASE creates it automatically whenever you insert the first memo field into a database structure

8. NAD.DBF

9. Status bar displays current database file name

INTEGRATING SKILLS CHECK

1. CTRL-A, CTRL-C, ENTER, **DBASE** ENTER, ENTER

2. None

3. Five spaces

4. C, ENTER, ENTER, **TEMP** ENTER, **FIELD1** ENTER, ENTER, **20** ENTER, **FIELD2** SPACEBAR, ENTER, **FIELD3** ENTER, SPACEBAR, SPACEBAR, ENTER, **FIELD4** SPACEBAR three times, ENTER, **FIELD5** SPACEBAR four times, ENTER, CTRL-END

5. Y, **Toby Friar** ENTER, **100, 122589**, T, **Said he needed money for a book.**, CTRL-W, CTRL-N

6. C, ENTER, ENTER, **MEMO** ENTER, **NOTES1** ENTER, SPACEBAR four times, ENTER, **NOTES2** SPACEBAR four times, CTRL-ENTER, ENTER, N

7. U, ENTER, CTRL-HOME, **This is the first memo field**, CTRL-W

8. U, ENTER, DOWN ARROW, CTRL-HOME, CTRL-K, R, **C:\CONFIG.SYS** ENTER, CTRL-W

5 SKILLS CHECK

1. (At the DOS prompt) **DBASE** ENTER four times (highlight NAD), ENTER, N

2. U, DOWN ARROW, F1 (view information), ESC, DOWN ARROW, F1 (view information), ESC, DOWN ARROW, F1 (view information), ESC

3. P, UP ARROW, F1 (view information), ESC

5.1 EXERCISES

1. No

2. No

3. U, DOWN ARROW, ENTER

4. PGDN, PGDN

5. PGUP, PGUP, **Bill Bailey** ENTER

5.2 EXERCISES

1. No

2. You can view the relationship between fields and records in a more graphic layout. You can position yourself within a group of records and view, compare, or edit information in related records. You can scroll through the same field in separate records and view, compare, or edit information in a single field. You can lock specific fields on your screen so they always appear regardless of what other fields you're viewing. You can freeze a field so it's the only field you can change

Appendix B   Answer Section   **375**

3. No

4. It means displaying a different group of fields on screen. When you pan to the right, a new field appears on the right and an old field disappears on the left. When you pan to the left, a new field appears on the left and an old field disappears on the right

5. Pressing END moves your cursor to the right in the currently displayed fields. When it gets to the rightmost field, it moves down the right margin of your screen. Pressing CTRL-RIGHT ARROW displays a new field on the right of your screen and causes the previously leftmost field to disappear

EXERCISES   5.3

1. Bottom, Top, Lock, Record No., and Freeze.

2. Press CTRL-HOME while viewing the Browse screen.

3. Locking a field means locking it into the current Browse screen display. Freezing a field means making that field the only one you can edit

4. CTRL-RIGHT ARROW (until FIELD10 is displayed), CTRL-HOME, L, **10** ENTER

5. CTRL-HOME, L, ENTER

6. CTRL-HOME, F, **FIELD10** ENTER

7. CTRL-HOME, F, ENTER

5.4 EXERCISES

1. The pointer

2. The Position menu, the command Goto Record

3. P, UP ARROW, ENTER, DOWN ARROW, ENTER

4. ENTER, UP ARROW, ENTER, 3 ENTER

5.5 EXERCISES

1. You can check the contents of a record quickly without having to enter the Browse or Edit screen

2. No

3. P, UP ARROW, ENTER, ENTER (make sure record 1 shows on status bar), U, DOWN ARROW, DOWN ARROW, ENTER (view display), any key

4. P, UP ARROW, ENTER, ENTER (make sure the last record number is displayed on the status bar) U, DOWN ARROW, DOWN ARROW, ENTER (view display), any key

MASTERY SKILLS CHECK

1. The Edit command opens the Edit screen, where you can change the contents of a single record. The Browse command opens the Browse screen, which displays information for corresponding fields in a sequence of adjacent records. You can change information in the displayed fields or reposition the fields in the Browse screen you want to work with

Appendix B   Answer Section   377

The Replace command lets you replace information in a single record or related records quickly but doesn't allow you to observe the changes taking place

2. U (highlight Edit), ENTER (view Edit screen), ESC, DOWN ARROW, DOWN ARROW, ENTER (view Browse screen), ESC, UP ARROW, UP ARROW, ENTER (view Edit screen)

3. U (highlight Browse), ENTER, CTRL-HOME, R, 7 ENTER, ESC (highlight Edit), ENTER, **Alan Vogle** ENTER, ESC (highlight Display), ENTER (view results), any key

INTEGRATING SKILLS CHECK

1. U, DOWN ARROW, F1 (read information), ESC, DOWN ARROW, F1 (read information), ESC, DOWN ARROW, F1 (read information), ESC, DOWN ARROW, F1 (read information), ESC

2. (Make sure NAD is showing on the status line) U (highlight Append), ENTER, **Carol Hannah** ENTER, **205 Martin** ENTER, **Aptos** ENTER, **CA, 95003**, ESC (highlight Display), ENTER (view results), any key

3. C, ENTER, ENTER, **AREA** ENTER, **CITY** ENTER, ENTER, **20** ENTER, **STATE** ENTER, ENTER, **2** ENTER, **CODE** ENTER, ENTER, **3** ENTER, UP ARROW, CTRL-END, ENTER, Y, **San Francisco** ENTER, **CA, 415, Seattle** ENTER, **WA, 206, Honolulu** ENTER, **HI, 808**, CTRL-END, U (highlight Browse), ENTER (scan the database)

SKILLS CHECK   6

1. **DBASE** ENTER three times (highlight NAD), ENTER, ENTER (check status line to make sure NAD is current), U (highlight Edit), ENTER, PGDN three times (make sure record 4 is displayed)

2. DOWN ARROW (nine times), CTRL-HOME, **This is the memo field for record 4**, ENTER, CTRL-W

3. ESC (check Rec: label on status bar), P (highlight Goto Record), ENTER (check Rec: label again)

4. S, ENTER, ENTER (highlight SAMPLE), ENTER, N, U (highlight Browse), ENTER, CTRL-HOME, B, CTRL-HOME, T, CTRL-HOME, R, 3 ENTER, ESC

5. P (highlight Goto Record), UP ARROW, ENTER, 4 ENTER, U (highlight Replace), ENTER, ENTER, **Ziggy Zagare** ENTER, LEFT ARROW, ENTER (dBASE should display "1 record replaced"), any key

6.1 EXERCISES

1. You use it to move to different positions in the current database

2. Seek, Locate, Continue, Skip, and Goto Record

3. It opens the Search/Scope menu

4. It lets you repeat the command Locate

6.2 EXERCISES

1. It moves you over, or skips, a specified number of records

2. It adds the number you enter to the current record number, calculates the sum, and then moves you to the matching record number

3. Type a minus sign before the number you enter

EXERCISES 6.3

1. Scope specifies a range of records. Search specifies the type of information you're looking for

2. Select the field you want to search on, select the operator you want to use, and define the information you want to search for

3. Yes and no. They are ranked in alphabetical order according to the ASCII table code, where all uppercase letters come before all lowercase letters

4. After you've located at least one record

5. = Equal To, < = Less Than or Equal To, < Less Than, > Greater Than, > = Greater Than or Equal To, and < > Not Equal To

6. (Begin in the Assist screen and make sure NAD.DBF is the current database) P (highlight Locate), ENTER (highlight "Build a search condition"), ENTER, ENTER (highlight = Equal To), ENTER, **John McCord** ENTER, DOWN ARROW, ENTER, *any key*, LEFT ARROW, DOWN ARROW, ENTER (view results), any key

EXERCISES 6.4

1. Five

2. Default scope, ALL, NEXT, RECORD, and REST

3. The ALL command

4. Move to the record before the range you want to use. Use the NEXT command and type in the number of records in the range

6.5 EXERCISES

1. (Make sure NAD.DBF is current) P, UP ARROW, ENTER, ENTER (make sure record 1 is current), U (highlight Replace), ENTER, ENTER, **Claudio Abau** ENTER, ESC, ENTER (make sure replacement occurred), any key

2. (Highlight Display) ENTER (view results), any key

3. (Highlight Replace) ENTER, DOWN ARROW, ENTER, **123 Adams Street** ENTER, ESC, ENTER (make sure replacement occurred), any key

4. (Highlight Display) ENTER (view results), any key

5. (Highlight Replace) ENTER, DOWN ARROW, DOWN ARROW, ENTER, **Berkeley** ENTER, ESC, ENTER (make sure replacement occurred), any key

6. (Highlight Display) ENTER (view results), any key

6.6 EXERCISES

1. Numeric field information only

2. No

3. It calculates all numeric field values in all records of the current database

4. S, ENTER, ENTER (highlight VALUE), ENTER, ENTER, U (highlight Sum), ENTER, ENTER (view results), any key

5. U (highlight Sum), ENTER (highlight "Construct a field list"), ENTER (highlight UNITS), ENTER (highlight > Greater Than), ENTER, **25** ENTER (highlight "Execute the command"), ENTER (view results), any key

Appendix B   Answer Section   **381**

MASTERY SKILLS CHECK

1. CTRL-S, ENTER, ENTER, **NAD** ENTER, ENTER, P (highlight Locate), ENTER (highlight "Build a search condition"), ENTER (highlight MONEY), ENTER (highlight = > Equal To or Greater Than), ENTER, **01/01/90** ENTER (highlight "Execute the command"), ENTER (view the results), any key, U (highlight Display), ENTER (view the results), any key

2. (Highlight Continue) ENTER, any key, U (highlight Display), ENTER (view results), any key

3. U (highlight Replace), ENTER (highlight STATE), ENTER, **UT**, RIGHT ARROW (highlight "Build a search condition"), ENTER (highlight STATE), ENTER, ENTER, **AZ**, ENTER (highlight "Execute the command"), ENTER (view results), any key

4. ENTER, ENTER, **VALUE** ENTER, ENTER, U (highlight Sum), ENTER, ENTER (view results), any key (highlight Average), ENTER, ENTER (view results), any key

5. (Highlight Count) ENTER, ENTER (view results), any key

6. (Highlight Sum) ENTER (highlight "Build a search condition"), ENTER (highlight UNITS), ENTER (highlight = > Equal To or Greater Than), ENTER, **25** ENTER (highlight "Execute the command"), ENTER (view the results), any key

INTEGRATING SKILLS CHECK

1. S, ENTER, ENTER, **NAD** ENTER, ENTER, P (highlight Goto Record), ENTER, UP ARROW, ENTER, **10** ENTER, U (highlight Display), ENTER (view results), any key

2. U (highlight Replace), ENTER (highlight MONEY), ENTER, **0**, ENTER, RIGHT ARROW (highlight "Build a search condition"), ENTER (highlight MONEY), ENTER (highlight < Less Than), ENTER, **100** ENTER, ENTER (highlight "Execute the command"), ENTER (view results), any key

3. S, ENTER, ENTER, **VALUE** ENTER, ENTER, R (highlight Sum), ENTER (highlight "Build a search condition"), ENTER (highlight COST), ENTER (highlight > Greater Than), ENTER, **1** ENTER (highlight "Execute the command"), ENTER (view the results), any key

4. S, ENTER, ENTER, **NAD** ENTER, ENTER, R (highlight Average), ENTER, ENTER (view results), any key (highlight Sum), ENTER, ENTER (view results), any key

7 SKILLS CHECK

1. CTRL-A, ENTER, ENTER (highlight NAD), ENTER, ENTER, P (highlight Goto Record), ENTER, UP ARROW, ENTER, **10** ENTER, U (highlight Display), ENTER (view results), any key

2. (Check record number total on right side of status bar) R (highlight Count), ENTER, ENTER (view results), any key

3. U (highlight Browse), ENTER, CTRL-HOME, (B is the default) ENTER, CTRL-HOME, T, ESC

7.1 EXERCISES

1. No

2. No

3. Yes

Appendix B   Answer Section   383

4. (Make sure NAD.DBF is current) P (highlight Goto Record), ENTER, UP ARROW, ENTER, **10** ENTER (make sure record 10 appears on status bar), U (highlight Delete), ENTER, ENTER (you should see "1 record deleted"), any key

5. (Make sure record 10 is current), U (highlight Display), ENTER (look for asterisk), any key

6. U (highlight Recall), ENTER, ENTER (look for "1 record recalled"), any key

7. P (highlight Goto Record), ENTER, UP ARROW, ENTER, **11** ENTER (make sure record number appears on status bar), U (highlight Delete), ENTER, ENTER (you should see "1 record deleted"), any key (highlight Display), ENTER (look for asterisk), any key (highlight Recall), ENTER, ENTER (you should see "1 record recalled"), any key

EXERCISES 7.2

1. dBASE displays the number of records marked for deletion on the screen after it marks them. dBASE displays "Del" on the status bar in the Browse and Edit screens for marked records. dBASE displays an asterisk after the record number for all marked records when the records are displayed by using the Display command on the Update menu or the List command on the Retrieve menu

2. Yes, by using the ALL command on the menu for the command "Specify scope"

3. Press R, and then press ENTER to execute the command List

4. Press CTRL-S and then any key

5. (Make sure NAD.DBF is current) U (highlight Delete), ENTER (highlight "Build a search condition"), ENTER (highlight MONEY), ENTER (highlight > Greater Than), ENTER, **500** ENTER, ENTER (highlight "Execute the command"), ENTER, any key

6. (Highlight Recall), ENTER (highlight "Specify scope"), ENTER (highlight ALL), ENTER, any key

7.3 EXERCISES

1. Yes

2. No

3. Yes

4. One less than before you packed it

5. Make sure the database you want to pack is current. Press U, UP ARROW (to highlight Pack), ENTER (view the results), any key

MASTERY SKILLS CHECK

1. Mark the record for deletion and then pack the database

2. Between the marking and the packing

3. P (highlight Goto Record), ENTER, ENTER, U (highlight Delete), ENTER, ENTER (view results), any key (highlight Display), ENTER (look for asterisk), any key (highlight Recall), ENTER, ENTER (view results), any key

Appendix B

4. P (highlight Goto Record), ENTER, ENTER, U (highlight Delete), ENTER, ENTER (view results), any key (highlight Display), ENTER (look for asterisk), any key (highlight Pack), ENTER (view results), any key

INTEGRATING SKILLS CHECK

1. CTRL-S, ENTER (highlight VALUE), ENTER, ENTER, P (highlight Goto Record), ENTER, DOWN ARROW, ENTER, U (highlight Delete), ENTER, ENTER (view results), any key, P (highlight Goto Record), ENTER, ENTER, U (highlight Delete), ENTER, ENTER (view results), any key, R, ENTER (look for asterisks), any key, U (highlight Recall), ENTER, ENTER (view results), any key

2. CTRL-S, ENTER (highlight NAD), ENTER, ENTER, U (highlight Browse), ENTER, CTRL-U, DOWN ARROW, CTRL-U, DOWN ARROW, CTRL-U, DOWN ARROW, PGUP, CTRL-U, DOWN ARROW, CTRL-U, DOWN ARROW, CTRL-U, DOWN ARROW, ENTER, ESC (highlight Edit), ENTER, CTRL-U, ENTER, ESC (highlight Display), ENTER (view results), any key (highlight Recall), ENTER, ENTER (view results), any key

3. CTRL-S, ENTER, ENTER (highlight Value), ENTER, ENTER, U (highlight Delete), ENTER (highlight "Specify scope"), ENTER (highlight ALL), ENTER (highlight "Execute the command"), ENTER (view results), any key (highlight Pack), ENTER (view results), any key

SKILLS CHECK 8

1. DBASE ENTER four times (highlight NAD), ENTER, ENTER (make sure NAD appears on the status bar)

2. T (highlight "List structure"), ENTER, ENTER (observe structure), any key

386 Teach Yourself dBASE III PLUS

3. U (highlight Browse), ENTER (scan the first screenful of records), PGDN (scan second screenful), ESC

8.1 EXERCISES

1. No

2. No

3. No

4. CTRL-END, ENTER (to confirm)

5. Name: FAX. Location: Below the PHONE field. Type: Character. Width: 12 spaces

6. (Make sure NAD.DBF is current), M, ENTER (highlight CHARGES), CTRL-N, **FAX** ENTER, ENTER, **12** ENTER, CTRL-END, any key

7. M, ENTER, PGDN, CTRL-N, **FIELD1** ENTER, ENTER, **10** ENTER, **FIELD2** ENTER, ENTER, **10** ENTER, CTRL-END, ENTER (compare screen to Figure 8-5)

8.2 EXERCISES

1. Yes, most definitely

2. The name of the field, the type of the field, and the size of the field

3. Save the new structure each time you change the name of a field

Appendix B   Answer Section   **387**

4. (Make sure NAD.DBF is current), M, ENTER (highlight PAID), ENTER, SPACEBAR, SPACEBAR, ENTER, CTRL-ENTER, ENTER, T (highlight "List structure"), ENTER, ENTER (view results), any key

5. M, ENTER (highlight PAID), ENTER, SPACEBAR four times, (make sure Logical shows), ENTER, CTRL-END, ENTER, U (highlight Browse), ENTER (view results), ESC

6. M, ENTER three times, **25** ENTER three times, **25** ENTER (view results)

7. UP ARROW, ENTER, ENTER, **35** ENTER three times, **35** ENTER, CTRL-END, ENTER, T (highlight "List structure"), ENTER, ENTER (view results), any key

EXERCISES   8.3

1. Yes

2. No. The backup copy always contains all the information in the previous version of your database

3. (Make sure NAD.DBF is the current database) M, ENTER (highlight FIELD2), CTRL-U, ENTER, CTRL-END, ENTER

4. (Make sure NAD.DBF is current), M, ENTER (highlight FIELD2), CTRL-U, ENTER, CTRL-END, ENTER, T (highlight "List structure"), ENTER, ENTER (view results), any key

MASTERY SKILLS CHECK

1. S, ENTER, ENTER (highlight VALUE), ENTER, ENTER, M, ENTER, CTRL-N, **NEW-FIELD** ENTER, ENTER, **10** ENTER, CTRL-END, ENTER, any key

2. M, ENTER (highlight QUANTITY), **NUMBER** ENTER, CTRL-END, ENTER

3. M, ENTER, T (highlight PRICE), CTRL-U, ESC, ESC

4. M, ENTER (highlight NUMBER), **QUANTITY** ENTER, CTRL-END, ENTER

5. T (highlight "List structure"), ENTER, ENTER (view results), any key

INTEGRATING SKILLS CHECK

1. C, ENTER, ENTER, **SAMPLE** ENTER, **NAME** ENTER, ENTER, **10** ENTER, **NUMBER** ENTER, SPACEBAR, ENTER, **1** ENTER, ENTER, **DATE** ENTER, SPACEBAR, SPACEBAR, CTRL-END, ENTER, Y, **Record 1** ENTER, **1** (cursor moves down automatically), **010190** (cursor moves down automatically), **Record 2** ENTER, **2** (cursor moves down automatically), **010290** (cursor moves down automatically), **Record 3** ENTER, **3** (cursor moves down automatically), **01/03/90** (cursor moves down automatically), PGUP, CTRL-END, ENTER, any key

2. M, ENTER, CTRL-U, (make sure field name NAME disappears), ESC, ESC, T (highlight "List structure"), ENTER, ENTER (view structure on screen; NAME field should still exist), any key

3. M, ENTER, DOWN ARROW, ENTER, SPACEBAR four times, ENTER three times, SPACEBAR three times, CTRL-END, ENTER, T (highlight "List structure"), ENTER, ENTER (view list), any key, U (highlight Browse), ENTER (view contents), ESC

4. M, ENTER, CTRL-U three times, CTRL-END, ENTER, any key (look at status bar)

9 SKILLS CHECK

1. **DBASE** ENTER three times, (highlight NAD), ENTER, ENTER, U (highlight Browse), ENTER (view contents), ESC

Appendix B   Answer Section   **389**

2. P (highlight Goto Record), ENTER (highlight RECORD), ENTER, **10** ENTER (check status bar for record 10), U (highlight Edit), ENTER, ESC

3. P (highlight Goto Record), ENTER, ENTER, R, ENTER (press CTRL-S, then any key intermittently as you look for asterisks next to any record numbers in the displayed list of record contents), any key

EXERCISES 9.1

1. A separate disk file

2. No

3. Yes

4. Yes. The precedence is determined by the order in which you attach them to a database

5. Logical and memo fields

6. The master index is the first or primary index

7. Eight. You can't use the logical field PAID or the memo field NOTES

8. (Make sure NAD.DBF is current), O, ENTER, F10 (highlight MONEY), ENTER, RIGHT ARROW, ENTER, **MONEY** ENTER, any key

9. S, ENTER, ENTER (highlight NAD), ENTER, Y (highlight MONEY), ENTER, LEFT ARROW, U (highlight Browse), ENTER, PGUP (view results), ESC

9.2 EXERCISES

1. The database you want to search in must be active, and a current index based on the field you want to search through must be attached

2. The command Seek is the fastest way to locate individual records

3. (Make sure NAD.DBF is current and NAME.NDX is attached to it) P, ENTER **"Carol McGinnis"** ENTER (view current record number), any key

9.3 EXERCISES

1. Yes

2. No, it's a database file

3. A duplicate copy of the original database in which the records are saved to disk in the sorted order

4. A sorted database is a database file. An index is a file based on information in a database file. A sorted database responds more quickly than an indexed one to movements between records. A sorted database takes up more disk space since it is a duplicate of another database. A sorted database must be re-sorted whenever records are added or updated.
   An indexed database is more flexible than a sorted database. You can create different indexes and attach them in various ways to reorganize the records in the database. Indexes attached to a database are updated automatically as the database is updated. If an index is not attached to a database when you update the database, you must rebuild the index

Appendix B   Answer Section   **391**

5. (Make sure NAD.DBF is current) O, DOWN ARROW, ENTER (highlight MONEY), ENTER, LEFT ARROW, ENTER, **NADMONEY** ENTER, any key, S, ENTER, ENTER (highlight NADMONEY), ENTER, ENTER, U (highlight Browse), ENTER (view results), ESC

EXERCISES 9.4

1. Four

2. You can copy a duplicate file. You can select fields to copy. You can select records to copy. You can select a combination of fields and records to copy

3. By using the Search/Scope menu attached to the Copy command on the Organize menu

4. (Make sure NAD.DBF is current) O, UP ARROW, ENTER, **MONEY** ENTER (highlight "Build a field list"), ENTER (highlight NAME), ENTER (highlight PHONE), ENTER (highlight MONEY), ENTER, LEFT ARROW (highlight "Execute the command"), ENTER, any key

5. (Make sure NAD.DBF is current) O, UP ARROW, ENTER, **OWES** ENTER (highlight "Build a search condition"), ENTER (highlight MONEY), ENTER (highlight > Greater Than), ENTER, **499** ENTER (highlight "No more conditions"), ENTER (highlight "Execute the command"), ENTER, any key

MASTERY SKILLS CHECK

1. (Make sure NAD.DBF is current) O, ENTER, F10 (highlight DATE), ENTER three times, **DATE** ENTER, any key, U (highlight Browse), ENTER (view results), ESC

2. (Make sure NAD.DBF is current) O, ENTER, F10 (highlight DATE), ENTER, +, F10 (highlight PAID), ENTER, ENTER, ENTER, **DATEPAID** ENTER, any key, U (highlight Browse), ENTER (view results), ESC

3. (Make sure NAD.DBF is current) O, DOWN ARROW, ENTER, F10 (highlight ZIP), ENTER, ENTER, **ZIP** ENTER, any key, U (highlight Browse), ENTER, PGUP (view results), ESC

4. (Make sure NAD.DBF is current) O, DOWN ARROW, ENTER, F10 (highlight ZIP), ENTER, F10 (highlight NAME), ENTER, ENTER, **ZIPNAME** ENTER, any key, U (highlight Browse), ENTER, PGUP (view results), ESC

5. (Make sure NAD.DBF is current) O, UP ARROW, ENTER, UPDATE, ENTER (highlight "Build a field list"), ENTER, ENTER (highlight PHONE), ENTER (highlight MONEY), ENTER, RIGHT ARROW (highlight "Build a search condition"), ENTER (highlight MONEY), ENTER (highlight > Greater Than), ENTER, **499** ENTER (highlight "No more conditions"), ENTER (highlight "Execute the command"), ENTER, any key

INTEGRATING SKILLS CHECK

1. O, F1 (read help display), ESC

2. O, DOWN ARROW, F1 (read help display), ESC

3. C, ENTER, ENTER, **NAME** ENTER, **NAME** ENTER, ENTER, **30** CTRL-END, ENTER, Y, **Walrus** ENTER, **Minnow** ENTER, **Anteater** CTRL-END, ENTER, O, ENTER, F10, ENTER, ENTER, **NAME** ENTER, any key, U (highlight Browse), ENTER, PGUP (view results), ESC

4. S, CTRL-C, ENTER (the DOS prompt should appear), **dBASE** ENTER three times (highlight NAD), ENTER, ENTER (make sure NAD appears on status bar)

Appendix B   Answer Section   **393**

5. U, ENTER, **Aardvark** ENTER, UP ARROW, CTRL-END, S, ENTER, ENTER, (highlight NAME), ENTER, Y (highlight NAME), ENTER, LEFT ARROW, U (highlight Browse), ENTER

6. The record for Aardvark doesn't show because it was added after the index NAME.NDX was created, and NAME.NDX was not updated. Press any key

7. (Make sure NAME.DBF is current) O, DOWN ARROW, ENTER, F10, ENTER, LEFT ARROW, ENTER, ENTER, **NEWNAME** ENTER, any key, U (highlight Browse), ENTER, PGUP (view results), ESC

8. S, ENTER, ENTER (highlight NAD), ENTER, ENTER, O, UP ARROW, ENTER, **DEBTS** ENTER (highlight "No more conditions"), ENTER, any key

SKILLS CHECK   10

1. S, ENTER, ENTER, **NAD** ENTER, ENTER, U (highlight Edit), ENTER (view results), ESC

2. U (highlight Browse), CTRL-HOME, B, CTRL-HOME, R, **10** ENTER, CTRL-HOME, T, ESC

3. On the right side of the status bar after "Rec:"

4. P, UP ARROW, ENTER, DOWN ARROW, ENTER (view results), ENTER, UP ARROW, ENTER, **10** ENTER (view results), ENTER, ENTER (view results)

5. S, ENTER, ENTER (highlight NAD), ENTER, Y (highlight NAME), RIGHT ARROW

6. S, ENTER, ENTER (highlight NAD), ENTER, ENTER

10.1 EXERCISES

1. No. You can use it in all DOS-based programs

2. (View the Assist interface) SHIFT-PRT SCR

3. P (highlight Goto Record), ENTER (highlight RECORD), 8 ENTER, U (highlight Edit), ENTER, SHIFT-PRT SCR, ESC

10.2 EXERCISES

1. (Make sure NAD.DBF is current) R (highlight List), ENTER (highlight "Construct field list"), ENTER five times, LEFT ARROW (highlight "Execute the command"), ENTER, Y

2. R (highlight List), ENTER (highlight "Build a search condition"), ENTER (highlight MONEY), ENTER (highlight > Greater Than), ENTER, **500** ENTER, ENTER (highlight "Execute the command"), ENTER, ENTER (view results), any key

3. R (highlight List), ENTER (highlight "Construct a field list"), ENTER, ENTER, LEFT ARROW, ENTER (highlight MONEY), ENTER (highlight > Greater Than), ENTER, **500** ENTER (highlight "Execute the command"), ENTER (view results), any key

10.3 EXERCISES

1. R (highlight Display), ENTER, ENTER (highlight Specify Scope), ENTER, ENTER (highlight Record), ENTER, **20** ENTER (highlight "Execute the command"), ENTER (view results), any key

Appendix B   Answer Section   395

2. (Make sure record 1 is current) R (highlight Display), ENTER (highlight "Construct a field list"), ENTER, ENTER (highlight PHONE), ENTER, LEFT ARROW (highlight "Execute the command"), ENTER (view results), any key

3. R (highlight Display), ENTER (highlight "Specify scope"), ENTER (highlight NEXT), ENTER, 3 ENTER (highlight "Execute the command"), ENTER (view results), any key

4. R (highlight Display), ENTER (highlight "Construct a field list"), ENTER, ENTER (highlight MONEY), ENTER, LEFT ARROW (highlight "Build a search condition"), ENTER (highlight MONEY), ENTER (highlight > Greater Than), ENTER, 500 ENTER, ENTER (highlight "Execute the command"), ENTER (view results), any key

5. The Display command displays up to 15 records on screen and then holds the screen. The List command displays one or more records in a continuous scrolling list. The Display command sends output only to the screen. The List command can send output to the screen or the printer

MASTERY SKILLS CHECK

1. (Check the status bar for NAD) R, ENTER three times (watch list scroll), any key (highlight Display), ENTER (highlight "Specify scope"), ENTER (highlight RECORD), ENTER, 1 ENTER (highlight "Execute the command"), ENTER (view results)

2. CTRL-PRTSC (view results), any key

3. R (highlight List), ENTER (highlight "Construct a field list"), ENTER six times, LEFT ARROW (highlight "Execute the command"), ENTER, Y

4. R (highlight Display), ENTER (highlight Specify Scope), ENTER (highlight RECORD), ENTER, **20** ENTER (highlight "Execute the Command"), ENTER (view results), any key

INTEGRATING SKILLS CHECK

1. R (highlight List), F1 (read description), ESC (highlight Display), F1 (read description), ESC

2. S, ENTER, ENTER (highlight VALUE), ENTER, ENTER, R (highlight List), ENTER three times (view results), any key, ENTER, ENTER, Y

3. S, ENTER, ENTER (highlight NAD), ENTER, Y (highlight NAME), RIGHT ARROW, R (highlight Display), ENTER (highlight "Specify scope"), ENTER (highlight NEXT), ENTER, **15** ENTER (highlight "Execute the command"), ENTER (view results), any key

11 SKILLS CHECK

1. S, ENTER, ENTER (highlight NAD), ENTER, T (highlight "List structure"), ENTER (view display)

2. The results should look as follows:

Field	Field Name	Type	Width	Dec
1	NAME	Character	35	
2	ADDRESS	Character	35	
3	CITY	Character	20	
4	STATE	Character	2	
5	ZIP	Character	5	
6	PHONE	Character	12	
7	MONEY	Numeric	6	2
8	DATE	Date	8	
9	PAID	Logical	1	
10	NOTES	Memo	10	

3. Any key

EXERCISES 11.1

1. C, (highlight Format), ENTER, ENTER (type name of format file), ENTER

2. One is .SCR, which stands for "screen," because format files control the way database field names and information will appear on your screen. The other is .FMT, which stands for "format." dBASE creates this file from the .SCR file

3. No

4. E and CTRL-F

5. S and CTRL-A

EXERCISES 11.2

1. Yes

2. No

3. Yes

4. Use the Set Up menu in the Create screen for format files, and then select the command Select Database File

5. S, ENTER (highlight NAD), ENTER

6. Press M to open the Modify menu and check the entry in the Source field

11.3 EXERCISES

1. You create a .SCR by using the Create screen for format files. dBASE creates the matching .FMT file when you save the .SCR file to disk. You use the .SCR file to create and modify the display. dBASE uses the .FMT file to modify its screen display when you use a format file

2. No

3. The blackboard

4. F10

5. C (highlight Format), ENTER, ENTER, **QUICK** ENTER, ENTER (highlight NAD), ENTER (highlight Load Fields), ENTER, ENTER (highlight PHONE), ENTER (highlight MONEY), ENTER, F10 (make sure fields are inserted), F10, E, ENTER, U (highlight Edit), ENTER (view results), ESC

6. Yes, but only if you save it first

11.4 EXERCISES

1. None except the name of each screen as shown on the left side of the status bar

2. Yes

3. Text characters, single and double lines, and single- and double-line boxes

4. Place the cursor in the field width and press ENTER, and then move the cursor to the new position and press ENTER a second time

Appendix B Answer Section **399**

5. On the navigation line, or the second line from the bottom of your screen

EXERCISES 11.5

1. Field names and their locations by column and row in the format file

2. To your disk in the current directory

3. A simple ASCII text file that you can view with a word processor or text editor

4. Converts existing characters to a different type of display

5. Allows only certain types of characters to be entered into a field

6. The Modify menu

7. You might reduce the size of a field such that existing information is truncated or deleted

8. No

MASTERY SKILLS CHECK

1. C (highlight Format), ENTER, ENTER, **CHECK** ENTER, ENTER (highlight NAD), ENTER, UP ARROW, ENTER (highlight NAME), ENTER (highlight PHONE), ENTER (highlight MONEY), ENTER, F10

2. (Place cursor under N in NAME field name) SPACEBAR four times, LEFT ARROW four times, **Name** (place cursor under P of PHONE field

name), SPACEBAR five times, (move cursor to first space of PHONE field width), ENTER, (move cursor to Row 00 Col 57), ENTER, LEFT ARROW six times, **Phone**

3. (Place cursor under M of MONEY field name), SPACEBAR five times, (place cursor on first space of MONEY field width), ENTER, F10, O (highlight "Single bar"), ENTER (move cursor to Row 04 Col 20), ENTER (move cursor to Row 03 Col 19), ENTER (move cursor to Row 05 Col 26), ENTER

4. F10, E, ENTER (in the Assist screen), U (highlight Edit), ENTER (view results), any key

5. M (highlight Format), ENTER, ENTER (highlight CHECK.SCR), ENTER, F10 (move cursor to Row 07 Col 10), **Call if this amount passes $500**, F10, E, ENTER

INTEGRATING SKILLS CHECK

1. C, DOWN ARROW, ENTER, ENTER, **VALUE** ENTER, ENTER (highlight VALUE), ENTER, UP ARROW, ENTER, ENTER, DOWN ARROW, ENTER, DOWN ARROW, ENTER, DOWN ARROW, ENTER, F10, SPACEBAR four times (move cursor under first space of ITEM field), ENTER (move cursor to Row 00 Col 20), ENTER, LEFT ARROW five times, **Item** ENTER, SPACEBAR eight times (move cursor under first space of QUANTITY field width), ENTER (move cursor to position Row 01 Col 20), ENTER, LEFT ARROW nine times, **Quantity** ENTER, SPACEBAR five times (move cursor under first space of PRICE field width), ENTER (move cursor to Row 03 Col 20), ENTER, LEFT ARROW six times, **Price** ENTER, SPACEBAR four times (move cursor under first space of COST field width), ENTER (move cursor to Row 04 Col 20), ENTER, F10, E, ENTER (in the Assist screen), U (highlight Edit), ENTER (view results), any key

2. C (highlight Format), ENTER, ENTER, **MY** ENTER (highlight Create a New Database File), ENTER, **MY** ENTER, ENTER (highlight MY), ENTER, F10, F10 (highlight Content), ENTER, ENTER, **NAME** ENTER (highlight Width), ENTER, **30** ENTER (highlight Content), ENTER, ENTER, **ADDRESS** ENTER,

Appendix B

ENTER, ENTER, **CITY** ENTER (highlight Width), ENTER, **20** ENTER (highlight Content), ENTER, ENTER, **STATE** ENTER (highlight Width), ENTER, **2** ENTER (highlight Content), ENTER, ENTER, **ZIP** ENTER (highlight Width), ENTER, **5** ENTER (highlight Content), ENTER, ENTER, **PHONE** ENTER (highlight Width), ENTER, **12** ENTER, CTRL-S (highlight Load Fields), ENTER (highlight NAME), ENTER (highlight PHONE), ENTER, F10, F10, E, ENTER

SKILLS CHECK 12

1. S, ENTER, ENTER (highlight NAD.DBF), ENTER, ENTER, C, UP ARROW, UP ARROW, F1 (read description), ESC

2. T (highlight "List structure"), ENTER, ENTER (view structure on screen), any key

3. M, UP ARROW, UP ARROW, F1 (read description), ENTER

4. S, ENTER, ENTER (highlight NAD.DBF), ENTER, Y (highlight NAME.NDX), ENTER, LEFT ARROW

5. R, ENTER three times, (view results), any key

6. R, DOWN ARROW, DOWN ARROW, F1 (read description), ESC

EXERCISES 12.1

1. Five

2. They're not strictly commands; they're settings into which you can enter text, whose numeric values you can change, or that can be toggled on or off

3. The report format area

4. Right brackets indicate current left margin setting. Dashes fill out the line to show the current page width setting

5. C (highlight Report), ENTER, ENTER, **TEST** ENTER, G, DOWN ARROW, DOWN ARROW, ENTER

6. LEFT ARROW (highlight "Left margin"), ENTER, **10** ENTER

7. ESC, ESC (or E, DOWN ARROW, ENTER), ESC, Y

12.2 EXERCISES

1. It lets you insert text that will appear at the top of every page

2. Open the Columns menu, press PGDN to move to the next column number you want to use, and insert one or more fields into the Contents setting

3. The current column number appears on the right side of the status bar

4. Highlight the Contents setting on the Columns menu. Press ENTER and then F10 to open a list of fields. Highlight the field name you want to insert and press ENTER twice

5. C, UP ARROW, UP ARROW, ENTER, **TEST** ENTER (the Create Report screen appears for TEST.FRM), C, ENTER, F10, ENTER, ENTER

6. DOWN ARROW, ENTER, **Name of Debtors** CTRL-END

7. PGDN (Column 2 should appear on status bar), UP ARROW, ENTER, F10 (highlight PHONE), ENTER, ENTER, DOWN ARROW, ENTER, **Phone Number** ENTER, CTRL-END

8. E, ENTER

EXERCISES 12.3

1. No

2. Yes

3. (Make sure NAD.DBF is current) R (highlight Report), ENTER, ENTER (highlight NAD.FRM), ENTER (highlight "Build a search condition"), ENTER (highlight STATE), ENTER (highlight = Equal To), ENTER, CT ENTER (highlight "Execute the command"), ENTER, ENTER (view results on screen), any key

4. No

5. The fields you can print have been inserted into the report form. You can't override the report form fields

EXERCISES 12.4

1. No

2. No

3. No

4. If you insert field names from the current report, they might not match field names in the database that you want to use

5. M (highlight Report), ENTER, ENTER (highlight NAD.FRM), ENTER (highlight "Left margin"), ENTER, 0 ENTER

6. RIGHT ARROW (highlight "Summary report only"), ENTER, E, ENTER

7. R, DOWN ARROW, DOWN ARROW, ENTER, ENTER (highlight NAD), ENTER three times (view results), any key

8. Only a summary of the report is printed

MASTERY SKILLS CHECK

1. A report can display database information in a more graphically attractive format. You have more control over the information that's displayed in a report

2. (Make sure NAD.DBF is current) C (highlight "Report"), ENTER, ENTER, **NAD1** ENTER, C, ENTER, F10, ENTER (NAME should show after Contents setting), ENTER, PGDN, ENTER, F10 (highlight MONEY), ENTER, ENTER, E, ENTER

3. R (highlight Report), ENTER, ENTER (highlight NAD1.FRM), ENTER three times (view results), any key

4. R (highlight Report), ENTER, ENTER (highlight NAD1.FRM), ENTER (highlight "Build a search condition"), ENTER (highlight MONEY), ENTER (highlight > Greater Than), ENTER, **100** ENTER, ENTER (highlight "Execute the command"), ENTER, ENTER (view results), any key

5. M (highlight Report), ENTER, ENTER (highlight NAD1.FRM), ENTER, C, PGDN, PGDN, ENTER, F10 (highlight PHONE), ENTER, ENTER, E, ENTER

6. R (highlight Report), ENTER, ENTER (highlight NAD1.FRM), ENTER three times (view results), any key

Appendix B   Answer Section   **405**

INTEGRATING SKILLS CHECK

1. Make VALUE.DBF current

2. S, ENTER, ENTER (highlight VALUE), ENTER, ENTER

3. C, (highlight Report), ENTER, ENTER, **VALUE** ENTER, C, ENTER, F10, ENTER, ENTER, PGDN, ENTER, F10, DOWN ARROW, ENTER, ENTER, PGDN, ENTER, F10, DOWN ARROW, DOWN ARROW, ENTER, ENTER, PGDN, F10, UP ARROW, ENTER, ENTER, E, ENTER

4. (Make sure VALUE .DBF is current) R (highlight Report), ENTER, ENTER (highlight VALUE .FRM), ENTER three times (view results), any key

5. M (highlight Report), ENTER, ENTER (highlight VALUE), ENTER, ENTER, **Report on All Items in VALUE.DBF**, CTRL-END, E, ENTER

SKILLS CHECK   13

1. S, ENTER, ENTER (highlight NAD), ENTER, ENTER, C, UP ARROW, F1 (read description), ESC

2. M, UP ARROW, F1 (read description), ESC

3. R, DOWN ARROW three times, F1 (read description), ESC

4. S, ENTER, ENTER (highlight NAD), ENTER, Y (highlight NAME), ENTER, RIGHT ARROW

5. R, ENTER three times (view results), ESC

6. T (highlight "List structure"), ENTER, ENTER (view results), ESC

13.1 EXERCISES

1. Three

2. (Check status bar for NAD) C, UP ARROW, ENTER, ENTER, **NAD** ENTER

3. O, DOWN ARROW, DOWN ARROW, ENTER, **10** ENTER

4. RIGHT ARROW or C

5. Ten, because the "Label height" setting governs the height of a label as measured in lines

6. O (highlight "Left margin"), ENTER, **5** ENTER

7. ESC, ESC or E, DOWN ARROW, ENTER or ESC, Y

13.2 EXERCISES

1. Select one of five different predefined label sizes to use

2. On the various lines in the Contents menu

3. Open the Contents menu, highlight the line where you want to insert a field, and press ENTER and then F10 to open the list of fields for the current database. Highlight the name of the field that you want to insert and press ENTER twice

4. Insert the first field name the usual way, insert a plus sign (+), and then insert the next field. Make sure field names are separated with a plus sign

5. E, ENTER

Appendix B　　　　　　　　　　　　　　　　　　　　　Answer Section　　**407**

EXERCISES 13.3

1. Yes

2. Yes

3. (Make sure NAD.DBF is current) R, ENTER, ENTER (highlight NAD.LBL), ENTER (highlight "Build a search condition"), ENTER (highlight STATE), ENTER (highlight = Equal To), ENTER, **CA** ENTER, ENTER (highlight "Execute the command"), ENTER, ENTER (view results), any key

4. No

5. The fields to be printed in labels have been inserted into the label format. You can't override the label file fields

EXERCISES 13.4

1. No

2. No

3. M, UP ARROW, ENTER (highlight NAD.LBL), ENTER six times (3 1/2 x 15/16 by 2 should appear), ENTER, E, ENTER

4. R, DOWN ARROW three times, ENTER, ENTER (highlight NAD.LBL), ENTER three times (view results), ESC

5. The current label layout displays a two-column format. The previous label layout displayed a three-column format

MASTERY SKILLS CHECK

1. Creating labels requires a specific type of report, a report using the format for printed labels

2. When you want to print database information on slips of paper, or labels, that you can affix to items, such as letters, boxes, and folders

3. (Make sure NAD.DBF is current) C (highlight Label), ENTER, ENTER, **AMOUNT** ENTER (make sure "Predefined size" shows 3 1/2 x 15/16 by 3), C, ENTER, F10, ENTER, ENTER, PGDN, ENTER, F10 (highlight MONEY), ENTER, ENTER, PGDN, ENTER, F10 (highlight DATE), ENTER, ENTER, E, ENTER

4. R (highlight Label), ENTER five times (view results), any key

5. (Make sure your printer is on, filled with paper, and connected to your computer) R (highlight Label), ENTER four times, Y

INTEGRATING SKILLS CHECK

1. S, ENTER, ENTER (highlight VALUE.DBF), ENTER, ENTER, C (highlight Label), ENTER, ENTER (highlight ITEM), ENTER (make sure "Predefined size" shows 3 1/2 x 15/16 by 1), C, ENTER, F10, ENTER, ENTER, PGDN, ENTER, F10 (highlight PRICE), ENTER, ENTER, E, ENTER

2. R (highlight Label), ENTER, ENTER (highlight ITEM), ENTER three times, (view results), any key

3. O, ENTER, **ITEM** ENTER, ENTER, **ITEMNAME** ENTER, any key (completes ITEMNAME.NDX), ENTER, **PRICE** ENTER, ENTER, **PRICE** ENTER, any key (completes PRICE.NDX)

Appendix B

4. S, ENTER, ENTER (highlight VALUE.DBF), ENTER, Y (highlight ITEM-NAME), ENTER, RIGHT ARROW, R (highlight Label), ENTER, ENTER (highlight ITEM), ENTER, ENTER, Y

5. S, ENTER, ENTER, (highlight VALUE.DBF), ENTER, Y (highlight PRICE), ENTER, RIGHT ARROW, R (highlight Label), ENTER, ENTER (highlight ITEM), ENTER, ENTER, Y

SKILLS CHECK 14

1. (Make sure NAD.DBF is current) P, ENTER (highlight "Build a search condition"), ENTER (highlight STATE), ENTER, ENTER, **CA** ENTER, ENTER (highlight "Execute the command"), ENTER (view results), any key

2. R, (Highlight "Continue"), ENTER (view results), any key

3. R, ENTER (highlight "Build a search condition"), ENTER (highlight STATE), ENTER, ENTER, **CA** ENTER, ENTER (highlight "Execute the command"), ENTER (view results), any key

4. R, ENTER (highlight "Build a search condition"), ENTER (highlight MONEY), ENTER (highlight > = Greater Than or Equal To), ENTER, **500** ENTER, ENTER (highlight "Execute the command"), ENTER (view results), any key

5. R, ENTER (highlight "Build a search condition"), ENTER (highlight STATE), ENTER, ENTER, **CA** ENTER (highlight Combine with .AND.) ENTER (highlight MONEY), ENTER (highlight > = Greater Than or Equal To), ENTER, **500** ENTER, ENTER (highlight "Execute the command"), ENTER (view results), any key

14.1 EXERCISES

1. Three: the Set Filter, Nest, and Exit menus

2. C, (highlight Query), ENTER, ENTER (highlight NAD.QRY), ENTER

3. D, ENTER

4. RIGHT ARROW

5. ESC, ESC

14.2 EXERCISES

1. You need to know the structure of the database you want to use and have a good idea of the records you want to view in the database

2. Yes. You use the Display command to do this

3. (Make sure NAD.DBF is current) C (highlight Query), ENTER, ENTER, **200-400** ENTER, ENTER (highlight MONEY), ENTER, ENTER (highlight > More Than), ENTER, ENTER, **200** ENTER, ENTER (highlight Combine with .AND.), ENTER, ENTER (highlight MONEY), ENTER, ENTER (highlight < Less Than), ENTER, ENTER, **400** ENTER

4. D, ENTER

5. E, ENTER

6. S (highlight Query), ENTER, ENTER (highlight 200-400.QRY), ENTER, U (highlight Browse), ENTER (view results), ESC

EXERCISES 14.3

1. No

2. Highlight Line Number, press ENTER, type the line number of the query form that contains the filter condition you want to change, and press ENTER

3. (Make sure NAD.DBF is current) M (highlight Query), ENTER, ENTER (highlight 200CA.QRY), ENTER (highlight Constant/Operator), ENTER, BACKSPACE four times, **AZ** ENTER, E, ENTER

4. .NOT.
   .AND.
   .OR.

MASTERY SKILLS CHECK

1. (Make sure NAD.DBF is current) C (highlight Query), ENTER, ENTER, **SAMPLE**, ENTER, ENTER (highlight MONEY), ENTER, ENTER (highlight > More Than), ENTER, ENTER, **500** ENTER

2. D, ENTER, PGDN, PGDN

3. E, ENTER

4. S (highlight Query), ENTER, ENTER (highlight SAMPLE.QRY), ENTER, U (highlight Browse), ENTER (view results), ESC

5. M, (highlight Query), ENTER, ENTER (highlight SAMPLE.QRY), ENTER (highlight Constant/Expression), ENTER, BACKSPACE three times, **200** ENTER, ENTER (highlight Combine with .AND.), ENTER (highlight Field Name), ENTER (highlight MONEY), ENTER, ENTER (highlight < Less Than), ENTER, ENTER, **800** ENTER

6. E, ENTER, U (highlight Browse), ENTER (view results), ESC

INTEGRATING SKILLS CHECK

1. S, ENTER, ENTER (highlight VALUE.DBF), ENTER, ENTER, T (highlight List structure), ENTER, ENTER (view results), any key

2. C (highlight Query), ENTER, ENTER, **VALUE** ENTER, ENTER (highlight UNITS), ENTER, ENTER (highlight > More Than), ENTER, ENTER, **500** ENTER

3. D, ENTER, PGDN, PGDN, E, ENTER, S (highlight Query), ENTER, ENTER (highlight VALUE.QRY), ENTER, U (highlight Browse), ENTER (view results), ESC

4. S, ENTER, ENTER (highlight NAD.DBF), ENTER, ENTER (highlight Query), ENTER, ENTER (highlight VALUE.QRY), ENTER (view message), any key

15 SKILLS CHECK

1. S, ENTER, ENTER (highlight NAD.DBF), ENTER, ENTER, T (highlight List structure), ENTER (view results), any key, S, ENTER, ENTER (highlight VALUE.DBF), ENTER, ENTER, T (highlight List structure), ENTER (view results), any key

2. T, F1 (read definition for Set drive command), ESC (highlight each command in turn and press F1 to display definition)

3. S (highlight "Quit dBASE III PLUS"), ENTER (reload dBASE), T (view results); the command "List structure" is disabled

Appendix B

EXERCISES 15.1

1. The current drive letter is displayed in the middle of the status bar

2. No

3. (Make sure C is the current drive) T (highlight Directory), ENTER, ENTER (highlight *.fmt Format Files), ENTER (view results), any key

EXERCISES 15.2

1. Yes

2. T (highlight Copy file), ENTER, ENTER (highlight VALUE.DBF), ENTER, ENTER, **BACKUP.DBF** ENTER (watch for completion), any key

3. (Highlight Rename) ENTER, ENTER (highlight BACKUP.DBF), ENTER, **OTHER.DBF** ENTER (watch for completion), any key

4. (Highlight Erase) ENTER, ENTER (highlight OTHER.DBF), ENTER (watch for completion), any key

EXERCISES 15.3

1. PFS:File data files only

2. In most cases, yes. In some cases, such as when you work with particularly large databases or data files, or with databases with unusually large fields or records, you should check the restrictions for the format you're converting to

MASTERY SKILLS CHECK

1. T, ENTER (highlight A), ENTER (check status bar), ENTER (highlight C), ENTER (check status bar)

2. DOWN ARROW, ENTER, ENTER (highlight VALUE.DBF), ENTER, ENTER, **TEST.DBF** ENTER, any key

3. DOWN ARROW, ENTER, ENTER (highlight *.dbf Database Files), ENTER (view results), any key

4. DOWN ARROW, ENTER, ENTER (highlight TEST .DBF), ENTER, **MY.DBF** ENTER (view progress), any key

5. S, ENTER, ENTER (highlight MY .DBF), ENTER, ENTER, T (highlight Export), ENTER, ENTER, **NEW.TXT** ENTER, any key

6. (Highlight Import) ENTER, ENTER, **NEW.TXT** ENTER, any key

7. (Highlight Erase) ENTER, ENTER (highlight TEST.DBF), ENTER (view success), any key, ENTER, ENTER (highlight MY.DBF), ENTER (view success), any key, ENTER, ENTER (highlight NEW.DBF), ENTER (view success), any key (highlight Directory), ENTER, ENTER (highlight * . All files), ENTER (view results), any key

INTEGRATING SKILLS CHECK

1. T (highlight Copy File), ENTER, ENTER (highlight NAD.DBF), ENTER, ENTER, **EXAMPLE.DBF** ENTER, any key

2. S, ENTER, ENTER (highlight EXAMPLE .DBF), ENTER, ENTER, T (highlight List structure), ENTER, ENTER (view results), any key

3. M, ENTER, CTRL-N, **ACCT_NU** ENTER, ENTER, 5 ENTER, CTRL-END, ENTER

Appendix B

4. P (highlight Goto Record), ENTER, ENTER (make sure record 1 shows on right side of status bar), U (highlight Edit), ENTER

5. 1 ENTER, PGDN, 2 ENTER, PGDN, 3 ENTER, PGDN, 4 ENTER, PGDN, 5 ENTER, PGDN, CTRL-END

6. U (highlight Browse), ENTER, PGUP (view results), ESC

7. R, ENTER three times, CTRL-S (view results), ESC

8. (Highlight Display) ENTER (highlight "Build a Search Condition"), ENTER, ENTER (highlight > Greater Than), ENTER, 0 ENTER, ENTER (highlight "Execute the command"), ENTER (view results), any key

9. S (highlight "Quit dBASE III PLUS"), ENTER, **DBASE** ENTER, ENTER, T (highlight Rename), ENTER, ENTER (highlight EXAMPLE.DBF), ENTER, **ACCOUNTS.DBF** ENTER, any key

10. ENTER, ENTER (highlight EXAMPLE.DBT), ENTER, **ACCOUNTS.DBT** ENTER, any key

11. S (highlight "Quit DBASE III PLUS"), ENTER

ASCII Character Chart
▶C◀

Decimal Value	Hexadecimal Value	Control Character	Character
0	00	NUL	Null
1	01	SOH	☺
2	02	STX	☻
3	03	ETX	♥
4	04	EOT	♦
5	05	ENQ	♣
6	06	ACK	♠
7	07	BEL	Beep
8	08	BS	◘
9	09	HT	Tab

Decimal Value	Hexadecimal Value	Control Character	Character
10	0A	LF	Line-feed
11	0B	VT	Cursor home
12	0C	FF	Form-feed
13	0D	CR	Enter
14	0E	SO	♫
15	0F	SI	☼
16	10	DLE	▶
17	11	DC1	◀
18	12	DC2	↕
19	13	DC3	‼
20	14	DC4	¶
21	15	NAK	§
22	16	SYN	▬
23	17	ETB	↨
24	18	CAN	↑
25	19	EM	↓
26	1A	SUB	→
27	1B	ESC	←
28	1C	FS	Cursor right
29	1D	GS	Cursor left
30	1E	RS	Cursor up
31	1F	US	Cursor down
32	20	SP	Space
33	21		!
34	22		"
35	23		#
36	24		$
37	25		%
38	26		&
39	27		'
40	28		(
41	29		)

Appendix C

ASCII Character Chart

Decimal Value	Hexadecimal Value	Control Character	Character
42	2A		*
43	2B		+
44	2C		,
45	2D		-
46	2E		.
47	2F		/
48	30		0
49	31		1
50	32		2
51	33		3
52	34		4
53	35		5
54	36		6
55	37		7
56	38		8
57	39		9
58	3A		:
59	3B		;
60	3C		<
61	3D		=
62	3E		>
63	3F		?
64	40		@
65	41		A
66	42		B
67	43		C
68	44		D
69	45		E
70	46		F
71	47		G
72	48		H
73	49		I

Decimal Value	Hexadecimal Value	Control Character	Character
74	4A		J
75	4B		K
76	4C		L
77	4D		M
78	4E		N
79	4F		O
80	50		P
81	51		Q
82	52		R
83	53		S
84	54		T
85	55		U
86	56		V
87	57		W
88	58		X
89	59		Y
90	5A		Z
91	5B		[
92	5C		\
93	5D		]
94	5E		^
95	5F		—
96	60		`
97	61		a
98	62		b
99	63		c
100	64		d
101	65		e
102	66		f
103	67		g
104	68		h
105	69		i

Appendix C ASCII Character Chart **421**

Decimal Value	Hexadecimal Value	Control Character	Character
106	6A		j
107	6B		k
108	6C		l
109	6D		m
110	6E		n
111	6F		o
112	70		p
113	71		q
114	72		r
115	73		s
116	74		t
117	75		u
118	76		v
119	77		w
120	78		x
121	79		y
122	7A		z
123	7B		{
124	7C		¦
125	7D		}
126	7E		~
127	7F	DEL	⌂
128	80		Ç
129	81		ü
130	82		é
131	83		â
132	84		ä
133	85		à
134	86		å
135	87		ç
136	88		ê
137	89		ë

Decimal Value	Hexadecimal Value	Control Character	Character
138	8A		è
139	8B		ï
140	8C		î
141	8D		ì
142	8E		Ä
143	8F		Å
144	90		É
145	91		æ
146	92		Æ
147	93		ô
148	94		ö
149	95		ò
150	96		û
151	97		ù
152	98		ÿ
153	99		Ö
154	9A		Ü
155	9B		¢
156	9C		£
157	9D		¥
158	9E		Pt
159	9F		*f*
160	A0		á
161	A1		í
162	A2		ó
163	A3		ú
164	A4		ñ
165	A5		Ñ
166	A6		ª
167	A7		º
168	A8		¿
169	A9		⌐

Appendix C

ASCII Character Chart

Decimal Value	Hexadecimal Value	Control Character	Character
170	AA		⌐
171	AB		½
172	AC		¼
173	AD		¡
174	AE		«
175	AF		»
176	B0		░
177	B1		▒
178	B2		▓
179	B3		│
180	B4		┤
181	B5		╡
182	B6		╢
183	B7		╖
184	B8		╕
185	B9		╣
186	BA		║
187	BB		╗
188	BC		╝
189	BD		╜
190	BE		╛
191	BF		┐
192	C0		└
193	C1		┴
194	C2		┬
195	C3		├
196	C4		─
197	C5		┼
198	C6		╞
199	C7		╟
200	C8		╚
201	C9		╔

Decimal Value	Hexadecimal Value	Control Character	Character
202	CA		┴
203	CB		┬
204	CC		├
205	CD		═
206	CE		╬
207	CF		⊥
208	D0		⊥
209	D1		┬
210	D2		┬
211	D3		└
212	D4		└
213	D5		┌
214	D6		┌
215	D7		╫
216	D8		╪
217	D9		┘
218	DA		┌
219	DB		■
220	DC		▬
221	DD		▮
222	DE		▮
223	DF		▬
224	E0		α
225	E1		β
226	E2		Γ
227	E3		π
228	E4		Σ
229	E5		σ
230	E6		μ
231	E7		τ
232	E8		φ
233	E9		Θ

Appendix C

ASCII Character Chart

Decimal Value	Hexadecimal Value	Control Character	Character
234	EA		Ω
235	EB		δ
236	EC		∞
237	ED		$\varnothing$
238	EE		ϵ
239	EF		$\cap$
240	F0		$\equiv$
241	F1		$\pm$
242	F2		$\geq$
243	F3		$\leq$
244	F4		$\lceil$
245	F5		$\rfloor$
246	F6		$\div$
247	F7		$\approx$
248	F8		$\circ$
249	F9		$\bullet$
250	FA		.
251	FB		$\sqrt{}$
252	FC		η
253	FD		^{2}
254	FE		■
255	FF		(blank)

▶ Index ◀

A

Action line, 18
Answers to exercises, 363-415
Append screen, 68
    appending with, 66-70
    Help information, 69
    Update menu, 66-67
Assist screen, 8
    deleting fields in. *See* Deleting fields
    menus, 20, 21-22
    working with, 14-18

B

.BAK extension, 162
Browse screen, 93
    deleting fields in. *See* Deleting fields
    editing key controls, 94
    features, 91-97
    freezing field, 99-102
    locking field, 98-101

428   Index

Browse screen, *continued*
    menu bar, 97-99
    using, 97-102

C

Calculating information, 129-135
    screen results of Average, 133
    screen results of Count, 134
    screen results of Sum, 132, 136, 137
Character fields
    defined, 39-40
    inserting, 42-48
Character string defined, 121
Copying database files, 200-205
Create Database screen, the, 43, 45
    creating databases, 38-54
Create Format screen, the, 232
    creating formats, 231-245
Create Label screen, the, 296
    creating labels, 295-305
    editing key controls, 300
    settings definitions, 302
Create Query screen, the, 317
    building filter conditions, 319
Create Report screen, the, 266
    creating reports, 264-291
    help instructions, 269
    menu settings defined, 278-280

D

Data, importing and exporting foreign, 345-348.
    See also PFS:File
Databases
    appending records to, 61
    Append screen with, 66-70
    becoming familiar with, 4-5
    creating, 38-54
    Create Database screen, the, 43, 45
    creating "on the fly," 54-55

Databases, *continued*
    creating, in format file, 253-259
    copying, 200-205
    defined, 4-5
    entering information in, 60-61
    indexing, 185-193
    inserting information in, 70-76
    loading, 60
    memo fields, inserting information in, 76-81
    naming a new file, 65
    opening, 60-66
    printing, 210-226. *See also* Printing database information
    saving and viewing structure of, 54-55
    selecting, 236-239
    sorting, 196-200
Date fields
    defined, 39-40
    inserting, 51-52
dBASE III PLUS
    features, defined, 5-7
    loading and unloading, 7-11
    quitting, 9, 11
    system requirements, 7, 357
.DBF extension, 61
.DBT extension, 52
Deleting fields
    in Assist screen, 177-179
    in Browse screen, 95
Deleting records
    marking a single record, 140-147
    marking a group of records, 147-152
    packing database and, 152-154
    query. *See* Query files
    recalling a single record, 141, 147
    recalling a group of records, 147-152
Directories, listing, 338-340
Displaying records, 104-106, 143-144, 222-226
    defined, 210
    query file, 325-327

Displaying records, *continued*
    See also Printing database information
Dot prompt, using the, 26-28
Drives, changing, 22, 338-341

E

Edit screen, 87
    editing key controls, 88
    using the, 86-91
Exporting and importing foreign data, 345-348
Extensions. *See* the relevant individual extension

F

Fields
    basic characteristics, 167
    deleting fields. *See* Modify Database file screen
    determining types of, 60
    memo. *See* Memo fields
    modifying. *See* Modify Database file screen
Files
    copying, 341-343
    erasing, 341-343
    exporting, 345-348
    extensions, 61
    field names, 40
    giving names, 169
    importing, 345-348
    listing names, 338-341
    names, 62, 64
    renaming, 341-343
.FMT extension, 232-233
Format files
    blackboard, defined, 241-242
    blackboard screen, 241
    Character Input Symbols menu, 257
    Create Format screen, the, 232
    creating, 231-236

Format files, *continued*
    creating a database within, 253-259
    Date functions menu, 258
    designing, 239-245
    drawing lines and boxes, 247, 250
    modifying, 246-251
    text file, generating, 252, 256
    using, 244-245
.FRM extension, 265

H

Help, accessing 28-34
    in Create Database screen, 44
    in main menu, 32

I

Importing and exporting foreign data, 345-348
Index file
    defined, 184
    creating, 185-193
    key field, defined, 195
    master, 189
Index key expression, defined, 186
Information
    entering, 60-61
    inserting, 70-76
    inserting in memo fields, 76-81
Insert mode, 71
Installing dBASE III PLUS, 352-362
    list of steps, 352
    making backup copies, 354-356
    on a floppy disk, 360-361
    on a hard disk, 359-360
    package contents, 352-354
    placing on DOS path, 361
    reading README.TXT file, 356-357
    running ID program, 358
    running tutorial, 362

Installing dBASE III PLUS, *continued*
    system requirements, 7, 357
Interface
    choosing Assist or dot prompt, 14
    defined, 5, 15
    nested menu-driven, 14

K

Key field, 195

L

Labels files
    creating, 295-305
    defined, 210
    modifying, 309-312
    printing, 305-309
.LBL extension, 295
Listing structure, 166
Listing fields, 215-221
    defined, 210
Logical field
    defined, 39-40
    inserting, 51-52

M

Memo field
    defined, 39-40
    editor keys and functions, 79
    inserted text, saving, 80
    inserting information into, 76-81
    inserting into records, 51-53
    editor screen, 80
Menu bar, 16
Menus
    Assist, 20, 22-23
    key controls, 21
    nested, 14-15
    Organize, 184

Menus, *continued*
    pop-up, defined, 15
    Position, 111
    pull-down, defined, 15
    Search/Scope, 111-113
    working with, 19-25
Message line, 16
Mode, insert or typeover, 71
Modify Label screen, 309
Modify Query screen, 331
Modify Report screen, 289
    modifying reports, 288-291
Modify Database file screen, 160
    deleting fields, 177-179
    existing fields, changing, 167, 175
    inserting fields, 159, 166

N

Navigation line, 17
.NDX extension, 187
Numeric fields
    calculating. *See* Calculating information
    defined, 39
    inserting, 48-49

P

PFS:File, 345, 347
    See also Importing and exporting foreign data
Printing database information
    DOS print screen, 212-214
    display. *See* Displaying records
    labels, 305-309
    listing to paper, 217
    listing to screen, 216, 219, 220, 221
    reports, 283-287

Q

.QRY extension, 317

Query files
    building filter conditions, 319
    connecting operators, 324
    creating, 316-329
    defined, 316
    displaying a record, 325-327
    filter conditions, 321, 331-335
    modifying, 329-335
    operators, defined, 322-323
    order of precedence, 333-335
    using, 326-329
Query form, defined, 318

R

Records
    adding, 61
    appending, 66-70
    displaying, 104-106
    going to, in Assist screen, 102-104
    going to, in Browse screen, 95, 97-99
    locating, 117-123
    replacing information. *See* Replacing record information
    skipping, 115-116
Replacing record information, 126-129
    replace windows, 128
    screen results, 127
Report files
    Create Report screen, the, 266
    creating, 265-275
    defined, 210
    designing, 275-282
    Modify Report screen, the, 289
    modifying, 288-291
    printing, 283-287
Reports, creating, 264-291
.RPT extension, 61

S

Saving
    inserted text in Memo field, 80
    structure of a database, 54-55
Scope conditions
    defined, 117
    specifying a scope, 124-125
.SCR extension, 232
Search conditions
    conditional operators, 118, 122
    defined, 117
Search/Scope menu, 111-112
    using, 110-114
Seeking records, 194-196
Sort
    defined, 184
    creating, 196-200
Status bar, 18
    showing file name, 64
Structure
    designing, 39-40
    modifying. *See* Modify Database file screen
    saving and viewing, 54-55

T

TSR programs, 213
Typeover mode, 71

U

Undeleting files, 342-343

V

.VUE extension, 61

The manuscript for this book was prepared and submitted to Osborne/McGraw-Hill in electronic form. The acquisitions editor for this project was Elizabeth Fisher, the associate editor was Gwen Goss, the technical reviewer was Michael Katz, and the project editor was Janis Paris.

Text design by Judy Wohlfrom and Roger Dunshee, using Baskerville for text body and Swiss boldface for display.

Cover art by Bay Graphics Design, Inc. Color separation and cover supplier, Phoenix Color Corporation. Screens produced with InSet, from InSet Systems, Inc. Book printed and bound by R.R. Donnelley & Sons Company, Crawfordsville, Indiana.